DATE DUE			
DEC 2 '85			
MAR 1 5 1990			

The Nuremberg Trial

The Nuremberg Trial

A HISTORY OF NAZI GERMANY AS REVEALED
THROUGH THE TESTIMONY AT NUREMBERG

JOE J. HEYDECKER *and* JOHANNES LEEB

TRANSLATED AND EDITED BY R. A. *Downie*

GREENWOOD PRESS, PUBLISHERS
WESTPORT, CONNECTICUT

Library of Congress Cataloging in Publication Data

Heydecker, Joe Julius, 1916–
    The Nuremberg trial.

    Translation of Der Nürnberger Prozess.
    Reprint of the ed. published by World Pub. Co.,
Cleveland.
    1. Nuremberg Trial of Major German War Criminals,
1945–1946. 2. Germany—Politics and government—
1933–1945. 3. World War, 1939–1945—Germany.
I. Leeb, Johannes, 1932–   joint author.
II. Title.
Law   943.086   75-9111
ISBN 0-8371-8131-3

Originally published in German under the title *Der Nürnberger Prozess*

Originally published in 1962 by The World Publishing Company,
Cleveland, Ohio

Reprinted with the permission of Verlag Kiepenheuer & Witsch
GmbH & Co., KG

Reprinted in 1975 by Greenwood Press, Inc.,
51 Riverside Avenue, Westport, Conn. 06880

Library of Congress catalog card number 75-9111
ISBN 0-8371-8131-3

Printed in the United States of America

10 9 8 7 6 5 4

CONTENTS

CONTENTS

CONTENTS

FOREWORD

This book is an attempt to make the material of the Nuremberg Trial available to a wider public in a comprehensible form. The verbatim reports of the court proceedings alone run to forty-two volumes; in addition, there are tens of thousands of written and printed pages of further documents, which at the time of the Trial were not yet written or were not yet available, but which today must be taken into consideration if an objective picture of events is to be obtained. Finally, the authors have attempted to re-create for the reader the atmosphere of the immediate postwar period and a picture of the general circumstances of the time, as well as to describe the developments leading up to the Trial.

On the other hand, the authors have decided—and this decision was forced on them by the wealth of material—to leave many aspects untouched; for example, the ramifications of the "indicted organizations," such as the Nazi government, the Corps of Political Leaders, the SS, SD, Gestapo, SA, the General Staff, and the Supreme Command of the Army. However, the actions laid at the door of these organizations have made their appearance under other headings during the Trial.

Furthermore, everything relating to the problems of jurisdiction and international law has been intentionally omitted, although they touch upon some extremely interesting points made during the lengthy pleadings and arguments of the prosecution and defense. In concentrating almost completely on the factual contents of the Trial, the authors have attempted to present the history of the Trial itself in all its aspects, based on documents, depositions, records, and historical facts. They have left nothing to speculation or imagination; they have strictly avoided all romantic embellishments and additions. Thus everything in this book is historically accurate, every action and reaction of the protag-

9

onists is vouched for by eyewitnesses, every event provable, every quoted word was actually spoken.

To achieve this accuracy and documentary fidelity, the authors, besides studying the material of the Trial and the relevant literature, made many journeys in Germany and beyond to the far-scattered sources and archives; they have sought out those who took part in the Trial—officials, witnesses, court and prison staff—to find out details; they have played over old recordings of voices from the Trial; and they have disinterred many hitherto unpublished accounts of examinations for their work. One of the authors, Mr. Heydecker, also drew on his personal experiences and knowledge of the milieu, since he was present for the whole ten months of the Trial in the courtroom as a newspaper and radio reporter.

The Trial of the International Military Tribunal now belongs to history. And yet it affects the present and the future. A passage from the opening speech by Mr. Jackson, the Chief Prosecutor, is characteristic of the ideas that inspired the proceedings:

"Modern civilization puts limitless weapons of destruction into the hands of mankind. . . . Every recourse to war, to any kind of war, is recourse to measures which by their very nature are criminal. War is inevitably a web of killing, invasion, loss of freedom, and destruction of property. . . . Human reason demands that the law should not be considered adequate if it punishes only petty crimes of which lesser people are guilty. The law must also reach the men who seize great power and deliberately combine to make use of it to commit an evil which affects every home in the world. The last step in preventing the periodic outbreak of war, which is unavoidable with international lawlessness, is to make statesmen responsible before the law."

1

The Great Hunt

SHOULD ADOLF HITLER
BE SHOT?

"If a British soldier met Hitler, would it be his duty to shoot him or to take him alive?" This question was put in the House of Commons on March 28, 1945, by the Labour Member for Keighley, Mr. Ivor Thomas.

A few minutes earlier Mr. Anthony Eden, then Foreign Minister, had stated that Adolf Hitler would be treated as the leading war criminal, and that he headed a list compiled by the War Crimes Commission in London.

"I am quite satisfied," answered Mr. Eden, "to leave the decision completely to the British soldier concerned." Laughter and applause.

In the House of Commons, all over England, and throughout the world everyone knew that Germany's last hour had struck. American, British, and Soviet troops were advancing irresistibly, and with them advanced the specialists of the intelligence services, charged with the task of finding and catching the Nazi leaders.

The War Crimes Commission had put a million Germans on their lists. Every bomb site, every farmhouse, every prison, every column of refugees on the highways was to be searched for them.

"The greatest manhunt in history is under way from Norway to the Bavarian Alps," Mr. Eden announced in the House of Commons. Never before had a million men at a time been sought and hunted. But the men who were later to appear in the dock at Nuremberg were not found at first. In the chaos of the German collapse even the intelligence experts on the staffs of General Eisenhower and Field Marshal Montgomery were unable to form a clear picture. In those days, no one knew what had become of Hitler, Goebbels, Ribbentrop, Bormann, or Goering.

THE END OF
JOSEPH GOEBBELS

Wilhelm Frick, the former Minister of the Interior, was "picked up" by officers of the American Seventh Army near Munich. There was still no trace of the other Nazi leaders.

On the morning of April 21, 1945, Berlin was shivering under an ice-gray cloud of dust, smoke, and sticky fog. A hundred thousand fugitives roamed the streets in desperation. The ruthless drive of the advancing Russians had swept them westward. Members of the Hitler Youth, women, and old men were building barricades. The thunder of guns announced the nearness of the front. Smoke rose from the remains of the flattened houses. The smoldering, biting stench of collapse hung over Berlin.

Through the chinks of the nailed-up windows the chilly April wind penetrated the private cinema of the Minister for Popular Enlightenment and Propaganda in Hermann Goering Street. Some two dozen men had gathered in the twilight of the desolate room. Five candle stumps cast a flickering light upon the serious faces of those present; there was no electric current.

This was the scene of the last conference that Dr. Joseph Goebbels held with his subordinates; it has been chronicled for history by an eyewitness, the Nuremberg defendant Hans Fritzsche. The Minister was wearing a punctiliously formal dark suit, his white collar shining in the gloom, which struck Fritzsche, the radio commentator, as being in glaring contrast to the somber room and the whole cruelly ruined city.

Dr. Goebbels lowered himself into an armchair and began to speak. What he said was not the subject of a conference of ministerial colleagues. He was talking to another audience. He pronounced a condemnation of the whole German people; he spoke of treason, reaction, cowardice.

"The German people have failed," Goebbels declared. "In the East they are running away, in the West they are obstructing our soldiers in their fight and greet the enemy with white flags." His voice rose as though he were still speaking in the Sport Palace. "What am I to do with a people whose men refuse to fight even when their women are raped?" Then he calmed down again. An ironical twitch played at the corner of his mouth. "However," he said, "the German people has chosen its own fate." And with a slight movement of his hand he continued: "Well, the venture has failed."

One or two colleagues jumped up, ready to remonstrate with Goebbels. The Minister gave them an icy look, and continued, "Yes, this may be a surprise for many, even for my colleagues. But I have never forced anyone to be my colleague, as we have never forced the German people. The people itself entrusted me with our task. Why have you worked with me? Now they'll cut your little throats."

Goebbels rose. He smiled imperceptibly at the expressions which his last cynical words had brought to the faces of those present. He limped to the tall red-and-gold door of the cinema, turned round once more, and said melodramatically: "But when we depart, then the earth shall tremble!"

But only the door trembled as he slammed it shut. The others had got up from their seats. No one spoke. They looked at each other, perplexed. It was clear to all of them that the end had come. They turned up their coat collars and went out into the street.

The Russian artillery was covering the government quarter with heavy fire. Fritzsche ran, doubled over, along the walls of the ruins, groping his way through debris and back streets. He felt as though awakened from a dream. He hurried through the town, looking for anyone who could give him reliable information about the situation, and in the end he returned in despair to the villa of Dr. Goebbels.

Here he found only some foulmouthed SS men, a couple of bewildered secretaries, empty rooms, ransacked writing tables and desks, discarded trunks. The chief of the Minister's staff, Curt Hamel, stood looking lost in his hat and coat. When he saw Fritzsche he said: "Goebbels has gone to the Führer's bunker. His last words were, 'It's all over.' The Russians have reached the

Alexanderplatz. I am going to try now to get through to Hamburg. Are you coming? There is an empty seat in the car."

Fritzsche declined. He wanted to stay in Berlin. He hastened to the Propaganda Ministry and closed down the radio division, dismissing his subordinates. Then he took his car from the garage and drove toward the Alexanderplatz to see if the Russians were really already there. Artillery fire and a tank battle between the Danziger Strasse and the railway forced him to turn back. At the Radio Center he heard that the defense of Berlin was to continue.

For a few more days, the center of the city held out. Then Fritzsche, his ear pressed to a weakening battery set, heard the news of Hitler's death from the Hamburg station. With Werner Naumann, Secretary of State of the Propaganda Ministry, he ran across to the Chancellery. He had a fixed plan. Berlin must capitulate at once. But he still hesitated to voice this suggestion to Martin Bormann.

In the garden of the Führer's bunker, between smoke-blackened walls, among gasoline cans and burning secret documents—for what else could it be?—Bormann called some SS men together and ordered them in Fritzsche's presence: "The Werewolf is dissolved. All Werewolf operations are to cease, and the execution of death sentences."

Fritzsche stumbled back to the Ministry of Propaganda. At 9:00 P.M. all those who were still in the bunker of the Chancellery were to make an attempt at a break-out. Thereafter, Fritzsche, as head of a government department, would be the last high official of the administration remaining in the capital of the German Reich. In this capacity he would offer the capitulation of Berlin to Marshal Georgi Zhukov.

He informed some military hospitals, command-post bunkers, and army units of his decision. Then he wrote a letter to the Soviet Marshal. The interpreter of the German News Agency, Junius, translated it into Russian.

Suddenly the door was flung open. General Wilhelm Burgdorf, Hitler's last adjutant, stormed into the shelter, his eyes flaming.

"You want to capitulate?" he shouted at Fritzsche.

"Yes," Fritzsche answered dryly.

"Then you will have to shoot me first!" Burgdorf screamed. "In his Testament the Führer has forbidden any capitulation. We must fight to the last man."

"And to the last woman?" Fritzsche asked.

The General drew his revolver. But Fritzsche and a radio technician were too quick for him. They threw themselves upon Burgdorf. There was the crack of a shot, which ricocheted from the wall to the floor. With their combined strength they threw the General out.

Burgdorf tried to return to the Chancellery. But on the way he turned his weapon on himself and put an end to his life.

Fritzsche's letter managed to cross the fighting lines to the Russian side. In the gray dawn of May 2 the emissaries met at the Propaganda Ministry: a Soviet lieutenant colonel, several other Russian officers, and a German colonel as a guide. The Russians invited Fritzsche to meet Marshal Zhukov.

The group marched in silence through a Berlin that no longer bore any resemblance to the former capital city. Dead horses, ruins, burned-out vehicles, corpses of soldiers, hanging telegraph wires, dead Hitler Youths, discarded antitank guns, smashed furniture, stinking cellar holes, lined the path of the emissaries. At the Anhalt Station they crossed the front line. A Russian jeep was waiting.

Opposite the entrance to Tempelhof Airport Fritzsche was led into a villa where the Soviet staff was quartered. There the government official learned that in the meantime one of the last commandants of Berlin, General Helmut Weidling, had also turned up to offer the capitulation of Berlin.

With Weidling's move Fritzsche's self-appointed mission had come to an end. Now, however, the Russians wanted him for something else. On May 4 they took him on a motor trip; the destination was a small settlement between Berlin and Bernau. Fritzsche was led down the steps of a low, damp basement. The officers with him brought him to a dimly lit room. There was a horrible sight. On the floor lay an almost naked corpse. The skull was badly charred but the body was well preserved. Of the clothing only the collar of a brown uniform and a lapel with a gilt party badge had remained.

Near the dead man were the corpses of five children. All were dressed in nightshirts and looked as though they were peacefully asleep.

Hans Fritzsche recognized the corpses of Dr. Joseph Goebbels and his children. He was so upset by what he saw, so embittered at the cheap way out his chief had chosen, that he did not even notice the seventh corpse, a woman—apparently Magda Goebbels.

The Soviet officers were satisfied with the identification. Fritzsche was brought out into the fresh air—but not to freedom. He was kept a prisoner in a cellar in Friedrichshagen together with other Germans. It was a strange state of suspended legality, which was given a juridical form only several days later when a Soviet NCO sought Fritzsche out, drew a crumpled piece of paper from his pocket, and from it laboriously read three German words: "You are arrested."

It was to be a long time before Fritzsche regained his freedom. His path led to Lubjanka prison in Moscow, and from there to the dock at Nuremberg.

FIELD MARSHAL
HERMANN GOERING
GIVES HIMSELF UP

The great manhunt was on. It was particularly energetic in the Bavarian Alps. Two principal districts were marked on the maps of the Allied search parties: in the north, the area between Hamburg and Flensburg; in the south, the district between Munich and Berchtesgaden. A group of leading Nazis had attempted to get through to Admiral Doenitz from the ruins of Berlin; Himmler, Ribbentrop, Rosenberg, and Bormann appeared to be among them. The rest were presumed to be in Bavaria.

Still, it came as a surprise to the 36th Division of the American Seventh Army when on the morning of May 9 a German colonel reported to an advanced post. It was known that the Alps were swarming with German soldiers who wanted to go on fighting on their own until they saw the hopelessness of their position and surrendered. But in this case things were quite different.

The German colonel gave his name: Bernd von Brauchitsch. Then he added, "I have come on the orders of Field Marshal Hermann Goering."

The American post sprang to life. So their division would have the glory of catching one of the biggest fishes! Colonel Brauchitsch was put into a jeep and rushed to Divisional Headquarters.

A telephone call had already announced the German emissary. There was no delay. The Division Commander, Major General John E. Dahlquist, and his second in command, Brigadier General Robert J. Stack, were at once available.

Bernd von Brauchitsch told the American generals that he had been commissioned by Hermann Goering to offer his surrender. The Field Marshal, said the Colonel, was in the Radstadt area near Zell am See.

In fact Goering was in a certain quandary. Over his head hung Hitler's death sentence, and it was possible that in spite of the general collapse some fanatical SS men might hunt him down and carry out the Führer's order to shoot him.

"My Führer," Goering had broadcast a few days earlier to the man in the beleaguered Reich Chancellery, "do you agree that according to your decree to persist in the defense of Berlin, on the basis of the Law of June 29, 1941, I now take over the total control of the Reich with complete powers both internal and external? If I receive no reply by 10:00 P.M., I shall assume that you have been deprived of your freedom to act and will regard the conditions of the above law as fulfilled."

The answer came at 10:00 P.M., but it was not addressed to Goering. It said:

"Goering has been dismissed from all offices, including that of successor to Hitler, and is at once to be arrested on a charge of high treason." Further it was ordered that on the death of the Führer "the traitor of April 23 was to be liquidated."

Later, the last Chief of Staff of the Luftwaffe, General Karl Koller declared, "The SS had evidently been afraid to carry out the sentence on the Field Marshal."

"I was kept in a room in which there was an officer," Goering stated at an examination in Nuremberg. "Outside the door there was an SS guard. Then they took me to Austria with my family on the fourth or fifth of May, after the air attack on Berchtesgaden. Airborne units marched through the town—it was called Mauterndorf—and freed me from the SS."

General Koller, in whose charge Goering then was, knew of Hitler's order to shoot him.

"But I was against any murder," he told the Nuremberg defense lawyer Werner Bross, "as I have always been against the murder of political opponents. For that reason the order was never carried out."

The German Luftwaffe sergeant Anton Kohnle, who was the guard at the Mauterndorf hunting lodge where Goering was prisoner with his wife, his daughter, valet, lady's maid, and cook, was soon able to see the Field Marshal. He stated:

"I reported to him, and he stopped in astonishment and looked me over. He asked me where I came from, and told me, in a very unofficial way, that everything would have been different if they had only listened to him. He gave me to understand that Hitler had suffered from delusions of grandeur. But now, with the end of the war, he, the Field Marshal himself, would take over the government of Germany.

"After this conversation," Kohnle added, "Goering walked about twenty steps away from me, and fell suddenly to the floor. It needed a great effort to raise this colossus to his feet again. Goering was a morphine addict, and I suppose his fit was caused by the fact that during his captivity the SS had withheld the drug from him."

At that time, of course, the Field Marshal could not foresee how things would turn out. Would the SS still be able to strike back and get him again? Under the circumstances it was indeed better to surrender to the protection of the Allies.

Brigadier Stack went personally to the place indicated by Colonel Brauchitsch. At the bend of a narrow country road the American's jeep met Goering's bulletproof Mercedes.

The cars stopped some distance from each other. The General jumped onto the roadway, Goering climbed with some difficulty from his car. He raised his marshal's baton, indicating a salute, and went toward the Americans. General Stack raised his hand to his cap and also went a few steps forward. Everything was strictly correct. The two men met halfway and shook hands.

Goering was brought to Divisional Headquarters where Major General Dahlquist himself received the important prisoner. The Headquarters of the Seventh Army was informed, and its Intelligence Chief, Brigadier General William W. Quinn, promised to come to the Division at once and personally take over the rare prize.

Meanwhile the commander of the 36th Division had had time to have a chat with Goering. John E. Dahlquist was an old soldier. He listened with astonishment to Goering's tale.

"Hitler was narrow-minded," the Field Marshal declared, "Rudolf Hess was an eccentric, and Ribbentrop a scoundrel. Why was Ribbentrop Foreign Minister? I heard once of a remark of Churchill's to this effect: 'Why do they keep sending me this man Ribbentrop instead of some smart chap like Goering?' Well, here I am. When are you going to take me to Eisenhower's headquarters?"

Dahlquist realized that Goering in fact believed that he could negotiate with the Allies as Germany's delegate. How ridiculous this idea was just never occurred to him. Did this man, once the most powerful after Hitler, really misinterpret the situation to such an extent?

He spoke at length about his powerful Luftwaffe, unaware of the fact that his successor in office, Field Marshal Robert Ritter von Greim, had already been taken prisoner in Kitzbühel. Greim identified himself with the classic words: "I am the Chief of the German Air Force—but I have no Air Force."

Meanwhile Goering applied himself to a dish of chicken, mashed potatoes, and beans, which had been brought in. With an appetite that filled Dahlquist with amazement the Field Marshal devoured the lot, helped himself to a plateful of fruit salad, and praised the American coffee.

The news of Goering's capture alerted the war correspondents throughout a wide area. They hastened to Kitzbühel, for Quinn, who was friendly toward the press, had promised them an interview with the Field Marshal.

Meanwhile Hermann Goering had expressed himself as satisfied with his accommodation in a private villa which had been put at his disposal. The rest of his family arrived—so did his luggage, filling sixteen trucks. It was almost as if he were moving into a hotel.

The Field Marshal took a bath at his ease and then dressed in a leisurely manner, in his favorite light green uniform with the gold insignia which he loved to sport.

How greatly all this contrasted with places in which, at the same moment, hundreds of thousands of German soldiers were herded together, in rain and mud, without food, without water, without sanitation.

Goering probably never gave them a thought. Freshly shaved, and in good humor, he walked with a springy step out of the house and into the friendly noonday sun, nodding amiably to the two dozen reporters who had assembled.

The newspapermen had formed a semicircle. A small round table and an armchair with floral upholstery stood against the wall of the house. Here, the famous prisoner took his seat. A microphone was set up, and the cameras clicked.

"Hello, Marshal, give us a smile!"

Goering obliged, but showed his impatience.

"Please hurry," he told the photographers, "I am hungry."

Then the questions began. At first they were the usual: Where is Hitler? Do you believe he is dead? Why was no landing in England attempted? How strong was the Luftwaffe at the beginning of the war?

"I believe that it was the strongest air force in the world," Goering answered proudly.

"About how many planes did you have?" a reporter wanted to know.

"That was six years ago," Goering said, "and I am not prepared for that question. I couldn't tell you now."

"Did you order the bombing of Coventry?"

"Yes. Coventry was an industrial center, and I had reports that it had large aircraft factories."

"And Canterbury?"

"The bombing of Canterbury was ordered from higher up in retaliation for the attack upon a German university town."

"Which university town was that?"

"I don't remember."

"When did you first believe that you had lost the war?"

"Very soon after the Normandy landings and the breakthrough of the Russians in the East."

"What contributed most to this result?"

"The continual air attacks."

"Was Hitler told of the hopelessness of the war?"

"Yes. Various military leaders explained to Hitler that the war might be lost. Hitler reacted quite negatively to this, and conversations on this subject were later forbidden."

"Who forbade them?"

"Hitler himself. He refused even to consider the possibility that the war might be lost."

"When was that?"

"When people first began to speak of it, about the middle of 1944."

"Do you believe that Hitler named Admiral Doenitz as his successor?"

"No! The telegram to Doenitz bore Bormann's signature."

"Why did so colorless an individual as Bormann have such a great influence on Hitler?"

"Bormann stayed with Hitler day and night and gradually brought him so much under his will that he ruled Hitler's whole existence."

"Who ordered the attack on Russia?"

"Hitler himself."

"Who was responsible for the concentration camps?"

"Hitler personally. Everyone who had anything to do with the camps was directly responsible to Hitler. The authorities had nothing to do with them."

"What future do you foresee for Germany?"

"If no living space can be found for the German people I foresee a very black future for Germany and the whole world. Everyone wants peace, but it is hard to see what will happen."

The correspondents dashed away to cable the interview to their papers. But on General Eisenhower's order the censor at Allied Headquarters held up the telegrams and this decision was final. Only nine years later, in May 1954, did Brigadier General Quinn release a transcription of the Goering interview to an American magazine for publication.

One question, however, which was put to Goering at the press conference, slipped through the censor and appeared in the American press:

"Do you know that you are on the list of war criminals?"

"No," Goering answered. "That surprises me very much, for I cannot imagine why."

ADMIRAL DOENITZ
TAKES OVER

At 10:00 P.M. on May 1, 1945, Radio Hamburg surprised Germany and the world with the announcement: "It is reported from the Führer's Headquarters that our Führer, Adolf Hitler, died for Germany at his command post in the Chancellery this afternoon, fighting against Bolshevism to his last breath. The Führer named Admiral Doenitz as his successor on April 30."

With this announcement, which tried to disguise Hitler's suicide as a hero's death, the German people's tragedy of the Nazi period came to an end, making way for a new piece on the old, dilapidated stage: the short-lived tragicomic attempt at government of the "Reich President" Karl Doenitz.

Four men, who were later to sit in the dock at Nuremberg, were the protagonists in this farcical finale of the Greater German Reich: the Commander in Chief of the Fleet, Admiral Doenitz; the Chief of Staff of the Supreme Command of the Armed Forces, Field Marshal Wilhelm Keitel; the Chief of Operations of the Armed Forces, General Alfred Jodl; and the Reich Minister of Armaments and Munitions, Albert Speer.

There was complete chaos in Germany. American, British, French, and Soviet troops were occupying the remaining parts

of the country. Millions of Germans were on the move, fleeing from the Red Army. Endless columns of uprooted humanity roamed the countryside. In the towns heavy bombing had smothered life. Swarms of disorganized soldiers were sweeping aimlessly toward the West. Fanatical execution squads were hanging deserters from the trees of the highways. Bridges were blown up.

Yet in Flensburg they "governed." There were no ruins here, no end-of-the-world atmosphere. Here everything was under control. In the reflected splendor of the past, Doenitz's battalion of guards marched out of an unpretentious brick building, reminiscent of a small-town school. It now housed the German government and the Supreme Command of the Armed Forces. It was the seat of Germany's last national leader.

How did this remarkable episode of German history come about? On April 16, 1945, Doenitz had been in Berlin. That morning, the capital was startled by a tremendous roar. At Küstrin and Frankfurt an der Oder all the Russian batteries had opened fire at the same moment—four hundred guns to every mile of the front. The thunder of the long-awaited offensive told Berlin that the end was near.

In the Führer's bunker at the Chancellery Hitler's trembling hands quivered restlessly to and fro over the maps. He sought a way out, operating with armies that existed only in his imagination. Walter Lüdde-Neurath, Adjutant to Admiral Doenitz, who observed Hitler in these last ghastly hours, reported, "Physically he gave the impression of a stricken and broken man; bloated, bent, weak, and nervous."

The position was hopeless. Eisenhower had encircled the Ruhr district and had shattered the divisions of Army Group B; 325,000 of its men had been captured. American tank spearheads were approaching Magdeburg, Nuremberg, and Stuttgart; British troops were storming toward Bremen and Lauenburg; the pincers of the Red Army were closing in on Berlin.

For three days the Russian fire had plowed up every yard of ground where German resistance was still active. For three days German antiaircraft, infantry, home guards, armed civilians, marines, and police had resisted. It was no use.

But Hitler still believed in victory. With undertones of contempt in his voice he declared, "The Russian is at the end of his tether. Now he is fighting only with soldiers of fortune, liberated prisoners of war, and men recruited from the districts he has overrun, a choice collection. The last assault from Asia will be smashed just as the attack from the West will be beaten back, in spite of everything."

Keitel seized on Hitler's optimistic mood and declared, "Gentlemen, it is an old military principle that an attack peters out if a successful breakthrough is not achieved by the third day."

"I don't agree," muttered Doenitz and ordered his Adjutant, Lüdde-Neurath, to remove the headquarters of the Navy from the danger zone within the next sixty minutes, setting it up somewhere else.

The Russian army, however, ignored Hitler's prophecies and Keitel's military wisdom. They forced the breakthrough on the fourth day. The last German front had ceased to exist.

Doenitz had acted correctly. He was charged by Hitler with the defense of the northern area in case the Russian and American wedges should split Germany into two parts. Now the small column of cars of the Commander in Chief of the Fleet rolled out of Berlin, through the night, at their head the five-ton bullet-proof armored car of the Admiral.

Doenitz transferred his command to Plön. Two days later, the Supreme Command of the Armed Forces also left the Berlin district for the north. Keitel and Jodl arrived with a swarm of adjutants, officers, ministers, and secretaries of state at Rheinsberg, and then later set out for Flensburg. Schleswig-Holstein was thus to be the scene of the last act.

On April 30, 1945, at 6:35 P.M., Doenitz in Plön received a startling radio message from the Berlin Chancellery: "The Führer appoints you, Herr Admiral, as his successor, in place of the former Field Marshal Goering. Authority in writing follows. From now on it is up to you to take all measures which the present situation requires." The message was signed with the name of Bormann. The next day, at about 3:00 P.M. a further radio message reached Plön: "Admiral Doenitz. Top secret. Personal delivery. Testament of April 29 transfers to you the post of Reich

President, to Minister Goebbels that of Chancellor, to Reich Leader Bormann that of Party Minister, to Seyss-Inquart that of Foreign Minister. Bormann is trying to reach you today to explain the situation. Form and time of announcement to the troops and publication left to you." Signatories were Goebbels and Bormann.

Doenitz, the new President of the Reich appointed by radio message, had no illusions about his position. He issued orders that Bormann and Goebbels should be arrested as soon as they turned up at his headquarters. He had no use for Party officials. He had to make peace, and he knew that the Allies would not deal with any government that included leading National Socialists.

He managed to get the civil and military departments to recognize him as head of the state. The Supreme Command of the Armed Forces and even Heinrich Himmler and the SS bowed to the orders of the "radio president." The members of the old government, so far as they were in Schleswig-Holstein, resigned in order to give Doenitz a free hand, among them the Party philosopher and "Minister for the Occupied Eastern Regions," Alfred Rosenberg, as well as Foreign Minister Joachim von Ribbentrop.

Doenitz formed a new cabinet. It was as nonpolitical as possible, carefully designated as "Acting Government of the Reich." He had difficult decisions to face. In his hands was a copy of a map. It came from the British secret dossier *Eclipse*, photographed by the German Secret Service: it showed the exact line of demarcation between East and West on which Roosevelt, Churchill, and Stalin had agreed at the Yalta Conference. This was the basic plan for the later division of Germany into zones. It provided Doenitz with the necessary information for negotiating the German surrender.

He wanted to keep up resistance in the East to allow as many troops and civilians as possible to retreat to behind the *Eclipse* line while surrender was being negotiated in order to avoid further sacrifices on this front. The men in Flensburg believed that they could win General Eisenhower over to this line of action, although it was known that the Allies intended to accept only a simultaneous surrender of all German troops on all fronts.

Thus Doenitz decided, as he put it, "against the Asiatic East" and "for the Christian West."

Events overtook him. At midday on May 2, 1945, Captain Lüdde-Neurath, the Admiral's adjutant, happened to be telephoning from Flensburg to a firm in Lübeck. The man at the other end asked him to speak up. "I can't hear a thing," he shouted, "there is such a noise here in the street, with one tank after another rumbling past . . ."

"What kind of tanks?" asked Lüdde-Neurath.

"Noisy English ones—do you want to hear?" And the man in Lübeck held the telephone to the open window. Thus the German High Command first learned of the breakthrough of the British.

UNCONDITIONAL
SURRENDER

It was time to consider surrender seriously. Doenitz sent Admiral Hans-Georg von Friedeburg, General Eberhard Kinzel, Rear Admiral Gerhard Wagner, and three other officers to the headquarters of Field Marshal Montgomery at Lüneburg.

Montgomery received the offer of surrender with scarcely a word. The armistice signed by von Friedeburg sometime later silenced the guns in the whole of the northern area at 8:00 A.M. on May 5.

Friedeburg flew into France and took part in the Reims negotiations with Eisenhower's staff. Soon afterward, General Jodl had to deal with Eisenhower's Chief of Staff, General Bedell Smith, about the question of capitulation in the East.

Eisenhower wrote in his memoirs, "To us it seemed clear that the Germans were playing for time so that they could transfer behind our lines the largest possible number of German soldiers. I told General Smith to inform Jodl that unless they instantly ceased all pretense and delay I would close the entire Allied front and would by force prevent any more German refugees from entering our lines. I would brook no further delay in this matter."

Jodl radioed to Doenitz: "General Eisenhower insists that we sign today. Otherwise the Allied fronts will be closed to all persons who wish to surrender individually and all negotiations will be broken off. I see no alternative except chaos or acceptance."

In a bare schoolroom at Reims the unconditional surrender was signed during the night of May 7, 1945. The American war correspondent, Drew Middleton, was one of the few people present at this historic moment. He writes: "Present were Major General Walter Bedell Smith for General Eisenhower, Major General François Sevez for General Alphonse-Pierre Juin, and Major General Ivan Susloparov for the Soviet Command.

"Jodl, his arrogant eyes glassy from strain, stood stiffly to attention, the harsh light revealing the worn marks of his grey uniform.

" 'I want to say a word,' he said to General Smith in English. Then he went on in German: 'General! With this signature the German people and the German Armed Forces are for better or worse delivered into the victor's hands. In this hour, I can only hope that the victor will treat them with generosity.'

"General Smith, his face drawn with fatigue, looked at him. There was no reply. Then the documents were signed. The time was 2:41 A.M."

Finally, Jodl was led into Eisenhower's office. The American Commander in Chief asked him through an interpreter if he thoroughly understood all provisions of the document he had signed.

Jodl answered, "Ja."

"You will, officially and personally, be held responsible," said Eisenhower, "if the terms of this surrender are violated, including its provisions for German commanders to appear in Berlin at the moment set by the Russian High Command to accomplish formal surrender to that government. That is all."

Jodl saluted and left.

The war was over.

What happened a day later in the Soviet headquarters at Berlin—Karlshorst was really only a confirmation. Field Marshal William Keitel flew from Flensburg to Berlin to sign the second document of surrender. In his company were General Paul Stumpf for the Luftwaffe and Admiral von Friedeburg for the German fleet.

Ten minutes after midnight on May 9, 1945, the Germans were shown into the conference room. At a large table sat Marshal Zhukov and the Soviet Foreign Minister, Andrei Vishinsky; next to them the British Air Chief Marshal, Sir Arthur Tedder, General Carl Spaatz as Eisenhower's representative, and the French General Jean de Lattre de Tassigny. A separate table for the Germans was placed near the door.

"At 12:10 Keitel walked in, followed by Friedeburg and Stumpf," wrote the American war correspondent Joseph W. Grigg, Jr. "Keitel, haughty and self-possessed, his face slightly flushed, slammed his marshal's baton down on the table and took a seat, looking straight ahead, ignoring the photographers. Once or twice he fingered his collar and nervously licked his lips.

"Air Marshal Tedder arose and said in a cold voice in English: 'I ask you, have you read this document of unconditional surrender? Are you prepared to sign it?' After the translation, Keitel picked a copy of the document off the table and replied in a harsh Prussian accent in German, 'Yes, I am ready.'

"Marshal Zhukov then motioned to him to come over to the table. Keitel picked up his cap, his marshal's baton, his gloves, slowly and carefully inserted his monocle in his right eye, walked over and sat down to sign in a long, scrawling hand the single name, 'Keitel.' "

Then, while the others signed, Keitel tried once more to win some time for the refugees who were streaming west. He beckoned the Russian interpreter to him and told him that because of bad communications the cease-fire order would need at least twenty-four hours to reach the front line troops.

The interpreter did not know what to do. He turned to an officer on Zhukov's staff and translated Keitel's words into his ear, but there was no answer. Zhukov stood up and said coldly in Russian: "I now request the German delegation to leave the room."

Everybody rose. Keitel shut the attaché case with the fateful document, tucked it under his arm, and left the room after a slight clicking of his heels by way of salute. A few days later, on May 13, he was arrested in Flensburg.

THE END OF THE
FLENSBURG GOVERNMENT

In Flensburg the government of Doenitz was still in session. In spite of the unconditional surrender they were allowed to remain in office. An Allied Control Commission appeared to supervise the operation of the surrender at the Army Command. In other respects the district of Flensburg remained undisturbed. The small district was thus the last spot where even after the surrender German soldiers and officers strutted about in full uniform and armed. But not for long.

Keitel's arrest showed Doenitz that the end of the Flensburg government would now only be a matter of days. He had dissolved the Werewolf, and finally also the Nazi Party, in order to demonstrate his good will—but these were measures that had already been overtaken by events.

Why was Keitel arrested? Brigadier General Lowell W. Rooks, the American head of the Allied Control Commission at the German High Command, gave no reason. He only carried out an order. However, Keitel himself knew more about it. As Lüdde-Neurath stated, the Commander in Chief of the Army himself gave the answer when he reported to Doenitz for the last time. According to Lüdde-Neurath, Keitel's arrest was apparently "connected with the shooting of fifty British R.A.F. officers in April, 1944." This crime was to play an important part at the Nuremberg Trial.

Doenitz appointed General Alfred Jodl as Commander in Chief of the Army in Keitel's place. It was his last act in office.

On May 17, the Soviet delegates arrived at the Allied Control Commission in Flensburg. Soon afterward, the "Government of the Reich" was ordered to report on board the laid-up German passenger steamer *Patria* at 9:45 A.M. on May 23.

"Pack your things," said Doenitz when he got the order. He knew that the end had come.

In the saloon bar of the *Patria*, at the appointed hour, began the last act of the Greater German Reich. The American Control Chief Lowell Rooks, the British Brigadier General Foord, the Soviet Major General Truskov, and the New York interpreter Herbert Cohn seated themselves solemnly around the table.

"It is quite clear what they are planning," Doenitz whispered to Jodl. They took their places.

"Gentlemen," said Lowell Rooks formally, "I have received instructions from General Eisenhower to summon you before me this morning to inform you that the Acting German Government and the High Command of the German Army with their various officials are to be arrested as prisoners of war. The Acting German Government is hereby dissolved. From this moment, you must regard yourselves as prisoners of war. When you leave this room, an Allied officer will be assigned to you and will accompany you to your quarters where you will pack, have a meal, and put your affairs in order."

The war correspondent Drew Middleton, who was present, writes that during this ceremony Admiral Doenitz sat stiffly, but General Jodl seemed to shrink in his chair, his nose becoming even redder than usual and angry purple blotches breaking out on his face. The general rubbed and squeezed his hands.

"He [General Rooks] then asked General Truskov if he had anything to say. The Russian General shook his head. Admiral Doenitz, replying to the same question, said, 'Any word would be superfluous.' "

A company of the 159th Brigade of the 11th Division of the British Second Army dashed with fast armored vehicles into the neighboring town of Glücksburg. Doenitz's Minister of Economy and Production, Albert Speer, had his office there. He, too, was on the list of war criminals.

Speer was a rational man—perhaps the only Nazi leader who judged the position calmly and correctly. When the British officer came to arrest him he surrendered without fuss.

Meanwhile, Doenitz was walking up and down outside his official residence in Flensburg-Mürwick. He had packed his bags and was waiting for transport to the prison camp. At his side was Admiral Friedeburg. Both men had their hands clasped behind their backs and walked up and down the small garden path in silence. The cars pulled up. The prisoners were to be taken to Flensburg police headquarters with their luggage.

Before Friedeburg left with his cases he asked his English guard if he could go to the toilet He disappeared behind the door and locked it. Minutes passed. There was no sound. The soldiers began to feel uneasy. They knocked. No answer. A sturdy corporal forced the door. There was the last Commander in Chief of the German Fleet, lying on his back. His body was trembling under the effects of the cyanide he had taken; his eyes were wide open, but he was no longer conscious.

The soldiers lifted the dying man from the floor, carried him into another room, and laid him on a bed. One of them ran for a doctor, but Admiral Friedeburg was dead before the call for help was answered.

Meanwhile, Doenitz, Jodl, and Speer were waiting for their transport in the courtyard of the police headquarters, with the muzzle of a British machine gun pointing at them. A handful of uniformed war correspondents had found their way to them and tried to obtain interviews, but with little success. Jodl answered the first question that was put to him brusquely and icily: "I am a prisoner of war and need only give my name and rank—nothing else."

The military trucks arrived and took the prisoners to the airfield, guarded by armored cars. For Jodl, Doenitz, and Speer this was the beginning of the road to the dock at Nuremberg, and from there to the gallows or to Spandau prison.

With the end of the German High Command and Government the fate of Germany was completely in the hands of the Allies.

VICE CHANCELLOR
FRANZ VON PAPEN AND
GOVERNOR GENERAL
HANS FRANK

"The greatest manhunt in history" was still under way. The number of Germans sought—originally a million—was raised to close to six million by the War Crimes Commission of the Allied Nations.

Where was Heinrich Himmler? Where were Ribbentrop, Rosenberg, Ley, Bormann, Frank, Streicher?

They had gone to earth, vanished from the scene, swallowed by the chaotic streams of refugees, by the ruins of the bombed cities. Their pictures, the warrants for their apprehension hung in every barracks, but there was no trace of them. American and British service posts knew that almost every day Moscow Radio criticized the slowness of the search action in the West. This lack of success threatened to turn into a political scandal. In the end, Moscow requested officially that the hunt for the missing Nazi leaders should be intensified. But Eisenhower's and Montgomery's agents were no miracle workers. They had to content themselves with the second-rank Nazis they succeeded in capturing. They already had quite a crowd; many of them were later to appear at Nuremberg.

There was, for example, Franz von Papen, called "the man who held the stirrup for Hitler." The former Chancellor, Vice Chancellor, and German Ambassador to Vienna and Ankara was arrested in Westphalia, in the stormy days when the American Ninth Army drove into the Ruhr. Franz von Papen and his family, to the last under Gestapo supervision because Hitler did not trust the old "gentleman diplomatist," had fled to Baron Max von Stockhausen, his son-in-law, when the Western front collapsed. There, at a lonely log cabin in the forest, the men had kept watch with shotguns, among them Papen's son, Friedrich Franz von Papen. The district was rife with deserters and liberated foreign slave workers. The women and children in the log cabin had to be protected until the arrival of the Americans. Franz von Papen was sure that that would mean for him the hour of liberation. But it turned out quite differently. Troops of the Ninth Army discovered the lonely hunting lodge; a sergeant entered it with a drawn pistol, and the men inside were taken prisoner.

"And who are you?" the sergeant asked the old man who was sitting on a wooden bench in the corner.

"Franz von Papen," he replied and held out his identification papers.

"You are a prisoner too," said the sergeant brusquely.

"But I don't hold any military post, and I am over fifty years old—"

"Never mind," said the man with the pistol, "you're under arrest."

Papen submitted to his fate. He invited the sergeant to sit down, and was given permission to have a plate of soup and to pack his belongings in a rucksack. Then the former Chancellor of the Reich was packed into a jeep with the other prisoners, and taken to Divisional Headquarters at Rüthen.

The officers there treated him with strict courtesy but held out no hopes. First his name had to be checked against the Allied list of wanted men. At Eisenhower's headquarters they wanted to see this important captive. All this took its time. Papen remained in custody—and was to remain so until long after the Nuremberg Trial.

The American Seventh Army, too, had its success story to report to the Commander in Chief's headquarters. On May 6, 1945, its 30th Infantry Division took over two thousand prisoners, a gray, undistinguishable mass of humanity, at Berchtesgaden. The men were searched, registered, and allocated to the barracks. It was purely a matter of routine, not a special action.

In the middle of the night, the telephone rang for Captain Philip Broadhead, chief of Berchtesgaden Military Control. The officer on duty at the prisoners' quarters was on the line.

"One of these guys tried to commit suicide," the lieutenant reported.

"So what?" Captain Broadhead asked morosely. He did not like to be awakened on account of trifles.

"Seems to me to be a big shot," said the officer, unimpressed. "Guilty conscience or something."

"What's his name?"

"Just a moment. Yes, Frank, Hans Frank."

Broadhead leaped out of bed. A few minutes later he was in the improvised first-aid room of the barracks beside the unconscious former Governor General of Poland.

Frank's left arm was bandaged to the finger tips. His round face was white as chalk and shrunken. His breathing was slight and scarcely audible.

"A razor slash, Captain," said the doctor. "But we'll pull him through."

They pulled him through. Frank's left hand and arm remained immobilized. In opening his artery he had also severed the nerves.

The news of Frank's identification took the whole world by surprise. With his name were associated horror and systematic mass-murders. He was known as the "Hangman of Poland," the "Jew-Butcher of Cracow." Yet Frank was one of the few who, at Nuremberg, took their guilt upon themselves and did not try to shift the responsibility for their deeds to other officials over or under them.

Frank volunteered to show the Americans where he had hidden the art treasures taken from Poland. According to the first valuation by experts they were worth "several million dollars." Frank also of his own free will surrendered his diary to the Americans. It comprised thirty-eight volumes and formed the most terrible indictment that a man had ever composed against himself. In them one reads with loathing sentences like these: "If I had gone to the Führer and had told him: 'My Führer, I report that I have destroyed a further 150,000 Poles,' then he would have said, 'That is good if it was necessary.'" . . . "If we win the war, then as far as I am concerned the Poles and the Ukrainians and the rest can be turned into mincemeat." . . . "Here we began with three and a half million Jews, of whom there remain only a few labor gangs; the others have—shall we say—emigrated." . . . "We should remember that we all appear together in Mr. Roosevelt's list of war criminals. I have the honor to be Number One."

Clearly, Frank knew what he was doing. He knew why in the night following his arrest he had opened his artery. But now he was to be nursed back to health—for Nuremberg.

SCHACHT, NEURATH, FUNK, KALTENBRUNNER, SEYSS-INQUART, KRUPP, AND SAUCKEL

The arrest of another Nuremberg defendant was effected in a much more friendly atmosphere. It was really more like a liberation. Hjalmar Schacht, the former president of the German Reichsbank, was at the time of his arrest by American troops a prisoner of Hitler.

He had made a long journey through prisons and concentration camps. In 1944, he was arrested by the Gestapo in connection with the July 20 assassination attempt. Ravensbrück, Moabit, and finally the extermination camp of Flossenbürg were his stopping places. "No one gets out alive from this camp," Schacht whispered to his fellow prisoners when he was brought in.

Through the open door of a shed in the camp, there was a view of the scaffolding of the gallows. Every night Schacht heard the screams and shots which left no doubt what was happening. Many a morning, as he took his exercise, he could count up to thirty dead being carried away on stretchers from the places of execution.

Only much later Schacht learned that the commandant of Flossenbürg had been expressly ordered to shoot him as soon as the Allies came anywhere near the camp. But it did not come to that. In the face of imminent defeat the SS suddenly attempted to introduce a more humane treatment, perhaps in the hope of thereby saving themselves.

Thus Schacht, together with other prisoners, was transferred first to Dachau and later to Austria when the Americans advanced. As the transport halted at the Pragser Wildsee the Ninth Army liberated him, and with him a number of others who were internees and "V.I.P. prisoners" of Hitler: the French Socialist leader, Léon Blum; the last Austrian chancellor, Kurt Schuschnigg; Pastor Martin Niemöller; the Ruhr industrialist, Fritz Thyssen; the deposed regent of Hungary, Nicholas von Horthy; Molotov's nephew, Alexei Kokosin; the generals Franz Halder and Alexander von Falkenhausen; the princes Philipp von Hessen and Friedrich-Leopold of Prussia; the sixty-two-year-old cousin of the British Prime Minister, Captain Peter Churchill; the Frenchmen Edouard Daladier, Paul Reynaud, Maurice Gamelin; and many others.

"Why did Hitler put you in jail?" Schacht was asked by the Americans.

"No idea," answered the banker.

He also had no idea why he was not set free, but kept under arrest. He was well treated, he had excellent food, and was allowed to walk unguarded by the Pragser lake. But then he was moved again, and by various stages reached eventually the overcrowded prisoner-of-war camp of Aversa near Naples.

Hjalmar Schacht, the financial genius with the old-fashioned stand-up collar, had changed sides several times. Now he was on his way to the prison at Nuremberg.

The wave of arrests continued; more and more thousands of people went into captivity. Scarcely a day passed but one of those later to appear at Nuremberg was caught in the net. On May 6, the French arrested the former Protector of Bohemia and Moravia, Konstantin von Neurath, in their zone. On May 11 in Berlin, Schacht's successor, Minister for Economics Walther Frank, was captured. On May 15, American troops in Austria seized Ernst Kaltenbrunner, the chief of the once-dreaded Security Headquarters. His boss, SS Leader Heinrich Himmler, however, could not be traced despite intensive efforts.

The Canadian Army caught a German E-boat. On board they

found Arthur Seyss-Inquart, nominally still "Commissar for the Occupied Netherlands." An American paper gave its report the headline, "The Trojan Horse of the Nazis Arrested!" The journal reminded its readers pointedly that it was Seyss-Inquart who, in 1938, helped Hitler to help himself to Austria.

The E-boat of the Commissar was not taken in flight. On May 3 the acting head of the Government, Karl Doenitz, had invited all the civil military commanders of the German occupied areas to Flensburg—from Bohemia, Holland, Denmark, and Norway. The purpose of the meeting was to carry out a rapid, bloodless surrender in these countries.

Bad weather kept Seyss-Inquart in Flensburg longer than planned. On May 7 he was at last able to start back to the Netherlands. The sea route was the only way still open. The Canadians picked him up.

Thus, Seyss-Inquart did reach Holland, but as a prisoner. Near the castle of Twickel at Hanglo, where he had once resided as a Commissar, a new place was built for him: a British prison tent, erected on a deserted football field among puddles.

The arrests went on. The British put Gustav Krupp von Bohlen und Halbach, head of the largest German armament concern, under house arrest. The elderly, infirm industrialist had to leave his feudal palace and take up quarters in the gardener's house of his lordly domain. Eventually, a decision had to be reached as to whether he was fit to appear at Nuremberg.

The arrest of the man chiefly responsible for the labor forces, Fritz Sauckel, went almost unnoticed in the daily spate of news.

ROBERT LEY,
ALFRED ROSENBERG, AND
JULIUS STREICHER

Another piece of sensational news hit the headlines of the world's press: "Dr. Robert Ley Arrested!"

"The capture of Ley is more important than the imprisonment of Goering," wrote *The New York Times*, "for Ley was the man behind the Werewolf."

Even today, the Werewolf, the abortive Nazi partisan movement, is still overestimated; so is Ley's importance. For a long time the leader of the German Labor Front had not been as influential as it was still assumed abroad. Ley was given to drink; he loved, in his own philistine way, a life of luxury which found expression in such things as a black-tiled bath with golden faucets in his villa. When his brain was examined after his death, the surgeons found signs of a severe mental disease.

When the Nazi bubble was about to burst, Ley tried to disappear in the Bavarian Alps. He chose a mountain hut south of Berchtesgaden as his secret refuge, but the Americans were given a hint by the local residents. Soldiers of the American 101st Airborne Division went to the place on May 16. With their submachine guns at the ready they forced their way into the hut.

In the semidarkness of the room a man was cowering at the edge of the wooden bed. He stared at the soldiers with feverish eyes, his jaw sagging. His face was framed by a four days' growth of beard, and his body was shaking with nervous tremors.

"Are you Dr. Ley?"

Ley stood up and shook his head vigorously. "You are m-m-mistaken," he replied. "I am Dr. Ernst D-Distelmeyer."

"O.K.," said the American. "Come with us."

The former leader of the Labor Front put up no resistance. He was wearing blue pajamas; he kept them on, hung a coarse woolen cape around his shoulders, put on brown shoes with thick soles, and donned a green Tyrolean hat. In this array he was shortly afterward delivered to Divisional Headquarters in Berchtesgaden. There he was thoroughly examined for ampules of poison and razor blades. Then the interrogation began.

"You are not Dr. Ley?"

"N-no. Here are my papers." They showed the name of Dr. Ernst Distelmeyer. The Intelligence Officer put some photographs of Dr. Ley in front of him. "That isn't me," Ley insisted.

"I will tell you something," the American said to him in perfect German, "and this will surprise you. I am a member of the secret service, and my duty in the last thirteen years has been exclusively to watch Dr. Robert Ley. I know you well enough."

Ley turned a shade grayer. Then he bluffed: "You are mistaken."

"All right," said the officer. He made a sign to a soldier, who went out of the room and returned with an old man. It was the eighty-year-old Franz Xavier Schwarz, formerly the powerful treasurer of the Nazi Party, now in American custody.

Schwarz did not know why he had been brought into the room. He gave full play to his surprise when he saw the prisoner. "Well, Dr. Ley!" he cried sympathetically. "What are you doing here?" Then, realizing his mistake, he looked helplessly from Ley to the Americans. The officer smiled.

"Now," he turned to Ley, "do you still call yourself Distelmeyer?" The Leader of the Labor Front gave no answer. His chin had sunk to his breast. At a sign from the officer, a second witness was brought in. It was Franz Schwarz, son of the treasurer. "Do you know this man?" he was asked.

"It is Dr. Robert Ley," said the younger Schwarz without hesitation. He had sized up the situation at a glance, realizing that lies were of no use.

"What do you say now?" the American asked quietly.

"You have won," answered Ley. With his head still bent he trotted out to the jeep. Lieutenant Walter Rice took him to the prison at Salzburg.

"We National Socialists will carry on," said Ley during his first examination. He had recovered from the shock of his arrest and was once again the true henchman of Hitler. At least he would keep up appearances.

Ley's arrest was overshadowed by a new event. The news came from the Headquarters of the British Second Army in northern Germany. There an intensive search for SS Leader Heinrich Himmler had resulted in the arrest of another leading member of the Party, the Nazi theorist, philosopher, and one-time Minister for the Occupied East, Alfred Rosenberg.

Rosenberg, editor of the Party bible, *The Myth of the Twentieth Century*, had eventually made his way to Doenitz in Flensburg. Apparently he had hoped to find a new post there, and to enjoy a certain measure of Allied protection as a member of a non-Nazi German government.

Doenitz, however, had declined his aid, and suggested to him that he surrender voluntarily to the British. Rosenberg did not follow this advice, or rather he was unable to so do. On the day after his talk with Doenitz he got drunk and sprained his ankle, which restricted his movements. So he stayed in the Naval School at Flensburg, then a hospital. On May 19 tanks and infantry surrounded the building. The British had orders to search the hospital for Heinrich Himmler. They did not find the SS leader, but got Rosenberg as a consolation prize. A few months later, the Party philosopher was to sit in the Nuremberg dock with the others; not because of the *Weltanschauung* he had propagated, but because of his actions as Minister for the Occupied Eastern Regions.

After the Flensburg intermezzo southern Bavaria again became the main scene of the great manhunt.

On May 23, 1945, four Americans in a jeep, soldiers of the 101st Airborne Division, drove toward Berchtesgaden. Major Henry Blitt was squatting in the back seat of the vehicle, looking thoughtfully at the beautiful mountain scenery, and thinking perhaps how good it would be to tour the country not as a soldier but on a holiday. The mountain folk in their local garb looked picturesque and peaceable. A pity that they were all Nazis, mused Blitt. The old man on the porch of his farmhouse, for instance, sitting in the sun, his face framed by a white beard. An easel stood nearby. Cowbells were tinkling in the field.

Suddenly, Major Blitt felt an irresistible urge to have a drink of milk here—genuine farmhouse milk, still warm from the cow, not the sterile, pasteurized product of the New York cardboard containers. Blitt stopped the jeep, and the Americans went into the farmhouse. The Major had his milk. He spoke Yiddish, for that was his mother tongue, but he could make himself understood with it in Germany. He began to talk to the bearded old man.

"How's it going, papa?"

"Good, good," answered the man.

"Are you the farmer?"

"No," said the bearded one. "I only live here. I'm an artist, you see, a painter—"

"What do you think of the Nazis?" Blitt asked with a smile. The old man nodded: "I don't understand these things. I am an artist and have never bothered about politics."

"But you look like Julius Streicher," Blitt joked. Something about this painter had in fact reminded him of the photograph on Streicher's warrant. The old man stared at him, an expression of surprise and shock on his face. Then he asked: "How did you recognize me?"

It was all pure accident. Streicher had taken the Major's joke seriously and had given himself away. "My name is Sailer," Streicher said quickly, in the hope of being able to correct his mistake. But it was too late. Major Blitt called his men.

"You are under arrest," he said to Streicher, who put on a morose expression. Nothing remained of the pose of a harmless painter. He looked much older than his fifty-nine years. His shaggy beard and uncombed hair, his collarless, blue-striped shirt, and his ragged trousers made him look slovenly.

An American correspondent witnessed Streicher's arrival at Divisional Headquarters. "Julius Streicher," he wrote in his paper, "the publisher of the anti-Semitic rag *Der Stürmer*, was the greatest Jew-hater in history. Now he has been discovered and taken prisoner by a Jew."

The London War Crimes Commission was now able to publish an interim balance sheet of the manhunt for the Nazi leaders. The majority of them had now been captured; only two were still missing, the most important ones—the former Foreign Minister Joachim von Ribbentrop and SS Leader Heinrich Himmler.

SS LEADER
HEINRICH HIMMLER

In the latter half of February 1945, a Swedish official of the Red Cross was traveling through stricken Germany in a plainly marked white car. It was Count Folke Bernadotte who, three years later, was murdered when acting as Arbitration Commissioner for the United Nations in Jerusalem.

He was seeking a meeting with Heinrich Himmler, the dreaded chief of the dreaded SS, the brain of the uncanny secret police, the ruler of the murder camps, the gas chambers, and the mills of death. Bernadotte wanted to persuade him, as chief of the German police and the home forces, to set free all Danish and Norwegian prisoners from the concentration camps so that they could be taken to Sweden by the Red Cross.

On February 19, the Count met Himmler in a hospital at Hohenlychen near Berlin. The SS leader had taken refuge there because his many duties and the imminent collapse of Germany had become too much for him. He played the sick man, and left it to others to get the country out of the mess. The meeting took place in the room of the notorious chief surgeon, Karl Gebhardt. "When I suddenly saw Himmler before me in the green Waffen SS uniform," Folke Bernadotte wrote in his memoirs, "without any decorations and wearing horn-rimmed glasses, he looked like a typically unimportant official and one would certainly have passed him in the street without noticing him. He had well-shaped, delicate hands which were carefully manicured, although this was forbidden in the SS. He was to my great surprise extremely affable and amusing and frequently made use of a joke when conversation was threatening to become awkward or heavy. Certainly there was nothing diabolical in his appearance. Nor did I observe any sign of that icy hardness in his look, of which I had heard so much."

So this was the man before whom the whole of Europe had trembled for years, the man whose nod was enough to condemn millions of people to extermination; a man full of narrow-minded fanaticism, irresolution, and sadistic lust for power. A man of respectable family—his father had been tutor to Prince Heinrich of Bavaria, and the SS leader owed his Christian name to the fact that he was a godson of the Prince.

Himmler had once tried his hand, unsuccessfully, as a poultry farmer and fertilizer salesman, became interested in the Mongol tyrant, Genghis Khan, marched with the *Freikorps* of the twenties, was secretary to the rebel Gregor Strasser, advocated the cultivation of curative herbs when he was already Germany's most powerful man after Hitler, and himself ordered ghastly experiments to be carried out on living beings. His sole aim was to concentrate gradually all power in his own hands, to be able to give orders without restraint, and to assume the succession after Hitler.

How did he react to the humane mission of Bernadotte? Himmler at first turned down the suggestion to have Scandinavian concentration camp prisoners taken to Sweden. "If I agree to your proposal," he said, "the Swedish papers would announce in large headlines that the war criminal Himmler was trying to buy himself off at the last moment to appear blameless before the world because he feared the consequences of his actions." Thus he sized up the general situation and his own position perfectly correctly. In the police, the SS, the Gestapo, and the reserve army he was still holding the strongest instruments of power in his hands. He could have carried out a *coup d'état* without fear of encountering much resistance. We now know that he often toyed with that idea. But he hesitated, unable to make up his mind, as always throughout his life. He wanted to be faithful to Hitler and at the same time get his own head out of the noose.

"I am prepared to do anything for the German people," he said to Count Bernadotte at a second meeting at the beginning of April, "but I must continue the fight. I have sworn allegiance to the Führer, and I am bound by this oath."

"But don't you see that Germany has already lost the war?" Bernadotte asked him bluntly. "A man who finds himself in your position and predicament can no longer obey his superiors blindly. He must have the courage to take steps that will be of service to his people."

Himmler was called to the telephone and broke off the conversation. But through a man he trusted, the SS Group Leader Walter Schellenberg, he made another proposal to Bernadotte: the Count should go to Eisenhower and offer the capitulation of the German front in the West.

Count Bernadotte was amazed. Then he put forward conditions. Two of them were rather unusual: one, Himmler must first publicly announce that he had taken over from Hitler as the latter was prevented from carrying out his functions due to illness; and two, Himmler must disband the Nazi Party and immediately dismiss all Party officials.

These points seemed difficult to accept, but to Bernadotte's great surprise the SS leader agreed to them. The Count did not know what had happened in the meantime behind the scenes.

Himmler knew that the war was already lost. He had known it since 1943. At that time he had secretly tried, through the German industrialist, Arnold Rechberg, to get in touch with the Western powers and discuss the possibility of a separate peace. Bormann and Ribbentrop, however, had frustrated Himmler's move.

Now, before the door finally closed, he was almost prepared to do anything to save his skin. While he was still issuing orders to hold fast and having thousands of retreating soldiers hanged for desertion he was carrying on a very dubious game on the side of negotiating, through an intermediary—Arnold Rechberg—who was to put out peace feelers in the West on his behalf. Himmler, the greatest destroyer of Jews in history, was also corresponding secretly with Dr. Hillel Storch, the Stockholm representative of the World Jewish Congress. Himmler arranged for the Jewish spokesman, Dr. Norbert Masur, to fly from Sweden to Berlin, under his personal safe-conduct to discuss the release of Jewish concentration camp prisoners. Furthermore, he was negotiating with the former Swiss President, Jean-Marie Musy, about the transport of Jews from the concentration camp at Belsen to neutral countries. He was trying, through the Swedish banker Jakob Wallenberg, to get into touch with the Western powers to start peace talks.

Now he was attempting to draw Count Folke Bernadotte into this game, and therefore he agreed to the requested liberation of the Scandinavian prisoners.

In the face of Germany's certain collapse Himmler was obsessed with a fixed idea: after having had millions of men exterminated he now thought that he could play the part of the great protector and angel of peace. He was convinced that he would be accepted in this role by the whole world. He would not see that he would forever remain a monster and mass-murderer.

For all that he still walked in fear of Hitler. He was afraid that the Führer would hear of his double-dealings and strike him down at the last moment. For this reason he planned a *coup d'état* in Germany, together with Schellenberg. Himmler wanted to make Hitler's bad health the main reason. In talks with Schellenberg he spoke of the increasingly bent posture of the Führer, his weary expression and trembling hands. Professor Max de Crinis, head of the psychiatric department of a Berlin hospital, was taken into confidence, also the "national health leader," Dr. Leonardo Conti. The doctors expressed their opinion that Hitler had Parkinson's disease, an ailment that produces a masklike rigidity of the face and paralytic symptoms in the limbs.

Himmler asked Schellenberg to come with him for a walk in the woods. Out of everyone's hearing he turned the conversation on the matter that concerned him most: "I don't think that we can work with the Führer much longer. He is no longer up to his task. Do you think that de Crinis is right?"

"Yes," Schellenberg replied.

"But what am I to do?" Himmler asked irresolutely. "I can't just have the Führer murdered or poisoned or imprisoned in the Chancellery—"

"There is only one thing to do," Schellenberg advised. "You must go to Hitler, explain everything to him, and then force him to abdicate."

"That is out of the question," said Himmler, scared. "The Führer would go raging mad and have me shot on the spot."

"Then you must take certain measures to prevent that," said Schellenberg calmly. "You have at your disposal a considerable number of leading SS men who would be able to carry out an arrest of this kind. And if nothing else works, the doctors must help."

But Himmler could not force himself to any decision. During the ninety minutes that they walked in the woods he could think only about all the things he would do when he had taken over from Hitler. "The Nazi Party will be immediately disbanded," he told his companion. "A new party must be founded. What name would you give it, Schellenberg?"

"Party of the National Assembly," suggested Himmler's confidant.

But this *coup d'état* never took place. Events at the front gave no further breathing space. The Red Army was knocking at the door of the capital. Himmler was frightened. "Schellenberg," he said in another talk with him, "I shudder when I think what is now going to happen—"

In the night of April 20–21, 1945, the SS leader again met Count Folke Bernadotte at Hohenlychen. Himmler seemed gray and harassed. "He gave the impression that he could no longer keep still," the Swede recorded. "Restlessly he wandered about trying to overcome his nervousness."

"The military situation is serious, very serious," Himmler repeated time and again. He urged Count Bernadotte to convey the offer of capitulation in the West to Eisenhower, and to arrange a meeting between himself, Himmler, and the American Commander in Chief.

"I greatly doubt whether the Allies will accept a capitulation only on the Western front," Bernadotte said later to Schellenberg. "Even if this should be the case, it would not make a meeting between Himmler and Eisenhower necessary. It is out of the question that Himmler should play any part in the Germany of the future."

Three days later Bernadotte and Himmler met again—for the last time. The meeting took place at the Swedish Consulate in Lübeck. It was the night of April 24, 1945. "As long as I live I shall never forget that night with its atmosphere of impending disaster," wrote Bernadotte. Air-raid warnings forced the men down to the shelter. Swedes and Germans were squatting there on the bunks. No one recognized Himmler. About one in the morning the All Clear sounded. The talks began at last in a room of the Consulate. A pair of candles lit up the scene, for the electricity had failed.

"Hitler is probably already dead," began Himmler. "If it hasn't happened yet, he is sure to die in the course of the next few days. Up to now my oath has bound me, but now the position is changed. I admit that Germany is beaten. And what comes now?"

Himmler was convinced that he would be named by Hitler as

his successor. All his statements assumed this: "In the situation that now exists I have a free hand. I am ready to surrender on the Western front so that the troops of the Western Powers can advance to the East as fast as possible. But I am not prepared to surrender on the Eastern front."

Once again he requested Count Bernadotte to arrange a meeting with Eisenhower. He even discussed with Walter Schellenberg how he should behave at a meeting with the American Commander in Chief: "Shall I only bow to him, or shall I offer my hand?"

In his midnight talk with Folke Bernadotte Himmler let his imagination run riot: "This is what I shall say to Eisenhower: 'I declare that the Western Powers have defeated the German Army. I am ready to surrender unconditionally on the Western front.'"

"And what will you do if your offer is rejected?"

"In that case I will take command of a battalion on the Eastern front and die fighting."

"It is generally known," Folke Bernadotte added in his memoirs, "that he did not carry out this plan."

The Vice-President of the Swedish Red Cross finally declared himself ready to send Himmler's offer of surrender to the Swedish Foreign Minister. If his government was willing to agree, the Allies would be informed from Stockholm.

"That was the grimmest day in my life," said Himmler at half past two in the morning as he left the Consulate. He took the steering wheel of his armored car himself. "I am going now to the Eastern front," he said to Folke Bernadotte as he left, adding with a faint smile, "It isn't far away."

President Harry S. Truman himself answered Himmler's proposals. He refused the partial surrender and ended his telegram with the words: "Wherever resistance continues, the attacks of the Allies will continue relentlessly until complete victory is won."

Himmler's last hopes had been dashed. He made his way to the Army Headquarters, which at that time were in Plön. Hitler's excommunication followed him: "I herewith expel before my death the former SS Leader and Minister of the Interior, Heinrich Himmler, from the Party and from all offices of state. By their secret dealings with the enemy as well as by their efforts to seize power in the State, Goering and Himmler have done unimaginable harm. . . ."

Himmler heard nothing of his expulsion. He did not know that Hitler had learned of his dealings with Folke Bernadotte through foreign broadcasts. He was still convinced that he would be the Führer's successor.

Doenitz was to rob him of this illusion. The Admiral invited Himmler to a confidential talk. Before the arrival of the SS leader, Doenitz took certain precautions. He rightly feared the power that Himmler still exercised. A strong company of reliable U-boat men mounted guard. Heavily armed guards were posted in the house and in the garden behind bushes. It was a few minutes after midnight on May 1, 1945.

The meeting between Doenitz and Himmler was completely private. But the substance of it has been preserved in a report which the Admiral himself dictated later. Concealed on his writing table among his papers Doenitz had a Browning with the safety catch off. He was ready for anything as he handed Himmler the radio message in which Hitler named the Admiral his successor and President of the Reich.

Himmler read the lines and turned pale. He thought it over a few seconds. Then he stood up and congratulated Doenitz. It was a dramatic moment.

"Let me be the second man in the State," he asked, after a pause, in a hoarse voice. Doenitz declined. He explained to Himmler that in his new government he could not use any person who was politically suspect. Himmler saw things quite differently. "He was completely unrealistic and full of fantastic ideas," Walter Lüdde-Neurath reported. "He considered himself as the proper spokesman and delegate for the negotiations with Eisenhower and Montgomery. According to him they were already waiting for the chance to talk to him."

But in the end Himmler had to admit that he had lost the game. Doenitz wrote: "He set off between two and three in the morning, fully aware that he could not be employed by me·in any prominent position."

For a week Himmler remained in contact with the acting government. Then, on May 6, officially relieved of all his offices by Doenitz, he departed forever.

"Later Doenitz was to regret that he let Himmler go," Lüdde-Neurath admitted. "Under the pressure of the Nuremberg Trial he declared that he would have had Himmler arrested at the time of his departure if he had known of the mass-murders and the conditions in the concentration camps."

Too late! Himmler was not to appear in the dock at Nuremberg. He was unable to summon the courage of shouldering the responsibility for his acts and orders.

Where did he hide after he had left Doenitz? Apparently at first in Flensburg itself, along with his two adjutants, Werner Grothmann and Heinz Macher. The home of a mistress of Himmler is said to have served them as a hide-out. SS Brigade Commander Otto Ohlendorf claimed to have seen the former SS Leader in Flensburg as late as May 21.

The Allied secret service agents were surprised that the name of Himmler had suddenly disappeared from the news on the Flensburg radio. Their best man and more than a hundred thousand soldiers were put on the alert. It was regarded as certain that the mass-murderer would try to escape, unknown, through the Occupied Zone to the West. The net was drawn tight round the miniature state of Flensburg, and eventually Himmler was caught in it.

He had shaved off his mustache, and stuck a black patch over his left eye. He carried an identity card of the German Secret Military Police in the name of Heinrich Hitzinger in his pocket. He was naive enough to regard this cheap masquerade as an effective disguise. The former chief of the German police acted like a school boy who had read too many thrillers. Moreover he appeared not to know that the German Secret Military Police was listed by the Allies among the organizations whose members were to be automatically arrested.

With his two adjutants, like him wearing a mixture of uniforms and civilian clothing, Himmler reached the British control point at Meinstedt near Bremervörde on May 21.

Thousands of people thronged the place—refugees, casualties, discharged soldiers, liberated prisoners of war, and foreign workers. Everyone who wished to cross the bridge over the Oste had to pass this control point.

Himmler and his companions shuffled along in line. When his turn came, the former Nazi leader showed his papers. The British soldier looked at them in surprise, cast a suspicious glance at the man with the eye patch, and told him to wait at the barrier.

"Himmler had made the mistake of producing his papers—most of the men who passed through the control point had none," said the report of the British Second Army HQ. "If he had come with bag and baggage, without papers, and had said that he wanted to get home, no doubt he would have been allowed to pass without hindrance. His policeman's maxim—that a man with papers is a man beyond suspicion—had made him suspect."

But no one knew yet that the suspect man was Himmler. For the moment he was only a man with a too good and too new identity card, who belonged to the Secret Military Police, and was called Heinrich Hitzinger. He remained in custody, and was rushed through two prisons in quick succession, Bremervörde and Zeelos. In the third one, Westertimke, he was placed temporarily in solitary confinement.

Meanwhile, the Intelligence Officers of the Second Army had been told of the case of one Hitzinger. It was not difficult to draw the right conclusion. On the morning of May 22, Headquarters at Lüneburg were already fairly certain that this man must be Heinrich Himmler. Toward nine in the evening three high-ranking officers made their way to Westertimke to view the prisoner in the flesh. But before they arrived, Himmler had already admitted his identity. No one can explain what made him do so. He asked for an interview with the camp commandant, Captain Tom Sylvester, who agreed and had the prisoner brought to his office. He dismissed the guard.

"Well?" he asked. The prisoner took off his eye patch and put on his glasses.

"I am Heinrich Himmler," he said. "I want to speak to Field Marshal Montgomery." He still believed that he could carry on negotiations.

"I shall inform the Army," replied the Captain. Then he had Himmler led away without a further word, and placed him under extra guard. After a while, some officers from Headquarters arrived. They took over the prisoner and brought him to Lüneburg. There, in the early morning hours of May 23, Himmler realized at last that he would not have a chance of discussing anything with the British, and that he could not expect to enjoy any privileges.

At the Information Center in Ulzener Strasse, in a private house commandeered by the military, Heinrich Himmler had to strip naked. His clothing and his body were examined by an Army doctor, Captain Wells, for poison or other aids to suicide. In a pocket of Himmler's jacket the doctor found a capsule containing cyanide of potassium, half an inch long and thinner than a cigarette. The prisoner had to put on an old English uniform and was locked in an empty room.

In the evening, Colonel M. L. Murphy of Montgomery's Intelligence Department arrived at the Information Center. He had been ordered to supervise all matters concerning Himmler, and to carry out a first interrogation of the prisoner. Murphy listened to the officers' reports. "Was any poison found?" he wanted to know.

"Yes, a capsule in his pocket," replied the doctor. "It has been removed. He cannot commit suicide."

"Was his mouth searched?" Murphy further inquired. Dr. Wells said no. "Then attend to that at once," ordered the colonel. "Perhaps he put that capsule in his pocket only to distract your attention."

Himmler was brought from his cell. The military doctor ordered him to open his mouth. The eyes of the SS leader contracted into small slits. His jaws made a chewing movement. He was crunching something between his teeth. A moment later, he fell to the ground as though struck by lightning. Captain Wells quickly knelt beside him and tried to get the remains of the capsule from the mouth of the dying man. Orders rang out. An emetic was given to the unconscious, twitching Himmler. A tube was inserted into his stomach and the contents removed. But all was in vain. The struggle lasted for twelve minutes. At 11:04 P.M., Dr. Wells gave up the fight. Heinrich Himmler was dead.

During the whole of the next day he remained lying on the floor in the room where he had died. Several hundred British soldiers, a dozen war correspondents, and photographers saw him there. They walked in silence past the corpse, stared into the face of the dead monster, went out again, and took a deep breath.

What was to be done with the dead Himmler? It was seriously considered at Montgomery's Headquarters that he be given a military burial in the presence of high-ranking German officers, and some chaplains argued the question whether he should have a Christian burial. Apparently the decision was made by Montgomery himself: Heinrich Himmler would be buried without any military or religious ceremony in a place that was to be kept secret. His last resting place should never become a national shrine for the Germans.

Meanwhile, a staff officer telephoned a British post at the Bergen-Belsen concentration camp. He wanted something special —one of the wooden boxes in which the bones of the camp prisoners had been collected and interred. But he had no success with his efforts to procure a fitting container for Himmler's remains.

On the morning of May 26, Himmler was taken away in a one-ton truck to an unknown destination. Two sergeants gripped his head and feet and swung him onto the floor of the truck.

A senior intelligence officer had decided on the location of the secret burying place somewhere in a wood near Lüneburg. A major and three sergeants went with him. These five men are the only ones who know the place.

Some earth was carefully removed. The three sergeants shaped a grave with their spades. Himmler's body was laid in it, dressed, as it had been since May 23, in a British Army uniform, an open service shirt, and gray German army socks.

The men looked into the grave once more, and one of the sergeants said, "Let the worm join the worms!" Then they completed their task in silence. The sod was relaid; no scar, no mound marks the place. No trace has been left of the man whose place at Nuremberg remained empty, who could have told more than any of the other defendants.

There was, however, an epilogue. Under a barn at Berchtesgaden, American troops found Himmler's buried private hoard, valued at about a million dollars and consisting of an unusual mixture of currencies. Captain Harry Anderson of the Control Commission counted 132 Canadian dollars, 25,935 English pounds sterling, 8,000,000 French francs, 3,000,000 Algerian and Moroccan francs, 1,000,000 Reichsmarks, 1,000,000 Egyptian pounds, two (!) Argentine pesos, half a Japanese yen, and 7,500 Palestinian pounds.

RIBBENTROP, SCHIRACH, RAEDER

Almost all the prominent figures of the Third Reich had been arrested or were dead. There remained only a few puzzles for the Allied search parties to solve, one of the most important being— where was Ribbentrop? He had remained in northern Germany, as Admiral Doenitz was about to form his nonpolitical government. The new "President of the Reich" was in urgent need of an uncommitted man who could be entrusted with the office of Foreign Minister. It had to be someone whom the Allies would not reject out of hand as a party to negotiations.

Ribbentrop got wind of the matter, approached Doenitz, and promised to help him in his search. He said he was going to think it over, but the results of his meditations were merely that next day he proposed to Doenitz no one else but himself as Foreign Minister. The Admiral, however, refused, and entrusted Count Schwerin von Krosigk with the post. Ribbentrop disappeared from the scene.

He made his way to Hamburg, rented some rooms on the fifth floor of an unpretentious apartment house, and under the eyes of the British Military Government began to lead the life of a harmless private citizen. While dozens of secret agents and intelligence officers were looking for him, while warrants with his photograph were hanging in all barracks and police stations, Ribbentrop, in an elegant double-breasted suit, with a black felt hat and very dark sunglasses, took leisurely strolls through Hamburg. He tried to get in touch with former connections from his unspectacular period as a champagne salesman in an effort to find anonymity in some firm or other.

Time and again his path led to the office of an almost forgotten business friend of old. Here the man with the sunglasses, who now called himself Reiser, began some mysterious negotiations.

"I have been given a posthumous order by the Führer," he whispered to his old friend, looking anxiously over his shoulder to make sure that no one in the shop was listening. "You must hide me until the time is ripe. . . . The future of Germany is at stake. . . ."

The wine merchant hesitated. But his son did not; he went to the police. Allied plain-clothes men quickly took up the trail of the mysterious stranger. Next morning, on June 14, 1945, the last dramatic scene of the great manhunt began. Three British soldiers and a Belgian soldier mounted the steps of the unpretentious apartment house to a room on the fifth floor. They knocked at the door. Nothing stirred. Then they kicked with their boots against the door. Suddenly, Sergeant Major R. C. Halloway whistled in surprise. The door had opened a little. Through the gap the men saw a young woman, a brunette. The scanty negligee scarcely concealed an attractive figure. Her unkempt hair hung about her face which was shiny with cold cream. The soldiers pushed the door open and shoved the woman aside. They searched the rooms. In the fourth room the Belgian soldier found an unmade bed. He drew the cover aside.

"There's a man in here!" he shouted. The man in the bed seemed to be sleeping like a log. He had not heard the knocks at the door. Even the boots and the voices of the soldiers had not wakened him. Or perhaps he didn't want to hear it all.

"Hey, get up."

Lieutenant Adams shook the sleeping man by the shoulder. He had to shake a long time before the man came to life. He turned round slowly, blinked at the light, and gazed incredulously at the foreign soldiers beside his bed.

What's the matter?" he asked in a faint voice.

"Get up," said Adams, "and get dressed—quickly."

Joachim von Ribbentrop, former Foreign Minister of the

Greater German Reich, threw back the blanket. Without saying a word he got out of bed.

"What is your name?" the lieutenant asked.

"You know very well who I am," Ribbentrop answered with a bad-tempered smile. He made a stiff bow and said ironically: "I congratulate you!"

"All right, Herr von Ribbentrop," said Lieutenant Adams. "Get dressed. You're under arrest."

"I would like to shave first."

"There will be time for that later. Now you have to come with me." Ribbentrop dressed, combed his hair carefully in front of the mirror, and threw some things into an army kit-bag.

At the British Headquarters Joachim von Ribbentrop was searched thoroughly and completely. That was one of the measures to which the Allies had become accustomed since some prominent men had slipped through their fingers with the help of those infernal German poison capsules. They found a capsule of potassium cyanide which the prisoner was carrying in a secret place on his body. In Ribbentrop's bag the British discovered, neatly bundled, several hundred thousand Reichsmark.

"I wanted to hide," Ribbentrop stated at his first hearing, "until public opinion had quieted down."

"Do you mean public opinion in Germany?"

"Yes, that too, but above all world opinion. I know that we are all on the list of war criminals, and I can see that in the present state of world opinion only one verdict can be expected—sentence of death."

"You wanted to wait until the storm had blown over, and then reappear?"

"Yes."

There must have been utter confusion in Ribbentrop's mind. One of his coat pockets contained three letters: one to Field Marshal Montgomery, one to Foreign Minister Eden, and one addressed to "Vincent" Churchill. There is no more convincing proof of the amateurish way in which the Foreign Minister of the Third Reich went about his job than this slip—Vincent instead of Winston. And that man had been responsible for the foreign policy of a nation!

Ribbentrop was taken to Lüneburg and from there later to an internment camp "somewhere in Europe."

Apart from two stragglers everyone who was soon to sit in the dock at Nuremberg was now in Allied hands. One was Baldur von Schirach, former Youth Leader and finally Gauleiter and Defense Commissar for Vienna. When the Russians marched into the Austrian capital, Schirach, with a newly grown beard, set out for Schwaz in the Tyrol. He boarded under the name of Richard · Falk in a farmhouse. Here he felt fairly secure, for the Americans believed erroneously that he was dead; there was a report that the Viennese had hanged their Defense Commissar from the Florisdorf Bridge over the Danube during the last days of the Nazi regime.

Thus Schirach was even able to work, unrecognized, as an interpreter for an American unit. In his spare time he was busy as an author, typing industriously away at a manuscript; he had put the title of a detective story on the first page: "The Secret of Myrna Loy." Inside, however, was hidden the history of the last days of Vienna.

His farmhouse hosts suspected nothing. The occupation authorities in Schwaz were all the more surprised when, on June 5, 1945, they received a letter from the man they had believed to be dead: "Of my own free will I surrender to American imprisonment, so as to have the opportunity to vindicate myself before an international court of law. Baldur von Schirach."

"But Schirach is already dead," cried the local commanding officer. Still, he sent off a jeep. On the way to the farmhouse, Schirach met the soldiers. He had shaved off his beard.

Why did he surrender voluntarily? Henriette von Schirach, Baldur's wife, tried to find out more and came upon a witness who told her: "On June 5, 1945, there was a radio announcement: All Hitler Youth Leaders were to be arrested and the whole Hitler Youth regarded as a criminal organization; even the sixteen-year-old members were to be charged. Now he did not want to be Richard Falk any longer, living comfortably in hiding, but to emerge again as the Reich Youth Leader placing himself dramatically at the head of his organization."

"But he had nothing more to do with the Hitler Youth," Frau Schirach objected. "Axmann had already succeeded him as Youth Leader."

"Everybody believed that Axmann was dead," the witness told her, "and so he felt again responsible."

"Why didn't you escape?" asked Frau Schirach when she saw her husband in his cell shortly after his arrest. "You could have gone to Spain. You had been reported dead. You could have disappeared."

"But you know that I wouldn't do that," answered Schirach. "I have thought everything over very carefully. I had time to think, no one was looking for me. I want to speak before a court of law and take the blame myself. Through me, youth has learned to believe in Hitler, I taught them to have faith in him; now I must free them from this. When I have had the opportunity to say this before an international court of law, then they can hang me!"

"Hang?" asked his wife, shocked. Baldur von Schirach had no illusions. "They will hang all of us," he replied. Was he thinking of the things he had not mentioned in his touching little speech, but which at Nuremberg were to be brought to light by the prosecution?

The great manhunt came to an end on June 23, 1945, with the arrest of the last straggler. Six Soviet officers under the command of Colonel Pimenov turned up at the house of the former Admiral Erich Raeder at Babelsberg near Berlin. The former Commander in Chief of the German Navy, removed from office by Hitler in 1943 and succeeded by Doenitz, was living in the Russian sector, officially registered and so far undisturbed. Now there was a sudden interest in him.

With his wife, Erika, Raeder was taken to the Lichtenberg Prison. A fortnight later, the Russians flew them both to Moscow. Twelve miles from the capital, on an island in the Moskva River, they were put into a log hut. Why he had been arrested Raeder learned only when he was brought to Nuremberg early in October 1945.

RUDOLF HESS

In the front row of the Nuremberg dock there was a man who, during the whole of the Trial, presented a whole series of problems to the international tribunal and to all taking part in it— Rudolf Hess.

His external appearance prompted the question whether the accused was in full command of his faculties, or whether he should not rather be in a mental hospital. Hess himself claimed that he had lost his memory and could not remember anything; but he also claimed that he had only simulated this mental condition.

The American prison psychiatrist, Douglas M. Kelley, had been studying Rudolf Hess for many months, and had spent innumerable evenings in his cell. The chief conclusions from his observations may be summed up in these words: during the whole of the Nazi period, Hess had always played second fiddle; he was merely "the Deputy." This must have wounded his pride, and as he saw no chance of ever rising higher in the Nazi hierarchy, he took the drastic step of his sensational flight to England. As angel of peace, mediating between the warring powers, Hess hoped to become the world's "Number One" overnight.

Kelley believed that Hess, by reason of his secondary position, had developed an "inhibition complex" which expressed itself in all kinds of physical complaints. He had, in fact, tried out new doctors, new remedies and cures for years, but had quickly given up each attempt when there was no miracle cure after a week or two. In the end he had lost all faith in orthodox medicine, and sought help from nature doctors, cranks, quacks, charlatans, and astrologers. The stomach pains about which Hess complained most frequently never subsided.

From all that Kelley could find out, it appeared that Hess had quickly deteriorated after 1938; he lost weight and his resilience was waning. Witnesses confirmed that he would sit for hours at his desk, gazing idly into space.

The psychiatrist believed that he knew the deeper cause of this: about that time, Hess must have realized that Hitler, to whom he looked up as to an idolized father, was in fact not worthy of respect. Hess was really in a mental crisis; but the solution which he attempted in the end was just as odd as his whole intellectual and spiritual condition. In a talk with Kelley he admitted that an astrologer had prophesied in 1940 that he was chosen to bring peace to the world.

Hess had decided to fly off to England to conduct peace negotiations single-handed. He prepared his coup in complete secrecy. Hitler, of course, had to be kept completely in the dark. Hildegard Fath, who was Hess's secretary, said in a deposition:

"From the summer of 1940 onward, on Hess's orders, I had to get secret weather reports about conditions in the British Isles and the North Sea for him. I got the reports from a Captain Busch. Sometimes I obtained them from Fräulein Sperr, who was Hess's secretary at his Liaison Office in Berlin."

Several times Hess carried out secret trial flights. The German aircraft manufacturer, Willy Messerschmitt, made a statement to the press about these events in 1947: "In the late autumn of 1940, he told me in Augsburg that he wanted to try out new fighter planes. At first I refused, but Hess insisted and declared that his position entitled him to this, and in the end I gave permission for 'the Führer's Deputy' to fly the Me-110 plane. Hess, an outstanding pilot, carried out some twenty flights from the Augsburg airfield. After each flight he reported to me and my engineers what faults he said he had discovered in the machine, in the hope that this would lead the engineers to design a special machine for the secretly planned flight to Britain. After one such flight Hess said to me, 'This fighter plane is excellent, but it is only suitable for short flights. I bet that it will lose all its maneuverability if you put additional fuel tanks in the wings.' Shortly after this, Hess tried the same tactics with regard to a radio set which he wanted to have greater range. In order to show that the installation of a heavier radio set did not affect the flying qualities of the machine, I had one put in. Pretending that his interest was a purely technical one, Hess gradually got us to build for him an ideal machine for the flight he had planned."

On May 10, 1941, Hess set off from Augsburg with the special plane, never to return. He had been told by his Munich astrologer that the chosen day was propitious.

On that evening, at eight minutes past ten, an enemy aircraft was sighted by British observers off the coast of Northumberland, a type that had not been seen before in that area. The report aroused incredulity at headquarters: an Me-110 on the coast of Northumberland—it seemed impossible, for these machines did not carry enough fuel to fly there and back. However, the report was followed up, and a fighter squadron was alerted to chase the mysterious aircraft.

At 11:07 P.M. came the message that the plane had crashed near Eaglesham in Scotland and gone up in flames. The pilot had baled out, landed in an open field, and been taken prisoner by the Home Guard.

A farmer, Mr. David McLean, was the first person to meet Rudolf Hess on British soil. He had heard the plane circle above his house several times, saw it crash and burst into flames, and ran out to investigate, armed with a hayfork. In the darkening sky he made out the mushroom shape of a parachute, and a man touching down in a nearby field. As the farmer approached he saw him lying on the ground and helped him up. Hess had sprained his ankle but was still able to walk.

"I am looking for the house of the Duke of Hamilton," he told the farmer in fluent English. "I have an important message for the Royal Air Force. I am alone and unarmed." McLean led the unexpected guest to his house, where he offered him a cup of tea.

"No, thank you," said Hess, "I don't drink tea so late." His name, he said, was Alfred Horn. While he was sitting on a chair rubbing his ankle, a rattletrap car drew up at the farmhouse. It belonged to Robert Williamson, a special constable, who had seen the plane crash from Eaglesham. In the same car was a man by the name of Clark, a neighbor of Williamson and a member of the Home Guard. Both men entered McLean's farmhouse. Williamson was wearing a steel helmet with the inscription

Police. Clark was armed with an old-fashioned pistol, a relic of the First World War.

Thus accoutered, they confronted Hess and arrested him. "We had no idea who he was," Williamson remembered, "but somehow he seemed important."

Hess was taken by car to Busby. From there the men had to go some distance on foot to a Home Guard barracks off the main road. Williamson was in the lead, Hess limped along in the middle, and Clark formed the rear guard.

"My chief concern was Clark's revolver," Williamson said later, "and I think our prisoner felt the same way."

The event surprised the Home Guard in their sleep. The men tumbled out in nightshirts, underclothes, wearing slippers or barefoot when Williamson gave the alarm. Hess was brought in, and was held in the guardroom for further orders. "I am a German officer," he protested. Clark waved his revolver. "In you go" was all he said. Hess obeyed. At that moment began his imprisonment.

The capture of the German Captain Horn was duly reported. So was the prisoner's statement that he had come to England on a "special mission" and wished to speak to the Duke of Hamilton.

This request was, in fact, granted, and the next morning the Duke of Hamilton turned up to find out what was the matter with this character Alfred Horn. The Duke reported:

> On Sunday, May 11, I came to Maryhill Barracks with an Intelligence Officer, and there we first inspected the personal effects of the prisoner. Among these were a Leica camera, photographs of himself and a young child, some drugs, and visiting cards of Dr. Karl Haushofer and his son, Dr. Albrecht Haushofer.
>
> I entered the prisoner's cell accompanied by the Intelligence Officer and the officer in charge. The prisoner immediately asked if he could speak to me alone. I therefore asked the other officers to retire.
>
> The German began by telling me that he had made my acquaintance during the Olympic Games in Berlin in 1936 and that I had once dined at his house.
>
> "I don't know if you remember me," he said, "but I am Rudolf Hess."
>
> He said further that he had come on a mission for mankind: the Führer did not wish to destroy England and wanted to end

the war. His friend, Albrecht Haushofer, had told him that I was an Englishman who would appreciate his point of view. He went on to say that he had tried three times to fly to England, the first time in the previous December, but he had turned back each time on account of bad weather.

The Führer, Hess also maintained, was convinced that Germany would win the war, possibly soon, but certainly in one, two, or three years. Hess himself wished to stop the futile carnage.

How that could be done, Hess himself did not exactly know. He proposed to the Duke that he should bring together members of his political party in order to work out peace proposals. Hitler's condition for peace, he told the Duke of Hamilton, was that England should change her traditional policy.

On the evening of May 11, Winston Churchill happened to be in Ditchley, resting at the home of some friends. They were watching a private movie.

"The merry film clacked on," Churchill writes in his memoirs, "and I was glad of the diversion. Presently a secretary told me that the Duke of Hamilton wished to speak to me from Scotland. The Duke was a personal friend of mine, but I could not think of any business he might have with me which could not wait till morning. However, he pressed to speak with me, saying it was an urgent matter of Cabinet importance."

In this way Churchill learned the astonishing news. "It was as if my trusted colleague, the Foreign Secretary, who was only a little younger than Hess, had parachuted from a stolen Spitfire into the grounds of Berchtesgaden," he commented..

What was to be done with Hess? Churchill himself gave the necessary instructions. Hess was brought to the Tower of London until some more congenial accommodation could be found for him in a country house.

All this must have been crushing for Hess. Instead of being welcomed as the great peacemaker, he was treated as a prisoner of war. His illusions were shattered. And there was the obvious question: could a man like Rudolf Hess, the "Führer's Deputy," have flown to Britain in full possession of his senses? Was he so out of touch with the actual political situation? The British authorities, in any case, felt that first the doctors should have a look at him.

A few days after the landing an outstanding specialist, Dr. J. R. Rees, reported to Churchill:

> Hess said he was horrified at the heavy raids on London in 1940, and loathed the thought of killing young children and their mothers. This feeling was intensified when he contemplated his own wife and child, and led to the idea of flying to Britain and arranging peace with the large anti-war faction which he thought existed in this country.
>
> It was with such thoughts in his mind that he was impressed on hearing his teacher and paternal friend, the "geopolitician" Karl Haushofer, express similar sentiments, and mention the Duke of Hamilton as a person of common sense, who must be horrified at the senseless slaughter. The older Haushofer had also told Hess that he had seen him on three occasions in a dream piloting an aeroplane to an unknown destination. These remarks, coming from such an admired man, awakened in Hess the feeling that he had a mission—that of flying to this country as an emissary of peace, and to speak to the Duke of Hamilton, who would conduct him to King George. The present British Government would be thrown out of office and a peace party installed in its place.
>
> He was insistent that he would have no dealings with the "clique"—the government now in power—who would do everything possible to thwart him, but he was very vague as to what statesmen should replace them, and seemed to be extremely ill-informed as to the names and relative importance of our politicians.

The British press reveled in the sensation. The BBC broadcast the news—and now the secret could no longer be kept in Germany. Dr. Goebbels' Propaganda Ministry had to tell the German people that the Führer's Deputy, in the midst of the war, had disappeared into enemy country.

Dr. Henry Picker, one of Hitler's stenographers, has told of the impact of the news in the Führer's circle: "Hitler learned of the flight of his deputy to Scotland as he was sitting by the fire talking to Goering and Ribbentrop. He was called aside by Lorenz to hear some important news. Hitler himself dictated the first announcement to Lorenz and—after he learned of the first English report about midnight—compiled the detailed statement for Monday after discussions with Goering, Bormann, and Ribbentrop, which explained the flight by a long-standing ailment that had obviously affected Hess's mind."

On Monday, May 13, the German Information Office issued a report, which was printed by all German newspapers without comment:

> It is officially announced by the National Socialist Party that Party Member Rudolf Hess, who, as he was suffering from an illness of some years' standing, had been strictly forbidden to embark on any further flying activity, was able, contrary to this command, again to come into possession of an aircraft.
>
> On Saturday, May 10, at about 6:00 P.M., Rudolf Hess again set off on a flight from Augsburg, Bavaria, from which he has not yet returned. A letter left behind shows by its confusion traces of a mental disorder, and it is feared that he was a victim of hallucinations. The Führer at once ordered the arrest of the adjutants of Party Member Hess, who alone had knowledge of these flights and did not, contrary to the Führer's orders, of which they were fully aware, either prevent or report the flights.
>
> Under these circumstances it must be assumed that Party Member Hess either jumped from his aircraft or met with an accident.

The Nazi Party correspondent who wrote in the German newspapers on May 13 had more to tell:

> From an examination of the papers left behind by Rudolf Hess, it seems that he harbored the delusion that by a personal approach to English acquaintances he could still bring about an understanding between Germany and England. In point of fact, a report from London states that he has baled out of his plane over Scotland near the place he was seeking, and has been found there, apparently injured.
>
> Rudolf Hess, who for years has been known to suffer from severe pain, has lately had increasingly frequent recourse to all kinds of cures, to hypnotists, astrologers, and so forth. How far these persons are to blame for creating mental confusion in Hess is being investigated. But it is also conceivable that Hess has

been deliberately lured into a trap by the English. The whole nature of his action confirms the fact mentioned in the first announcement, namely, that he suffered from delusions. He knew better than anyone else the numerous peace proposals put forward honestly by the Führer. But apparently he has deluded himself into thinking that, by a personal sacrifice, he could prevent those developments which would end only with the complete destruction of the British Empire. Hess, whose duties, as we all know, lay exclusively within the Party, had no clear idea about his venture, still less of its consequences.

Willy Messerschmitt, in the interview already mentioned, described how Hermann Goering reacted to the disappearance of Hess. The first news reached the aircraft manufacturer about eight o'clock the same evening when he stopped at a hotel in Innsbruck. Two hours later Goering telephoned him and excitedly ordered him to attend a meeting in Munich. Next morning, Messerschmitt called on Goering in his special train at Munich Central Station.

> Goering pointed his marshal's baton at my stomach. He shouted: "So as far as you are concerned, anyone can apparently fly off in a Messerschmitt!" I asked him what he meant, to which Goering replied: "You know this fellow Hess very well!" I answered, "But Hess is not just anybody."
>
> Goering, who was gradually cooling down, said: "You should have made inquiries before you put a machine at the disposal of such a man." I answered: "If you came to my factory and asked for a plane, should I first ask the Führer for permission to give it to you?" That angered Goering again, and he countered sharply: "That is entirely different. I am the Air Minister." I replied, "And Hess is the Führer's Deputy."
>
> "But you should have noticed, Messerschmitt, that the man was mad!" I replied dryly, "How could I assume that a madman could occupy such a high position in the Third Reich? I think they should have made him resign, Herr Field Marshal." Goering laughed. "You are incorrigible, Messerschmitt. Go back and get on making aircraft."

Messerschmitt remained free, but Hess's adjutants were thrown into concentration camps. Letters which Hess sent from Great

Britain by way of the Red Cross were of course stopped by the censor.

"Hitler is still very annoyed," stenographer Picker noted a year later, "that he was told nothing about the trial flights which Hess made before his escape to England. Hitler regards the return of Hess to Germany as out of the question as there would be only the alternative 'lunatic asylum or firing squad.' Hess will have to build for himself a new existence abroad."

The head of the Party office, Martin Bormann, wrote to SS Leader Heinrich Himmler in a letter found after the war: "Even in the earliest statements by the adjutants Pintsch and Leitgen, and by General Haushofer, as well as in one of the first letters of Frau Hess herself, there is a possible explanation of the flight— R. H. wanted to shine because he suffered from an inferiority complex." This agrees exactly with the conclusion of the American prison psychiatrist Kelley. Bormann then gives in his letter some details about the married life of Rudolf Hess, not sparing the latter's wife: "In the opinion of the Führer, these are in fact the real causes. Only now it has become known that R. H. has been treated again and again for impotence, even at the time when the son called *Buz* was produced. Before himself, before his wife, and before the Party and the people, R. H. believed that by this undertaking he could prove this virility. . . . As his actions show, R. H. himself believed a hundred per cent in the success of his talks when the so-called dream of truth was told to him by General Haushofer, and later Schulte-Strathaus and Nagengast prophesied luck and success for him from his horoscope. Hess believed in such things, all the more as he had been foretold success from three quarters.

The Munich physician, Dr. Ludwig Schmitt, who treated Rudolf Hess from 1936 to 1939 for various ailments, told a reporter of *The New York Times* after the war: "Hess had a tendency to schizophrenia and was slightly psychopathic." These tendencies must have grown stronger after the failure of his flight to England. When, four years later, Hess sat in the dock at Nuremberg, the doctors would again be concerned with him.

2.

The Road to Nuremberg

SOMEWHERE IN
EUROPE

Somewhere in Europe—that was the mysterious description when the Allies did not want to specify a definite place. Somewhere in Europe: in this case it was Bad Mondorf in Luxemburg, the last stage before the prisoners were brought to the dock in Nuremberg. At Bad Mondorf there began the preliminary investigation with its innumerable examinations. A German doctor, Ludwig Pflücker, himself a prisoner at Mondorf, has described the place as follows: "The situation of the prisoners at Mondorf was good. Their accommodations, mostly on the second floor in fine hotel rooms with a view of green fields, was not bad. The hotel grounds were available for walks in the fresh air, and since the weather was generally good, some strolled about in groups while the others talked together or rested on deck chairs and garden seats. Their sojourn in this hotel, with its garden and the surrounding park with its tall, old trees, was idyllic."

The officer in command of the prison was an American colonel, Burton G. Andrus, later security chief of the Nuremberg Palace of Justice. Colonel Andrus was no friend of the prisoners. Little wonder that a minor war developed between the colonel and his prisoners.

As a rule, the interrogations lasted for hours at a time. The intelligence officers kept returning to the same points, jumping from one subject to another, interspersing harmless questions, and watching for contradictions. There was always a stenographer present, taking down every word.

Werner Bross, temporary assistant to Goering's defense counsel Stahmer, later published parts of two of these interrogations of June 1945, five months before the Trial began:

QUESTION: "What is your full name?"
ANSWER: "Hermann Wilhelm Goering."

71

"What was your function?"

"Officer and Commander in Chief of the Luftwaffe, Air Minister, President of Prussia, President of the Reichstag, Minister for Forestry, with the rank of Reichsmarshal."

"Obviously you were one of the most successful Nazis since you have managed to survive?"

"I don't know what you think of the situation, but there are still a lot of Nazis about."

"You are the last of the leading Nazis. How have you managed to stay alive? Why weren't you killed?"

"It was quite by chance. I was taken prisoner and was to be shot. It was by chance that I wasn't."

"What do you think of Schacht?"

"He talks only about himself."

"Don't you think that you yourself, too, talk only about yourself? Can't you tell us anything else about Schacht?"

"He was a clever man. Even before the Party came to power he worked for it."

"He must have been cleverer than you, for he resigned from the Party before the war."

"Some people have no principles."

"Can we trust Schacht?"

"I leave that to you."

"Is he a man without principles?"

"I wouldn't exactly say that, but it is known that Schacht has often changed his views."

"Are you a man of integrity?"

"I have always stood for my convictions."

"What is your chief conviction?"

"To work for my country. I won't condemn Schacht, I was only asked for my personal view."

"Did you sign a decree in 1938 imposing on the Jews a levy of a thousand million reichsmarks?"

"That was ordered by Hitler."

"Are you ashamed of it?"

"I don't think that the law was just."

"Then you are ashamed of having signed that document? Or is a German field marshal never ashamed?"

"Under the Geneva Convention I don't need to answer that question."

"You are no longer a prisoner of war. The war with Germany is over. Germany has surrendered unconditionally to the Allied Nations. Will you answer the question?"

"I regret it. But you have to think of the time when the law was made."

"Who kept your checkbook?"

"My secretary and I."

"Who paid the costs of your mansion, Karinhall?"

"The Air Ministry and the Ministry of State."

"How were the funds for the purchase of a picture provided?"

"Always in cash."

"Where did the cash come from?"

"I was the second man in the country, I had always plenty of money. I myself confirmed the order."

"Did you get all your foreign currency in this way?"

"Yes. I was the supreme authority."

"Was there a regular procedure, and were records kept?"

"It was merely a matter of getting permission—and in my case that was totally unnecessary."

"Would you call yourself a poor man now?"

"I don't know what is left. I have no control over anything."

"You haven't buried anything in a hole?"

"No, nothing."

"Did you keep a diary?"

"I kept a diary occasionally. My adjutant kept one in recent years. It was burned at Karinhall, where all these things were kept. My people or the Russians have burned it, for I gave the order that everything was to be burned. The Russians advanced between Berlin and Karinhall. We had to flee in a hurry. A lot of stuff is also buried there."

"Tell us where it is and we will get it."

"I have been told where it is buried, but it would be difficult to get it. Furthermore the Russians wouldn't let you dig there. It is almost impossible to describe from here, because the articles are scattered and a map would be difficult to draw."

"Is there a plan of the place?"

"No."

"Who knows besides you where the things are buried?"

"The soldiers who were with me and who carried out my orders. I don't know what became of the soldiers. I believe it would be impossible even if. we got hold of one of the soldiers, for the Russians would never let us dig anything up without taking it themselves. I hope that we can perhaps recover the things later."

"Did you in April 1945 draw out money to put it into another bank?"

"I gave an order to send half a million to a bank in South Germany. If it had been done I would have been notified, but I haven't heard anything about it."

"Have you made a will?"

"I am doing it now, but it isn't necessary, for by law everything goes to my child."

"Are you leaving your secretary anything?"

"The list is ready, and my wife will look after everything."

"Where is the list?"

"It was packed with the library. We did it on the train. I had two trains. One was my headquarters. The second train stood in a safe place in a tunnel siding. When things began to get hot, the guards disappeared and many things were stolen. Jewel boxes were opened and stones were taken out, but the settings were left lying about."

"Did you examine the train?"

"An American officer has told me about it."

"What is your annual income?"

"Twenty thousand marks a month as Reichsmarshal, 3,600 marks a month as Commander of the Luftwaffe, tax paid. Also 1,600 marks as President of the Reichstag. Then I had my authorship—there were profits of about a million marks from all my books."

"Didn't your living expenses amount to more than that?" ·

"A number of my expenses were paid from another quarter. Berlin and Karinhall were kept by the state."

"Didn't you pay large sums for pictures—more than you earned?"

"I had some money of my own."

"Have you any brothers or sisters?"

"Yes. A half brother in Wiesbaden, who is seventy-four years old. His name: Major Wilhelm Goering. Then there is Professor Dr. Heinrich Goering, ophthalmologist in Wiesbaden. Some brothers and sisters have long been dead. My eldest brother Karl died in the last war. Sisters Olga and Paula: don't know where they are—perhaps with the Russians. Albert is in a prison camp, but was never a Party member."

"No one will harm your relatives, we don't work that way."

"The Americans won't do anything to them, but the Russians."

"How long do you think you would live if you were handed over to the Russians?"

"Not very long."

The interrogators of the Allied Commission of Inquiry took their time. Every day they asked new questions, and every day they returned to the old ones. Often a prisoner exclaimed in a temper: "I have already told you that ten times." But that left the officers cold. They went on asking—for weeks and months on end.

The legal documents piled up. To the reports of the interrogations were added many hundreds of tons of official papers which had been found by special search parties all over Germany. These documents were turned into ammunition for the prosecution at Nuremberg.

TO THE FURTHEST CORNERS
OF THE EARTH

No one in Germany knew about the dispute that was going on between Moscow, London, and Washington before the war was over. The differences of opinion were fundamental. All the participants wanted to avoid a spectacular international trial, except the United States. London, Paris, and Moscow, on the other hand, felt uneasy about the idea of putting German politicians, soldiers, and industrialists in the dock, thus granting them the right of defense before a court of law.

There were many steps that led to the Trial, almost against the will of its originators. On several occasions during the war, the Allied Powers and the exiled governments had expressed their determination to bring those guilty of criminal offenses against international law to trial and punishment.

Only the small circle around Hitler and Goebbels, to whom foreign news was available, learned of these developments abroad. The German people must not know—listening to foreign broadcasts was punishable by death. No one must hear of the Allies' warning: "Let those whose hands are not yet stained with the blood of the innocent avoid joining the ranks of the guilty, for the three Allied Powers will definitely pursue them to the furthest corners of the earth and deliver them to their judges so that justice may be done," said the Moscow Declaration of November 1, 1943, drawn up by the American Secretary of State, Cordell Hull; the British Foreign Minister, Anthony Eden; and the Soviet Foreign Minister, Molotov. The official signatures of this document simply say: Roosevelt, Churchill, Stalin.

The two most important points of the Moscow Declaration state:

1. War criminals who have perpetrated their crimes in a limited area will be handed over to the country concerned to be judged according to its laws.

2. War criminals whose acts cannot be localized geographically because they affect several countries will be punished by a common decision of the Allies.

The second point was the basis of the dispute which broke out among the victorious powers immediately after the end of the war. How was the "common decision" to be reached?

STALIN'S TOAST AND CHURCHILL'S OBJECTION

"Common decision on punishment" did not mean that a trial had to take place. What Stalin understood by punishment had been known to the Western Powers since the Teheran Conference. This conference took place toward the end of November 1943. It was the first time that Roosevelt, Churchill, and Stalin had met. In Europe the die was cast: the end of the German Sixth Army at Stalingrad had given the war a new turn. The downfall of Germany was looming on the horizon of history.

Elliott Roosevelt had accompanied his father to Teheran, where he had sat in on all the meetings of the Big Three. To him we owe an exhaustive account of the events.

The dispute broke out during a dinner party. Stalin was the host; white wine, Russian champagne, and vodka were served with the meal. Churchill, however, got his usual brandy.

Elliott Roosevelt has impressively described what a Russian banquet is like: almost every sentence of the conversation takes the form of a toast.

For instance, one of the Russians said. "I would like to drink a toast to the future delivery of war materiel," whereupon everyone rose and drank to it. This went on for hours. Toward the end of the banquet Stalin rose. He had already proposed about a dozen toasts. But now he introduced a new note into the festivities.

"I drink," he said, "to the quickest possible justice for all German war criminals. I drink to the justice of a firing squad."

A heavy silence fell upon the banquet hall. Stalin continued, unperturbed, "I drink to our determintion to settle with them as soon as they are captured, all of them. There must be at least fifty thousand of them."

Churchill leaped from his seat "like lightning," as Elliott Roosevelt put it. "Such a procedure," replied the Prime Minister, "is in complete opposition to the British conception of justice. The British people will never approve such a mass murder."

"I watched Stalin," writes Elliott Roosevelt. "He seemed to be highly amused, even though his face remained serious. His eyes twinkled suspiciously as he took up the Prime Minister's challenge and pulled its arguments to pieces in a courteous tone, appearing not to notice Churchill's ill humor."

"Stalin intended," wrote Churchill himself, "that the German General Staff was to be liquidated. The whole striking force of Hitler's mighty armies depended upon some fifty thousand officers and experts. If at the end of the war they were captured and shot, Germany's military power would be forever broken."

"The British Parliament and British public opinion," Churchill retorted to Stalin, "will never approve mass executions. The Soviet must not be under any delusion on this point."

"Fifty thousand must be shot," Stalin insisted, and raised his glass again.

"I take the opportunity," said Churchill, "to declare that in my opinion no one, whether Nazi or not, should be led summarily before a firing squad without legal trial and consideration of the relevant facts and proofs. Rather would I here and now be led out into the garden and shot than that my honor and that of my country should be smirched by such baseness."

Franklin Delano Roosevelt, the third in this Conference of the Big Three, followed the exchange with an anxious expression. When Stalin turned to him to hear his opinion he said jokingly, "It is clear that a compromise between your attitude and that of the Prime Minister must be found. Perhaps we could say that a smaller number, say about 49,500 war criminals only, should be summarily executed."

The Americans and Russians laughed. The British held back, so as not to offend their chief. Foreign Minister Eden made a reassuring gesture with his hand to Churchill to indicate that it had been only a joke. But the Prime Minister would not calm down. He left the table and went alone into an adjoining room that was almost in darkness. There, his head lowered, he stared out at the dusky garden.

"I was there a few minutes," he wrote in his memoirs, "when from behind someone put a hand on my shoulder. It was Stalin, and beside him stood Molotov. Both were laughing heartily, and maintained that they had only been joking."

Was it really a joke? Churchill continues: "Although I was neither convinced then, nor am I today, that they were not in earnest, I went back into the other room."

Once again, more than a year after Teheran, the controversial question came up between Churchill and Stalin. The scene this time was the Crimea. On the ninth day of the Yalta Conference, on February 9, 1945, the agenda contained the item "Punishment of War Criminals."

Churchill reminded Stalin and Roosevelt of the Moscow Declaration and the "common decision" that was still to be reached. It was a most unwelcome subject. Stalin's face did not betray his thoughts. He knew that here they were merely discussing theories, while in the areas which the Russians had reoccupied, practical measures had already begun on December 13, 1943, at Kharkov, the first "War Crimes Trial" had taken place against three German officers. After a show examination, the accused had been shot. Why a longer trial?

Joseph Stalin turned to Churchill with a diplomatic smile. Through the interpreter he asked him, "Are you thinking also of Rudolf Hess, who is in your hands—what is he doing?"

"Hess is being treated like any other prisoner of war in Britain," the Prime Minister replied.

"Yes, yes," said Stalin absent-mindedly. "I should like to suggest that we leave this matter to our foreign ministers for later consideration. Now let us discuss the Allied offensive in the West."

A pair of attaché cases were shut, and another pair moved into their places.

ROBERT H. JACKSON

Still Britain and France were not very enthusiastic about the idea of a trial, but Washington was. The Soviet Union was still for putting the Nazis up against a wall and shooting them. There seemed to be no solution—until one man took all the tangled threads in his clever hands, with good humor, patience, and energy. He came to Europe on a special mission for President Truman, journeyed to and fro across bombed and hungry Germany, and held secret conferences in London and Paris.

His name was soon to be known throughout the world: Robert H. Jackson, Justice of the United States Supreme Court. Jackson succeeded in getting the representatives of America, Britain,

France, and the Soviet Union to gather round a table. On June 26, 1945, the delegates of the four victorious powers sat down together in London in order to reach a "common decision." They were: for the United States, Justice Robert H. Jackson, acting for President Truman, and ten assistants; for Britain, Attorney General Sir David Maxwell Fyfe, Lord Chancellor Jowitt, and eleven assistants; for France, Counsel at the Court of Appeal, Robert Falco, the international legalist, Professor André Gros, and two assistants; for the Soviet Union, General Iola J. Nikitchenko, Vice-President of the Supreme Court at Moscow, and two assistants.

The discussions took place behind closed doors. Opinions were so divergent and conflicted so strongly that it often looked as though the conference would end in failure. But in the end agreement was reached on most of the points at issue. The last question to be discussed was that of the place of the Trial.

The Russians suggested London or Berlin. The British wished to hold the proceedings at Munich. In the end, Jackson flew to Frankfurt to see General Lucius D. Clay, the military governor of the American Zone, to ask him about a suitable place with suitable accommodation. Clay suggested Nuremberg and its almost undamaged Palace of Justice. Thus the town whose name was to be forever linked with the Trial was mentioned for the first time—Nuremberg, the city of the mass Party meetings, the scene of Hitler's great triumphs. Jackson flew back to London. After long delays even the Soviet expressed themselves satisfied with Nuremberg, on the condition that the permanent seat of the court should be in Berlin and that only the first trial should take place at Nuremberg. They were still thinking in terms of a whole series of international trials; they had in mind some 200,000 individual actions. Jackson had great trouble in weaning them from this fantastic idea. He proposed, as a way out, that different groups of people should be charged together, for example, the SA and SS, in order to avoid actions against every individual member. This was agreed.

One item was not raised in the official proceedings: that of the air raids. All those taking part fought shy of this sticky problem. After the First World War the Allies had planned to bring German airmen before the international courts. The British were thinking of the zeppelins which had dropped bombs on London. In 1918 this idea was quickly dropped, and there is no record that the London Conference of 1945 dealt with the question of the air raids. But many years later Jackson admitted that the problem had in fact been discussed. The delegates, however, agreed to drop the controversial question because it would have been difficult to distinguish between indiscriminate bombing and "military necessity," and there would have been countercharges against the Allies.

On August 8, 1945, the Big Four Powers signed an agreement on the International Military Tribunal and on the Statute of the Court in London. It laid down the rights and duties of all the participants, the procedure of the Trial, and the principles which the judges were to observe. Article 24 said:

The proceedings of the Trial shall take the following course:

a. The Indictment shall be read in court.

b. The Tribunal shall ask each defendant whether he pleads "guilty" or "not guilty."

c. The Prosecution shall make an opening statement.

d. The Tribunal shall ask the Prosecution and Defense what evidence, if any, they wish to submit to the Tribunal, and the Tribunal shall rule upon the advisability of any such evidence.

e. The witnesses for the Prosecution shall be examined, and after that the witnesses for the Defense. Therafter such rebutting evidence as may be held by the Tribunal to be admissable shall be called by either the Prosecution or the Defense.

f. The Tribunal may put any question to any witness and to any Defendant at any time.

g. The Prosecution and the Defense shall interrogate and may cross-examine any witnesses and any defendant who gives testimony.

h. The Defense shall address the court.

i. The Prosecution shall address the court.

j. Each Defendant may make a statement to the Tribunal.

k. The Tribunal shall deliver judgment and pronounce sentence.

While the London Conference was discussing and deciding, those who were to be charged were still living as internees at Bad Mondorf. When the members of the Tribunal met in Berlin on October 18, 1945, for the first time—in the hall of the former People's Court, where Judge Freisler once condemned the men of the 20th of July to death—the prisoners had an opportunity to study the bill of indictment, which was delivered to them the same day.

It comprised 25,000 words and was divided into four main parts:

1. *Conspiracy.* The accused had pursued a common plan to seize unlimited power and conspired for the committing of all further crimes.

2. *Crimes against peace.* The accused had broken 26 international treaties in 64 cases, had begun a war of aggression, and had caused a world war.

3. *War crimes.* The accused had instituted a horrible blood bath and had ordered or permitted mass murder, tortures, slave labor, and economic exploitation.

4. *Crimes against humanity.* The accused had persecuted political opponents, racial and religious minorities, and made themselves responsible for the destruction of whole groups of the population.

The pages of this document are filled with such incredible, revolting details as even the most morbid imagination could not conceive.

IN THE CELLS AT
NUREMBERG

How did the prisoners take the frightful document? On August 12 they had been flown from Mondorf to Nuremberg in two planes; here they had an opportunity to nominate defense counsel of their own choice, but counsel could not relieve their minds of the oppressive burden of the charges. This they had to bear themselves.

The American court psychologist, Gustave M. Gilbert, observed the accused men in their cells, spoke with them, and kept a detailed diary. Gilbert spoke German well. His first act was to administer an intelligence test. He put questions to them, tested their powers of memory, had them solve various problems, put psychological games in their hands, and got them to explain the significance of symbolic pictures. From the results he calculated the so-called intelligence quotient. The IQ of the average person is between 90 and 110.

Among those accused at Nuremberg, according to Gilbert, Schacht was top with an IQ of 143, then came Seyss-Inquart with 141 and Goering with 138. At the bottom of the list were Sauckel with 118, Kaltenbrunner with 113, and Streicher with 106. These IQ figures do not, of course, represent moral or character evaluations. Even criminals may have higher-than-average intelligence quotients.

Gilbert made a further test. He asked the prisoners to write, in a few words, in the margin of the document, their attitude toward the bill of indictment. These remarks, in the psychologist's view, reflect their characters quite clearly.

Fritzsche, von Papen, and Schacht, the three accused who were later to be acquitted, displayed rather dissimilar attitudes in their notes.

> HANS FRITZSCHE: "It is the most horrible indictment of all time. Only one thing is more horrible: the German people's indictment of those who betrayed their idealism."
>
> FRANZ VON PAPEN: "The accusation amazed me, for these reasons: (1) The irresponsibility with which Germany was cast into this war and a world-wide catastrophe; (2) the vast number of crimes which some of my countrymen have committed. The last point is psychologically inexplicable. I believe that paganism and the years of the totalitarian regime are chiefly to blame. Both turned Hitler into a pathological liar in the course of time."
>
> HJALMAR SCHACHT: "I quite fail to understand why I have been accused."
>
> FRANK (who, with Kaltenbrunner, was indicted for the majority of the atrocities): "I am awaiting the trial as the world's judgment, ordained by God, to examine the terrible time of suffering under Adolf Hitler, and to bring it to an end."

KALTENBRUNNER: "I do not consider myself guilty of any war crimes. I only did my duty in the service of state security, and I refuse to be judged as a substitute for Himmler."

DOENITZ: "After all, none of the points of the indictment apply to me. Typical American sense of humor."

KEITEL: "To a soldier, orders are orders."

RIBBENTROP: "The wrong people have been indicted!"

SPEER: "The trial is necessary. There is such a thing as common responsibility for such terrible crimes—even under an authoritarian system."

HESS: "I can't remember."

GOERING gave vent to his wit: "The victor will always be the judge, and the vanquished always the accused."

Goering's hand was trembling as he wrote this. He could hardly concentrate and had to strike out a word, even in such a simple sentence, because he had misspelled it. He was in a bad state. He had lost weight, and suffered from febrile bronchitis, a heart condition, and the effects of the treatment of his drug addiction.

"When Goering came to us at Mondorf," Colonel Andrus told the psychologist, Gilbert, "he was a grinning, slavering simpleton with two suitcases full of drugs. I thought he was a drug salesman. But we have broken him of the habit and made a man of him for the first time."

His daily dose of drugs was drastically reduced. When Goering complained, Dr. Pflücker encouraged him by playing on his vanity, "A strong man like you can bear this much better than a weakling."

Goering held out; the cure was successful. The weakness produced by the drugs disappeared, his will and his mind regained their powers of concentration, his energy returned. The man who finally appeared in the courtroom had been freed from the stupor of drugs, and his mind was clear.

ROBERT LEY,
GUSTAV KRUPP,
MARTIN BORMANN

There was only one man who collapsed under the burden of the indictment—Dr. Robert Ley.

Once the powerful chief of the German Labor Front, surpassed only by Streicher as a rabid anti-Semite, Ley worked out a fantastic scheme in prison in the form of a memorandum for the Americans. In it he proposed:

1. Germany should become part of the United States.

2. America should introduce a National Socialist regime cleansed of anti-Semitism, and thereby insure its leading role in the world.

3. Dr. Robert Ley should be intrusted with the execution of this plan; he and his collaborators would direct the whole operation from the Nuremberg prison.

When he discovered that his scheme aroused merely derision and pity, he wrote a letter to Henry Ford. He recalled his experiences in building up the Volkswagen factory and asked for a job with the American automobile king "as soon as the trial is over."

Only the indictment was able to shake him out of his fancies. He could not comprehend that he was held responsible for the transportation of millions of foreign workers to Germany and for their inhuman treatment. Ley lost his nerve. He paced restlessly in his cell day after day. He wore felt slippers and an American army shirt.

On the evening of October 25, 1945, the American sentry who looked from time to time through the peephole into Ley's cell was watching the restive, perturbed prisoner. "Why don't you sleep?" he asked him. Ley came close to the peephole, staring at the sentry. Tears ran unchecked down his sunken cheeks.

The sentry continued his rounds. The next time he looked into Ley's cell he noticed that the prisoner had gone into the corner where the toilet was. Only his legs were visible. It was a common sight for the sentry.

The next time Ley was still in the corner. The sentry looked at his watch. It was 8:10 P.M. He became suspicious. "Hey, Doctor Ley!" he shouted through the peephole.

No answer. The sentry informed the sergeant of the guard. He came with two soldiers. The cell door was opened and the four Americans entered.

It was a sorry sight. Ley was hanging over the seat of the toilet, his face blue-red. He had made a loop from the zipper of his army jacket and fixed it to the lever of the water tank. Twisted strips of a towel formed the noose round his neck.

The soldiers cut him down and laid him on the wooden bunk. The doctors were called.

Ley's mouth was choked with scraps of his underclothing. He had gagged himself so that the sentries would not be alerted by the death rattle from his throat. He had even stopped up his nose and ears with wads of cloth.

A few minutes after this discovery, the German prison physician, Dr. Ludwig Pflücker, entered the cell, and immediately after him the dentist, Dr. Heinz Hoch. Pflücker noticed that Ley's body was still warm. He gave him two injections, one cc. of Cardiazol and one cc. of Lobulin, and tried artificial respiration, but without success.

Colonel René Juhli, the American prison doctor, confirmed that Ley was dead. Ley's suicide was at first kept strictly secret by order of the security officer, Andrus. He feared that the event would have a contagious effect on the other prisoners. However, they heard about it, but did not feel inclined to follow his example.

"Thank God," said Goering, quite unimpressed when the news reached him, "he would only have been a disgrace to us."

Ley's place in the dock was not the only one to remain empty. Two other men managed to stay away from the Court: Gustav Krupp von Bohlen und Halbach and the mysterious Martin Bormann. To the prosecution, Krupp represented the entire German armament industry. The bill of indictment accused the industrialist ". . . that he assisted the seizure of power by the Nazi conspirators, strengthened and increased their control over Germany, and assisted the preparations for war. He took part in the military and industrial plans and preparations of the Nazi conspirators for a war of aggression; he approved and committed war crimes and crimes against humanity, especially the exploitation and misuse of human beings for work in aid of a war of aggression, and took part in these crimes."

The indictment reached Krupp on his sickbed in Castle Blühnbach near Werfen in Austria. He was unable to grasp what was going on. Krupp's legal representative, the lawyer Theodor Klefisch, submitted a petition to the Court: "The accused does not know of the existence of the indictment, and is therefore incapable of instructing his counsel on his defense." Klefisch accordingly petitioned the Court that the charges against Krupp should be dropped. Jackson, however, opposed this petition vigorously. An international medical commission was appointed to examine Krupp and submit an authoritative report to the Court. They came to this conclusion: "It is our unanimous, considered medical opinion that it would be impossible for the patient, Gustav Krupp von Bohlen, by reason of his mental condition, to follow the proceedings at a court of law. The physical condition of the patient is such that he could not be transported without danger to his life."

In spite of this emphatic report the prosecuting authorities did not relent. Perhaps it was possible to proceed against Gustav Krupp in his absence? Or, if this was impracticable, could not the son of the accused, Alfred Krupp, take his place among the accused?

These petitions were in fact presented; but the Court was determined to follow an independent path. In a preliminary hearing, on November 14, the prosecution, which had submitted the first of these petitions, suffered an embarrassing setback. "Do you believe," Lord Justice Lawrence asked Jackson, the American chief prosecutor, "that it would serve the interests of justice to sentence a man who, on account of illness, is not in a position to conduct his defense properly?"

Jackson had to answer in the negative. "Thank you," said Lord
Justice Lawrence. Then he turned to the British counsel, Sir
Hartley Shawcross: "Do you agree with me that according to
the law of Great Britain—as well as the law of the United States—
a man in Gustav Krupp's mental and physical condition would
be pronounced incapable of pleading?"

SIR HARTLEY: Yes, indeed.

LAWRENCE: Do you now propose that in the present circumstances proceedings should be taken against Gustav Krupp in his
absence, in view of the medical report that now lies before us?

SIR HARTLEY: I agree with the view that according to British
law he would not be capable of pleading.

LAWRENCE: And that law serves the interests of justice?

SIR HARTLEY: That I cannot deny.

Jackson and Shawcross had suffered a moral defeat. Charles
Dubost, the French prosecutor, now had the task of proposing,
in the name of his colleagues, the other possibility to the Court:
that the son of the sick Krupp should take his place.

This time, the French judge, Donnedieu de Vabres, took the
lead and asked his compatriot bluntly, "Do you really believe
that you can request the Court to substitute one name for another on the bill of indictment?"

Dubost gave a negative answer.

"Thank you," said Lawrence curtly.

The case of Krupp was settled, the proceedings against him
were suspended—and the prosecuting authorities knew from that
day on that the court was really a court of justice. Krupp's place
in the dock remained empty.

So did the place of the accused Martin Bormann. He was
tried in his absence, for in his case the Court was of the opinion
that he could turn up of his own free will if he was still alive.

Bormann, Hiltler's private secretary, had remained out of sight
since the last survivors had tried to escape from the bunker of
the besieged Berlin Reich Chancellery. The question what had
become of him puzzled the Allied Secret Service and the public.

Bormann was the man who, in the last period of the Third
Reich, had undoubtedly the strongest influence on Hitler, who

ousted everybody else from Hitler's immediate circle, and eventually managed to increase his power so much that it was difficult to tell whether certain decisions and orders were his own or Hitler's.

Major General Hans Baur, Hitler's pilot, said after his return from Soviet captivity in 1955: "Hitler's last order to me was to convey Martin Bormann to safety in a Condor which was kept ready at Zechlin. But Bormann was killed when he attempted to break through the Soviet lines around Berlin."

The Spaniard, Juan Pinar, who, as a member of the "Blue Division," also returned from Soviet captivity in May 1945, said that he dragged Bormann's body from a tank in Berlin. According to Pinar, Bormann had been killed by a direct hit on the tank.

The widespread doubts about Bormann's death seem to have been answered by these and other witnesses in the course of the years, and Bormann's death was accepted as a fact. On October 26, 1954, his name was entered under number 29223 in the *Register of Deaths* in the registry office at West Berlin.*

In 1945, Bormann's death was still doubtful. During the preliminary London Conference, Jackson said, "We are still without Bormann, but we have heard that the Russians have got him." General Nikitchenko answered, "Unfortunately we haven't got him at the moment."

Thus the Court of Justice later felt obliged to call upon Martin Bormann in official announcements to give himself up. For four weeks the summons was read over all broadcasting stations in the four occupied areas of Germany. Two hundred thousand notices with Bormann's name were printed, every newspaper published the appeal several times, and in the British Zone alone almost five million copies of the announcement were distributed.

All these efforts were in vain. Bormann was not found, and his place in the dock at Nuremberg remained empty.

* After Adolf Eichmann's capture in the Argentine in 1960, rumors were again revived that Bormann, too, was—and still is—in that country under an assumed name.—Translator.

3
Power and Folly

THE TRIAL
BEGINS

On November 20, 1945, the Palace of Justice in Nuremberg resembled a beehive. The press box held 250 newspapermen who had come from all over the world to witness the opening session and to cable their impressions of the historic occasion to their readers. But only five German press representatives were admitted.

At the courtroom door, guards checked the identity cards. War correspondents in American, British, and French uniforms hurried up the wooden steps to the entrance—reporters of all nationalities, Indians, Russians, Australians, Africans, Swiss, Brazilians. Some well-known faces were among them. John Dos Passos, Thomas Mann's daughter Erika, Erich Kästner.

The courtroom was filled with the hum of the ventilating system and the murmur of several hundred voices. Fluorescent lighting illuminated the scene frigidly, but the dock and the judges' bench were specially lit up for the photographers and newsreel cameramen by twenty-two powerful floodlights.

The accused sat in two rows on long wooden benches, and spoke briskly among themselves or with their lawyers, whose desks had been set up in front of the dock.

Opposite them, on the other side of the room, was the oblong table of the judges on a raised dais, and behind it were the windows, with the flags of the United States, Great Britain, France, and the Soviet Union on the wall spaces between them. In front of the judges' dais, but at floor level, sat the stenographers for the four official langauges. The Germans and the Russians used pencil and notebook; English and French, small, noiseless stenotyping machines were used.

The stands for the press and the public, slightly above floor level, were to the right of the benches of the accused, and the

93

prosecutors' benches were placed at the foot of the stands. Projecting into the room were a table and lectern for the use of the prosecution and defense counsel.

To the left of the accused, behind glass walls, sat the interpreters for the four official languages. Every word was simultaneously translated into the other three languages, and every seat in the room was fitted with earphones and a dial which permitted the listener to switch to any of the four languages.

Just next to the interpreters' cubicles, near the center of the front wall, was the slightly raised witness stand. Witness stand, lectern, and judges' dais were fitted with small, colored lamps, a yellow one and a red one. The interpreters could switch them on. The yellow lamp indicated "Please speak more slowly," the red one was a warning that the translators were unable to follow.

Everything about the Nuremberg Trial transcended normal experience. There were 218 full days of proceedings, and in this it was surpassed only by the longest trial in history, the parallel trial at Tokyo, which lasted 417 days. Altogether, the proceedings at Nuremberg comprised 4,000,000 words and filled 16,000 pages. The prosecution produced 2,630 documents, the defense 2,700. The Court took the statements of 240 witnesses and checked 300,000 sworn statements. The accused had the services of 27 leading counsels, 54 assistants, and 67 secretaries. The duplication of all written matter in the four languages consumed 5,000,000 sheets of paper, weighing more than twenty tons. The photographic laboratory of the Court produced 780,000 copies on 13,000 rolls of photographic paper. Eighty-one thousand feet of magnetic tape and 7,000 disks recorded every word of the trial for comparison with the shorthand transcriptions. The news agencies with permanent representatives in the Palace of Justice sent out almost 14,000,000 words over their teletypes to the far corners of the earth.

"Attention! The Court!"

Everyone rose. It was three minutes past ten on the morning of November 20, 1945.

The four judges and their four deputies emerged in single file from a door in the main wall of the hall. Six of them wore black gowns; the two Russians at the end of the procession were in uniform.

With a slight bow toward the defending lawyers the members of the Court sat down. The trial began.

Seen from the dock, the men at the judges' table, from left to right, were:

The Russians: First, Deputy Judge Lieutenant Colonel Alexander F. Volkhkov, a fleshy-lipped young man with wavy hair; on the right, Judge Major General Iola J. Nikitchenko, thin-lipped, with rimless glasses.

The British: Deputy Judge Sir Norman Birkett, with a forelock that tended to fall over his brow; next to him the President of the Court, Lord Justice Sir Geoffrey Lawrence. He was the central figure of the Trial: bald, with glasses that kept slipping down his nose, a full, often grumpy-looking face, brightened every now and then by the smile of his dry wit. Sir Geoffrey held the reins of the trial firmly in his hands; his decisions showed that he was a man of feeling and wisdom.

The Americans: First, Judge Francis A. Biddle, a smooth, re-fined-looking man with a dark Clark Gable mustache; next to him, the Deputy Judge, John J. Parker, gray-haired, with an avuncular double chin and rimless glasses.

The French: First the aging Judge Henri Donnedieu de Vabres, with sparse hair, dark horn-rimmed glasses, and a heavy walrus mustache; next to him, at the end of the line of judges, Deputy Judge Robert Falco, his black hair neatly parted, a full mustache above his usually smiling lips.

Long before the opening of the Trial, Goering had visualized how in that historic hour he would dominate the Court. In fact, things turned out rather differently.

The whole of the first day of the Trial went by with the reading of the extensive bill of indictment, which was already known to the twenty-one accused. Goering sat quietly on the corner of his bench, leaning on the balustrade with his elbows wide apart, his chin cupped in his hands. There was nothing of the magnilo-quent pose he had visualized for himself.

The other defendants, too, remained quiet, trying to settle down in their new surroundings. Frick and Fritzsche were reading at-

tentively the German text of the indictment. Papen and one or
two others had put on their headphones, playing occasionally with
the switches to hear what the translations into the other languages sounded like. Keitel sat bolt upright on the bench, his
arms folded, displaying an impenetrable expression. Hess never
bothered about the proceedings. Before the beginning of the Trial
he said to Goering, "You'll see that this whole ghastly business
will disappear, and within a month you'll be the leader of Germany." Then he turned to a book which he had brought with
him from the prison library, and went on reading it without
paying the slightest attention to the proceedings. The book was
called *Der Loisl*. At one apparently amusing part of the story
Hess broke into loud laughter. Soon after this he had an attack
of stomach cramps, and the Court gave him permission to leave
the room and return to his cell.

Hess was one of the two defendants to be missing on the first
day: Ernst Kaltenbrunner stayed in prison because he was suffering from a cerebral hemorrhage.

There was a third casualty in the afternoon. Joachim von
Ribbentrop suddenly turned pale and fainted during the reading
of the atrocities and crimes against humanity.

The rest of the accused spent the day in more or less candid
examination of the crowded press box and in trying to size up the
judges who would eventually pass judgment upon them.

On the second day of the Trial the twenty-one prisoners were
asked to come up to the microphone one after the other, and
plead either guilty or not guilty. It was a formality. They nearly
all used the official formula: "Not guilty." There were, however,
some variations. Schacht said with emphasis, "I am in no way
guilty." Sauckel said, "I declare myself, in the meaning of the
indictment, before God and the world and especially before my
people, not guilty." Jodl said, "Not guilty. For what I did and
what I had to do I can answer with a clear conscience before
God, history, and my people." Papen said, "In no way guilty."
Fritzsche said, "Of *this* charge—not guilty." Hess simply said,
"No," and the President interjected, "Let that be recorded as
'not guilty.'" Some of the press laughed, and the President said,
"Anyone who disturbs the court must leave the room."

Then it was Goering's turn. He began, "Before I answer the question of the High Court, as to whether I am guilty or not . . ."

Goering believed that his big moment had come, but the President interrupted him. For the moment it was merely a question of pleading guilty or not guilty, and Goering gave in: "I declare myself not guilty of the charge."

Later, Goering was to have ample opportunity to make lengthy speeches on the witness stand. For nine whole days he was given a chance to speak almost without interruption. As the self-appointed representative of all the other accused he undertook to fill in their common political background, and to relate the historical events as he saw them—as he wanted to have seen them: the beginnings of Hitler and of the National Socialist Party, the Munich Putsch, the struggle for power.

Next, the prosecution submitted to the Court the prehistory of the German tragedy. Quietly and without emotion, the voices of the interpreters told the story into their microphones, from the distant, unexciting beginnings to the catastrophic avalanche.

It was on a fateful day in January 1933 that the thunder of that approaching avalanche rang out for all the world to hear.

HITLER
IN POWER

At 11:15 A.M. on January 30, 1933, Hitler took the solemn oath of allegiance to the Weimar Constitution, before the aged President of the Reich, Paul von Hindenburg, and after him the new members of his Cabinet did the same.

Hitler's "millennium" had begun.

But his power was not yet secure. There were still political parties in Germany, there was still a Reichstag with elected members and legislative powers—and in this Parliament, Hitler and his Party did not have a majority. In the November election of 1932 the Nazi Party had, in fact, lost two million votes, and the number of its Reichstag members had fallen from 230 to 196.

On March 5, 1933, new elections for the Reichstag were to take place. Would Chancellor Hitler then get a majority—or would he be rejected by the will of the people? Would he then have to retire as quickly as his transient predecessors, Brüning, Papen, and Schleicher?

Everything depended on these elections. A week before election day, on the evening of February 27, 1933, President von Hindenburg was dining as guest of honor at the club of the Vice-Chancellor Franz von Papen. The club had its rooms not far from the Reichstag building.

Suddenly, the guests noticed a red glow in the sky above the roofs. Hindenburg rose stiffly from his chair and went to the window. His gaze fell on the cupola of the Reichstag. It was in flames—the Reichstag was burning!

Strange things happened on that night. Although the election was in the offing and the leaders of all parties were traveling across Germany, speaking at one meeting after another, the three most important men of the Nazi Party "happened" to be in Berlin— Hitler, Goering, and Goebbels.

Only a few moments after the fire alarm had been given, Hitler and Goering met on a balcony in the burning Reichstag. The Chief of the Gestapo, Rudolf Diels, also happened to be there. Goering said to him dramatically, "This is the beginning of a Communist rising!" Then Hitler began to rave. Diels recalled that "his face was flaming red from excitement and from the heat." Diels had never before heard him scream in such an uncontrolled manner. "We shall give no pardon! Whoever stands in our way will be struck down. Every Communist functionary will be shot wherever he is found. And there will be no pardon for Social Democrats either!" How did Hitler and Goering know already who had started the fire? Twelve years later in Nuremberg the American chief prosecutor, Robert H. Jackson, revealed the truth. He turned to Goering who was sitting on the witness stand.

JACKSON: There was a great purge following that fire, was there not, in which many people were arrested?

GOERING: The arrests which you attribute in the Reichstag fire are the arrests of Communist functionaries. These arrests . . . had nothing to do with the fire. The fire merely precipitated the arrests.

JACKSON: In other words, you had lists already prepared at the time of the Reichstag fire of persons who should be arrested, did you not?

GOERING: We had always drawn up beforehand fairly complete lists of Communist functionaries who were to be arrested. That had nothing to do with the fire in the German Reichstag.

JACKSON: They were immediately put into execution—the arrests, I mean—after the Reichstag fire?

GOERING: Contrary to my intention of postponing this action for a few days . . . the Führer ordered that same night that the arrests should follow immediately.

At 9:17 P.M. the first police car drew up at the burning Reichstag. Police Inspector Emil Lateit, several other police officials, and Inspector Scranowitz rushed into the building. In one of the gloomy corridors, where burning sofas and leather seats spread a flickering light, a ghostlike apparition staggered toward the men: a young man, naked to the waist and glistening with sweat, with disheveled hair and a crazed look in his eyes. He ran about among the smoldering furniture, an insane, happy smile on his face.

Scranowitz went up to the stranger and told him that he was under arrest. Police Inspector Lateit felt in the man's trouser pockets and found a table knife and a foreign passport. Then the arrested man was taken out of the building by the police. A few minutes later, at the police station, Commissar Walter Zirpins carried out a first interrogation. The man turned out to be a Dutch national, Marinus van der Lubbe.

"He was quite an intelligent fellow," Zirpins stated after 1945. "He even spoke good German. When we wanted to get a Dutch interpreter for him he was annoyed and said, 'I know German as well as you do!'" He refused cigarettes and alcohol, but ate masses of sweets and oranges. From time to time he asked for coffee. He spoke fluently, and would not pass any sentence of the record of the interrogation that he had not himself formulated.

When the report was completed after three hours, about fifty to sixty pages with seven carbon copies, van der Lubbe signed every single page."

The eight copies of this weighty factual document disappeared in some mysterious way; they were never seen again.

Fire Brigade Chief Ludwig Wissell questioned the crew of Fire Brigade No. 6, who had been the first at the scene of the fire, and wrote in his report: "In order to provide light for the firemen who were following, one of the firemen examined the possibility of switching on the electric light. He went into a lumber room. From there, some steps led downward. When the fireman descended these steps, groping with his hands along the wall, his left hand touched a small light switch, which he turned on. He then saw a fanlight from which some panes, about 15 by 20 inches in size, had been broken out. Looking out, the fireman saw several revolver muzzles being aimed at him; the weapons were held by men dressed in brand-new police uniforms who ordered the fireman to retire at once or they would shoot. The fireman retreated and reported the matter at once to his officer."

The Fire Chief of Berlin, Walter Gempp, grew suspicious when he read these reports. On the site of the fire he satisfied himself that a conflagration of such an extent could not have been started by one man alone. Moreover, Gempp discovered that the President of the Reichstag, Hermann Goering, had expressly ordered that the Reichstag buildings should be left that night without the usual night guard. All officials had been told to leave by 8:00 P.M. No one was allowed to remain after that time.

Gempp recorded his findings dutifully in his report, and took the occasion to remark that the efforts to overcome the fire had been handicapped by an order from Goering not to give the general alarm at once. Shortly afterward, Gempp was relieved of his post. In accordance with the new era that had been ushered in, he was accused of "permitting Marxist and Communist subversive activities among firemen." Gempp met with a tragic end of which more will be said later.

Martin H. Sommerfeldt, Goering's press officer in the Prussian Ministry of the Interior, received an order from his chief at the scene of the fire to draw up at once an official statement for the papers. Sommerfeldt wrote an account of some twenty lines, in which he mentioned quite factually the events of the fire, the work of the fire brigades, and the first police findings. He gave this account to Goering for him to read in the Ministry a short while later.

"That is rubbish!" Goering screamed at him. "That is a police report, not a political communiqué."

Goering read in Sommerfeldt's account that the weight of the incendiary material was estimated at about a hundredweight.

"That is complete nonsense!" he shouted. "A hundredweight of incendiary material? Ten, a hundred hundredweights!" He took his red pencil and wrote a bold "100" on the sheet. Then he sent for a secretary and dictated a new account to her:

"This arson is the most monstrous act of Bolshevist terror in Germany up to now. After this, government buildings, castles, museums, and vital factories are planned to be set on fire. Reichsminister Goering has met this terrible danger with the severest measures. The whole of the security police and criminal police in Prussia has immediately been placed in the highest state of readiness. The auxiliary police have been called up. Communist newspapers, pamphlets, and posters are banned for a period of four weeks through the whole of Prussia. All newspapers, journals, pamphlets, and posters of the Social Democrat Party are banned for two weeks . . ."

Thus, just a week before the decisive Reichstag elections, all means of propaganda were to be denied to Hitler's most powerful opponents.

Goering wrote his large G under the report and sent Sommerfeldt to Koch Street where the domestic and foreign correspondents were awaiting new information about the fire. Sommerfeldt showed them the communiqué, but the newspapermen found it uninteresting. They had already cabled or telephoned the same story to their journals two hours before.

"But who gave you all this information?" asked Goering's press officer, nonplussed.

"Herr Berndt," he was told, "Alfred Ingmar Berndt, Dr. Goebbels' representative."

Naturally, the Gestapo had information about everything. In his memoirs, Hans Gisevius, of the Berlin Secret State Police, wrote: "The most sensational thing for us was that not Goering but Goebbels was the real incendiary. Goebbels had the original idea. Goebbels understood very well what the silencing of the press of the Left would mean at that time. Goebbels had worked closely with Goering, intimating to him somewhat mysteriously that the Führer agreed—something sensational had to happen, perhaps an attempted political murder, perhaps a fire, but Hitler wished to be surprised."

President Hindenburg was told of the "Bolshevist danger" a few hours after the fire alarm. The senile Head of State was talked into believing that the burning Reichstag was the signal for a Communist rising. Hindenburg wanted to save his people from the blood bath of a civil war. He fell for the Nazi leaders' story, and signed an emergency decree in which important articles of the constitution were suspended: personal liberty, the free expression of opinion, the freedom of the press, the right of assembly, the privacy of postal communications, the protection against house search and arrest without a legal warrant.

With this, the President of the Reich signed the death sentence of German democracy and opened the doors for Hitler's dictatorship. With this scrap of paper carrying Hindenburg's stiff signature, the first wave of Nazi terror was unleashed in Germany on the very night of the Reichstag fire. Thousands were arrested. The lists had long been ready. The prisons filled up. The first concentration camps were built. Newspapers inimical to Hitler were banned, opposition meetings dispersed, the leaders of the opposition arrested.

Under these conditions the German people went to the polls on March 5, 1933. Hitler had practically eliminated his opponents; the Reichstag fire had frightened the people who feared a Red revolution—was there any choice but to vote for Germany's saviors, the Nazis?

But in spite of the election terror and the civil war bluff, the German people were not stampeded: the Nazi Party received only 44 per cent of the vote. It was a setback for Chancellor

Hitler. He had to think up a new trick in order to gain unlimited power.

On March 24, 1933, the newly elected Reichstag assembled. At that session Hitler wanted to pass a bill that would empower him in future to rule without parliamentary control or constitutional hindrance. He knew that the legally elected majority of the Reichstag would never approve this law. Once again, therefore, terror had to come to his help: Hitler had a number of opposition members arrested, thus intimidating the rest of them. His tool for this move was the emergency decrees signed by Hindenburg on the night of the fire.

At the Nuremberg Trial, the American prosecutor, Frank B. Wallis, said: "On March 14, 1933, the defendant Frick (then already Minister for the Interior) stated: 'When the Reichstag meets the 21st of March, the Communists will be prevented by urgent labor elsewhere from participation in the session. In concentration camps they will be re-educated for productive work. We all know how to render harmless permanently, subhumans who don't want to be re-educated.' During this period . . . a large number of Communists, including party officials and Reichstag deputies, and a smaller number of Social Democrat officials were placed in protective custody. On March 24, 1933, only 535 out of the regular 747 deputies of the Reichstag were present. The absence of some was unexcused; they were in protective custody in concentration camps. Subject to the full weight of the Nazi pressure and terror, the Reichstag passed an 'Enabling Act' . . . with a vote of 441 in favor. This law marks the real seizure of political control by the conspirators."

With the Enabling Act, Hitler became absolute dictator. Weimar was dead, democracy strangled.

But the Reichstag fire spread further. In the early months of 1933, the Hitler regime still had to maintain the appearance of legality, for other countries followed the events in Germany with special attention. On September 21, 1933, the Reichstag Fire Trial opened at Leipzig. Before the judges in the scarlet robes stood five defendants: Marinus van der Lubbe; the parliamentary leader of the Communists, Ernst Torgler; and the Bulgarians, Georgi Dimitroff, Vassil Taneff, and Blagoi Popoff.

Torgler and the three Bulgarians were outspoken. Although Goering's police made every effort to prove that these four Communists were van der Lubbe's collaborators, they were not successful, and in those days the law was still mighty enough to return a verdict of not guilty.

Van der Lubbe was sentenced to death. He offered a pitiful spectacle. The same young man who after his arrest had stood up to three hours' police questioning, dictated the statement himself, and signed several hundred pages of the duplicated sheets—that man was now a human wreck. Throughout the entire three months of the trial he sat in the dock completely indifferent and hunched up, and never said a word beyond an occasional "yes" or "no."

Charles Reber, an internationally known specialist on poisons, wrote of this pathetic case: "If a man who is mentally and physically fit is given a daily dose of from a quarter to a half milligram of scopolamine, then that man will degenerate to a condition of complete indifference and stupor. His brain is practically paralyzed, and he is in a constant state of twilight sleep. His back becomes more and more bent, and he laughs foolishly without reason."

This is an exact picture of van der Lubbe. He had been the only person who was actually in the burning Reichstag. There is only one explanation: others had persuaded the muddle-headed young man to lend them a hand, and had then left him at the site of the fire while they themselves disappeared.

Twice in the course of the trial van der Lubbe raised his head from his knees and mumbled, "The others—" Then he sank back into his dull silence. The broken man could say no more. During the trial he was a living corpse who was to take his secret with him to the scaffold. But another man spoke up for him. Very much to the annoyance of the President of the Court, the aged Senator Wilhelm Bünger, the accused Dimitroff turned prosecutor. He attacked witnesses, even important ones such as Dr. Joseph Goebbels and Hermann Goering. Dimitroff was self-confidence personified. His questions were like judo holds, and Goebbels and Goering were not equal to them.

"I have the impression," said Goebbels, "that Dimitroff wants to make propaganda for Communism in this court."

DIMITROFF: Have the National Socialists defended themselves?

GOEBBELS (in a temper): Of course we have defended ourselves.

DIMITROFF (calmly): Do you not believe that we Communists also have the right to defend ourselves?

Much more dramatic was his conflict with the witness Goering. The President of the Reichstag and Premier of Prussia had had a new uniform made for that day. As he spoke, the sweat beaded his brow, his voice cracked, and he repeatedly wiped his face with a handkerchief. He tried to justify the official version of the Bolshevist arson, and stormed against the criminal creed of Communism.

DIMITROFF: Does the Premier of Prussia know that this criminal creed rules one sixth of the earth, namely the Soviet Union?

GOERING (enraged): I will tell you what the German people know. The German people know that you are behaving impertinently, and that you have come to this country to set the Reichstag on fire. In my eyes you are a rogue who should go straight to the gallows.

THE PRESIDENT: Dimitroff, I have already told you that you must not carry on any Communist propaganda here. It is not surprising that the witnesses are annoyed. I forbid this propaganda strictly. You may only ask factual questions.

DIMITROFF: I am very satisfied with the answer of the Prussian Premier.

THE PRESIDENT: Whether you are satisfied or not is a matter of indifference to me. I forbid you to speak.

DIMITROFF: I have a further factual question to ask.

THE PRESIDENT: I forbid you to speak.

DIMITROFF: You are afraid of my questions, Herr Prime Minister of Prussia.

GOERING: What are you talking about, you rogue, you tramp!

THE PRESIDENT: Out with you!

GOERING: Out, tramp, out!

DIMITROFF: You are afraid of my questions.

The bailiff seized the accused man and hustled him out of the courtroom. On the way to the door Dimitroff shouted above the tumult: "You really are afraid, Herr Prime Minister!"

The most remarkable fact about the Reichstag Trial is that three experts—a fire specialist, a heat engineer, and an analytical chemist—affirmed unanimously that van der Lubbe could not possibly have started the extensive fire in such a short time; there must have been other hands at work. Van der Lubbe had used a few fire kindlers for domestic use, with which at the most he could have started a few small local fires in the large complex of the Reichstag buildings. But the firemen found wide areas of conflagration in the large plenary chamber, in the galleries and the corridors. The Court's chemical expert, Dr. Schatz, stated that some liquid, self-inflammatory fuel must have been used.

At that moment the apathetic van der Lubbe raised his head, shaking with silent laughter. What was this man's secret?

At the Nuremberg Trial twelve years later, this question was raised again, and again Goering was on the witness stand. The American prosecutor, Jackson, subjected him to a cross-examination. But how different was the scene!

JACKSON: Who was Karl Ernst?

GOERING: Ernst was the SA leader of Berlin.

JACKSON: And who was Helldorf?

GOERING: Count Helldorf was the subsequent SA leader of Berlin.

JACKSON: And Heines?

GOERING: Heines was the SA leader of Silesia at that time.

JACKSON: Now, it is well known to you, is it not, that Ernst made a statement confessing that these three burned the Reichstag and that you and Goebbels planned it and furnished the incendiary materials, liquid phosphorus and petroleum, which were deposited by you in a subterranean passage for them to get, which passage led from your house to the Reichstag building? You knew of such a statement, did you not?

GOERING: I do not know of any statement by the SA leader, Ernst.

JACKSON: But there was such a passage from the Reichstag building to your house?

GOERING: On one side of the street is the Reichstag building, opposite is the Palace of the Reichstag president. The two are connected by a passage along which the wagons run which carry the coke for the central heating.

JACKSON: You were generally being accused of burning the Reichstag building. You knew that, did you not?

GOERING: That accusation . . . came from a certain foreign press. That could not bother me because it was not consistent with the facts. I had no reason or motive for setting fire to the Reichstag. From the artistic point of view I could not at all regret that the assembly chamber was burned; I hoped to build a better one. But I did regret very much that I was forced to find a new meeting place for the Reichstag, and, not being able to find one, I had to give up my Kroll Opera House, for that purpose. The opera seemed to me much more important than the Reichstag.

JACKSON: Have you ever boasted of burning the Reichstag building, even by way of joking?

GOERING: No. I made a joke, if that is what you are referring to, that after this I should be competing with Nero, and that probably people would soon be saying, that dressed in a red toga and holding a lyre in my hand, I looked on at the fire and played while the Reichstag was burning. But the fact was I nearly perished in the flames, which would have been very unfortunate for the German people, but very fortunate for their enemies."

JACKSON: You never stated that you burned the Reichstag?

GOERING: No. I know Herr Rauschning said in his book which he wrote that I had discussed this with him. . . .

Hermann Rauschning, President of the Senate of Danzig, had published his *Gespräche mit Hitler* (*The Voice of Destruction*) in exile. The passage in the book to which Goering referred runs: "Shortly after the Reichstag fire Hitler wanted a report from me on the situation in Danzig. Before we were admitted to the

Chancellery we had an opportunity, in the waiting room of what were then Hitler's offices, to talk to some of the leading Nazis. Goering, Himmler, Frick, and several Gauleiters from the West were talking together. Goering gave details of the Reichstag fire. The secret of the fire was still strictly guarded in the Party at that time. From that conversation I learned for the first time that the Reichstag fire had been started by no one else but the National Socialist leaders. Goering described how his 'boys' reached the Reichstag by an underground passage from the President's palace, and how they only had a few minutes' time, and how they were almost discovered in the act. He regretted that 'the whole shack' was not burned down. In their haste they were unable to 'complete the job.' Goering, who was ranting in grand style, finished his account with the truly significant words: 'I have no conscience. My conscience is called Adolf Hitler.' "

It was a rather different story which he told on the witness stand at Nuremberg.

GOERING: I saw Herr Rauschning only twice in my life, and only for a short time on each occasion. If I had really set fire to the Reichstag, I would presumably have let it be known only to my closest circle of confidants, if at all. I would not have told it to a man whom I did not know and whose appearance I could not describe at all today. That is an absolute distortion of the truth.

JACKSON: Can you remember the luncheon on Hitler's birthday in 1942 at the headquarters of the Führer?

GOERING: No.

JACKSON: You do not remember that? I will ask that you be shown the affidavit of General Franz Halder and I call your attention to his statements which may refresh your recollection. "On the occasion of a luncheon on the Führer's birthday in 1942, the people around the Führer turned the conversation to the Reichstag building and its artistic value. I heard with my own ears how Goering broke into the conversation and shouted, 'The only one who really knows the Reichstag is I, for I set fire to it.' And saying this, he slapped his thigh."

Later Halder continued: "I sat in Hitler's immediate vicinity, and on his right side sat Goering. Every word was clear and easy to understand. Also the effect of Goering's words proved the importance of his statement. There was complete silence at the table. Hitler was obviously annoyed. Several minutes went by before the conversation was resumed slowly by the company."

GOERING: This conversation did not take place, and I request that I be confronted with Herr Halder. A statement of this type is utter nonsense. How Herr Halder came to make that statement, I do not know. Apparently that bad memory, which also let him down in military matters, is the only explanation.

Obviously Goering did not care to go down in history as an incendiary. Jackson was disarmed. He did not press Goering any further.

In the preliminary hearing, the American prosecutor, Kempner, had put many questions about the fire to Goering. Parts of this report were also read out at the trial.

KEMPNER: How could you tell your press agent, one hour after the Reichstag caught fire, that the Communists did it, without further investigation?

GOERING: Did the public relations officer say that I said this at that time

KEMPNER: Yes. He said you said it.

GOERING: It is possible when I came to the Reichstag, the Führer and his gentlemen were there. I was doubtful at that time, but it was their opinion that the Communists had started the fire.

KEMPNER: Looking back on it now, and not in the excitement that was there once, wasn't it too early to say, without any investigation, that the Communists had started the fire?

GOERING: Yes, that is possible, but the Führer wanted it this way.

KEMPNER: Tell us what you were going to say.

GOERING: Whatever was done or planned in this affair, I can only assume it came from some other quarters.

KEMPNER: What do you think in this connection, for example, of Police President Ernst [the SA chief of Berlin]. Tell us frankly your opinion of Ernst.

GOERING: Yes, I had him in mind—if there was another hand in the game. So far as Ernst is concerned, I believe that anything was possible. I would like to know what interest Ernst could have had in it. Supposing that he said to himself, "Let us set fire to the Reichstag and say that it was the Communists." Perhaps the SA expected then to be able to play a bigger part in the government.

This explanation tallies with the statement made by another witness at Nuremberg, the former Gestapo official, Hans Bernd Gisevius. On April 25, 1946, Gisevius said in Nuremberg under oath: It was Goebbels who first thought of setting the Reichstag on fire. Goebbels discussed this with the commander of the Berlin SA brigade, Karl Ernst, and he suggested in detail how it should be done. A certain chemical known to every maker of fireworks was chosen. After spraying it, it ignites after a certain time—hours or minutes. In order to get inside the Reichstag, one had to go through the corridor leading from the palace of the Reichstag President to the Reichstag itself. Ten reliable SA men were provided and Goering was informed of all the details of the plan. Goering—and he gave assurances that he would do so—was to put the police on wrong trails in the first confusion. From the very beginning it was intended that the Communists should be accused of this crime.

JACKSON: What became of the ten SA men who carried out the Reichstag fire?

GISEVIUS: So far as we are aware, none of them are still alive. Most of them were murdered on June 30 under the pretext of the Röhm revolt. Only one, a certain Heini Gewehr, was taken over by the police as a police officer, and we tracked him down as well. He was killed in the war, while a police officer on the Eastern Front.

Thus, all those who had been in the know, and all who had unconsciously come upon the facts of the fire, had lost their lives. Fire Chief Gempp was strangled soon after his dismissal from his post. A right-wing member of the Reichstag, Ernst Oberfohren of the National Party, who was said to have written a report on the true facts about the fire, was found shot at his desk. Erik Hanussen, a clairvoyant who said at a séance two days before the fire that he saw "a large house in flames," was murdered a short while later in the Gruenwald. Hanussen's presumable informant, the engineer Georg Bell, who had his information from the highest Nazi circles, escaped to Austria, but before leaving he gave some secret Nazi papers to a Munich newspaper editor, Fritz Michael Gerlich. But his office was likely to be searched, and so those papers had to disappear as quickly as possible. The last to see them was the former State President of Württemberg, Eugen Anton Bolz. Gerlich's secretary, Miss Breit, clearly remembered the contents of the documents. They contained: detailed facts about the Reichstag fire; an agreement between the Nazi Party and the British oil millionaire, Deterding, concerning the secret backing of the SA in return for preferential treatment of his German interests; a list of witnesses to the fact that Hitler had murdered his niece Geli Raubal; plans for discrediting the Church; plans of SA Chief of Staff Roehm for getting rid of Hitler after the Nazis' seizure of power.

The men who had seen these dangerous documents had to die. Bell was ferreted out by SA unit commander Uhl in Austria and was there dispatched with six pistol shots. Uhl himself was murdered on June 30, 1934, in Ingolstadt. On the same day, Gerlich was killed. State President Bolz was executed shortly before the end of the war in connection with the plot of July 20, 1944. Another man, Paul Waschinsky, who seems to have recruited van der Lubbe for the arson plot, was likewise killed in 1934. Captain Roehrbein, who boasted in some prison to have been one of the SA men involved in the fire, was shot. SA chief Ernst, who led the troops through the underground passage, committed the folly of writing a letter to his superior officer Edmund Heines, which began with the words: "I hereby give an account of the Reichstag fire, in which I took part." Ernst was murdered.

There was still one more accomplice, the ex-convict and SA man Rall. He was naive enough to make a statement about his complicity before a local court. The report was sent to the higher court in Leipzig, but was intercepted by the Gestapo who had received their information from the recording clerk of the lower court, an SA man named Reineking.

Rall was disposed of. One night he was taken by an SA murder squad by car to an empty field near Berlin. There they strangled him and left him for dead. The murderers, of whom Reineking was one, dug a grave. But when they went to throw Rall in, the "dead" man had disappeared. He had revived and run away across the field, clad only in his shirt. They caught up with him, strangled him again, and then buried him. Reineking himself was murdered at the Dachau concentration camp toward the end of 1934.

That was the bloody trail of the Reichstag fire in those years of darkness, till in the end all voices had been silenced. But at Nuremberg, one of the dead came back to life!

The witness Gisevius had in fact been mistaken: one of the incendiaries, SA man Heini Gewehr, who was thought to have been killed on the Eastern front, was discovered by Goering's defense: he had survived the war, and was now in American captivity at Hammelburg, near Bad Kissingen. His appearance caused a sensation; for if Goering had really nothing to do with the fire—and at least his defense had to assume this—then Heini Gewehr would only have to say, "Everything is pure invention. I know nothing of a team of incendiaries, I have in any case not been one of them," and the trustworthiness of the witness Gisevius would have been severely shaken. Goering would have triumphed.

The lawyer Werner Bross, an assistant of Goering's defense counsel, Dr. Otto Stahmer, brought the good news to the accused in prison. Bross writes in his memoirs: "But Goering, far from being happy, became rather disturbed. 'This matter must be handled extremely carefully,' he said. 'With such witnesses you have to be careful. Even if the SA actually did set fire to the Reichstag, that is not to say that I knew anything about it.'"

Could the troop of incendiaries use the underground passage, whose entrance was in Goering's palace, without his knowledge? Could an SA chief of the comparatively humble rank of Karl Ernst have carried out such an extensive operation without the consent of the Party leaders?

Goering said to Bross, "Who guarantees that this witness will not buy his freedom with a statement that condemns me?" The matter was dropped. "He showed no inclination to follow up this new clue, or even to discuss the subject further in conversation," wrote Bross.

THE BLOODY
SEED

"After they had achieved complete political control," said the American prosecutor, Frank B. Wallis, "the Nazi conspirators set about making it secure. The first step was the ruthless suppression of political opponents by means of concentration camps or murder. Concentration camps first appeared in the year 1933 and were used as a means of removing political opponents, who were taken into so-called protective custody. This system of concentration camps grew and spread throughout Germany."

The decisive months of 1933 were full of unrest. Things that happened in the open street, while ordinary Germans dared not look, went on in the name of "political co-ordination."

The National Socialist Revolution was on the march. Raymond H. Geist, First Secretary of the American Embassy, lived through those days in Berlin. He submitted his impressions to the Nuremberg Court as a sworn statement. Prosecuting counsel Wallis read out parts of it:

"As early as 1933, concentration camps were built and the Gestapo were in charge. The first wave of terrorism began in March 1933, accompanied by unusual activity on the part of the mob. After the National Socialist Party had won the election in March 1933, the pent-up passions broke out on the morning of March 6, in the form of large-scale attacks upon Communists, and also against Jews and other people. Hordes of SA men roved about in the streets, striking, robbing, and even murdering men. For those Germans who were taken into 'protective custody' by the Gestapo, there was brutality and horror. There were hundreds of thousands of victims all over Germany."

Goering, placed under oath on the witness stand by his defending counsel, Dr. Otto Stahmer, was interrogated about these events.

GOERING: Naturally cases of undue interference occurred in the beginning, naturally here and there they affected innocent people, naturally here and there people were struck and acts of brutality were committed, but measured by the magnitude of the events this German revolution for freedom was the least bloody and the best disciplined of all previous revolutions in history.

DR. STAHMER: Did you supervise the treatment of those arrested?

GOERING: Naturally I gave instructions that such things had to cease. I have just said that they did occur everywhere to a greater or lesser extent.

DR. STAHMER: Did you interfere in cases of which you were informed?

GOERING: I took personal charge of the concentration camps until the spring of 1934. I would like just to touch on the case of Thälmann, because he was the most striking, for Thälmann was the leader of the Communist Party. I cannot say today who told me that Thälmann had been beaten up. I had him brought directly to my room, immediately and without informing the authorities, and questioned him very closely. He told me that he had been beaten especially at the beginning of the interrogations. I told him: "My dear Thälmann, if you had got into power I do not think that I would have been beaten up, but you would have cut off my head at once."

He admitted this; then I told him that in future he could communicate quite freely with me if anything of that kind happened either to him or to others. I could not always prevent it, but it was not my wish that any act of brutality of any kind should be carried out against them.

While Goering was making this statement he did not care to remember a speech which he had made in public on March 3, 1933. The British prosecutor, Harcourt Barrington, read parts of it:

"Fellow Germans! My measures will not be mellowed by any

legal considerations. My task is not to carry out the law, but only to destroy and exterminate, and nothing else!"

Were the concentration camps, as Goering claimed, really a relatively harmless institution at first? One man who must have known was the former Gestapo chief Rudolf Diels. His statements played an important part at Nuremberg. He said about measures taken in 1933:

"For the setting up of the concentration camps there were no orders or instructions; they were not 'installed,' they were just there one day. The SA chiefs built 'their' camps because they would not intrust their prisoners to the police or because the prisons were overfilled. There were beatings throughout the country."

Everywhere, SA groups built concealed places of torture with their own hands, so-called "bunkers," in which the brown revolutionaries gave vent to their hatred of their defenseless opponents. The news quickly spread beyond the German borders and shocked the world. Something had to be done to wipe out the bad impression. Hitler still put some value on foreign opinion. The "wild" camps and SA cellars had to be organized systematically. But the SA were not inclined to let themselves be pulled up suddenly. A trial of strength was bound to come. Gestapo chief Diels had heard of a place of torture on the fourth floor of the local Berlin headquarters of the SA in Hedemann Street. "Here, some tortured people had escaped their persecutors by suicidal jumps from the windows. The resident of a nearby house had reported this," said Diels. "A courageous officer of the Wecke detachment was prepared to help me in closing down the place of torture. A number of policemen armed with hand grenades surrounded the building. Inside, the SA men too took up positions. They set up machine guns in the entrance of the house and in the windows."

Diels called to the SA men that Goering had ordered them to get out. "When I pointed to the police officers armed with hand grenades, they roared with laughter," continued Diels. "But in the end they had to hand over their prisoners, and I entered the torture rooms with the policemen. The floorboards of several empty rooms in which the torturers had done their work were covered with straw. The victims that we found were almost starved to death. They had been locked, standing up, in narrow racks for days at a time, in order to extract 'confessions' from them. The 'hearings' had begun and ended with beating; a dozen brutes had thrashed the victims with rods of iron, rubber truncheons, and whips at intervals of a few hours. Teeth that had been knocked out and broken bones were evidence of the tortures.

"When we entered, these living skeletons lay in rows upon the filthy straw with festering wounds. There was not one victim whose body did not show, from head to toe, the blue, yellow, and green marks of inhuman thrashings. The eyes of many of them were closed by swellings, and under their nostrils were crusts of clotted blood. Every one of them had to be carried into the police van; they were no longer capable of walking. In the police prison I ordered a medical examination. The official medical report could make the strongest man feel sick.'

Diels reported on numerous SA holes of this kind, which could only be wiped out gradually by force. It was more difficult to force the "wild" concentration camps under state supervision. Here, too, the SA or even the SS often opposed the police with arms. One of these places was at Papenburg. Diels reported:

"At Papenburg the burgomaster had informed me of the excesses of the SS toward the inhabitants. The SS men pillaged the district like the Swedes in the Thirty Years' War. They robbed, arrested people who displeased them, and started fights."

Diels wanted to take over the camp. "Goering's deputy, Secretary of State Grauert, authorized us to take along fifty Berlin policemen, armed with carbines. The SS in the camp let the police know that they would be met with machine-gun fire if they came near the place."

Grauert collected two hundred men of the Osnabrück municipal police and marched to the camp. The police and the SS were now facing each other, ready to fire.

Diels hastened to Hitler. It was an ugly situation. He asked if the police could now proceed by force of arms against the SS. Hitler ordered that army artillery should be brought up and the whole camp "ruthlessly leveled to the ground." Faced with this threat, the SS surrendered. But soon Diels received new alarm signals, this time from the Kemna camp near Wuppertal.

"There, the SA had found an especially 'original' way of treating captured Communists," reported the Gestapo chief. "They were forced to drink herring brine, and then they would gasp in vain for a drink of water in those hot summer days. One of my commissars reported that the SA there had practiced the 'joke' of making the prisoners climb trees; they had to stay for hours in the treetops, calling 'cuckoo' from time to time."

The Kemna Trial, which took place in 1947, established that groups of prisoners of twenty-five each were locked into shelters that had only room for five. At night they were taken out singly and "given a hearing"—in other words, beaten until they were unconscious. Their screams were drowned by the noise of a phonograph playing "Deutschland über Alles." The SA men had built a special bench on which the prisoners had to lie; one tormentor took the head of the victim between his legs, a second held the feet, and then he was thrashed. Some got burning cigars stuffed into their mouths, which they had to swallow.

That was 1933. But it was no more than a foretaste of the horrors to come in later years.

The "wild" concentration camps were gradually dissolved or taken under state control. Goering succeeded in putting things in "order." For reasons of humanity? On the witness stand at Nuremberg he spoke about such a camp, one near Breslau: "In any case it was not a camp authorized by me. I immediately closed it and dissolved it." Thus it was only a matter of internal power politics, of "authorization," and not of humanity. "Wild" camps were superseded by "authorized" ones—that was the only difference. Murdered prisoners were said to have been "shot while trying to escape"—the official formula. Many committed suicide. Germany had become a land of silence.

Pyres were kindled in the towns—the burning of the books. Thousands of works which had contributed to Germany's standing in the world of science and literature were reduced to cinders. Goebbels dictated what should appear in the papers; the truth was being told only in whispers. In other countries the press was still free, and the news which came from Germany aroused horror

and indignation. Boycott Germany! That was the cry which arose
as a natural reaction abroad. Don't buy any more German goods!

In a few months, Hitler had succeeded in bringing down the
respect for Germany in the world like the mercury column of a
thermometer that is suddenly plunged into cold water. But
Goebbels had his answer ready; it was all only a malicious invention of foreigners, an evil atrocity story spread by "international
Jewry."

A counterboycott was to take place throughout the whole of
Germany on April 1, 1933, a "retaliation for false foreign news."
The Jews were to be the victims.

"What can you tell us about this, and what part did you play
in it?" attorney Dr. Hanns Marse asked his client, the defendant
Julius Streicher, who had made the persecution of the Jews his
aim in life. On the witness stand, however, he told this naive
story: "A few days before the first of April I was ordered to the
Brown House in Munich. Adolf Hitler told me what I already
knew. A terrible slander campaign was under way in the foreign
press against the new Germany, and now we had to tell world
Jewry: 'Thus far and no further.' Hitler said that April 1 would
be a Counterboycott Day, and he wanted me to take charge of it.
I ordered that no Jewish life should be attacked, and that outside
each Jewish shop there should be one or more pickets who would
be responsible for seeing that no property was damaged. It is a
fact that the Counterboycott Day passed without any major
incidents."

Everything was well organized: the Star of David was smeared
on the shop windows of all Jewish firms, SA men prevented cus-
tomers from entering, pickets stood before the offices of Jewish
lawyers and doctors, posters were displayed everywhere: "Don't
buy from the Jews!" The whole day trucks rattled through the
streets, packed with SA men who chanted in chorus Streicher's
slogan: "*Juda verrecke*," "Perish Judah!"

Meanwhile, the machinery for issuing new decrees and laws
had started up. The Journal of Federal Law for 1933, which was
produced at the Nuremberg Trial, shows that the defendants
Frick and Neurath signed the order depriving immigrant Jews
of their German nationality; Frick excluded Jews from all public

offices and government posts, from journalism and radio, banned
them from the universities, and from the medical and legal professions as well as from agricultural occupations.

Nazi maneuvers in the sphere of foreign politics distracted the
attention of the world from these developments at home. Germany left the Disarmament Conference and the League of
Nations. Hitler wanted to have his hands free. He was already
reaching for his next objective—rearmament.

The old German Reichswehr, with its one hundred thousand
men, grew into the forces of the Wehrmacht. Here, however,
Hitler had to overcome an obstacle: what was to become of the
millions of his revolutionary army of the SA? Roehm and his
SA were a source of trouble. The Führer could not tolerate any
other power beside him. All opposition had to be swept away.

"Concerning the crushing of the opposition, the blood bath
of June 30, 1934, must not be forgotten," says the Nuremberg bill
of indictment. "It is known as the Roehm Putsch and it reveals
the methods that Hitler and his closest collaborators, among
them the defendant Goering, were prepared to apply in order to
overcome any resistance and to consolidate their power. On that
day, Roehm, Chief of Staff of the SA since 1931, was murdered
on Hitler's order, the old guard of the SA were butchered without
trial and without warning. On this occasion a large number of
other people, who had opposed Hitler at some time or another,
were also killed."

Once again it was Hermann Goering who, at the Nuremberg
Trial, was given the opportunity to present his version of the
bloody events of June 30, 1934, still invested with many secrets.
He was one of those chiefly involved. This was his official version:

"The chief reasons for the differences between Roehm and us
were that Roehm wanted to follow a stronger revolutionary line.
After we had taken over, Roehm set his cap at getting control
of the War Ministry. This was flatly refused by the Führer. A
few weeks before the Roehm Putsch, a subordinate SA chief confided to me that he had heard that an action against the Führer
and those loyal to him had been planned. I know Roehm well.
I sent for him and spoke to him openly about the things I had
heard. I reminded him of the old days when we had fought to-

gether and exhorted him to be absolutely faithful to the Führer. He assured me that he had of course never dreamed of doing anything against the Führer.

"Shortly afterward I received further information that he was in close contact with those circles which had always been strongly opposed to us, such as the circle of the former Chancellor, Schleicher; the circles around an ex-member of the Reichstag who had been expelled from the Party, the former chief of organization of the Party, Gregor Strasser. I felt obliged to talk to the Führer about it. To my surprise the Führer told me that he already knew of the matter and regarded it as very menacing. But he would await further developments and watch things carefully. The next act followed more or less as the witness Körner has described it."

Goering's former private secretary, Paul Körner, had answered questions of the defending counsel, Dr. Otto Stahmer, two days earlier:

DR. STAHMER: What do you know of the events regarding the Roehm Revolt?

KÖRNER: I found out that a Roehm Revolt was planned while I stayed with the Field Marshal at Essen, where we were present at the wedding of Gauleiter Terboven. During the wedding festivities Himmler arrived and made a report to Hitler. Later the Führer took the Field Marshal into his confidence.

DR. STAHMER: What information did Goering receive?

KÖRNER: The Führer told him to return to Berlin immediately after the wedding, as the Führer himself was going to southern Germany to follow up these reports in person.

Goering continued the story: "I was given the order to proceed immediately against the men of Roehm's circle in northern Germany. Some of them were to be held as prisoners. In the course of the day the Führer ordered the execution of SA Chief Ernst and two or three others. Hitler himself went to Bavaria, where a conference of a group of Roehm and some of his officers was taking place, and personally arrested Roehm and his men at Wiessee. The situation had already grown quite serious; several SA formations, under cover of false orders, had been armed and were kept in readiness. In one instance only a short fight occurred, and two SA chiefs were shot. When the headquarters of SA Chief Ernst was raided in Berlin, more submachine guns were found in the cellar than were in the possession of the whole of the Prussian police.

"No orders had been given to shoot the rest of the arrested men. It did, however, happen that during the arrest of the former Chancellor, Schleicher, both he and his wife were killed. An inquiry established that during the arrest Schleicher grabbed a pistol, perhaps in order to shoot himself. At that both the men who had come to arrest him raised their revolvers, and Frau von Schleicher threw herself at one of them to get hold of him, and he stated that his gun went off as a result. We greatly regretted this mishap.

"In the course of the evening I heard that other people had been shot as well, including some who had nothing whatever to do with the Roehm uprising. The Führer returned to Berlin the same night. When I heard that I went to him the next day and asked him to issue an order at once that all executions were forbidden by him, the Führer, under all circumstances, although a couple of people who were involved and whom the Führer had condemned to death were still alive. As a result these two were spared.

"I begged him to do this because I was afraid the matter might get out of hand, as had indeed already happened to some extent. I suggested to him that there should be no further bloodshed under any circumstances. The Führer then issued the order in my presence. The action was reported to the Reichstag and was approved by President Hindenberg and the Reichstag as a measure of national emergency."

Later, Goering was questioned about these events by Jackson in cross-examination:

JACKSON: What was it that Roehm did that he was shot?

GOERING: Roehm planned to overthrow the government, and it was intended to kill the Führer also. He wanted to follow it up by a revolution, directed in the first place against the Army.

JACKSON: And you had evidence of that fact?

GOERING: We had sufficient evidence of that fact.

JACKSON: But he was never tried in any court where he would have a chance to tell his story as you are telling yours, was he?

GOERING: That is correct. He wanted to bring about a Putsch and therefore the Führer considered it right that this thing should be nipped in the bud—not by a court procedure, but by smashing the revolt immediately.

JACKSON: Who actually killed Roehm? Do you know?

GOERING: I do not know who personally carried out this action.

JACKSON: Among those who were killed was also Erich Klausener, who had been Chief of the Catholic Action of Germany?

GOERING: Klausener was among those who were shot. Actually, it was Klausener's case which caused me, as stated recently, to ask the Führer to give immediate orders to cease any further action, since in my opinion Klausener was quite wrongfully shot.

JACKSON: And when it got down to a point where there were only two left on the list yet to be killed, you intervened and asked to have it stopped. Is that correct?

GOERING: No, that is not entirely correct. I intervened when I saw that many were shot who were not concerned with this matter. And when I did so, two persons were left who had taken a very active part, and the Führer himself had ordered that they be shot.

A witness at Nuremberg debunked Goering's fairy tale. Dr. Otto Pannenbecker, defending counsel for the accused Wilhelm Frick, once Minister for the Interior, called Hans Bernd Gisevius, who was then in the Police Department of the Ministry of the Interior. What Gisevius had to say, under oath, sounded rather different: "I must first of all say that there never was a Roehm Putsch. On June 30 there was only a Goering-Himmler Putsch. I am in a position to give some information about this because I worked on this affair in the Police Department. The SA did not revolt, although I would never say a word to lessen the guilt of the SA leaders. The position was simply this: on one side there were the SA with Roehm at their head, and on the other, opposing them strongly, were Goering and Himmler. It was carefully arranged that the SA were sent on leave a few days before June 30. The SA chiefs were cunningly invited by Hitler to a conference at Wiessee on June 30. It isn't the usual thing for conspirators about to revolt to travel to a meeting in a sleeper. They were arrested at the station and taken immediately to their execution.

"As to the so-called Munich Putsch, the Munich SA never turned up, and an hour by car from Munich the so-called traitors Roehm and Heines were asleep, having no idea that according to Hitler's and Goering's story a putsch had taken place on the evening before in Munich.

"I was able to observe the 'putsch' in Berlin very closely. It took place entirely without the knowledge of the public and of the SA. One of the leading 'rebels,' SA group chief Karl Ernst, was very worried four days before June 30 about the rumors that were going around in Berlin that the SA were going to revolt. He asked for an interview with the Minister for the Interior, Frick, to give him the assurance that no putsch was planned. I myself arranged this interview. Karl Ernst then set off on a holiday trip to Madeira. On June 30 he was brought back from the liner, which had not yet sailed, to Berlin to be shot. I was myself present at his arrival at the Tempelhof Airport, which I watched with interest since I had read the official announcement of his execution in the newspapers a few hours before. I was also present when the defendant Goering made a statement to the press about this affair on June 30. He said he had waited for days for a signal that had been arranged with Hitler. Then he had struck, 'like lightning' of course, but he had also 'exceeded his instructions.' This excess had cost a lot of innocent people their lives. I still remember General von Schleicher, who was murdered with his wife; von Bredow; the permanent secretary Klausener, and many others."

The background of the so-called Roehm Putsch was cleared up not only by the statement of the witness Gisevius. Historical research and various trials before German courts since 1945 have made the true picture emerge: Hitler, Goering, and Himmler, under pretense of an imminent SA revolt, got rid of all opposition in their own ranks on June 30. The "old guard," who had marched for twelve years for Hitler and wanted their reward, were simply shot. Uncomfortable sharers of secrets—like Schleicher, the Reichstag incendiary Ernst, and those of his comrades who were still alive—were reduced to silence forever.

Why had Hitler chosen June 30 as the day for the bloody massacre? Hindenburg was already fatally ill at the time. Any day could be his last—and so the question was indeed pressing: who was to be his successor as President of the Reich and Head of State? Chancellor Hitler himself wished to be Head of State, for only with this office did the supreme command of the Army fall into his hands. Roehm with his three million SA men was no doubt the gravest threat to Hitler's plans; therefore, Roehm had to die.

The defendant Hans Frank, in 1934 still Bavarian Minister of Justice, wrote in his prison cell at Nuremberg a description of how he had witnessed Hitler's decisive stroke in Munich:

> From six in the morning till about two in the afternoon, almost two hundred SA chiefs were brought in by the SS who, "by order of the Führer," were locked in cells as "state prisoners of the government." From their names I saw that almost the whole SA hierarchy from all over Germany and all sectional chiefs of the SA leadership were under arrest at the Stadelheim prison.
>
> An hour before noon, Roehm himself was brought in with his whole staff of aides and adjutants. These, too, were taken to their cells. I went along the corridors, where the elite of the old militant party were behind the cell doors, and thought of the sudden changes in human destiny. Yesterday, Roehm's name was a name that conjured up authority, strength, and influence—and now he was a man behind prison bars, robbed of all his power.
>
> I opened his cell and went in. He was very pleased and said: "What is all this? This morning, Adolf Hitler personally arrested me in Wiessee. He hauled me out of bed. What's going on? Dr. Frank, I am a soldier, and have always been nothing but a soldier. The Führer is under the influence of my deadly enemies. You just wait, he is about to destroy the entire SA. I don't care about my life, but please look after my family." He pressed my hand and added, "All revolutions devour their own children."

On the table of Roehm's cell was a revolver with which he was meant to shoot himself. He refused. "Hitler must shoot me himself," he bellowed.

Toward midday, a salvo echoed from the prison courtyard. The execution of the SA chiefs had begun. Roehm hammered on the door of his cell and demanded coffee. He was brought a metal mug. He drank, threw the mug in a corner, and screamed, "I want proper coffee, not your shitty prison coffee!"

A former member of the Bavarian police, Johann Mühlbauer, was a witness in a case before the Munich assizes against Sepp Dietrich and Michael Lippert in 1957. He described what the last act of the drama was like:

Two SS men went to Roehm's cell. One of them threw the door open and shouted: "Chief of Staff, get ready."

Roehm stood in the center of the cell, stripped to the waist. His eyes were closed.

One of the two SS men gave the command: "Fire!"

They both fired almost simultaneously. Roehm fell backward stiffly, his massive body hitting the stone floor.

"My Führer, my Führer," mumbled the dying man.

"You should have thought of that sooner, now it's too late," said one of the two murderers. Then he turned to the other: "Give him the *coup de grâce*." The other man bent over Roehm, put his revolver against his naked chest, and pulled the trigger.

Roehm was dead, and with him the SA—never again to play any part in German politics. All were dead who had seen behind the scenes, all who could have put a spoke in Hitler's wheel.

VIENNA,
JULY 25, 1934

"If every German murderer who was active abroad had been my responsibility, I would have had a lot on my hands." The speaker was Hitler's Foreign Minister, defendant Konstantin von Neurath, on the witness stand at Nuremberg.

Hitler had a clear path. Now he reached beyond Germany's boundaries; the incidents multiplied.

"On Monday, the 23rd July, 1934, a ship carrying explosive material was seized by the Swiss Police on the Bodensee. It was engaged in smuggling German bombs and munitions into Austria."

Sidney S. Alderman, of the American prosecuting counsel, was reading from the diary of the United States ambassador in Berlin, William E. Dodd. "That was, in my opinion, an evil omen," Dodd wrote. In fact, two days later the murderers of whom Neurath had spoken attempted a *coup d'état* in Vienna. From their shots the Austrian Chancellor, Dr. Engelbert Dollfuss, bled to death. He died slowly and painfully while his murderers were sitting beside him, smoking cigarettes, and refusing him any medical aid or the assistance of a priest.

At the same hour, Adolf Hitler was enjoying Wagner's *Das Rheingold* in a box at the Bayreuth Opera House. However, he listened only with one ear, for the other was turned to his adjutants Julius Schaub and Wilhelm Brückner, who whispered to him the latest news from Austria.

It was not so good. The operation of SS Unit 89 had failed, and Mussolini had marched his troops at once toward the Brenner Pass to assist Austria against Hitler.

"The Führer was very excited after the performance," wrote Friedelind Wagner, who witnessed the scene in Bayreuth. "It was frightful to see." Although he had plenty of things to attend to after the failure of the Austrian putsch, he hastened to the Opera House Restaurant. "I must spend an hour there," he said to his companions, "and let myself be seen. Otherwise people will believe that I had something to do with the affair."

"On the basis of factual proof," the British prosecuting counsel, Sir Hartley Shawcross, submitted at Nuremberg eleven years later, "very little doubt can remain that the murder of Dollfuss was planned in Berlin and was arranged by Hitler some six weeks previously."

The annexation of Austria—which was to succeed so brilliantly in 1938—miscarried in 1934, and with it failed Hitler's first attempt to extend the boundaries of his power. But the attempt had exposed once and for all the methods by which foreign policy would be carried on from then on. Everything that took place in Austria on July 25, 1934, was repeated in some form or another time and again.

What was the situation in Austria in 1934? At the head of the government was a man whose ambition and energy by far exceeded his physique. Dr. Engelbert Dollfuss was small in stature and, on this account, the butt of many jokes. Dollfuss collected these jokes and actually enjoyed them.

He was a Christian-Socialist dictator who took more than a leaf out of the book of Big Brother Benito Mussolini. He met the Italian head of state several times and listened to his advice. At that time, Mussolini was no friend of Hitler. On the contrary, he feared that Hitler's power and influence in Europe would become too great. He assured Dollfuss, on the other hand, that it was his aim "to free the people along the Danube from the hegemony of the German race."

He gave his Austrian colleague many political hints, a fact which became known only many years later when the secret correspondence between the two statesmen was published. Mussolini wanted a Fascist Austria, and called on Dr. Dollfuss to carry on a ruthless struggle against Social Democrats and National Socialists. Dollfuss, in danger of being crushed between the Left and Right, followed the advice from Rome. In February 1934, using the threat of a strike by the Social Democrats as a convenient excuse, he had the Viennese workers' quarters attacked with artillery cannon. He banned the Austrian Socialist Party as well as the Nazi Party. Eventually he had to resort to measures used by all dictators: he ruled by force, he oppressed and censored and struck down his opponents, and he set up concentration camps.

Hitler was in a difficult position. He wanted the *Anschluss*, the annexation of Austria, but at the same time he wanted to keep favor with Mussolini. So he declared in public that Austria must remain independent—to put Mussolini's mind at ease. More or less secretly, however, he assisted the Austrian Nazis as much as possible in the belief that events in the country would lead to a Nazi rising anyway without his having to intervene openly. His henchman, the national leader of the Austrian Nazi Party, Theodor Habicht, was given a free hand to carry out subversive activities and commit acts of terrorism.

July 25, 1934, was a bright, cloudless day. All was quiet in Vienna. In the office of the 16th police district, Inspector Johann Dobler had been handed a note with the words, "89—12:45 P.M.

Siebensterngasse No. 11. Municipal gymnasium." This was the
meeting place of the insurgents; they regarded Dobler as one of
them. He was to have taken part, but he felt pangs of conscience
at the last moment. He telephoned the headquarters of the
National Front, the party which supported Dollfuss.

"I have a very urgent matter to report," he said. "I am a police
inspector but I cannot give my name. Please send someone to
me outside the Café Weghuber in fifteen minutes."

The secretary of the National Front sent a reliable man, Karl
Mahrer, to the meeting place. They sat down at a table, and the
policeman showed his identity card, checked the other man's
credentials, and then told his fantastic-sounding story: "An
attempt to murder Dollfuss has been planned for this afternoon.
He must be warned at once. I have been asked to take part in
the conspiracy."

Mahrer was taken aback. An old friend of his, the former
Captain Ernst Mayer, happened to be sitting at a neighboring
table. Mayer played an important part in Dollfuss' semimilitary
organization and had some connections with people in the government. Mahrer invited the captain to his table, and Dobler
repeated his story.

Mayer then telephoned the second highest man in the government. Major Emil Fey. Mayer hinted vaguely at what was being
planned but told Fey that he could say no more over the telephone. A new meeting was arranged. Valuable time was lost
while Dobler, Mahrer, and Mayer went to another coffeehouse,
the famous Café Central. There they met an emissary of Fey's,
and Dobler had to tell his story yet a third time. Fey's confidential agent listened to everything, went away and reported the
matter to Fey, who listened without much surprise as he had
already heard some rumors from other sources. However, he
considered it advisable to inform the Chancellor. Dollfuss was
just presiding at a Cabinet meeting. He was on the point of
making a further journey to see Mussolini—his wife and children
had already set out for Riccione—and he wanted to settle all outstanding business in Vienna before leaving. Fey entered the
council chamber, bowed to Dollfuss, and asked him in a whisper
if he could speak to him in private for a moment. The two men

withdrew into the anteroom, and there Fey disclosed to the Chancellor what was going on.

It was later alleged that Fey had intentionally waited too long before informing the head of state of the imminent danger because he was on bad terms with him. There is, however, no proof of this allegation. At first, Dollfuss did not take the whole story very seriously. There had been stories of an imminent *coup d'état* by the Nazis for months but they had always turned out to be false alarms. "It will be the same again," said Dollfuss.

"No," Fey insisted. "This time it is serious." He had to argue with the Chancellor for quite some time before Dollfuss could be persuaded to take action. He called off the Cabinet meeting, explained matters to the ministers, and asked them to return to their offices. There they were to await further instructions.

The ministers dispersed. Dollfuss, Fey, and the director of security, Secretary of State Karl Karwinsky, remained in the Chancellery. In this way an important part of the plan to be carried out by SS Unit 89 was thwarted—the conspirators had plotted to arrest the whole government, an action which was to have taken place at the Cabinet meeting.

On the other hand, the countermeasures taken by Dollfuss and Fey were hesitant, dilatory, and ineffective. In the gymnasium in the Siebensterngasse the police detective Marek watched dozens of men taking off their clothes and putting on the uniforms of the famous Austrian Deutschmeister regiment. He rang his office. The police promised to send a few detectives, but nothing happened.

Meanwhile, two trucks crammed with insurgents had already reached the Chancellery. A further group, under the command of the Nazi leader, Hans Domes, was on the way to the radio station. They were to take possession of the transmitter. A third group, under the command of SS leader Max Grillmayer, drove in a private car toward Velden on the Wörther Sea, in order to arrest the President of Austria, Miklas, who was vacationing there.

The main group arrived without hindrance at the Ballhausplatz. In front of the Chancellery there was only a guard of honor with unloaded rifles. The heavy gates were promptly opened for the trucks. The uniforms of the conspirators aroused no suspicions.

The men were regarded as regular soldiers. The time was 12:53 P.M.

In the courtyard the disguised SS men jumped from the trucks. A couple of policemen on duty were disarmed without trouble. Then the insurgents stormed into the building. They had brought with them detailed plans of the complicated old Metternich Palace; all the key positions were quickly occupied. Some 150 Chancellery officials, guards, and assistants were seized and assembled in the courtyard. The doors of the whole building were bolted and secured against attacks from the outside.

The leaders of the conspiracy, eight men in all, hurried along the corridors and up the staircase to the rooms where they believed Dollfuss to be with the rest of the ministers. The noise of the attack had already reached the historical Congress Hall. The Chancellor understood at last that the situation was serious, and that the warnings had been justified. The director of security, Karwinsky, took Dollfuss by the arm and said to him in agitation, "Come with me to the third floor. There you will be safe."

Dollfuss went with him. On the way they were met by a porter, Hedvicek, a man who was really devoted to the Chancellor.

"No, no," he shouted to Dollfuss, "come with me. I will lead you by a secret door into the State Archives, and from there you can go straight down into the street."

Dollfuss hesitated. Karwinsky was still holding Dollfuss by one arm, Hedvicek seized the other. For seconds the head of state was pulled to and fro, while the boots of the murderers were heard hurrying up an iron spiral staircase. Dollfuss decided for Hedvicek's way of escape. They tried to open the secret door. It was locked. They turned back in confusion.

At that moment the opposite door opened. The conspirators rushed into the room. The first of them, Otto Planetta, quickly walked over to Dollfuss, his revolver drawn. The Chancellor raised his hands. Planetta fired at a distance of two feet. Dollfuss was hit in the armpit and reeled. Planetta fired a second time. The shot hit the Chancellor in the neck. He turned on his heel and fell backward on the floor.

"Help, help," he whispered.

"Stand up!" shouted Planetta.

"I can't," Dollfuss muttered. Then he lost consciousness.

Two of the assailants lifted the unconscious man, laid him upon a small sofa, and threw a chair cover over him. There they left him to his fate.

At the same time, Domes's group had reached the radio station. The SS men smashed the windows on the ground floor, knocked down Police Inspector Flick, and made their way to the studios. The engineers had to interrupt the midday concert, and the announcer was forced at gun point to read the statement: "Dr. Dollfuss has resigned. Dr. Rintelen has taken over as head of the government."

Dr. Rintelen, the "King of Steiermark," was meanwhile waiting at the Hotel Imperial. He was to form a new National Socialist government after the completion of the revolt. But he waited in vain.

At the War Ministry, the other members of the Cabinet whom Dollfuss had sent prematurely away from the meeting, had gathered to discuss the situation. They telephoned President Miklas, and the Minister of Education, Dr. Kurt Schuschnigg, was charged with the provisional direction of affairs. Schuschnigg was given full powers so that he was able to act against the rebels.

In several parts of Austria there were some sporadic shooting incidents which ended with a complete victory for the government. The radio station was retaken after a two-hour siege in which one SS man lost his life while the rest were taken prisoners. SS leader Grillmayer, who was to have taken the President prisoner at Velden, was arrested in Klagenfurt before he had reached his objective.

The revolt had collapsed. Only the Chancellor's office was still in the hands of the conspirators. Police and Army units loyal to the government had surrounded the building, but avoided an attack in order not to endanger the lives of the members of the government who were being held prisoner inside.

The insurgents were in a hopeless position. The leader of the insurrection, Gustav Wächter, and the "military head" of the action, Fridolin Glass, were not present because, strangely enough, they had turned up too late to take part in the revolt. Dr. Rintelen, too, who was to form the new government, did not appear at the scene of the putsch. He was arrested in the Hotel Imperial by an editor, Dr. Friedrich Funder, and tried to shoot himself the same evening. To the end of his life in 1946 he bore the marks of his attempted suicide.

The murder group in the Chancellery had only one weapon left: the hostages Dollfuss, Fey, and Karwinsky. Paul Hudl and Franz Holzweber, the leaders of the insurrectionists, were so witless that they turned to their captive, Major Fey, and admitted to him that they did not know what to do. Fey's behavior was later approved by an officers' court of honor as he acted under threat of death. But at the time his role was rather ambiguous. He telephoned Schuschnigg's provisional government and, with the permission of the rebels, sent them a note that Dollfuss wanted to avoid all unnecessary bloodshed, that Dr. Rintelen was Chancellor, and that he, Fey, had taken over the executive.

Schuschnigg and his ministers refused to recognize this, as the statement had apparently been made under pressure. They delegated the Welfare Minister, Odo Neustädter-Stürmer, to get in touch with the rebels and present them with an ultimatum: if they did not surrender voluntarily, government troops would attack them.

Dollfuss was still lying on the narrow sofa. One of the insurgents was sitting at the Chancellor's desk, smoking. Two prisoners, the chief of the police guard, Johann Greifeneder, and a certain Jellinek, were given permission by the conspirators to attend to the fatally injured man. They brought him back to consciousness with the help of wet towels.

"How are my ministers?" was his first, weak question. Then he asked Greifeneder to move his arms, as he himself could not move them. He asked for a doctor, for a priest. The rebels refused brusquely. A small wad of cotton was placed on the Chancellor's neck wound, that was all. He was bleeding to death internally.

"I am so thirsty," groaned Dollfuss.

Greifeneder moistened his lips with a wet pad. Then Dollfuss wanted to speak to the leader of the rebels. Hudl was brought. He bent over the Chancellor. Dollfuss asked if he could speak to Schuschnigg; he felt his end near. But Hudl interrupted him: "That doesn't interest us. Let's get down to business. You must give the order that no action must be taken against the Chancellery before Rintelen has taken over the government."

But even in the hour of his death, Dollfuss remained stubborn. He refused to become an instrument of the conspirators.

"A doctor," he murmured.

"A doctor has already been sent for," lied Hudl.

Dollfuss was scarcely able to speak. With an effort he requested to talk to Major Fey. Fey was brought in. He had to put his ear close to the Chancellor's mouth to understand the whispered words: "My love to my wife . . . Ask Mussolini . . . to look after my children." Minutes passed. Dollfuss opened his eyes once more. He saw the conspirators standing beside him. A gentle smile appeared on his pale features.

"Children, you are so nice to me," he said clearly. "Why aren't the others like that? I only wanted peace . . . we have never attacked . . . we must always be on guard . . . May God forgive them . . ."

Those were his last words. The time was 3:45 P.M.

Late in the afternoon, Minister Neustädter-Stürmer appeared outside the Chancellery. Major Fey went out on the balcony with two of the conspirators. The Minister in the street and the Major on the balcony carried on a grotesque conversation:

FEY: Where is Rintelen?

NEUSTADTER: If you don't leave the place by 5:55 P.M. it will be stormed.

FEY: I forbid it.

NEUSTADTER: You have nothing to forbid—you are a prisoner.

Meanwhile, Holzweber had telephoned the German ambassador Dr. Rieth from inside the building.

"Rebel Leader Friedrich." He announced himself by his code name. "The revolt has miscarried."

The German ambassador hastened to the Ballhausplatz to try to do something for the SS men. There the negotiations between Neustädter-Stürmer and the insurgents were continuing. The conspirators had threatened to kill their prisoners. But they were prepared to give themselves up if they were promised a safe-conduct to the German border. The Minister decided to give them this promise to save the lives of the hostages, and gave his word of honor that they could go unharmed.

The German ambassador appeared on the scene. "A mad business, this," he said by way of greeting.

"Excellency," the Minister replied, "I find it remarkable in the extreme that you can find no other word for this terrible affair. The guilt for what has happened lies on your side of our border."

Rieth turned to Neustädter-Stürmer and requested his mediation. "What has to be done here is our affair," said the Minister. "Besides, I don't consider it very commendable that you should interfere in our negotiations with the rebels."

"In that case there is nothing more for me to do," snapped Rieth.

At 7:30 P.M.—about the time that Hitler was listening to Wagner's music and to the whispered information from his adjutants at Bayreuth—the conspirators surrendered. Forces loyal to the government occupied the Chancellery. What happened then was only a brief sequel. A few minutes after the building had been taken over, the murdered Chancellor was found. The conspirators, in spite of the word of honor that the Minister had given, were not taken to the German border but arrested.

"I gave my word of honor as a soldier," Neustädter-Stürmer explained, as a witness at the ensuing trial. "A soldier's word of honor is given to soldiers. I leave it to the court to decide whether soldiers would have refused medical aid and spiritual comfort to a mortally wounded man."

Planetta, the Chancellor's murderer, admitted that he had fired the fatal shot. He and Holzweber were sentenced to death; so were five other insurrectionists, while Hudl, a highly decorated former officer, was given a life sentence. He was released after the *Anschluss* in 1938.

Planetta went to the gallows, shouting, "Heil Hitler." But his Hitler had already made a hasty *volte-face.* He described his tools as "dissatisfied elements," denied any connection with the affair, and even dissembled regret about it. At the last moment, the German Army and SS held back the Austrian Legion, a band of Austrian Nazi expatriates, which was already on the march. Propaganda Minister Goebbels had to cancel hastily his prepared announcements of the successful uprising. The compromised German ambassador was recalled from Vienna, was replaced by von Papen.

Yet four years later there was a memorial parade of the surviving insurrectionists in Vienna, and tablets were unveiled in their honor. At the Nuremberg Trial, therefore, the American prosecutor, Sidney S. Alderman, said with a good deal of justification: "In 1938, Germany proudly identified herself with the 1934 murder, reaped its harvest, and assumed full responsibility for it."

HITLER REVEALS
HIS PLANS

The prosecution at the Nuremberg Trial laid a new pile of papers upon their tables. The pages revealed a particularly dark chapter. Now for the first time the German people could learn the truth about Hindenburg's death in 1934.

On July 26, 1934, the health of the eighty-seven-year-old President of the Reich took a turn for the worse. On that day, Hans Heinrich Lammers, the head of the Reich Chancellery, was in Neudeck in order to inform the aged Head of State about events in Austria and the murder of Chancellor Dollfuss. He was carrying out Hitler's order to ca'm the old man. But Hindenburg seemed to see through all the subterfuges to the heart of the matter. Hardly four weeks had passed since the Roehm blood bath.

It was too much for the upright old man. After Lammers' visit he took to his bed. The political turmoil had broken his will to live. In vain the doctors, with Professor Ferdinand Sauerbruch at their head, sought to induce a turn for the better. Hindenburg's days were numbered, and for Hitler the time was now ripe for another major coup. He had long been determined to usurp the office of Head of State, because with it went the command of the armed forces. He needed the armed forces, he needed the existing Reichswehr and the late Wehrmacht for the plans which he was soon to pronounce quite openly. While Hindenburg was still alive, on August 1, 1934, Hitler and his subservient Cabinet decided:

"The office of President of the Reich will be combined with that of Reich Chancellor. In consequence, the former functions of the President pass to the Führer and Reich Chancellor Adolf Hitler."

It was also announced that the Army should at once take the oath to the new Head of State. In the afternoon, after he had already seized all power by these decrees, Hitler was ready to travel to Neudeck and to face the dying Hindenburg. World history knows few such deeply shameful moments.

What happened during the Field Marshal's last hours has been falsified by Hitler. According to his account, which was later published by Franz von Papen and had apparently, in the course of the years, been embellished by some legendary details, Hindenburg was lying in bed with his eyes closed when Hitler was led into the room. The President's son, Oskar von Hindenburg, told the dying man, "Father, the Chancellor is here."

Hindenburg did not react. His son repeated the words. "Why didn't he come earlier?" Hindenburg murmured, his eyes still closed.

"The Chancellor was unable to come earlier," said Oskar von Hindenburg.

"Oh, I understand," whispered the old man.

"Father," Oskar began again, "Chancellor Hitler wants to discuss one or two points with you."

Eventually the dying Hindenburg opened his eyes. He turned a long, enigmatic look on Hitler, but no word came from his lips. Then he closed his eyes again—forever.

If this story were true one might read into Hindenburg's silent look a fearful reproof. But Hitler, when he invented the story, intended that this look of Hindenburg's should be taken as a "last command."

In fact everything was quite different. Hitler entered the room in which the doctors and Hindenburg's two daughters were present. The President lay already in agony and to all appearances never recognized Hitler. His last words, scarcely intelligible, were: "My Kaiser . . . my German Fatherland."

At 9:00 A.M., on August 2, 1934, the doctors confirmed his death. Now at last Hitler could rule alone. Franz von Papen wrote in his memoirs, "The death of Hindenburg removed the last obstacle from the path of Hitler's total seizure of power."

Everything was already prepared: "On April 4, 1933, the Reich cabinet passed a resolution establishing a Reich Defense Council," the American prosecutor, Thomas H. Dodd, stated at the Nuremberg Trial. "The function of this council was secretly to mobilize for war and at the second meeting . . . the chairman was the defendant Keitel, then Colonel Keitel; and he stated that the Reich Defense Council would immediately undertake to prepare for war emergency.

"He stressed the urgency of the task of organizing a war economy and announced that the Council stood ready to brush aside all of their obstacles.

"Detailed measures of financing future wars were discussed and it was pointed out that the financial aspects of the war economy would be regulated by the Reich Finance Ministry and the Reich bank, which was backed by the defendant Schacht.

"On May 31, 1935, the defendant Schacht was secretly appointed plenipotentiary-general of the war economy, and he had the express function of placing all economic forces of the nation in the services of the Nazi war machine. He was in effect given charge of the entire war economy. In case of war, he was to be virtual economic dictator of Germany. . . . Thus every aspect of the German economy was being geared to war under the guidance particularly of the defendant Schacht."

Hitler himself had no conscience. In a conversation with Rauschning which was read in the courtroom at Nuremberg by the American prosecutor, Sydney S. Alderman, he said brazenly: "I liberated men from the filthy, humiliating, poisonous folly called conscience and morals."

On March 7, 1936, Hitler declared in the Reichstag: "We have no territorial demands to make in Europe. To begin with, we know that tensions in Europe cannot be solved by war."

On the day of that speech Hitler set off his *Operation Schulung*: the lightning occupation of the demilitarized zone of the Rhineland. The young German Wehrmacht marched into the districts which had been kept free of troops by international treaties. In Nuremberg, the prosecution read out how Hitler justified his action in the Reichstag: "France has responded to the many friendly approaches and peaceful assurances of Germany with a military pact with Russia directed exclusively against Germany. Germany thus regards herself as no longer bound by that discarded treaty. In the interest of the primitive right of a people to its own safety the German government from today has restored the full and unlimited sovereignty of the Reich in the demilitarized zone of the Rhineland."

With this reasoning, Hitler succeeded in presenting his actions before the German people and before the world as a spontaneous reaction to the conclusion of the Franco-Soviet Treaty. Only at Nuremberg was it proved by a captured document—again a secret order—that the occupation of the Rhineland, carried out on March 7, 1936, had already been planned since May 2, 1935.

It has often been said that the world would not have had to endure the agony of the following years if France, on March 7, 1936, had energetically opposed Hitler's first military move. In the evening after the hearing of the Rhineland case in the courtroom at Nuremberg, the psychologist, Gustave M. Gilbert, had a long talk with Wilhelm Keitel in his cell.

"Hitler must have been a destructive demon," Gilbert said to the former Commander in Chief of the German Army.

"Yes," Keitel admitted, "and at first he was favored by luck. It would have been much better if everything had not gone so well for him. Just imagine, we carried out the occupation of the Rhineland with three battalions—with only three battalions! I said at the time to Blomberg: 'How can we do it with three battalions? What if France resists?' 'Oh,' said Blomberg, 'don't worry. We are going to take our chance.' "

"I suppose," said Gilbert, "that at that time a single French regiment would have been able to throw out your troops."

Keitel snapped his fingers, as though he were chasing away an annoying fly: "They could have thrown us out just like that—and

I would not have been surprised. But after Hitler had seen how easy it all was . . . one thing led to another."

For the understanding of Hitler's mind November 5, 1937, is an important date. On that day, almost a year before the *Anschluss* of Austria, almost two years before the war began, Hitler disclosed the whole range of his plans.

While the German people and the world were lulled with empty words about peace, a secret conference took place in Berlin. Those whom Hitler had collected for the occasion were the War Minister Werner von Blomberg, Lieutenant Colonel Werner von Fritsch as Commander in Chief of the Army, Admiral Erich Raeder as Commander in Chief of the Navy, Hermann Goering as Commander in Chief of the Luftwaffe, Foreign Minister Konstantin von Neurath, and Hitler's personal adjutant, Colonel Friedrich Hossbach, who prepared a report on the proceedings of the meeting. It survived the war, was found by the Allied troops, and eventually found its way to the Nuremberg courtroom. "This document," said the American prosecutor, Alderman, "destroys any possible doubt about the well-laid plans of the Nazis in their crimes against peace. This document is of such tremendous significance that I feel in duty bound to read it through in its entirety."

The Hossbach Report was one of the so-called key documents, one of the weightiest pieces of evidence in the whole Nuremberg Trial: "The Führer began by stating that the subject matter of today's conference was of such importance that its detailed discussion would certainly, in other countries, take place before the Cabinet in full session. However, he, the Führer, had decided not to discuss this matter in the larger circle of the Reich Cabinet, just because of its very importance. His subsequent statements should be regarded as the result of his four and a half years in government; he desired to explain to those present his fundamental ideas on the possibilities and necessities of expanding our foreign policy, and in the interests of a farsighted policy he requested that his statements be looked upon, in the case of his death, as his last will and testament."

After this introduction Hitler gave his six listeners a long-winded account of the relations of power in Europe and the world. He presented a picture of how it seemed to him—and it was completely false and absurd, as we now know. Important only were the conclusions which Hitler drew from his inaccurate estimate of the situation. Hossbach goes on in his report: "The question for Germany is where the greatest possible conquest could be made at the lowest cost. Our problems can be solved only by force, and this is never without risk. The battles of Frederick the Great for Silesia and Bismarck's wars against Austria and France were tremendous risks, and the speed of Prussian action in 1870 prevented Austria from entering the war. If we place the decision to apply force with risk at the head of the following expositions, then all we have to do is to answer the questions 'when' and 'how.' We shall have to deal with three different cases.

"Case 1. Period 1943–45: After this we can only expect a change for the worse. In comparison with the rearmament which will have been carried out by that time by other nations, our relative power will have decreased. If we do not act, then, before 1943–45, any year could bring about a major food crisis, for the countering of which we do not possess the necessary foreign currency. Over and above that, the world will anticipate our action and will increase every year its countermeasures. What the actual position will be in 1943–45, no one knows today. Only one thing is certain—that we can wait no longer.

"On the one side, the large armed forces, with the necessity for securing their upkeep, the aging of the Nazi movement and of its leaders, and on the other side, the prospect of a lowering of the standard of living and a drop in the birth rate, leave us no other choice but to act. If he, the Führer, were still alive, then it would be his irrevocable decision to solve the German *Lebensraum* problem no later than 1943–45. The necessity for action before 1943–45 will come under consideration in Cases 2 and 3.

"Case 2. Should the social tensions in France lead to an internal political crisis of such dimensions that it absorbs the French Army and thus renders it incapable of employment in war against Germany, then the time for action against Czechoslovakia has come.

"Case 3 assumes that France would be so tied up by a war against another state that it cannot proceed against Germany. For the improvement of our military political position it must be our first aim, in every case of entanglement by war, to conquer first Czechoslovakia and Austria simultaneously, in order to remove any threat from the flanks in case of a possible advance westward.

"Assuming a development of the situation which would lead to a planned attack on our part in the years 1943–45, then the behavior of France, England, Poland, and Russia would probably have to be judged in the following manner: The Führer believed personally, that in all probability England and perhaps also France have already silently written off Czechoslovakia, and that they have got used to the idea that this question would one day be solved by Germany. The difficulties of the British Empire and the prospect of being entangled in another long, drawn-out European war, would be decisive factors in the nonparticipation of England in a war against Germany. The British attitude would certainly not remain without influence on France's attitude. An attack by France, without British support, is hardly probable. Naturally, we should in every case have to guard our western frontier during our operations against Czechoslovakia and Austria. . . . The annexation of the two states by Germany, militarily and politically, would bring considerable relief, owing to shorter and better frontiers, the freeing of fighting personnel for other purposes, and the possibility of reconstituting new armies up to a strength of about twelve divisions.

"No opposition to the destruction of Czechoslovakia is expected on the part of Italy; however, it cannot be judged today what would be her attitude in the case of Austria. The measure of surprise and the speed of our action would decide Poland's attitude. Poland will have little inclination to enter the war against a victorious Germany, with Russia in the rear. Military action by Russia must be countered by the speed of our operations; it is a question whether this needs to be taken into consideration at all, in view of Japan's attitude.

"Should Case 2 occur—paralyzation of France by a civil war— then the situation should be utilized at any time for operations against Czechoslovakia. However, the Führer sees Case 3 looming nearer; it could develop from the existing tensions in the Mediterranean, and should it occur, he has firmly decided to make use of it at any time, perhaps even as early as 1938. As to the war in Spain, the Führer does not see an early end to hostilities there. . . ."

The Hossbach Report proved five things beyond doubt:

1. Hitler's rearmament was not, as he always said, a question of national honor and equality of right, but the first step toward his plan of aggression.

2. After the session of November 5, 1937, the leaders of the armed forces and the Foreign Office and the defendants Goering, Keitel, Raeder, and Neurath knew that Hitler had formed the "unalterable decision" to use his forces in 1943–45 at the latest and to wage war.

3. Hitler was also resolved to sell his fellow dictators Mussolini and Franco. He was not concerned with his blood relations, the Austrians and Sudeten Germans, but with raw materials and supplies of men for new divisions.

4. All Hitler's assurances to the German people and to the world were deliberate deception: "We have no territorial demands in Europe." "We only want peace." "We know that tensions in Europe cannot be solved by war."

5. Hitler, who was praised by his Propaganda Minister Goebbels as "the greatest military genius of all times," had judged the military position completely wrongly. He had reckoned entirely without the United States of America.

THE ANSCHLUSS

Special Operation Otto: that was the code name for the *Anschluss*, the invasion of Austria by German troops, which took place in March 1938.

The beginning looked harmless enough. The Austrian Chancellor, Dr. Kurt von Schuschnigg, wrote in his memoirs: "Early in 1938, von Papen made inquiries as to how we would react to an invitation to Berchtesgaden for a conference with the Führer. I expressed my complete readiness."

On February 11, 1938, Schuschnigg, his Foreign Minister, Guido Schmidt, and his adjutant, Lieutenant Colonel Bartel, took the night express to Salzburg. Papen welcomed his guests cordially at Salzburg, where they left the train to continue the journey by car. The German passport officials greeted them with their hands raised in the Hitler salute.

"The Führer is waiting for you; he is in splendid form," Papen said with a smile, and added, "You won't mind that some generals happen to be staying at the Berghof?" As a guest, Schuschnigg could scarcely object to this, but at that moment he had a feeling that the meeting was not going to be a harmless one. Hitler had judged the situation correctly; the generals he had ordered to Berchtesgaden at the time of Schuschnigg's visit were the newly appointed Chief of the Supreme Command of the Wehrmacht, Wilhelm Keitel, then General of Artillery Walter von Reichenau, and General of the Air Force Hugo Sperrle. As was shown at the Nuremberg Trial, their presence served no official purpose. They were only there to make Schuschnigg nervous by their mere presence and to put him under pressure.

It must be remembered that at the time of the Schuschnigg visit an agreement existed between Germany and Austria, signed by Hitler on July 11, 1936. Point 1 of this agreement read: "In the spirit of the statement by the Führer and Reich Chancellor of May 21, 1935, the German government acknowledges the complete sovereignty of the State of Austria." That statement said that Germany had "neither the intention nor the desire to interfere in the internal affairs of Austria, still less to annex or join up with Austria."

But what did signed declarations matter? Shortly after the conference with Hitler, Schuschnigg wrote down what had been said. This conversation, here given in a shortened form, reveals the prelude for the *Anschluss*.

SCHUSCHNIGG: This room with its wonderful view has surely been the scene of many decisive conferences, Herr Reichskanzler?

HITLER: Yes, in this room my thoughts ripen. But we did not get together to speak of the fine view or of the weather.

SCHUSCHNIGG: First of all, Herr Reichskanzler, I would like to thank you that you have given me the opportunity for this meeting. I would like to assure you that we take the treaty between our two countries that we signed in July 1936 very seriously, and that we are most anxious to remove all of the remaining misunderstandings and difficulties. In any case, we intend to follow a policy friendly toward Germany in accordance with our own mutual agreement.

HITLER: So that's what you call a friendly policy, Herr Schuschnigg. . . . I am telling you once more things can't go on in this way. I have a historic mission: and this mission I will fulfill, because providence has destined me to do so. I am carried along by the love of my people. I can go about freely and without guard at any time in Germany.

SCHUSCHNIGG: Herr Reichskanzler, I am quite willing to believe that.

HITLER: And you know, I could call myself an Austrian with just as much reason, in fact with more reason than you, Herr Schuschnigg. Why don't you try a plebiscite in Austria, in which we two run against each other? You just try that.

SCHUSCHNIGG: Well, if that were possible. But you know yourself, Herr Reichskanzler, that this is impossible.

HITLER: That is what you say, Herr Schuschnigg. But I am telling you that I am going to solve the so-called Austrian problem one way or the other. . . . I have only to give an order, and in one single night all your ridiculous defense mechanisms are blown to bits. You don't seriously believe that you can stop me or even delay me half an hour, do you? Who knows? Perhaps you will wake one morning in Vienna to find us there—just like a spring storm. And then you'll see something.

SCHUSCHNIGG: Herr Reichskanzler, whether we like it or not, that would mean bloodshed. We are not alone in this world, and such a step would probably mean war.

HITLER: It is easy enough to talk of war while we are sitting here in our comfortable easy chairs. . . . The world must know that it is unbearable for a great Power like Germany to have every little state on her borders believe that it can provoke her. But now I give you once more, and for the last time, the opportunity to come to terms, Herr Schuschnigg. Either we reach a solution now, or else events will take their course. And we shall see whether you will like these events. . . . Think it over, Herr Schuschnigg, think it over well. I can only wait until this afternoon. I tell you that you will do well to take me literally. I don't believe in bluffing.

SCHUSCHNIGG: Herr Reichskanzler. . . . Now, what are exactly your wishes?

HITLER: That we can discuss this afternoon.

During lunch time, the Austrian Chancellor had the opportunity to talk to his Foreign Minister, Schmidt. Then both were invited into the anteroom where Papen and Foreign Minister Ribbentrop were waiting. Ribbentrop gave Schuschnigg the typewritten draft of a new agreement, and said, "That is the utmost that the Führer will concede to you." The paper contained conditions that were practically unacceptable. The Austrian Government was to undertake to appoint the National Socialist leader, Arthur Seyss-Inquart, as Minister of the Interior with restricted police control; it was to release all National Socialist prisoners, including those who had taken part in the murder of Dollfuss; the National Socialists were to be admitted to the Austrian Government party, the Patriotic Front, and so on.

Schuschnigg went on: "Herr Von Ribbentrop solicitously explained every paragraph and took notice of my objections, but he asserted again that the draft had to be accepted as it stood. We voiced our protest and Dr. Schmidt reminded Herr Von Papen of the agreement that only subjects of mutual agreement were to be brought up at the meeting at the Berghof. Von Papen said that he himself was completely taken by surprise. I asked whether we could count on the good will of Germany. Both Ribbentrop and Papen answered in the affirmative and assured me that it was Hitler's only aim to solve the Austrian problem quickly and peacefully so that he could turn his attention to other problems."

Some proof of this "good will" was given a few moments later. Hitler summoned the Austrian Chancellor again. The conference continued.

HITLER: Herr Schuschnigg, I have decided to make one last attempt. Here is the draft of the document. There is nothing to be discussed about it. I will not change one single iota. You will either sign it as it stands, or else our meeting has been useless. In that case I shall decide during the night what will be done next.

SCHUSCHNIGG: I have been informed of the contents of the document, and I can do nothing under the circumstances but take cognizance of it. I am also willing to sign it, but I want to make it quite clear that . . . according to our constitution, cabinet members are appointed by the head of the state, the president, just as it is only the president who can grant an amnesty. Therefore, my signature can only mean that I am ready to see the president and to see that the agreement is carried out, if the president should decide to accept it.

HITLER: Yes, I understand that.

SCHUSCHNIGG: Consequently, I can in no way guarantee that the time limit stipulated in the document, as for instance the three days for the amnesty—will be observed.

HITLER: You have to guarantee that.

SCHUSCHNIGG: I could not possibly, Herr Reichskanzler.

HITLER: You must!

SCHUSCHNIGG: I cannot.

Hitler was furious. He stood up, strode to the door, and opened it. "General Keitel!" he bawled. He dismissed Schuschnigg from the room with the words, "I shall have you called later." Schuschnigg went out, Keitel entered.

In the Nuremberg prison, Papen, in a talk with the Court psychologist Gilbert, re-created the whole scene, and the American wrote in his diary: "Von Papen repeated how Hitler put military pressure on the Austrian Chancellor Schuschnigg. Hitler yelled, 'Keitel!' so that he could be heard over the whole house. Keitel came running, out of breath, but in Hitler's room he was only asked to take a seat in a corner. The whole affair served only to intimidate Schuschnigg."

Faced with this devil's brew of military threats, bluff, and intimidation, Schuschnigg capitulated. Half an hour after the threatening call, "Keitel!" he signed what could be called the "unconditional surrender" of Austria.

All this was proved by numerous statements of witnesses and by documents. Only one of those who took part, Foreign Minister

Joachim von Ribbentrop, could not remember anything of it when he was questioned by the British prosecutor, Sir David Maxwell Fyfe.

SIR DAVID: Would you tell the Court under oath that you know nothing about the effects of all this in Austria?

RIBBENTROP: Yes, indeed, I know nothing of the effects.

SIR DAVID: I understand. Tell me, why did you and your friends keep Schuschnigg in prison for seven years?

RIBBENTROP: I don't know. But if you say prison—I know from my own experience that the Führer ordered several times that Schuschnigg should be treated especially well and decently.

SIR DAVID: You speak about prison. I would rather say Buchenwald and Dachau. He was in both. Do you believe that he would feel very well there?

RIBBENTROP: I have heard here for the first time that Herr Schuschnigg was in a concentration camp.

SIR DAVID: Then try for a change just to answer my question: Why did you and your friends keep Schuschnigg a prisoner for seven years?

RIBBENTROP: I cannot tell you anything about that. I can only tell you one thing, that I heard then that he was not in prison but in a villa and had all reasonable comforts he wanted.

What happened after Berchtesgaden? Downcast, Schuschnigg and Schmidt returned from the Obersalzberg to Vienna. Although the consequences were obvious, the Austrian President, Wilhelm Miklas, agreed with a heavy heart: he appointed Seyss-Inquart as Minister of Security and Police, and signed the amnesty by which all arrested National Socialists were set free.

Immediately Austria began to ferment. The new Austrian Minister, Seyss-Inquart, traveled to Germany to receive Hitler's instructions. On his return to Vienna he addressed the officials under him in a circular as "German Police in Austria." The internal dissolution had begun.

Schuschnigg made a last attempt to save the situation. He proclaimed a general plebiscite for March 13. The Austrian people should decide for themselves. The government slogan ran: "For a free and German, independent and social, Christian and united

Austria—for bread and peace throughout the land." Schuschnigg counted on a 70 to 75 per cent vote for the government. One may smile at this, but in Berlin no one smiled. There they were afraid that Schuschnigg might be right, and that would be an unbearable setback for Hitler, a decisive international defeat for National Socialism. The plebiscite had therefore to be prevented.

"Hitler is enraged beyond all bounds," Seyss-Inquart informed the Chancellor. "Goering demands that the plebiscite be canceled at once. He expects my phone call in an hour. If no decision reaches him by then he will assume that I am prevented from telephoning and will act on that assumption." Schuschnigg hurried to President Miklas. About half past eleven in the morning—it was March 11, 1938—he returned to his office. He asked Seyss-Inquart and Minister Glaise-Horstenau to come to his office.

"Please inform Herr Goering," Schuschnigg said to the two men, "that in view of the situation the demand is being met."

The plebiscite was canceled. The Ministers phoned Berlin. Then they returned to Schuschnigg's office. Seyss-Inquart had a note in his hand from which he read what Goering had just ordered on the telephone: "The situation can only be saved if the Chancellor resigns at once and Dr. Seyss-Inquart is appointed Chancellor within two hours. If there is any fruitless delay, German forces will invade Austria."

Schuschnigg went to the President again. Meanwhile friends and advisers urged him: "Call on the masses, let the Army march. Resist to the last. Call on the world to help—Paris, London! The Powers will not stand by and see such methods applied here in Europe. Today it is our turn, whose will it be tomorrow?"

"Italy! Let us turn to Mussolini!" said other advisers.

In 1934, when Dollfuss was murdered, Mussolini had rushed troops to the Austrian border in order to support the country against Hitler. But now, in 1938, there came from Rome only the cool reply: "The Italian government state that, if they are asked, they cannot offer any advice in the present situation."

Thus Schuschnigg, as Goering had demanded, announced his resignation to the President, and he stood by this decision when Miklas looked at him and said quietly: "So I see that I am left alone."

The only thing that Schuschnigg was prepared to do was to carry on business as the retiring chief of the government until a new Chancellor was appointed. But Miklas refused to make a National Socialist the head of the government; he refused to obey orders from Berlin, and appoint Seyss-Inquart. He alone resisted.

Schuschnigg decided to give a talk on the radio. It was his last official act. He closed with the words: "God save Austria!"

In Vienna, tens of thousands rejoiced in the streets. The police had put on swastika arm bands, and many were hoisted on the shoulders of the raging masses. Strangers embraced, processions started up from nowhere, *"Deutschland, Deutschland über alles"* was sung everywhere. A young student climbed the façade of the Chancellery and hoisted a swastika flag. Only one obstacle stood in Hitler's way: Miklas. The President repeatedly refused to appoint Seyss-Inquart as Chancellor. While there was rejoicing and marching, singing and dancing in the streets, while in the Leopoldstadt, the Jewish Quarter, thousands wept and hundreds prepared for flight, while the rest of the people, uneasy at heart, sat at home by their loud-speakers, while Schuschnigg was interned and began his seven-year journey through prisons and concentration camps, excited talks were going on between Goering in Berlin and his henchmen in Vienna. Surprisingly, transcriptions of these telephone conversations could be laid before the Nuremberg Court in 1945—"Thanks to the efficiency of the defendant Goering and his Luftwaffe organization," as the prosecutor, Alderman, put it. All the talks had been recorded by the listening service of the Air Ministry. The reports filled a voluminous dossier with the classification, "Secret State Matter," and the pages disclosed what happened behind the scenes of the joyful *Anschluss.* They showed how the "spontaneous rising of the people" in Austria was in fact engineered, and what pressure Hermann Goering brought to play to force Schuschnigg's government to resign.

At 5:00 P.M. on the decisive day, Goering telephoned from Berlin to the Austrian SS chief, Odilo Globocnik, in Vienna, and received from him, in his overanxiety to please, the false information that President Miklas had agreed to the demands from Berlin, and had appointed Seyss-Inquart as Chancellor. At 5:20 P.M. Goering learned the truth from a further talk with Seyss-Inquart

himself. The actual words spoken, as they were read before the
Court at Nuremberg, tell the whole story.

GOERING: Globocnik said that you had been given the Chancellorship.

SEYSS-INQUART: Me? When did he say that?

GOERING: An hour ago. He said you had the Chancellorship.

SEYSS-INQUART: No, that isn't true. I have made the proposal
to the President that I should be given the Chancellorship. He'll
take three or four hours to make up his mind. As far as the Party
is concerned, we have informed the SA and SS formations that
they will take over the maintenance of order.

GOERING: But that won't do. That won't do under any circumstances. The President must be told immediately that he must
hand over the power to you as Chancellor without delay, and that
he must accept the list of ministers as it was laid down.

SEYSS-INQUART: Herr Field Marshal, Mühlmann [one of the
intermediaries] has just arrived, he was there. May he report to
you?

GOERING: Yes.

MÜHLMANN: The situation is that the President still obstinately
refuses his approval and demands an official diplomatic action on
the part of the Reich. We wanted—as three National Socialists—
to speak to him personally in order to impress upon him that in
this hopeless situation the only possible thing to do was to say
yes. He would not even admit us. It looks as though he is in no
way inclined to give in.

GOERING: Give me Seyss-Inquart.

SEYSS-INQUART: I am here.

GOERING: Then act as follows: go at once with Lieutenant General Muff [the German military attaché in Vienna] to the President and say to him: if he doesn't meet our demands—you know
what they are—without delay, then tonight our troops already
stationed on the border will carry on with the invasion all along
the line, and Austria will cease to exist. General Muff must go
with you and ask to be admitted at once and tell him that. Please
give us immediate information on what grounds Miklas is resist-
ing. Tell him this is no time for shilly-shallying. Now the situation

is that this very night the invasion of Austria will start at all points. It wlll only be canceled if we hear by 7:30 P.M. that Miklas has handed over the Chancellorship to you. Order the immediate reinstatement of the Party with all its organizations and set the National Socialists free throughout the whole country. They should all be in the streets. Report back to me by 7:30 P.M. General Muff should go with you. I will give Muff the same instructions. If Miklas will not understand in four hours he will have to understand in four minutes.

"Yet another historical event was arranged by telephone," said prosecutor Alderman in Nuremberg. "I refer to the famous telegram which Seyss-Inquart sent to the German Government, in which he requested that it should send troops to Austria in order to help him with the suppression of disorder."

The conversation which took place at 8:48 P.M. the same evening between Goering and Keppler developed along the following lines:

KEPPLER: I would like to report briefly to you: President Miklas has refused to do anything. However, the Government has stopped functioning. I have spoken to Schuschnigg and he told me that they had given up their duties. Seyss has said on the wireless that he will carry on the affairs of state as Minister of the Interior. The old Government has given orders that the Army should offer no resistance. So there will be no shooting.

GOERING: Good! Now listen: the main thing is that Seyss-Inquart should now control the whole Government, the radio, and so on. And listen: Seyss-Inquart should send me the following telegram—write it down: "The provisional Austrian Government, which after the resignation of the Schuschnigg Government regards as its task the restoring of peace and order in Austria, appeals to the German Government with the urgent plea to help and assist them in preventing bloodshed. To this end they ask the German Government to send German troops as speedily as possible."

KEPPLER: The SA and SS are marching through the streets, but things are now very quiet.

GOERING: Listen: increase the frontier guards so that no one escapes with his fortune.

KEPPLER: Certainly.

GOERING: Seyss must form a provisional government at once. It doesn't matter what the President says.

KEPPLER: Yes.

GOERING: At any rate, our troops will cross the border today.

KEPPLER: Yes.

GOERING: Well, and he should send the telegram as soon as possible. Please show him the text of the telegram and do tell him—that we are asking him—well, he does not even need to send the telegram. All he needs to do is to say, agreed. He should call me at the Führer's or at my place. Heil Hitler!

An hour later, at 9:54 P.M., in a conversation between Dr. Dietrich in Berlin and Keppler in Vienna, Dr. Dietrich said: "I need the telegram urgently."

KEPPLER: Tell the General Field Marshal that Seyss-Inquart agrees.

DIETRICH: That is marvelous. Thank you.

But this conversation at 9:54 P.M. had no longer any real meaning, for an hour earlier, at 8:45 P.M., Hitler had already given the order for the invasion.. "Communications with Austria were now suspended," continued Alderman, "but the German military machine had been set in motion. To demonstrate that I now offer in evidence captured Document C-182, a directive of March 11, 1938, at 2045 hours from the Supreme Commander of the Armed Forces. This directive, issued by General Jodl and signed by Hitler, orders the invasion of Austria."

This secret command states, among other things: "To avoid further bloodshed in the Austrian towns, the entry of the German Armed Forces into Austria will commence at daybreak on March 12. I expect the set objectives to be reached by exerting all forces to the full as quickly as possible."

"It was getting toward midnight," Schuschnigg wrote in his memoirs. "No news reached us from the outside. In the Ministers' Council Room we were still talking to the President. Once more all the forceful reasons were discussed that seemed to support the appointment of Seyss-Inquart's government. Finally Miklas gave in and signed the list." The end of Austria had come.

At the Nuremberg Trial, prosecutor Alderman revealed yet another aspect of the *Anschluss*.

"At the very time that Hitler and Goering had embarked on this military undertaking, they still had a question mark in their minds, and that was Italy. Italy had massed on the Italian border in 1934 on the occasion of July 25, 1934—the *Putsch*. Italy had traditionally been the political protector of Austria. With what a sigh of relief did Hitler hear at 10:25 P.M. that night, from Prince Philipp von Hessen, his ambassador at Rome . . . that Mussolini had accepted the whole thing in a very friendly manner."

HITLER: I will never forget it, whatever should happen. If he should ever need any help, or be in any danger, he can be convinced that I shall stick to him whatever might happen, even if the whole world were against him.

PHILIPP: Yes, my Führer.

Now something had to be done in London to allay British fears. On the day after the invasion, on Sunday, March 13, 1938, Goering, who was in Berlin looking after government affairs, telephoned Ribbentrop in London. Hitler was in his native Austria. The conversation between Goering and Ribbentrop, as it was read in Court, is very long; the most important parts were these:

GOERING: You know that the Führer has entrusted me with the conduct of government affairs. And so I want to put you in the picture. There is an indescribable rejoicing in Austria, you can hear it on the wireless.

RIBBENTROP: Yes, it is fantastic, isn't it?

GOERING: The Führer wonders whether you can explain to people over there how things really are, as you happen to be on the spot. Most of all that it is completely untrue that Germany issued any kind of ultimatum. That was one of Schuschnigg's lies. It is also untrue that an ultimatum was presented to the President. There was, I believe, a military attaché present but only because Seyss-Inquart took him along to deal with some technical question. I also want to make it clear that Seyss-Inquart asked us to send German troops, both by word of mouth and then by telegram. The invasion was a result of this wish. The whole action has now taken a normal course—it has developed into a march of joy, as it were. Everything is wonderfully peaceful. Two nations are in each others' arms and rejoice and express their enthusiasm and pleasure. And I must also say that Mussolini has behaved fabulously.

RIBBENTROP: Yes, yes, so I have heard.

GOERING: I envy all those who were in Vienna yesterday. I have to sit here and hold the fort. Have you heard the Führer's speech in Linz?

RIBBENTROP: No, unfortunately not.

GOERING: It was for me the most interesting speech by the Führer that I have ever heard—it was quite short. This man, who is a master of words like no other, could scarcely speak.

RIBBENTROP: Was he very moved?

GOERING: Yes, terribly. I believe that the man has gone through some trying days. And the scenes that took place—Ward Price [the British journalist] was there with him.

RIBBENTROP: Yes, I have read his article this morning. The Führer turned round and asked him: "Is this oppression? Can you call this oppression and violence what you see here?"

Could you call this oppression and violence, Hitler asked Ward Price. But what are words? Only a day before, Goering had reassured the Czech ambassador; but soon after the tumultuous *Anschluss* the Nazi phonograph began to play a new record. It was put on by Dr. Goebbels and was broadcast daily on the radio: the "Egerland March." It was to be their marching song in the near future.

"PEACE
IN OUR TIME"

"I will under no circumstances be willing," Hitler declared on September 12, 1938, during the Party rally at Nuremberg, "to stand by quietly and watch the continued oppression of our fellow Germans in Czechoslovakia. The Germans in Czechoslovakia are neither defenseless nor are they abandoned."

Shortly after this speech there was bloodshed and unrest in the Sudetenland. Again a crisis was kindled which was soon to reach a violent climax. Since 1933, the antagonism between the racial groups of Czechoslovakia had steadily worsened; since the *Anschluss* it had become almost unbearable. The Sudeten Germans confidently believed that they would have to fight for their own justified claims. They did not suspect that they were only tools; Konrad Henlein, the leader of the Sudeten German Party, was only a subordinate. On March 28, 1938, Henlein received detailed instructions from Adolf Hitler himself in Berlin. In the report of that meeting it is stated unmistakably: "The tendency of the advice which the Führer has given to Henlein is that the Sudeten Germans must make demands which are not acceptable to the Czech government. Henlein has summarized his instructions as follows: We must always demand so much that we cannot be appeased. The Führer approved this line of action."

The Sudeten Germans, who thought they were fighting for their natural rights, were ruthlessly thrown into a bloody adventure. What Hitler really wanted to achieve, the ends to which unrest and bloodshed in the Sudetenland would act as a pretext, still lay locked in the secret archives in Berlin.

Operation Green: that was the code name for the actual plan— the destruction of Czechoslovakia. Hitler was not really interested in the Sudeten Germans and their "liberation." He was solely concerned with liquidating Czechoslovakia so as to create the strategic conditions for his further war plans.

On May 30, 1938, Hitler signed a document with the name "Green Study." This secret order said: "It is my unalterable decision to destroy Czechoslovakia by military action in the foreseeable future. To await or to induce the appropriate political and military situation is a matter for the political leadership. Accordingly, the preparations are to be put in hand without delay. The intended attack requires as preliminaries: (a) a suitable external motive, (b) a satisfactory political justification, and (c) a move unexpected by our adversary, which will find him in the worst possible state of preparedness. Militarily and politically, the most favorable action is a lightning move as a reaction to some incident by which Germany would be insufferably provoked, and which would justify military measures in the eyes of at least part of world opinion. *Signed:* Adolf Hitler."

The unrest inspired from Berlin continued, the natural reaction was counterpressure. The situation grew intolerable. Great Britain decided to send a mediator, the venerable Lord Runciman of Doxford. Runciman traveled through the Sudeten territory. He realized that war or peace depended upon his report. Greatly depressed, Runciman reported to his government on "this cursed country," as he put it. But even he saw no possibility of a solution.

It was clear that Hitler would march. Europe was trembling with fear of war. In Berlin, in Paris, in London, everywhere people expected the powder barrel to go up at any moment.

The French Prime Minister, Edouard Daladier, probed the feelings in London. A few lines from the report of his conversation with the British Prime Minister, Neville Chamberlain, will suffice to show the despair of the statesmen.

DALADIER: I believe that the peace of Europe can be saved if Great Britain and France declare now that they will not permit the destruction of the Czech State.

CHAMBERLAIN: As I listened to Mr. Daladier, I had the same sensation as he had. My blood boils when I see how Germany gets away with it time and again and extends its rule over the free nations. But such sentimental feelings are dangerous, and I must bear in mind the powers with which we are playing. We play not with money but with men. I cannot enter a conflict light-heartedly which will bring with it such fearful effects for families, women and children. We must therefore see whether we are strong enough to achieve victory. I say openly that I do not think that we are. . . .

After the Party rally the world awaited Hitler's blow. Then Chamberlain made a sensational move. He offered to visit Hitler in Germany to discuss with him the Sudeten question. On the very next day, September 15, 1938, Chamberlain was in Berchtes-gaden. Hitler had accepted the suggestion and had informed the British Prime Minister that he was entirely at his disposal.

"I quickly saw," Chamberlain wrote after the meeting, "that the situation was much more critical than I had assumed. I knew that his troops, tanks, and guns were ready to attack the Czechs at his word, and it was clear that quick decisions would have to be made."

However, Chamberlain gained some breathing space. He said that he had to consult the other members of his Cabinet, and Hitler agreed not to act until then. The Englishman flew back to London. Three days later, on September 18, 1938, Great Britain and France, in a common message to the Czechoslovak President, Eduard Beneš, suggested that he should cede the Sudeten districts to Germany. Beneš refused at first.

Paris and London put pressure on him. On September 21, 1938, the President's resistance collapsed. In a note to the Western Powers he said: "Forced by circumstances and under the most extreme pressure from the French and British Governments, the Government of the Czechoslovak Republic accepts with bitter-ness the Franco-British proposals. The Government of Czecho-slovakia points out with distress that they were never once con-sulted in the preparation of these proposals."

Peace seemed to have been saved, even if Chamberlain and Daladier had lost face. At a further meeting in Bad Godesberg, Chamberlain informed Hitler that Czechoslovakia was prepared to cede the Sudetenland to Germany. He explained the necessary formalities, but Hitler answered with a statement that was like a slap in the face: "I am sorry, Herr Chamberlain, but I cannot now go into these matters."

"With a jolt Chamberlain sat up in his chair," recalled the interpreter, Dr. Paul Schmidt. "The blood rushed to his face in anger." Hitler declared that the claims of Poland and Hungary to Czech territory must also be satisfied. Besides, he would not agree to the apparently tedious formalities for the surrender of the district. "The occupation of the surrendered Sudeten districts must take place at once," he said. The Hitler-Chamberlain talks came to a standstill. Once again there was alarm in the capitals of Europe. Eventually the negotiations got under way again. Hitler gave Chamberlain a memorandum, demanding an immediate withdrawal of the Czech Army from a region which he had marked on a map of the country. The evacuation of this region was to begin on September 26 and its surrender to Germany to take place on September 28.

Interpreter Schmidt translated. "That is an ultimatum," Chamberlain said in surprise. "With great disappointment and deep regret, I have to say that in my efforts to maintain peace you have not helped me in the slightest."

"But," said Hitler with some embarrassment, "this is headed 'Memorandum' and not 'Ultimatum.' "

At this moment a note was passed to him by an adjutant. Hitler read it, gave the paper to the interpreter, and said, "Read this note to Herr Chamberlain." Schmidt translated: "Beneš has just announced on the radio the general mobilization of the Czech Army."

A breathless silence fell. This was war, everyone thought. But Hitler showed himself suddenly conciliatory. He succeeded in persuading Chamberlain to forward the "Memorandum" to Prague; the British Premier believed that Beneš would agree. A weary struggle about dates and hours began. Eventually the British ambassador in Berlin, Nevile Henderson, dispatched Colonel Mason Macfarlane with the document to Prague.

Macfarlane traveled by car to the German-Czech boundary where hastily built trenches, barbed-wire fences, and machine-gun posts spoke of the threat of war. During the night he traveled on foot six miles by forest and field paths, "always in danger," as Henderson wrote, "of being shot as a guerrilla either by the Germans or the Czechs."

In this adventurous way Hitler's document finally reached the hands of the government in Prague. Beneš refused to accept its terms. On the same day, September 26, 1938, Hitler made his famous speech in the Berlin Sport Palace: "I have assured Herr Chamberlain that the German people want nothing but peace. I have further assured him and repeat it here, that—if this problem is solved—there exists no further territorial problem for Germany in Europe. And I have assured him also that I shall then have no further interest in the Czech State. And that will be guaranteed. We want no Czechs!"

To Chamberlain's adviser, Sir Horace Wilson, he said a few hours later: "The Czech government has only the alternatives of accepting or rejecting the German proposals. In the latter case I shall wipe out Czechoslovakia."

"Under these circumstances," Wilson replied, "I must carry out an instruction by the British Prime Minister. I have to ask you, Herr Reich Chancellor, to take notice of the following information: If France, in fulfillment of her treaty obligations, is involved actively in hostilities against Germany, then the United Kingdom will regard itself as obliged to support France."

Hitler shouted in a rage: "If England and France want to start a war, then let them do it. It is all the same to me. I am prepared for any eventuality. Then we shall all find ourselves at war next week."

France was determined to march for Czechoslovakia. In Paris, gas masks were distributed to the civilian population. In Berlin, the sirens sounded for air-raid exercises. In London, Chamberlain sat up half the night. He was working on his speech to Parliament. The time limit laid down by Hitler had run out. Next day the invasion would begin. Only one spark of hope remained: Chamberlain had sent a request to Mussolini to try to make Hitler postpone his plans. While the world was still asleep, at five o'clock in the morning on September 28, 1938, the British ambassador in Rome was called from his bed. Instructions had come from London to go at once to Mussolini and put Chamberlain's suggestion before him. Lord Perth forthwith sought out

Foreign Minister Ciano. At 11:00 A.M. Mussolini himself sat down at the telephone and called Bernardo Attolico, his ambassador in Berlin.

MUSSOLINI: This is the Duce speaking. Are you listening?

ATTOLICO: Yes, I am listening.

MUSSOLINI: Go at once to the German Chancellor and tell him the British Government have informed me through Lord Perth that they would welcome my intercession in the Sudeten German question. Tell the Führer that I accept his decision: he may be sure of that. But tell him I would regard the request for intercession very favorably. Are you listening?

ATTOLICO: Yes, I am listening.

MUSSOLINI: Then hurry up!

Attolico hurried up. Five minutes later the telephone rang in Ribbentrop's room in the Foreign Office. Attolico, forgetting all his ambassadorial dignity, cried into the telephone in English: "I have a personal message from Il Duce. I must see the Führer at once, very urgent, quick, quick!"

"Go at once to the Chancellery," he was told. "Put a large Italian flag on your car, so that you will be admitted at once." Time was indeed getting short. Hitler was called out of a conference. Again Attolico forgot all formality. Already in the corridor he blurted out to Hitler what he had to say.

"Tell the Duce," said Hitler after a short pause, "that I accept his suggestion."

In London, Chamberlain was already addressing the Lower House. He had decided to tell the British nation that there would be war. As he was speaking, a parliamentary secretary passed him a message. Chamberlain glanced at it. His face brightened. He picked up the notes for his grave war speech and tore them up before the eyes of the Members. Then he said calmly: "I have to tell the House that Herr Hitler has invited me to meet him in Munich tomorrow. Monsieur Daladier and Signor Mussolini are also invited. I hope that the House will allow me to go and see what I can make of this last attempt."

Eyewitnesses of this scene reported, "A storm of applause broke out in the Chamber. Nothing like it had happened since the day when Sir Edward Grey announced England's entry into the war on August 4, 1914."

"Chamberlain flew to Munich," said prosecutor Alderman in the Nuremberg courtroom, "where a meeting took place of Chamberlain, Mussolini, Daladier, and Hitler in the Brown House. It lasted until September 30, 1938, a Friday, on which the Munich Pact was signed. It will suffice if I say here that this agreement provided for the separation of the Sudetenland from Czechoslovakia. Czechoslovakia was asked to agree."

It was a dark hour for Europe. Britain and France had bought peace by sacrificing their friend, Czechoslovakia; they could not foresee that this sacrifice would be in vain. Hitler had no intention of being satisfied and permitting the world to live in peace. The word "Munich" was to become a political term of shameful surrender.

In the Nuremberg prison, Hermann Goering told the court psychologist, Gustave M. Gilbert, "It was so simple. Neither Chamberlain nor Daladier did in fact want to risk anything to save Czechoslovakia. The fate of Czechoslovakia was decided in three hours. Besides, Daladier found it difficult to pay much attention to the proceedings."

Meanwhile, the Czech delegation was waiting for the result in the Hotel Regina, guarded by the Gestapo. At 1:30 in the morning Hubert Masarik, Counselor at the Foreign Ministry, and two other men from Prague were brought to the Brown House. Only the British and French statesmen were present.

"The atmosphere was oppressive," wrote Masarik. "The French were obviously embarrassed, but Chamberlain yawned incessantly without any sign of embarrassment. We were brutally informed that no appeal against the verdict was possible. We took our leave and went." In Prague, the Czech Foreign Minister prophesied: "In any case, we are not the last. After us, the same fate will overtake others."

On October 1, 1938, the very day that Hitler had long before decided, the German Wehrmacht marched into the Sudetenland. Beneš resigned and went to England.

"Peace in our time," cried Chamberlain at his arrival in London holding up the Munich Agreement to the journalists who had come to meet him at the airport.

Peace in our time? "It is only the first sip, the first taste of the bitter chalice that will be put before us year after year," said Winston Churchill prophetically in the House of Commons.

"On the evening of March 14, 1939," Alderman continued in Nuremberg, "Herr Hácha, the new President of the Czechoslovak Republic, and Herr Chvalkovsky, the Foreign Minister, came to Berlin at the suggestion of the German ambassador in Prague. Since the previous weekend the Nazi press had accused the Czechs of using force against the Slovaks, against members of the German minority, and against citizens of the German Reich."

Emil Hácha and František Chvalkovsky had to wait until 1:15 A.M. before they were brought before Hitler. At the same hour the Wehrmacht had received the order to march on Prague.

"I made up my mind already last Sunday," said Hitler unabashedly to the Czech Head of State. "At six o'clock the German Wehrmacht will advance into Czechoslovakia from all sides."

Hácha was to sign an order that the Czech forces were to offer no resistance, and that the rest of Czechoslovakia was to place itself under Hitler's protection. Hermann Goering threatened the sixty-six-year-old Hácha that if he refused, German bombers would set out at once and turn Prague into a heap of rubble.

The time was 3:00 A.M. Hácha collapsed from a heart attack. Hitler's private doctor, Theodor Morell, gave him an injection. "I see that resistance is useless," Hácha whispered when he had been brought to. At 3:55 A.M. he signed the prepared document. The world looked on in fear and silence as Hitler drove into Prague the next day. Czechoslovakia had ceased to exist.

Among those whom Hitler had deceived, Chamberlain was the first to protest in anger: "What has become of the words, 'No further territorial claims'? What has become of the assurance, 'We want no Czechs'? How much trust can we put in the other assurances that come from the same source?"

Clearly, the patience of the Western Powers was exhausted. Each further step would lead irretrievably to war. But Hitler no longer saw realities. On May 23, 1939, he announced to the high officers of the Wehrmacht his new target, "to seize Poland at the first favorable opportunity." He was marching on blindly toward the abyss.

THE "CRYSTAL NIGHT"

Even before Hitler had completed his secret plans and plunged the world into the Second World War by his attack on Poland, another terrifying scene took place in Germany itself. The Court devoted several days to the details: "From the earliest days of the Nazi Party," said the indictment, "anti-Semitism had played a predominant part in National Socialist thought and propaganda. With the assumption of power in 1933, the persecution of the Jews became official national policy."

In the town of the Trial, Nuremberg, Hermann Goering had proclaimed the so-called Racial Laws on September 15, 1935. They banned marriage and extramarital relationships between Germans and Jews, they deprived the Jews of German citizenship.

"Did you proclaim the Nuremberg Laws?" Goering was asked on the witness stand by the chief American prosecutor Robert H. Jackson.

GOERING: Yes

JACKSON: On April 26, 1938, you published a decree providing for the registration of Jewish property and provided that Jews inside and outside Germany must register their property, did you not?

GOERING: If you have the decree there, and it is signed by me, there cannot be any doubt.

JACKSON: On April 26, 1938, you published a decree, did you not, that all acts of disposal of Jewish enterprises required the permission of the authorities?

GOERING: That I remember.

JACKSON: Then you published on November 12, 1938, a decree imposing a fine of a million marks for atonement on all Jews?

GOERING: I have already explained that all these decrees were signed by me, and I assume responsibility for them.

This cross-examination introduced the inquiry into one of the most frightful acts of the period before the war. On October 28, 1938, police knocked at the doors of 17,000 Jews all over Germany. These Jews had been Polish nationals until the previous day; but the Polish government had declared their passports no longer valid, and Hitler seized the opportunity to rid himself of these now stateless people. At once, Reinhard Heydrich, then head of the Security Service, carried out the first deportation of Jews in modern history.

On that day, almost a year before the beginning of the war, thousands of Jews were arrested and packed into trains and trucks throughout the Reich. Of their possessions they were not allowed to take more than they could carry. The wretched load of humanity was sent to the Polish border. At the border station of Benschen, the Jews were driven out of the trucks on some open ground and chased across the fields by Heydrich's men—eastward, toward Poland. Old men and women collapsed, and were roused with kicks; some remained dead on the spot. The Polish sentries were not prepared for this onslaught of thousands of hunted men. Hitler's first mass expulsion succeeded.

In this tragedy lay the seed of further trouble. Among those expelled were the cobbler Sendel Grynszpan and his wife and children. From Poland, where the family arrived empty-handed, they wrote a post card to Sendel's son, Herschel Grynszpan, who had emigrated to Paris, telling him what had happened. Herschel reacted in a way that was to have dreadful repercussions. The seventeen-year-old lad wanted to take his revenge for the injustice inflicted upon his family. On the morning of November 7, 1938, he bought a revolver in a shop in the Rue du Faubourg Saint-Martin. Then he made his way to the German Embassy in the Rue de Lille. He had made up his mind to kill the German ambassador, Count Johannes von Welczek.

By chance Welczek returned at that moment from an early morning walk. Grynszpan did not know the ambassador. He went up to him and asked where Count von Welczek was to be found. The ambassador referred him to an attendant by the name of Nagorka and continued on his way, without suspecting that he had just escaped assassination. Nagorka led the young man to the office of Ernst vom Rath, who was responsible for receiving visitors; he asked the unknown youth what he wanted.

Grynzpan shot several times at Rath who, severely wounded, crumpled up on the floor. Although Hitler sent two of his doctors to Paris as soon as the news of the attack was received, and although French soldiers immediately volunteered as blood donors, the German embassy official died soon afterward.

Interrogated by the French police, Grynszpan declared that the news of the brutal treatment of his family had driven him to the deed: "From that moment," he said, "I was determined to protest by killing a member of the German embassy. I wanted to avenge the Jews and draw the attention of the world to events in Germany."

He had followed an angry impulse without thinking of the catastrophic political consequences. His unfortunate deed provided Nazi Germany with an excuse and a cue for further persecutions of the Jews. Two days after the shots in the German embassy, on November 9, 1938, Hitler and his "old comrades" celebrated, as every year, their abortive Putsch of 1923. During the reunion dinner, toward nine o'clock, a messenger appeared and whispered to Hitler that Rath had died of his wounds in Paris. Hitler leaned over toward Goebbels who was sitting next to him, and spoke quietly to him for some time. Then he left the table, without delivering his usual speech.

No one knows what passed between Hitler and his Minister of Propaganda. But everything that followed, blow by blow, was obviously a consequence of those whispered words. While most Germans were asleep in their beds, the scene was set for a "spontaneous uprising of the people." Throughout the whole of Germany, Jewish places of worship suddenly went up in flames, over seven thousand Jewish shops were completely demolished, some were set on fire, tens of thousands of windowpanes were broken, and twenty thousand Jews were dragged from their beds and arrested.

Goebbels wanted to present these events as the German people's answer to the deed of Herschel Grynszpan. In fact, however, all this had nothing whatever to do with the German population. "These accounts of violence," said the American prosecutor, William F. Walsh, "were not localized anti-Semitic demonstrations, but were directed and ordered from a centralized headquarters in Berlin. This is established by a series of teletype messages sent by the Berlin Secret State Police headquarters to the chiefs of police throughout Germany. I shall quote the relevant part of one of these confidential orders, signed by Heydrich:

> Because of the attempt on the life of the Legation Secretary Vom Rath in Paris, tonight, November 9-10, 1938, demonstrations against the Jews ought to be expected throughout the Reich. The following instructions are given on how to treat these events:
>
> The Chiefs of the State Police or their deputies must get in telephonic contact with the political leaders who have jurisdiction over their districts and must arrange a joint meeting with the appropriate inspector or commander of the Order of Police to discuss the organization of the demonstration. At these discussions the political leaders have to be informed that the German police have received from the Reichsführer SS and the Chief of the German Police, the following instructions.
>
> (a) Only such measures should be taken which do not involve danger to German life or property. (For instance, synagogues are to be burned down only when there is no danger of fire to the surroundings.)
>
> (b) Businesses and private apartments of Jews may be destroyed, but not looted. The Police is instructed to supervise the execution of this order, and to arrest looters.

The defendant Walther Funk, then Minister for Economic Affairs, stated on the witness stand at Nuremberg: "When I drove to my Ministry on the morning of November 10, I saw on the streets and in the windows of the stores the devastation which had taken place and I heard further details from my officials at the Ministry. I tried to reach Goering, Goebbels, and, I think, Himmler. Finally I succeeded in reaching Goebbels. I told him that this terror was an affront against me personally, that valuable goods which could not be replaced had been destroyed, and

that our relations with foreign countries . . . would now be disturbed noticeably. . . ."

Funk spoke out plainly. According to a statement under oath
this is what he said to Goebbels: "Have you gone mad, Goebbels,
to do such filthy things? It makes one ashamed to be a German.
All our prestige abroad goes by the board. I labor day and night
to build up our national prestige and you have thrown it wantonly
out of the window. If this disgrace doesn't stop you can do your
dirty business without me."

But Funk was too weak to throw in his hand. The report of a
preliminary hearing was read out in the courtroom. Funk was
asked: "You knew that the looting and all that was done at the
instigation of the Party, didn't you?" Funk began to weep and
answered: "I should have resigned in 1938. That is why I am
guilty, I am guilty, I confess that I stand here guilty."

Like Funk, Goering expressed his indignation at the events
of that dreadful night. And like Funk he never thought of the
human side of those organized excesses. Quite naively, he told
the Nuremberg Court the real reasons for his indignation: "The
Führer arrived in Berlin in the course of the morning. Having
in the meantime heard that Goebbels had at least played an
important part as instigator, I told the Führer that it was impossible for me to have such events take place at this particular
time, that I was very much concerned in connection with the
Four-Year plan, in concentrating the entire economic field, and
that I had, in the course of my speeches to the nation, asked
that every old tooth-paste tube, every rusty nail, every bit of scrap
metal be collected and utilized. I said that it could not be
tolerated that a man who was not responsible for these things
[Goebbels] should disturb my difficult economic tasks by destroying so many things of economic value on the one hand and by
causing so much disturbance in economic life on the other hand.

"In the afternoon I had another discussion with the Führer.
In the meantime Goebbels had been to see him. The latter I
had told over the telephone in unmistakable terms, and in very
sharp words, my view of the matter. While we were talking,
Goebbels joined us and began to talk in his usual way. It was on
that occasion that he first made the suggestion that a fine should

be imposed . . . and he named an almost incredibly high sum. After a short discussion . . . one thousand million marks was set upon.

"I pointed out to the Führer that under certain circumstances that figure would have repercussions on the tax returns. The Führer then expressed the wish and ordered that the economic solution should also be carried through now. He ordered, in general terms, what was to be done. Thereupon I called the meeting of November 12 with those departments having jurisdiction over these matters."

It was a meeting at which, during its stormy course, the leading actors showed their true faces. At this meeting, the fate of the Jews was decided. Once again busy stenographers were at work to take down all the statements of those taking part. The report was later discovered, actually in the Berlin office of the Air Ministry where the meeting took place. The significant dossier was put before the Nuremberg Court. Any commentary to the verbatim report would be superfluous.

GOERING: Gentlemen, I have had enough of these demonstrations. They do not harm the Jews, but finally devolve on me, the highest authority for the German economy. If today a Jewish shop is destroyed, if goods are thrown into the street, the insurance company will pay the Jews for the damages. Furthermore, consumer goods are destroyed. It is absurd to empty and set fire to a Jewish store when a German insurance company has to cover the damage, and the goods, which I sorely need, are burned. I do not want to leave any doubt, gentlemen: we have not come together merely to talk again, but to make decisions; and I earnestly ask the competent departments to take trenchant measures for the Aryanizing of German economy and submit them to me as far as necessary. The State Trustee will estimate the value of business and decide what amount the Jew shall receive. Naturally, this amount is to be fixed as low as possible. The State Trustee will then transfer the business to Aryan ownership.

JACKSON: Now, you then speak at considerable length of the method by which you intended to Aryanize the Jewish businesses, is that right?

GOERING: Yes.

Further sections were read from the report on the meeting in Goering's Air Ministry:

JACKSON: You inquired how many synagogues were actually burned down, and Heydrich replied, "Altogether there were 101 synagogues destroyed by fire, 76 synagogues demolished, and 7,500 stores destroyed in the Reich." Then Dr. Goebbels interposed, "I am of the opinion that this is our chance to dissolve the synagogues. The Jew must pay for it. I consider it necessary to bring out an order now that Jews will be forbidden to visit German theaters, cinemas, and circuses. I believe we can carry this through on the grounds of the present state of the theater. The theaters are crowded anyway. . . . The Reich Ministry of Transport must issue an order that special compartments are set aside for the use of Jews. . . . Then an order must be made that Jews are forbidden to visit German baths and recreation grounds. . . . We must also consider whether it is necessary to forbid Jews to enter German forests. At present they run about in droves in the Grunewald. . . . Further, that Jews are not allowed to sit in German parks. . . . Finally, I consider it essential that Jewish children should be completely barred from German schools."

GOERING: I now wish to call in Herr Hilgard, the insurance expert. . . . Herr Hilgard, this is the matter at issue. As a result of the righteous anger of the populace against the Jews a certain amount of damage has been caused throughout the country. I assume that some of the Jews are insured. The matter would be greatly simplified if an order were made that this damage was not covered by insurance.

HILGARD: In the case of the insurance of glass, which plays an important part, by far the greater part of those who have suffered are Aryans. The ownership of premises is mostly in Aryan hands while the Jews as a rule have only rented their shops.

GOERING: Then the Jews must pay for the damage.

HEYDRICH: Through Aryanization and other restrictions the Jews will naturally be without work. What we are experiencing is that the Jews are turned into proletarians. I must therefore introduce measures that will isolate the Jews. To this end I suggest some police measures, for example, that every Jew must wear a distinctive symbol.

GOERING: A uniform?

HEYDRICH: A badge.

GOERING: One more question, gentlemen: how would you consider the situation if I announced today that the Jews must pay a fine of a thousand million marks as a contribution? I will choose the words that, as punishment for their ruthless crime and so on and so on, a contribution of a thousand million marks has been decreed for the German Jews as a whole. That will break them. The swine won't commit a second murder so quickly. Incidentally, I'd like to say that I wouldn't like to be a Jew in Germany today! If the German Reich in some measurable time comes into conflict in the international field, it is self-evident that we in Germany will carry out first of all a great reckoning with the Jews.

So much for the report. Its contents were not disputed by Goering on the witness stand; he turned it aside with some shallow or cynical subterfuges. Everything that was said in 1938 soon became frightful reality, including symbols, ghetto, and destruction.

DRESS REHEARSAL
IN SPAIN

Germany was waging war before the war began. Hermann Goering chose to say only a few sentences as a witness at Nuremberg about his first military adventure:

"When civil war broke out in Spain, Franco sent an appeal for help to Germany, especially for support in the air. The Führer hesitated and I strongly urged him to give the support under any circumstances—first, to combat the spread of Communism in that region, but also in order to try out my young Air Force on a number of technical points. With the Führer's approval I dispatched a large part of my transport fleet and also a number of

training units of my fighters and bombers, and also some antiaircraft guns; in this way I had the opportunity of testing under fire
whether the materiel had been developed in an efficient manner.
So that the personnel should also acquire practical experience I
arranged a steady rotation, repeatedly sending out new units and
recalling others."

These brief sentences disguise an unscrupulous enterprise,
knowledge of which was withheld from the German people right
up to the last act. This was the top secret Condor Legion.

The questions raised at Nuremberg show once more the true
face of Hitler's policy and that of his henchmen: on August 8,
1936, the German Chargé d'Affaires in London, Prince Otto von
Bismarck, assured the British Foreign Secretary in the name of
the German Government that no weapons or war materiel had
been, or would be, delivered to Spain.

He lied. German soldiers and German weapons had long been
on the way to Spain, were already being used there in action, and
continued to arrive in a steady stream. Germans were fighting in
a foreign land. Germans were compelled to lay down their lives
on a distant battleground. Mothers wept for their sons—but it
was strictly forbidden for the relatives to speak of the reasons for
their sorrow! Goebbels banned any information on this.

The war beyond the Pyrenees led in the end to momentous
mistakes by the High Command of the Luftwaffe in Berlin. What
went off well in Spain, so they reasoned erroneously, must also
succeed in the coming large-scale war. The fatal errors in these
conclusions lie in the following points:

1. In Spain a picked corps was fighting against a greatly inferior
enemy.

2. The field of operations covered only short distances.

3. The German units in the Spanish Civil War presented no
major problems of leadership.

4. Only a relatively small force was involved; there was no problem as regards supplies for it.

Spain was to be the great training ground for the German Army
and the model for future wars. In reality, however, it was an ideal
case which was not to be repeated. Because of this error by their
leaders, millions of German soldiers were later to lose their lives

in the wastes of Russia, in Africa, and in other extensive theaters of war.

How did this adventure come about? Spain had years of crises behind her: in 1931, King Alfonso XIII had abdicated, and by 1936 the succeeding republic had experienced twenty-eight changes of government. Finally, February 16, 1936, there was an election in which the Socialist Popular Front legitimately achieved power with 256 out of 473 seats in Parliament. Then the Generals revolted. In Spanish Morocco, the military rose against the new government. General Francisco Franco, C.O. of the Canary Islands, flew to Morocco and took over the leadership of the revolt. In northern Spain, General Mila rose. At the same time, General Queipo de Llano achieved a coup: he captured Seville with 180 men.

But in the other Spanish provinces, in Madrid and Barcelona particularly, the rising miscarried; the Government remained master of the situation. The insurrectionists were in a dilemma. They had either to capitulate or try to bring the Moroccan troops under Franco's command over from Africa to the Spanish mainland. Means of transport were lacking. The officers on board the Spanish naval ships who had supported the rising were quickly overwhelmed by the crews. Thus the Navy was entirely in the hands of the Government.

In search of help Franco applied to Mussolini and Hitler. Two German merchants who lived in Moroccan Tetuan acted as intermediaries. They hastened to Berlin and opened negotiations with Hermann Goering, who at once seized the chance offered: here at last he could try out his Luftwaffe. Hitler decided on armed intervention. To begin with, General Walter Warlimont was sent to Franco, but much more important was the help of the Luftwaffe. Since the Spanish Navy was not available there only remained the air route by which the troops could be brought from Morocco across the Mediterranean to Spain.

In fact, Goering now organized the first air lift in history. Disguised as a private firm, the *Hispano-Marokkanische Transport-Aktiengesellschaft—Hisma* for short—was set up. It carried out its business with two squadrons called Pablos and Pedros. The army units were given the code name of Imker. The whole thing was called the Condor Legion, and referred to in the secret Berlin documents by the significant code name, "Operation Fire Magic." In July 1936, a strange group of eighty-five young civilians went on board the steamer *Usaramo* in Hamburg. They were "tourists" of the Travel Company "Union": "businessmen," "technicians," and "photographers," as their passports stated. These travelers had a great deal of luggage. Unfortunately one of the cases broke in two while being loaded, and out of it fell a 550-pound shell. The ship's crew were alarmed but then accepted the explanation that it was a "special mission for the recovery of the German colonies."

From Hamburg, the *Usaramo* sailed to Cadiz in Spain. Among the "tourists" were ten pilots of the German Air Force, ten air crews and personnel. In Spain they met a second group who, on July 27, 1936, had flown directly to Seville with several Ju 52 transport planes. From Tetuan in Morocco to Jerez de la Frontera near Seville, Goering's Ju 52s in a short time brought 12,000 Moroccans and 285,000 pounds of ammunition across the Mediterranean. Only in this way could Franco start his civil war.

The German transport was sucked at once right into the maelstrom. After the loyal Spanish ship *Jaime I* had fired a pair of salvos among the suspected Junkers the planes were fitted with bombs, and it was not long before the *Jaime I* was severely damaged by a German air attack. In return the *Usaramo* was shot up by a Spanish Government cruiser on entering Cadiz, but was able to land its "businessmen," "technicians," and "photographers" with their luggage.

From Wilhelmshaven, the battleships *Deutschland* and *Admiral Scheer* set course for Spain. Their task was to give protection and transport to German nationals from the regions threatened by the civil war—for this civil war, first really set going by Goering's air lift, was plunging the whole of Spain into chaos, destruction, and terrible suffering.

British, French, American, and Italian warships now appeared along the coasts of Spain. All foreigners fled from the unhappy country. In Málaga alone, German and Italian steamers took some two thousand Germans on board under the protection of the battleships.

But while the Spanish Government Navy was restricted to its

task of escorting and protecting, the Luftwaffe took an active and direct part in the conflict. It was not alone in this: Mussolini had placed troops at Franco's disposal, and on the other side of the front line the Soviet Union had come to the aid of the Madrid Government with men and war materiel. Apart from those who had been sent to Spain by Moscow, Rome, and Berlin, there came many volunteers of their own free will—men who wanted to fight for their political convictions, but also mercenaries and adventurers from all over the world: Frenchmen, Englishmen, Poles, Americans, Czechs, Portuguese, Scandinavians. Some of them entered Franco's service, but the majority joined the International Brigade of the Popular Front Government. Spain had suddenly become the cockpit of the world. The insurrection of the generals had turned into the first "ideological" war of our century.

On August 6, 1936, the French Government proposed to the Powers a general ban on delivering arms to the warring parties. On August 31 Paris extended this proposal and suggested the formation of a general Nonintervention Committee. Twenty-six European states took part at the first meeting—among them Germany, Italy, and the Soviet Union. An elaborate apparatus was set in motion, plenary meetings and committee meetings were held, the delegates exchanged accusations and counteraccusations.

On December 7, 1937, Berlin affirmed anew that "there are no German troops in Spain." Joachim von Ribbentrop, Germany's representative on the Nonintervention Committee, claimed that 25,000 French and 35,000 Soviet volunteers were in Spain. Ivan Maiski, the representative of the Soviet Union, said in reply that six thousand well-armed Germans were fighting there.

In his memoirs, written in the Nuremberg prison, Ribbentrop said: "It would have been better to call this the Intervention Committee, for the whole activity of its members consisted in explaining or concealing the participation of their countries in Spain more or less convincingly. It was a most unpleasant task."

On March 8, 1937, the Nonintervention Committee finally decided to set up a land and sea control which would prevent foreign soldiers and weapons from reaching Spain. Great Britain, France, Germany, and Italy were entrusted with the control. To Germany fell the task of patrolling with her fleet the eastern

Spanish coast from Cap de Gata to Cap Oropesa: the poacher was appointed gamekeeper. While officially the farce of nonintervention and sea control was enacted, men and materiel poured in secretly and unchecked.

For three long years of this civil war with all its horrors and destruction, the Spanish people had to foot the bill for Stalin, Mussolini, and Hitler-Goering. The war could never have lasted so long without foreign intervention.

Goering's Luftwaffe unit in Spain, the Condor Legion, at first consisted of four squadrons of bombers, four squadrons of fighters, a reconnaissance squadron, and two squadrons of seaplanes; in addition there were several batteries of heavy antiaircraft artillery and air intelligence units. Major General Hugo Sperrle, disguised in Spain under the name of Sander, had little joy in the achievements of the units under his command. In this trial under fire the shortcomings of the Luftwaffe planning in Berlin soon became evident. Goering gave to the first German fighter unit in Spain six planes of the type He 51, single-engined biplanes reminiscent of the aircraft of the First World War. They were so slow that they could not even catch up with the bombers of the other side. The Martin bomber of the Popular Front Government, for example, was faster by thirty miles an hour, to say nothing of the Devoitines, Curtises, and the Soviet Ratas. Goering's airmen looked enviously at the modern Fiat fighters and Savoia bombers sent by Mussolini. By Christmas 1936 the first of the faster machines came from Germany: the Messerschmitt 109 fighters, fast bombers of the type He 111, and the first dive bombers. Then came the Do 17, as reconnaissance aircraft, and the He 59 seaplane.

In the summer of 1938, four months' heavy fighting raged along the Ebro. It was the biggest battle since the First World War. The turning point was near. The Condor Legion achieved supremacy in the air, especially with their modern Me 109s. The legitimate Spanish Government was in a hopeless plight after they had lost 75,000 men on the Ebro. At Christmas 1938 Franco began the attack on Catalonia, and to the Condor Legion fell the task of opening the offensive in the air. The rear lines of the Government forces were bombed incessantly. The confusion was terrible. On February 9, 1939, Franco stood as victor at the Pyrenees. A day later, he turned for the last time toward central Spain. With the fall of Madrid, on March 28, 1939, the civil war came to an end.

German soldiers were fighting for a thing that had become a lie like so many others, cooked up in Berlin to deceive them. For while they believed that they were risking their lives for national interests and for Franco's just victory, Hitler and his henchmen were pursuing quite different objectives. A document submitted to the Nuremberg Court made this quite clear: the Hossbach report of the secret conference held by Hitler on November 5, 1937. At this meeting Hitler said, "From the German point of view, a hundred per cent victory by Franco is not desired: we should be much more interested in a continuation of the war and the maintenance of tension in the Mediterranean."

Such are the facts of which the men of the Condor Legion knew nothing, facts which were played down by the official propaganda, for to Dr. Joseph Goebbels, too, the Spanish Civil War came as a favorable opportunity to try out his methods "under fire." He found it most convenient when on May 29, 1937, Spanish Government aircraft dropped two bombs on the battleship *Deutschland* which was anchoring off Ibiza. Twenty-three members of the crew were killed, eight more died later from their wounds. Hitler learned the news during the Bayreuth Festival. He returned immediately to Berlin and ordered the battleship *Admiral Scheer* to shell the Spanish Government port of Almería as a reprisal. The bombardment was duly carried out on May 31, 1937. The German papers were full of it. But they had been silent about another bombardment a few weeks earlier, on April 26, 1937. It is a memorable date, and one of the darkest pages in the annals of Hermann Goering.

On that day, Goering's Condor Legion appeared over the small Spanish town of Guernica: bombs fell—more and more bombs from more and more aircraft—and for the first time in history they were not aimed at fighting troops, military targets, or defense installations, but on residential quarters, on open streets and squares, on unprotected houses, on women and children. For the first time the guns of the low-flying planes were turned not against soldiers but against fleeing civilians. The horrors of the coming world war had their dress rehearsal in Spain.

While the Legion was on its way home to Germany, Hitler himself disclosed the secret of the silent crusade on April 28, 1939, in a speech to the Reichstag: "The German people will learn how bravely their sons have fought in that place for the freedom of a noble nation, and in the last resort for the salvation of European civilization."

"Come what may," Goering said in Hamburg to the members of the Legion on May 31, 1939, "you have proved that we are unconquerable." Twenty thousand legionaries marched on June 6, 1939, past Adolf Hitler in Berlin—openly, jubiliantly, and in the face of all the solemn assurances previously given that Germans had never fought in Spain. The unconquerables, as Goering called them, were soon thrown into other battles; a short three months after the victory parade in Berlin began the Second World War.

4
War

STALIN AND
THE CANNIBALS

"This document [also] is of such great importance historically
. . . that I feel obliged to read most of it," said the American
prosecutor, Sydney S. Alderman, introducing a new section of the
Trial. "The original of this document, when captured, found its
way through the complicated channels across the Atlantic to the
United States. There it was found by members of the staff of the
American Prosecution, by them taken to London, and thence to
Nuremberg. We think the document is of unquestioned validity.

"The document consists of minutes of a conference held on
May 23, 1939. The place of the conference was the Führer's study
in the new Reich chancellery. The defendant Goering was present. The defendant Roeder was present. The defendant Keitel was
present. The subject of the meeting was, I quote: 'Indoctrination
on the Political Situation and Future Aims.' "

The date, May 23, 1939, is important. Two months after Hitler's march into Prague, two months after the end of the Spanish
Civil War, and not much more than three months before the
outbreak of the Second World War, a decision was made which
affected the lives of millions of people.

"Where straightforward pressure is no longer considered to be
decisive, its place must be taken by the elements of surprise and
masterly handling," Hitler declared to those taking part in that
secret conference. "But that is not possible without invading foreign countries or taking possession of foreign property. The past
period has been well used. All our steps were taken purposefully.
The national political unity of Germany has been accomplished.
Further successes cannot be achieved without bloodshed."

Then Hitler developed his plans. "Danzig is not our objective.
It is more a matter of obtaining living space in the East and in-
suring our means of livelihood. In Europe there is no other pos-

sibility for action. If fate forces us toward a conflict with the West, it is useful to have a large eastern territory. The question whether Poland should be spared therefore does not arise; we have to attack the Poles on the first suitable occasion. A repetition of the case of Czechoslovakia is not to be expected. There will be fighting, and it is our job to isolate the Poles. The achievement of isolation is decisive. Therefore your Führer reserves for himself the final decision as to when the blow must be struck.

"It is not certain that in the course of a German-Polish conflict a war with the West is ruled out; it may arise with England and France. The fundamental thing is our settlement with the Poles, beginning with an attack on Poland. We can be sure of success only if the West stays out. If that is not possible, then it would be better to attack the West and finish Poland at the same time.

"What course would such a conflict take? The war with England and France will be a matter of life and death. The hope of getting off lightly is a dangerous fallacy: the possibility just doesn't exist. We must burn our bridges, and it will be no longer a matter of right or wrong but of the existence or nonexistence of eighty million people.

"The question is: a short war or a long one? Every army or government has to strive for a short war. But the government has to prepare for a war of ten to fifteen years' duration. There is no doubt that a surprise attack may lead to a rapid decision. But it is criminal if the government relied upon a surprise attack. The aim is to bring the enemy down with a decisive blow. Right or wrong or treaties do not matter here. Success is only possible if we are not led into a war with England over Poland.

"A long war must be prepared for, apart from the surprise attack; the destruction of England's chances on the Continent must be the aim. The Army has to take possession of the positions which are important for our fleet and the Luftwaffe. If we succeed in occupying and securing Holland and Belgium and knocking out France, that would create the basis for a successful war against England. Time is on our side against England. Germany cannot bleed to death on land. Important is the ruthless employment of all means. The aim is always to bring England to her knees."

Shortly after Hitler had explained his views they took tangible form in the Army. The Commander in Chief of the Army, Walther von Brauchitsch, gave detailed instructions to the Army groups for the conduct of the forthcoming operations. The order begins with the words: "The objective of the operations is the destruction of the Polish Army. Our political leadership demands that the war should open with severe surprise blows leading to rapid success."

Concurrent with these secret preparations, the "psychological warfare" was launched at full strength by Propaganda Minister Goebbels. On March 26, 1939, ten days after Hitler's entry into Prague, Goebbels issued to the German press the first reports of "excesses against German nationals in Poland." The world had meanwhile learned the meaning of such statements. Two days after Dr. Goebbels' propaganda story there was already a new focus of crisis in Europe. At its center was the Free City of Danzig, a political hybrid created in 1920, an old bone of contention between Germany and Poland. Danzig was under the international supervision of the League of Nations, but both Germany and Poland strove to add it to their country's territory. It was the fuse of the powder barrel. Joseph Beck, the Polish Foreign Minister, reacted quickly and irritably to Goebbels' propaganda attack. On March 28, 1939, he announced to the German ambassador in Warsaw, Count Helmuth von Moltke, that "any intervention of the German government aimed at an alteration in the existing status of Danzig would be regarded as an attack upon Poland." Beck announced immediate countermeasures on the part of the Polish government, but at the same time expressed his readiness to start talks.

"You want us to negotiate at bayonet point," Moltke said indignantly.

Beck replied coolly, "According to your usual method!"

With regard to the outbreak of the war, the Nuremberg Trial encountered problems which held surprises for all participants. The judges of the four victorious nations looked forward uneasily to the things that were now bound to be disclosed. The Soviet judges, Major General Iola T. Nikitchenko and Lieutenant Colonel Alexander F. Volkhkov, displayed, as always, inscrutable faces. But the Soviet prosecution, under their chief Lieutenant General Roman A. Rudenko, were prepared to oppose the German defending counsels: they wanted at any price to prevent things being brought to light by which the Soviet Union might be brought down to the same level as the defendant.

In order to understand this underlying conflict certain events must be remembered which all participants of the Trial remembered well enough, but which were scarcely mentioned:

1. Poland guessed that she would be Hitler's next victim. She was determined to defend herself. In Warsaw, however, they overestimated their own strength and underestimated the striking power of the new German army.

2. In London and Paris it was recognized that Poland could not be effectively helped from the West if she were attacked by Germany. The only Power that could help Poland against Hitler was the Soviet Union, because it bordered Poland in the East.

3. That help was emphatically declined in Warsaw. The Polish Government rightly recognized that in this way they would jump out of the frying pan into the fire—instead of Hitler, Stalin would eventually swallow up Poland.

4. In London and Paris this consequence was also considered. If Hitler went to war, so they reasoned, then after his defeat—about which they were quite confident—the Soviet Union would lay its hands upon the remains of eastern Europe. That was certainly not the wish of the West.

5. The only possible way of preventing an expansion of the Soviet Union toward the West lay in avoiding war. The West would have to collaborate with Moscow to dissuade Hitler from an attack on Poland.

6. In Moscow they were of exactly the same opinion. Only they drew different conclusions. If Hitler were dissuaded from going to war with Poland, the Soviet Union could not expand toward the West. Therefore Hitler must be encouraged to attack Poland.

On the basis of these ruthless political considerations the war machine was mercilessly prepared for action. Hitler, however, was unable to appreciate or understand the mental processes of the leading minds of the West or East. He could not follow their line of thought because it assumed his overthrow, and he never took this decisive point into his calculations.

In politically sensitive Rome, they were much more farseeing than in Berlin. The Italian ambassador in Berlin, Bernardo Attolico, was a brilliant expert on Germany's internal affairs. He did not believe a word of Hitler's protestations for peace, and was convinced that he was leading Italy by the nose. This corresponded exactly to the facts. When Hitler had at length decided on war, he convinced his ally Mussolini of his intention to keep the peace for at least another three years. Attolico, however, bombarded his government with so many warnings that the Italian Foreign Minister, Count Galeazzo Ciano, wrote in his famous diaries, "The persistence of Attolico makes me doubtful. Either he has lost his head completely, or he sees and knows something of which we have no inkling."

Ciano went to see Ribbentrop in an attempt at saving the peace, or at least at finding out Germany's real intentions. The meeting took place on August 11, 1939, at Ribbentrop's castle of Fuschl near Salzburg. Ciano, from the very beginning of the talks, was overwhelmed with unalterable facts by his German colleague. Ribbentrop tore aside the curtain of peace and allowed the Italian to see the naked, terrible reality. In Nuremberg, Sir David Maxwell Fyfe read out the dramatic extracts from Count Ciano's diary.

"It was in his castle of Fuschl, while we were waiting to sit down at table, that Ribbentrop told me of the decision to light the fuse of the powder keg, just as though he were telling me the most trivial and banal matter.

" 'Tell me, Ribbentrop,' I asked while we were walking together through his garden, 'what do you want? The Corridor or Danzig?'

" 'Neither any longer,' he replied. 'We want war.' "

This statement hit Ciano like a blow. In his report to Rome he wrote: "I pointed out how the present conditions of European politics appear to make the armed intervention of France and England inevitable, but in vain." To his diary he confided: "They are convinced that France and Britain will watch the murder of Poland without lifting a finger. On this Ribbentrop wanted to lay a wager with me during one of the gloomy meals I shared with him at a Salzburg hotel. If the English and French remained neutral I was to give him an Italian painting, if they entered the war he promised me a collection of antique weapons."

What had Ribbentrop to say about this on the witness stand?

SIR DAVID: You will no doubt remember that according to Count Ciano's diary he asked you, "What do you want, the Corridor or Danzig?" Then you looked at him and answered, "Neither—we want war." Do you remember?

RIBBENTROP: That is completely untrue. I said to Count Ciano at that time, "The Führer is determined to solve this problem one way or another." That was the phrasing that I had from the Führer. That I should have said we want war is absurd, for it is clear to any diplomat that one would say nothing of the kind, not even to one's best and most trusted colleague, and certainly not to Count Ciano.

Ciano learned the facts next day in Berchtesgaden from Hitler himself. As he wrote in his diary, "It was soon clear to me that nothing further was to be done. Hitler had decided to strike, and he would strike. Our protests would not deter him in the slightest. He now listens with but slight attention and is unmoved when I speak to him of the distress that a war would bring to the Italian people."

There was alarm in Rome. It was not certain that Hitler wanted war. Mussolini's first reaction to this information was a plan to break off all connections with Germany in order to keep Italy out of the forthcoming conflict. On the other hand, he feared Hitler's wrath, which might express itself in a military operation against Italy.

In order to keep out of the war Italy made an excuse of her shortage of raw materials. Hitler seemed to suspect what was going on in Rome. In a letter he asked Mussolini with what raw materials Germany could help Italy. Mussolini believed that this was a good loophole for him, and concocted with his experts a list of things which could not possibly be supplied by Germany. It comprised seventy million tons of the scarcest and dearest raw materials which would have required seventeen thousand freight trains for their transport from Germany to Italy. Late at night

Mussolini sat up with his Foreign Minister and son-in-law Ciano, completing the crazy catalogue. Ciano wrote in his diary: "We prepared the list: it would kill a bull if he could read it."

The extravagant document took the breadth away from the economic experts who read it in Berlin. "And when does Italy require all these raw materials?" Ambassador Attolico was cautiously asked. The Italian smiled and asked for the impossible with a single word: "*Subito*—at once."

Thus it became evident that the Italians could not be counted on, at least not at the outbreak of war. But now that seemed no longer important to Hitler. For in the meantime an event had occurred that shook the whole world like a bomb. Ribbentrop had flown to Moscow, and signed a treaty between Hitler and Stalin. Mussolini was thus unexpectedly pushed back to third place in the game of power politics.

In Nuremberg, the Soviet prosecutors took up defense positions. The pact between Hitler and Stalin and their joint seizure of Poland must have put the Soviet judges of the International Tribunal in a most difficult spot, and the prosecutors and judges of the other three victorious powers in an extremely embarrassing position.

What was the historical truth of the matter? Since August 12, 1939, British and French military leaders had been in conference with the Soviet Marshal Klement Voroshilov in Moscow. They wanted to bring about a treaty between the West and the Soviet Union. This pact was to protect Poland and discourage Hitler from further actions. The negotiations dragged on. Voroshilov stood by the militarily logical point of view that in case of war the Red Army could only march against Hitler if it were allowed to march through Poland. But that was refused, as usual, by the government in Warsaw.

As the talks came to a dead end on this point, the danger had been recognized in Berlin: a treaty between Britain, France, and the Soviet Union would have frustrated Hitler's plans. He saw only one solution; namely, for him to seek a treaty with the Soviet Union. The matter was broached by means of trade discussions which had been going on between Berlin and Moscow for some time.

On August 16, 1939, Ribbentrop proposed a visit to Moscow. The German ambassador accredited to the Kremlin, Count Werner Schulenberg, discussed it with the Soviet Foreign Minister, Molotov. But Molotov would not accept the idea. A treaty between the deadly ideological enemies, Communism and National Socialism, was unthinkable to him. But Stalin intervened. He was a much better chess player and saw many more moves ahead than his hidebound Foreign Minister. He instructed Molotov to invite the German ambassador to visit him, and to tell him that the Soviet government was prepared to receive Ribbentrop and to conclude a pact with him. At a secret meeting of the Politburo on August 19, 1939, Stalin delivered a speech in which he said:

> We are absolutely convinced that if we conclude a treaty of alliance with France and Britain, Germany will feel constrained to hold back from Poland. In this way war could be avoided, but the subsequent development could assume a character very dangerous to us. On the other hand, Germany, if we accept her proposal for a nonaggression pact, will certainly attack Poland, and the intervention of France and England would be inevitable. Under these circumstances we should have the best chance to remain out of the conflict, and could wait with advantage until it is our turn. That is exactly what suits our interest best. Therefore our decision is clear: we must accept the German offer, and send the Franco-British mission home with a polite refusal. I repeat that it is to our advantage if war breaks out between the Reich and the Anglo-French bloc. It is important for us that the war lasts as long as possible so that the two groups exhaust themselves. In the meantime we must intensify the political work in the warring countries so that we are well prepared when the war comes to an end.

Stalin's concept was fiendish, but none the less his reasoning was superior to that of Berlin, London, and Paris. Two days after the decisive meeting of the Politburo, the British-French Military Mission was sent home. And two days later, on August 23, 1939, Ribbentrop concluded the nonaggression pact between Germany and the Soviet Union in Moscow. The world was amazed at the sensational news, but it could never guess what lay behind it.

Exactly two years later, on August 23, 1941, two months after the beginning of the murderous war between Germany and the Soviet Union, Stalin said in a public speech: "One might ask: how could it happen that the Soviet government could conclude a nonagression pact with such faithless men and monsters as Hitler and Ribbentrop? Was an error committed? Of course not. A nonagression pact is a peace pact. I think no peace-loving country can refuse a peaceful agreement with a neighboring country, even when monsters and cannibals like Hitler and Ribbentrop are at the head of that country."

With these notable words Stalin tried to get his head out of the noose before the world. The Soviet prosecutors and judges at Nuremberg, however, could not get away with it so easily. The German defense lawyers in 1945–46 had no knowledge of Stalin's speech to the Politburo, which was only later made accessible to German historians. The defense had to confine itself to another document which was even more serious. It concerned the secret codicil to the nonaggression pact signed in Moscow. In this, the spoils of the forthcoming war against Poland were divided between Germany and the Soviet Union, termed "Delimitation of the Mutual Spheres of Interest in Eastern Europe" in the document:

> In the event of a territorial-political organization of the Baltic States (Finland, Estonia, Latvia, Lithuania), the northern boundary of Latvia will also be the boundary of the spheres of interest of Germany and the U.S.S.R. In the event of a territorial-political organization in districts belonging to the Polish state, the spheres of interest of Germany and the U.S.S.R. will be divided by the approximate line of the rivers Narev, Vistula, and San. With regard to southeast Europe, the Soviet interest in Bessarabia is stressed; Germany, on the other hand, reaffirms her complete lack of political interest in these regions.

The document, signed by Molotov and Ribbentrop, ends with the words: "This protocol will be kept in strictest secrecy by both sides."

In fact it remained secret till March 1946. About this time the German defense counsel in Nuremberg learned for the first time of its existence. The rumor spread through the Palace of Justice; in the rooms of the attorneys its effect was sensational. For the lawyers it meant that one of the adjudicating nations was guilty of a deed with which the defendants were being charged: preparations for a war of aggression. If it could be shown that the Soviet Union was a party to Hitler's war of aggression, then the whole Trial would collapse.

The wanderings of that secret document remained a mystery until the late 1950s. The defense counsel for Rudolf Hess, Dr. Alfred Seidl, who obtained the document in 1946, kept his knowledge to himself at the time. In March 1946, so Dr. Seidl revealed later, he got into conversation with an American journalist during a recess at Nuremberg. The latter had excellent connections with the Washington State Department, and managed to get a photostat of the document for Dr. Seidl.

Seidl was startled. No doubt chance had tossed a juridical atom bomb in his lap; he later came to the conclusion that the State Department had played with him the traditional game of "international leakage." At any rate, he hurried to Ribbentrop, who declared the document as genuine. The ambassador Dr. Friedrich Gaus, who was present in Nuremberg as a witness, also testified to the authenticity of the document. Next, Seidl approached the British prosecutor, Sir David Maxwell-Fyfe, who also recognized its importance and gave the lawyer the excellent advice that he should take it to the Soviet prosecuting officials. Seidl did so. He sought a meeting with the chief Russian prosecutor, Roman Rudenko, but was only able to speak to the assistant prosecutor, N. D. Zorya—the man who a little later, while the Nuremberg Trial was still on, shot himself "while cleaning his rifle." Zorya told Seidl: "The Soviet delegation does not see any reason for talking about the subject." Perhaps he spoke in good faith, and only after the "bomb" had been placed in the courtroom did General Rudenko learn, by inquiring in Moscow, that there really had been a secret codicil to the German-Soviet treaty.

On March 25, 1946, Dr. Seidl lit the fuse without any warning.

DR. SEIDL: A week before the outbreak of the war and three days before the planned invasion of Poland, a secret agreement was reached between Germany and the Soviet Union.

THE PRESIDENT: Dr. Seidl, I hope you have not forgotten the

rule of the Court that this is not the proper place for making a speech.

DR. SEIDL: I have no intention of making a speech, but I intend to make some introductory remarks about a document which I shall submit to the Court.

THE PRESIDENT: Dr. Seidl, we have not yet seen the document. Have you a copy for the prosecuting attorneys? Have the representatives of the defendants any objection to this document being read?

RUDENKO: Mr. President, I know nothing of the existence of such a document, and I oppose its reading. I do not know what secrets, what secret agreement the defending counsel of Herr Hess is talking about. I therefore request you not to permit the reading of the document.

DR. SEIDL: Under these circumstances I am forced to invite the Foreign Minister of the Soviet Union, Mr. Molotov, to attend as a witness.

THE PRESIDENT: Dr. Seidl, the first thing we must do is to have the document translated. We do not know what it contains.

DR. SEIDL: The document contains . . .

THE PRESIDENT: No; the Court is not prepared to hear from you what is in the document. We wish to see the document ourselves, in English and also in Russian. When that has been done we can deal with the matter.

But Dr. Seidl chose another course. On April 1, 1946, he questioned Ribbentrop as a witness.

DR. SEIDL: The preamble to the secret treaty signed on August 23, 1939, between Germany and the Soviet Union ran something like this: "In view of the present tension between Germany and Poland, in the event of a conflict the following has been agreed."

RIBBENTROP: I don't remember the exact words, but in general it went like that.

THE PRESIDENT: Dr. Seidl, what document are you reading from?

RUDENKO: I should like to remind the Court that we are not here to discuss questions about the policies of the Allied Powers, but we are here to deal with concrete accusations against the

German chief war criminals, and the questions of the defense counsel are only an attempt to distract the attention of the Court. I therefore consider it right to reject such questions as irrelevant.

THE PRESIDENT: Dr. Seidl, you may put the question.

By this decision of the President, Dr. Seidl was able to pursue the matter at last. Ribbentrop took up the story and said: "It was agreed that the eastern parts of Poland would be occupied by Soviet troops, the western by German troops. There is no doubt that Stalin could never reproach Germany with a war of aggression against Poland; for when it comes to talking about an attack, this was carried out by both sides."

With this statement, however, the sensation was over. On two more occasions, Dr. Seidl attempted to throw the secret codicil into the balance, but its final rejection by the Court was inevitable, with good reason: Seidl steadfastly refused to disclose how he had obtained the document. Thus it was for the Tribunal to regard it as "evidence of doubtful origin," and to refuse its acceptance for that reason.

Dr. Seidl's argument—that the Soviets, as fellow criminals, could not be judges as well—therefore fell flat. The Trial continued, but the secret document has since found entry into the history books as a historical fact.

No one knew that better than Hitler. For the ink of the signatures on that document was hardly dry when he started the war— but a couple of hours later he suddenly canceled the order to attack.

What had happened? For some mysterious reason Europe was given a few more days' grace. In Nuremberg, Birger Dahlerus, as Goering's chief witness, was questioned about this incident.

THE LAST HOPES

"Two speeches which Hitler delivered in Obersalzberg to the senior officers of the army on August 22, 1939, were found among the papers of the Supreme Command of the Army in Flensburg," declared the American prosecutor, Sidney S. Alderman, at Nuremberg. The important parts of Hitler's speeches were read out in the courtroom.

"I have called you together to give you some insight into the factors upon which my decision to act is based. It has been clear to me that sooner or later there would be a conflict with Poland. I made up my mind early this year." He made it quite clear to those present why he had decided to attack Poland now: "My reasons are—my own personality and that of Mussolini. Much depends on me, on my existence, on my political ability. Never again in the future will there be a man with more authority than I have. My existence is thus a great factor. But I may at any time be struck down by some criminal, by some madman. The second personal factor is the Duce. His existence, too, is decisive. The Duce is the man with the strongest nerves in all Italy. On the side of our opponents the picture is negative, so far as authoritative personalities are concerned. In England and France there are no personalities of any stature. Our opponents have leaders who are below average. No masters, no men of action.

"Apart from the personal factor the political situation is favorable for us. All these favorable conditions will no longer exist in two or three years. No one knows how long I shall live. Therefore, any conflict should be solved now. Relations with Poland have become unbearable. An attempt on my life or that of Mussolini could alter the position to our disadvantage. Now there is still a good chance that the West will not intervene. We must take the decision upon ourselves with ruthless determination. I am only concerned lest at the last moment some blackguard proposes a plan of mediation."

On the same day he developed his plans in a second speech to the same circle. "A long spell of peace will not benefit us. Thus it is necessary to reckon with every possibility. First of all, Poland must be finished. I shall supply a propaganda reason for starting the war, never mind whether it is plausible or not. The victor will not be asked afterward whether he spoke the truth or not. When the war is started and carried through, right doesn't matter; only victory matters. Hearts must be closed to sympathy. Brutal action. Might is right. Utmost severity. First requisite: drive through to the Vistula and the Narev. Our technical superiority will break the nerves of the Poles. Every flicker of Polish strength that might show itself must be snuffed out. Persistent attrition. Complete destruction of Poland is the military objective. Speed is the main thing. Pursuit to the point of complete annihilation. Beginning of hostilities to be ordered later, probably Saturday morning."

"Goering replied to the Führer with thanks and the assurance that the Army would do its duty." With that, the document ended.

On August 25, 1939, as he had forecast, Hitler issued the order to the Army that they should open the attack on Poland at 4:45 A.M. the next morning. But in the evening he suddenly canceled this order. The position had changed unexpectedly: news had come from London that Britain had concluded an alliance with Poland, which was quite clearly directed against a German attack. This made Hitler hold his horses for a moment. He himself had meanwhile concluded his pact with Russia, but the decision of the British Government to help Poland in the event of aggression made him hesitate. He took up an idea that he had discussed with his senior officers on May 23, 1939: "The task is to isolate Poland. To achieve her isolation is vital." Was there still a chance of driving a wedge between Poland and Britain? In other words: could he persuade the British Government, in spite of their alliance, to witness the destruction without acting?

At that moment, a man entered the stage of world politics who had never been heard of before. He was the Swedish engineer and industrialist, Birger Dahlerus, a private individual. Years before he had once met Hermann Goering; now, in Europe's great crisis, he thought that he could prevent a world war with his slender power. Six years later he was called to Nuremberg by Goering to give evidence as a witness for the defense. First he was interrogated by Goering's defense counsel, Dr. Otto Stahmer.

DR. STAHMER: Herr Dahlerus, will you tell the Court how as a private individual and a Swede you came to attempt an understanding between England and Germany?

DAHLERUS: I knew England very well as I had lived there for twelve years, and I also knew Germany very well. During a visit to England at the end of July 1939, I found everywhere an absolute determination that the British people would tolerate no further act of aggression by Germany. I considered it my duty, and a very worthwhile thing, to convey this definite British attitude to the highest circles in Germany. After I had discussed the advisability of a journey to Germany with my friends I set off, and had an audience with Goering on July 6, at four in the afternoon at Karinhall. I told Goering what I had heard in England, and appealed to him in the strongest terms that every effort should be made to avoid the possibility of a war. I proposed to him that a meeting should be arranged in which he and several other members of the German Government would have the opportunity to meet Englishmen who could be completely trusted.

On the eighth of July I received Goering's reply that Hitler was favorable to the plan. The meeting took place in Sönke-Nissen-Koog in Schleswig-Holstein, near the Danish border. The house belongs to my wife; seven Englishmen, Goering, General Bodenschatz, and Dr. Schöttl were present. That was on August 7, and the meeting began with Goering asking the Englishmen to put any questions to him.

The Englishmen left no one in doubt that if Germany should attempt to occupy foreign territory, the British Empire would stand by Poland. Goering declared upon his honor as a statesman and a soldier that although he commanded, and might be tempted to lead into battle, the strongest air force in the world, he would do everything in his power to prevent a war.

The Englishmen who had been present left Germany on the morning of August 9, and upon their return reported immediately to the Foreign Office. On August 21 I learned that a trade agreement had been concluded between Russia and Germany. Next day this was extended to an agreement to cover other political questions. On August 23 I was requested by Goering, via telephone, if possible to come at once to Berlin.

DR. STAHMER: Did he mention the urgency of the situation in this talk?

DAHLERUS: Yes, Goering said that the situation in the meantime had become very serious.

He was right, considering that only a day before Hitler had already fixed the beginning of hostilities for August 26.

DR. STAHMER: When did you meet Goering?

DAHLERUS: I reached Berlin on August 24 and met Goering in the afternoon. He told me that the position had become very serious, because any agreement between Poland and Germany had become impossible. He asked me if I would go to London and explain the situation.

DR. STAHMER: When did you travel to London?

DAHLERUS: On the next morning, August 25, a Friday. Late in the afternoon I had an important meeting with Lord Halifax. He informed me that Henderson, the British Ambassador in Berlin, had spoken with Hitler the same day. Lord Halifax expressed the opinion that an agreement was quite possible, and that he did not believe that my services would be required any further.

The date is important. It was August 25, on which day Hitler issued the order to attack in the morning, and canceled it in the evening after the announcement of the British-Polish Alliance.

DR. STAHMER: Did you have a telephone conversation with Goering the same evening?

DAHLERUS: Yes. About eight in the evening Goering informed me that the situation had become extremely difficult, and begged me to do everything I could to arrange a conference between representatives of England and Germany. I met Lord Halifax again on Saturday, August 26. I urged him to stress to the German Government that the British Government desired an understanding. I suggested that he should write a letter to Goering. I would travel immediately to Berlin and hand it over personally. Lord Halifax consulted Chamberlain and then wrote a most explicit letter in which he stated, clearly and distinctly, that His Majesty's Government desired to find a peaceful solution.

DR. STAHMER: Did you fly back with the letter to Berlin?

DAHLERUS: Yes, I reached Berlin in the evening. I met Goering in his railway train. I told him how things looked in London, and emphasized that there was no doubt that if Germany marched on Danzig, she would at once find herself at war with England. When I had told him this I gave him the letter. He opened it, and after he had read it he put it before me and asked me to translate it exactly, as it was of great importance that he should understand the contents accurately. He sent for his adjutant at once, stopped the train at the next station, and declared that in his opinion Hitler should at once be told of the contents of this letter.

I followed him to Berlin by car, and we reached the Chancellery at the stroke of midnight. Goering went in at once to talk to Hitler and I went to my hotel. About a quarter past twelve I had a visit from two officers who asked me to come with them to Hitler. I was received by him at once; he was alone with Goering.

Hitler began in his usual manner, explaining German politics to me at length. That lasted about twenty minutes, and I believed that my visit had been fruitless. While he was cursing England and the English I interrupted him and said that I had lived in Britain as a worker, as engineer, and as the director of industrial firms, that I knew the English people very well, and that I could not agree with his opinions.

The result was a long discussion. He asked many questions about England and the English people. Then he began to tell me how well the German forces were equipped. He seemed to grow very excited, strode about the room, and finally told me in a very agitated state that if it came to a war he would build U-boats, U-boats, and still more U-boats. He spoke as though he was not conscious that anyone was still in the room. After a time he screamed that he would build aircraft, aircraft, and still more aircraft, and that he would win the war. Eventually he quieted down, and asked me to go to London at once and expound his point of view there.

In fact, Dahlerus did fly back to London. He took with him some absurd offers of Hitler's such as: "England should help Germany with the annexation of Danzig and the Polish Corridor, and Germany would promise to defend the British Empire with the German Army, wherever it may be attacked . . . Germany wishes to conclude a treaty or alliance with England."

Dahlerus flew several times more to and fro between London and Berlin—quite fruitlessly, for he did not perceive that he was only a tool for Hitler's attempt to divert Britain from carrying out her treaty obligations, and to "isolate Poland." This was the very point which the British prosecutor, Sir David Maxwell-Fyfe, raised when he later cross-examined Dahlerus.

SIR DAVID: I would like to ask you to tell the Court one or two things which Goering did not discuss with you. He told you—or did he?—that two days earlier, on August 22, Hitler had announced to him and the other German leaders at Obersalzberg that a conflict with Poland was unavoidable.

DAHLERUS: I never received any indication or information about political intentions.

SIR DAVID: Did he tell you that the decision had been made to attack Poland on the morning of August 26?

DAHLERUS: No, not in any way.

SIR DAVID: Did Goering ever tell you why the plan of attack was put off from the 26th to the 30th of August?

DAHLERUS: No, he never said anything about plans of attack.

SIR DAVID: Now I want you to speak for a few moments about the German Foreign Minister. In general, I believe, you had the impression that Ribbentrop did everything he could to hinder and frustrate your efforts.

DAHLERUS: That is true.

SIR DAVID: But according to Goering's statement he did even more. If you remember, you were about to take leave of Goering, I believe, as you set off on your last visit to London. "Before we parted," you wrote in your book, [*The Last Attempt*] "he said that he would take the opportunity to thank me, in case we did not meet again. I was somewhat surprised at this parting and could not abstain from replying that in all probability we should meet again soon. Goering's expression changed, and he said solemnly, 'Perhaps certain people will do what they can to prevent you from coming out of this affair alive.' " And you write further, "At a meeting in October of the same year Goering said to me that Ribbentrop had tried to arrange that my plane would crash.

Hence Goering's serious expression when we parted." So much for the Foreign Minister.

Edouard Daladier, France's Premier, appealed to Hitler in a personal letter of August 26: "You were, like myself, a front-line fighter in the last war. You know as I do what horror and condemnation the devastations of war leave in the consciences of the nations, no matter how the war ends. . . ."

The French ambassador in Berlin, Robert Coulondre, took the letter to Hitler on the same evening. After the interview he returned to the embassy in deep depression, and wrote to Paris: "For forty minutes I commented on the Premier's moving letter. I said everything that my heart urged me to say as a man and a Frenchman, to persuade the Chancellor to agree to a very last attempt toward a peaceful settlement. . . . But I could not influence him. His mind was already made up."

"In this decisive hour," the Frenchman said to Hitler, "you are facing the judgment of history. Do not spill the blood of the soldiers, the women, and children."

A few seconds passed in silence. Then Coulondre heard Hitler murmur: "Ah, the women and children, I often think of them." Then he took Ribbentrop by the arm, and led him to a corner of the large room. "I lived through several minutes of mad hopes," Coulondre continued.

"It is no use," Hitler said finally. The interview was over.

In fact the situation was completely hopeless; only Britain still hoped to be able to arbitrate. London tried to bring about direct talks between Berlin and Warsaw, and Hitler pretended to be playing the game because it was still his aim to "isolate Poland." Poland had the example of the Czech President Hácha still vivid in her memory. Any representative who went from Warsaw to Berlin would in the end be subjected to pressure and would have to capitulate. So it was decided in Poland that it was better to fight—"even if we have to go under."

A heroic decision—and yet fatal; because in Warsaw the secret treaty between Berlin and Moscow was still unknown, because no one dreamed of Hitler's far-reaching plans, because the Polish Army believed that it could hold out against the German Wehrmacht, and because the Polish General Staff assumed that France would march at once and break through the German West Wall as if it were a matchbox. And so it was easy for Hitler to make out that "he had waited in vain for a Polish representative with full powers."

Ribbentrop went a step further. In a midnight meeting on August 30, he read to the British ambassador the peace proposals "which Germany would have put forward if a Polish representative had come." Ambassador Nevile Henderson wrote about the meeting: "I said to Herr von Ribbentrop that His Majesty's Government would do their best to arrange consultations. Herr von Ribbentrop's answer was to bring out a lengthy document, which he read out in German loudly and at high speed." Henderson was unable to understand the contents. "When I asked Herr von Ribbentrop for the text of these proposals," he wrote, "he stated that it was now too late, as Poland's representative had not reached Berlin by midnight."

In the Nuremberg Court, this affair was echoed in a statement by Birger Dahlerus:

"I called up Forbes of the British Embassy. He told me that Ribbentrop had refused to hand over the note after he had read it through a great speed. I went at once to Goering and told him that this was impossible, that one could not treat the ambassador of a world power in such a manner. I proposed to him that he should allow me to call up Forbes and tell him the contents of the note over the telephone."

DR. STAHMER: Did Goering stress the fact that he would assume a heavy responsibility if he gave you this permission?

DAHLERUS: Yes, indeed. I met Henderson on the Thursday morning, August 31, and talked to him about the note, and he urged me to call on the Polish ambassador, Lipski, without delay, and give him a copy.

DR. STAHMER: Did that happen?

DAHLERUS: He sent Forbes with me to Lipski, and I read out the note to Lipski; but he did not seem to understand the contents. I therefore left the room, dictated the note to a secretary, and handed it to him. In the meantime, Lipski told Forbes that he was not interested in discussing this note with the German Government. If it came to a war between Poland and Germany he knew that a revolution would break out in Germany and that the Poles would march on Berlin. Lipski was as white as a sheet, and acted in an extremely nervous and depressed manner.

SIR DAVID: Mr. Lipski was suffering under great stress during these very critical days?

DAHLERUS: He was very nervous.

SIR DAVID: And did not Sir George Forbes say that Mr. Lipski had expressed very clearly his view that the German offer was a violation of Polish sovereignty, and that Poland, if it were left alone, would fight alone and die alone? Was that the state of mind in which Lipski then was?

DAHLERUS: Yes.

DR. STAHMER: Then on September 1 you met Goering again?

DAHLERUS: Yes. After some hesitation he told me that war had broken out because the Poles had attacked the radio station of Gleiwitz and blown up a bridge at Dirschau. Later he gave me details from which I concluded that the entire German Army had been thrown into the attack on Poland.

The radio station of Gleiwitz, the bridge at Dirschau—these are the incidents of which Hitler had spoken to his commanders: "I shall supply a propaganda reason for starting the war, never mind whether it is plausible or not." The evidence which was produced in Nuremberg about these incidents might have come from the criminal annals of the police. But before they were placed before the Court, Dahlerus concluded his evidence.

SIR DAVID: I now ask you once more to open your own book. There is a description of the meeting on September 1, the afternoon of the day on which Poland was attacked. You write, "For him,"—that is, Goering—"everything was settled according to a plan which could no longer be canceled. He summoned the Secretaries of State, Körner and Gritzbach, gave them a long lecture, and presented each of them with a sword of honor which, he hoped, they would carry to glory in the war. One had the impression that all these people were in a state of drunkenness." Are those your words?

DAHLERUS: Yes. Their mental condition had changed in a very short time.

SIR DAVID: In other words: of the three leading people in Germany the Chancellor was an abnormal person, the Marshal was in an advanced state of drunkenness, and the Foreign Minister—according to Goering—was a murderer who wanted to make your aircraft crash. Many thanks.

FOUR FORTY-FIVE A.M.

At 4:50 on the morning of September 1, 1939, Major Sucharski, Commander of the Polish troops on the Westerplatte, near Danzig, reported by radio to Warsaw: "At 4:45 A.M., the battleship *Schleswig-Holstein* opened fire on the Westerplatte with all her guns. The firing continues."

That was the first news item which told the world that the war had begun. At the same time, the German Army, by Hitler's command, had left their forward positions and advanced on all fronts into Poland. At 10:00 A.M., Hitler delivered a speech in the Reichstag; it made the blood freeze in the veins of a good many Germans:

"Last night, for the first time, regular Polish soldiers fired their weapons on our soil. Since five forty-five"—and here in his ecstatic oratory he erred by an hour—"the fire has been returned, and from now on bomb will be repaid with bomb."

Polish soldiers had invaded German territory and fired their arms—that was, according to Hitler's words, the cause of the war! It was the cause of which he had already spoken to his commanders on August 22, 1939: "I shall supply a propaganda reason for starting the war, never mind whether it is plausible or not."

On the Nuremberg witness stand sat the former General Erwin Lahousen. Slowly he repeated the words of the oath which the president read out to him. The examination was conducted by the American prosecutor, John Harlan Amen.

AMEN: Where were you trained?

LAHOUSEN: In Austria, in the Military Academy in Wiener Neustadt.

AMEN: And you were assigned to the Intelligence Division?

LAHOUSEN: I entered the Austrian Intelligence Department, which corresponded to the Abwehr in the German army.

AMEN: After the Anschluss, what position did you assume?

LAHOUSEN: I was automatically taken into the High Command of the German Armed Forces, where I did the same work. I was then a member of the Abwehr and my chief was Admiral Canaris.

AMEN: Admiral Canaris was your immediate superior? From time to time did you act as his personal representative?

LAHOUSEN: Yes.

AMEN: Did Canaris keep a diary?

LAHOUSEN: Yes. Even before the beginning of the war—a diary to which I personally had to contribute and did contribute much.

AMEN: What was the purpose of Canaris in keeping such a diary?

LAHOUSEN: As a truthful answer to this question, I must repeat what Canaris himself said to me on this subject: "the purpose and intention of this diary is to portray to the German people and to the world, at some future date, the leaders who are now guiding the fate of our nation."

AMEN: And did you keep copies of the entries which you made in Canaris' diary?

LAHOUSEN: Yes, I kept copies, with Canaris' knowledge and approval.

AMEN: Was the Wehrmacht ever asked to furnish any assistance for the Polish campaign?

LAHOUSEN: Yes. . . . The name of this undertaking which took place just before the Polish campaign was "Undertaking Himmler."

AMEN: Will you explain to the Tribunal the nature of the assistance required?

LAHOUSEN: The affair on which I am now giving testimony was one of the most mysterious actions which took place within the Amt Ausland-Abwehr Division. I, as well as my Division, Division

II. . . . I believe it was in the middle of August, were given the task of providing Polish uniforms and equipment, such as identification cards and so on, for an undertaking Himmler. This request . . . was received by Canaris from the Wehrmacht operations staff or from the National Defense Department. . . . The name, Himmler, however, spoke for itself.

AMEN: To whom was the Polish material to be furnished by the Abwehr?

LAHOUSEN: The articles of equipment had to be kept in readiness, and one day some man from the SS or the SD—the name is in the official diary of the division—collected them.

AMEN: Did you . . . find out from Canaris what in fact had happened?

LAHOUSEN: The actual course of events was the following: When the first Wehrmacht communiqué spoke of the attack of Polish units on German territory, Piekenbrock, holding the communiqué in his hand, and reading it aloud, observed that now we knew why our uniforms were needed. On the same day or a few days later, I cannot say exactly, Canaris informed us that people from concentration camps had been disguised in these uniforms and had been ordered to make a military attack on the radio station at Gleiwitz.

AMEN: Did you ever find out what happened to the men from the concentration camp who wore the Polish uniforms and created the incident?

LAHOUSEN: It is strange . . . after the capitulation I spoke about these matters with an SS Hauptsturmführer—he was a Viennese—in the hospital where both of us were staying, and I asked him for details on what had taken place. The man—his name was Birkel—told me, "So far as I know, even all members of the SD who took part in the action were put out of the way, that is, killed." That was the last I heard of this matter.

A statement by the former SD member, Naujocks, was even more damning:

I, Alfred Naujocks, make the following statement under oath. From 1931 to October 19, 1944, I was a member of the SS and from its formation in the year 1934 a member of the SD. I served as a member of the Armed SS from February 1941 to the middle of 1942. About the 10th August 1939 Heydrich, the chief of the SD, ordered me to carry out an attack on the radio station at Gleiwitz near the Polish border, and to make it appear as though Poles had been the attackers. Heydrich said to me: "A realistic excuse for the attack on Poland is necessary for the foreign press and for German propaganda." My order was to seize the radio station and to hold it long enough so that a Polish-speaking German was able to deliver a speech in Polish over the radio. This Polish-speaking German was put at my disposal. Heydrich told me he would say in his speech that the time had come for a showdown between Poland and Germany, and that the Poles were united and any Germans who opposed them would be struck down. Heydrich then told me that he expected Germany to attack Poland in a few days.

Between the 25th and 31st of August I sought out Heinrich Müller, the chief of the Gestapo, who was then in the neighborhood of Oppeln. In my presence Müller arranged with a man called Mehlhorn plans for a border incident which should look as though Polish soldiers were attacking German troops. This other affair was to occur at a place which, I believe, was called Hohenlinden. Germans to the number of about a company were used. Müller said he had about twelve or thirteen condemned prisoners, who would be made to put on Polish uniforms, and whose corpses would be left at the scene of the incident to show that they had been killed during the attack. To this end a fatal injection was provided, which would be prepared by a doctor under Heydrich's orders; bullet wounds should also be inflicted on them. Müller told me he had orders to put one of these criminals at my disposal for my action at Gleiwitz. The code name by which he called these men was "Canned Goods."

The incident in Gleiwitz, in which I took part, was carried out on the evening before the German attack on Poland. At midday on August 31 Heydrich gave me by telephone the code word that the attack was to take place on the same evening at eight o'clock. Heydrich said: "Report to Müller for the canned goods to carry out the action."

I did this, and told Müller to deliver the man to me near the radio station. I got the man, and left him lying at the entrance to the radio station. He was still alive, but no longer conscious. I did not see any rifle wounds, only a lot of blood smeared all over his face. We took the radio station as ordered, had a speech of three or four minutes delivered over an emergency transmitter, fired off some revolver shots, and left the place.

That was the "Polish" attack on the Gleiwitz radio station, and that was how Hitler's war began. As could only be expected, Britain and France stood by their treaty obligations, even if at first these were merely expressed on paper. The two Western Powers demanded that Germany should cease all actions against Poland and withdraw her troops. On September 3, 1939, the British ambassador in Berlin told Hitler and Ribbentrop:

"I have the honour to inform you that if today, the 3rd September, by eleven o'clock in the morning British Summer Time, an assurance of peace is not issued by the German Government and received by His Majesty's Government in London, a state of war will exist between the two countries from that hour."

"Hitler sat at his writing table," wrote the German chief interpreter, Dr. Paul Schmidt, "while Ribbentrop stood at the window a little to the right of him. I was standing at a short distance from Hitler's table, and I then translated for him slowly the ultimatum of the British Government. Hitler sat as though made of stone, and stared in front of him. He sat completely still and motionless. After a time which seemed to me like eternity, he turned to Ribbentrop, who was standing at the window as though dazed. 'What now?' Hitler asked his Foreign Minister, with an angry look in his eyes, as though he would like to say that Ribbentrop had informed him wrongly about the reactions of the British. Ribbentrop replied in a quiet voice: 'I assume that the French will present us with a similar ultimatum during the next hour.'

"Even in the anteroom there was deathly silence at this announcement. Goering turned to me and said, 'If we lose this war, then may heaven help us.'"

On September 3, 1939, at eleven o'clock in the morning, British Summer Time, the attack on Poland turned into a European war, but not a single shot was fired in the West. Britain and France looked on while Poland was slaughtered.

Thus the Wehrmacht was able to carry out its first blitzkrieg.

On September 5, German troops crossed the Vistula, by the tenth of September they had reached the Narev and the Bug, on the eleventh they stormed over the San at Lemberg, and by the 18th of September Warsaw was cut off and its surrender demanded. In the East, the Red Army began to march into Poland on September 17. Thus the secret agreement which Stalin and Hitler had made about the division of the spoils became effective. For a further ten days, until September 27, the encircled capital held out. Under the blows of the artillery and the bombs of Goering's Luftwaffe, Warsaw was at last forced to capitulate.

Of this bombardment—the first in history to which a city of two million inhabitants was exposed—General Karl Bodenschatz stated at the Nuremberg Trial:

"I only know that Warsaw was a fortress which was occupied by the Polish Army, and very strongly occupied, equipped with a good deal of artillery, and that twice or three times Adolf Hitler had suggested that the city should be evacuated by the civilian population. That was declined; only the foreign legations were evacuated. The Polish Army was in the city and defended it obstinately with the help of its closely spaced fortifications. Even the outer forts were strongly manned, and heavy artillery was firing from the inner part of the city. The fortress of Warsaw was therefore attacked, also by the Luftwaffe, but only after that ultimatum, that demand of Adolf Hitler's had been refused."

The former Field Marshal Albert Kesselring, in his examination by Goering's defense attorney, Dr. Otto Stahmer, expressed himself in much the same way: "As chief of the Air Force I led this attack. Warsaw was in German eyes a fortress and moreover to a large extent defended from the air, and so fulfilled all conditions of the Hague war conventions. I was myself over Warsaw, and after nearly every bombing attack I spoke to the commanders about the execution of the raids; I can here assure you on the basis of my own observations and information that everything humanly possible was done to raid only military targets and spare civilian targets."

At first glance all this seems very correct, almost harmless. But the further statements of General Lahousen told a different story.

AMEN: Do you recall attending conferences with Canaris at the Führer's headquarters, just prior to the fall of Warsaw?

LAHOUSEN: Canaris and I took part in discussions in the Führer's special train, shortly before the fall of Warsaw . . . on September 12, 1939.

AMEN: Who was present on this occasion?

LAHOUSEN: The foreign minister, Von Ribbentrop; Keitel, the chief of the OKW; Jodl, head of the Wehrmacht Operations Staff, Canaris, and myself. . . . First of all Canaris had a short talk with Ribbentrop in which the latter explained the general political aims with regard to Poland. Canaris expressed his serious misgivings regarding the proposed bombardment of Warsaw. . . . Canaris stressed the devastating repercussion which this bombardment would have in the foreign political field. Keitel replied that these measures had been agreed upon directly by the Führer and Goering, and that he, Keitel, had no influence on these decisions. Secondly, Canaris very urgently warned them against the measures which had come to his knowledge, namely the proposed shootings and extermination measures directed particularly against the Polish intelligentsia, the nobility, the clergy, and, in fact, all elements which could be regarded as leaders of a national resistance. Canaris said, at that time . . . "One day the world will also hold the Wehrmacht, under whose eyes these events occurred, responsible for such methods."

The chief of the OKW [Keitel] replied . . . that these things had been decided upon by the Führer and that the Führer, the Commander in Chief of the Army, let it be known that should the Armed Forces be unwilling to carry through these measures . . . they would have to accept the presence at their side of the SS, the SIPO [security police], and similar units who would carry them through. . . . This, in outline, was our discussion on the proposed shooting and extermination measures, in Poland.

AMEN: What further discussions took place?

LAHOUSEN: After this discussion in the private carriage of the chief of the OKW, Canaris left the coach and had another short talk with Ribbentrop, who, returning to the subject of the Ukraine, told him once more that the uprising should be so staged

that all the farms and dwellings of the Poles should go up in
flames, and all Jews be killed.

AMEN: Who said that?

LAHOUSEN: The foreign minister of that time, Ribbentrop, said
that to Canaris. I was standing next to him.

AMEN: Is there any slightest doubt in your mind about that?

LAHOUSEN: No. I have not the slightest doubt about that. I remember with particular clarity the somehow new phrasing that
"all farms and dwellings of the Poles should go up in flames."
Previously, there had only been talk of "liquidation" and "elimination."

DR. FRITZ SAUTER: (defending Ribbentrop) Did Ribbentrop actually say that the Jews should be killed? Can you clearly remember?

LAHOUSEN: Yes, I can clearly remember, for Canaris spoke of it
not only to me but also to others and always called on me as a
witness.

Ribbentrop himself, whose usual reply to awkward questions
in cross-examination was that he could not recall the details, gave a
circumstantial explanation of this point:

"It has been stated here that I said houses must go up in
flames and Jews must be killed. I wish to assert quite categorically
that such a statement has never been made by me. Canaris was
with me in my carriage, and it is possible—of this I cannot now
be quite certain—that I saw him later in passing. He then received instructions issued by the Führer as to how he was to act
in Poland with regard to the Ukrainian problem and other matters. The statement which was attributed to me is quite meaningless, for in the Ukraine there were Ukrainian villages, there were
Ukrainians who lived there, they were our friends, they were not
our enemies. Thus it would have been quite meaningless for me
to say that these villages should go up in flames. So far as regards
the slaying of the Jews, I can only say one thing, that this completely contradicts my inner convictions, and that the question
of killing the Jews was not in anyone's mind or thoughts at that

time, and therefore I can sum up by saying that all this is completely incorrect."

Whether Ribbentrop remembered or admitted it or not, the actual events leave no doubt that after the beginning of the war terror actions were organized everywhere according to plan in the occupied territories.

What were Hitler's aims? His chief plan was to drive further East—exactly as he had laid it down as early as 1933 in his book, *Mein Kampf:* "We National Socialists must hold fast irrevocably to our political aims, namely to secure for the German people a fit and proper territory on this earth. When, however, we speak of new territory, we must in the first instance think only of Russia and the border states under her rule. This action is the only one that before God and Germany's posterity would seem to justify the shedding of blood."

Secretly the High Command of the Army prepared for an attack on the Soviet Union, with which Ribbentrop had signed a pact of nonaggression only a few weeks before. On this point Hitler had unblushingly said to his senior officers on November 23, 1939: "Treaties are only observed as long as they are useful."

The only thing that held him back from the attack on the Soviet Union after the conquest of Poland was the West. Britain and France were at war with Germany. But beyond a few skirmishes by reconnoitering troops there had been no real warfare in the West. Hitler could not risk putting his plans into action so long as he had the two Western Powers at his back.

"I hesitated a long time," he said at the same meeting of his senior officers, "whether I should strike first in the East and then in the West. I did not build up the Wehrmacht in order not to strike. The decision to strike was always in my mind."

The American prosecutor, Telford Taylor, read a further extract from the verbatim report of Hitler's speech at that meeting: "Everything points to the fact that the moment is now favorable. It is a difficult decision for me. I have to choose between victory or destruction. I choose victory. My decision is unalterable, I shall attack England and France at the most favorable and earliest moment. Infringement of the neutrality of Belgium and Holland is unimportant. No one will say a word about it when we have conquered. We shall not commit the infringement of neutrality so idiotically as it was done in 1914."

Thus Hitler left no doubt about his plans for the East and the West.

THE MAD DOG
OF BERLIN

The lightning war in Poland had given Hitler a deceptive feeling of unconquerable strength, and six months after the victory over their eastern neighbor, the Wehrmacht was again on the march. The British chief prosecutor at Nuremberg, Sir Hartley Shawcross, gave a summary of the events: "On April 9, 1940, the German armed forces invaded Norway and Denmark without warning and without declaring war. It was a breach of the most explicit assurance of peace that had been given.

"For several years, the defendant Rosenberg, in his capacity of Chief of the Foreign Political Office of the Nazi Party, had interested himself in the creation of a Fifth Column in Norway. He formed a close connection with the *Nasjonal Samling*, a political group run by the traitor, Vidkun Quisling. In August 1939, a special fourteen-day course was held for them in the school of the Foreign Policy Office in Berlin; it was attended by twenty-five members who had been picked by Quisling. These 'reliable' men were to be the regional and linguistic experts for Germany's special troops. The aim was to eliminate any military resistance from the start by means of a revolt, in which Quisling would arrest the leading opponents, including the King. Along with this activity Germany carried out her military preparations."

From all the evidence, Alfred Rosenberg appears to have been the first to develop the idea of extending German power in the "Germanic North." In his search for accomplices he turned to the Commander in Chief of the Navy, Admiral Erich Raeder. The fleet, so Rosenberg thought, should be interested in the North. In his memorandum to Raeder, which was read out in

Nuremberg, Rosenberg wrote after an exhaustive talk with Quisling: "Those who have been trained at the course of the Foreign Policy Office must go as quickly as possible to Norway. The occupation of some important centers in Oslo must follow at once; at the same time the German fleet with contingents of the German Army must occupy a bay from which the way to Oslo can be controlled, and hold itself ready for the emergency call of the new Norwegian government."

As early as October 3, 1939—a month after the attack on Poland—Raeder began to interest himself more closely in the "Rosenberg Plan." He circulated in the High Command of the Fleet a questionnaire from which the British prosecutor, Elwyn Jones, quoted some extracts at Nuremberg: "The following points are to be settled: 1. Which parts of Norway can be used as bases? 2. Can the seizure of these bases, if this is not possible without a fight, be enforced by the military against the will of the Norwegians?"

The officer in command of the U-Boat fleet, Karl Doenitz, was also active in the affair. He prepared a memorandum which was laid before the Court, and of which Elwyn Jones said: "Apparently it is connected with the questionnaire of the defendant Raeder. Its last section says: 'It is therefore proposed to prepare a base at Trondheim and a supply base at Narvik as an alternative.'"

The Norwegian invasion was in one respect not a typical Nazi act of aggression, insofar as Hitler had to be persuaded to permit it. It was mainly Raeder and Rosenberg who persuaded him. The occasion for this was offered by a conference of the Naval Staff in the Führer's headquarters on December 12, 1939. Besides Hitler and Raeder, Wilhelm Keitel and Alfred Jodl took part. The report of the meeting, written by Raeder himself, was read out by prosecutor Elwyn Jones at Nuremberg:

"The account is entitled 'Case Norway.' I call the attention of the Court to the fourth section, which runs: 'The Führer decided to speak to Quisling himself in order to form an impression of him. The Commander in Chief of the Navy (Raeder) proposed: If the Führer gains a favorable impression, the OKW (High Command of the Wehrmacht) should be given permission to work out plans with Quisling for the preparation and execution of the occupation: (a) by peaceful means—that is to say, the German Army will be called in by Norway; or (b) by force.'"

The report further states: "On the basis of the meeting of the Führer with Quisling in the afternoon of December 14, 1939, the Führer gave orders for the preparation of the Norwegian undertaking by the OKW."

As in all previous cases, Hitler here again tried to conceal his real intentions. Thus his secret order says: "It is essential to try to give the undertaking the character of a friendly occupation, which has as its purpose the protection of the neutrality of the northern states."

In spite of the unambiguous language of the documents produced, the defense in Nuremberg attempted to make the attack appear as a logical security measure against a landing in Norway planned by England. The date of the preparations, which go back, to September 1939, do not permit this interpretation.

The events themselves speak clearly. Elwyn Jones read from an announcement by the Danish Government. "At 4:20 A.M. on April 9, 1940, the German ambassador, accompanied by the air attaché of the embassy, appeared at the private residence of the Danish foreign minister. The ambassador at once declared that Germany possessed positive proof that England was planning the occupation of bases in Denmark and Norway. For this reason, German soldiers were now crossing the border. German aircraft would soon be over Copenhagen; for the present they had orders not to drop any bombs. It was now a matter for the Danes to avoid any resistance, as resistance would lead to the most terrible consequences."

The threat of bombing was not new: Prague and the Czech President Hácha had had to give in to it. It was another very easy *coup de main* for the German Army. The British ambassador in Copenhagen, Howard Smith, reported to London:

> Early in the morning, about five o'clock, three small transport ships steamed into the entrance of Copenhagen harbour while a number of aircraft circled over them. The northern battery fired a warning shot at the aircraft. With that exception, the Danes offered no resistance, and the German vessels tied up at

the quay. About eight hundred soldiers landed with full equipment and marched to the Kastellet, the old fortress of Copenhagen. The gate was locked, and the Germans forced their way in with explosives. The garrison offered no resistance, and it appears that they were taken completely by surprise.

After the occupation a detachment was sent to Amalienborg, the royal palace, where they attacked the Danish garrison and wounded three guards, one of them fatally. Meanwhile, a great number of aircraft flew at a low altitude over the city.

Such was Howard Smith's report. In Norway, things went somewhat differently. Rosenberg's idea, Raeder's preparation, Keitel's planning, and Hitler's order took effect on April 9, 1940. The German fleet landed at several points on the Norwegian coast. As in Denmark, here, too, complete surprise was achieved.

Trygve Lie, later Secretary General of the United Nations, then Commander in Chief of the Norwegian forces, prepared a report for the Nuremberg Court, from which Jones read: "The German attack came as a surprise, and all the towns along the coast were occupied according to plan with little loss of life. The plan [of Quisling] to take the King, members of the Government and of Parliament prisoner, miscarried in spite of the unexpected attack, and resistance was organized throughout the whole country."

Sir Hartley Shawcross said in conclusion: "But however brave the resistance, which was hastily organized throughout the whole country, nothing could be done against the long-planned surprise attack. On June 10 military resistance ceased. Thus a further act of aggression had been completed."

The effect of the invasion on the rest of the world was tremendous. Even the most charitable, who tried to excuse the attack on Poland on the grounds of German interests in Danzig and the Corridor, had learned their lesson. With the occupation of Denmark and Norway, Hitler had · united the entire world against Germany. Neville Chamberlain, the former British Prime Minister who had by now been replaced by Winston Churchill, gave expression to the feelings of the nations in his speech of April 16, 1940: "This is the latest crime of the fiend in Germany. Every victim of German brutality adds to those who have already con-

demned Germany, further millions of men who know that no
nation can be safe until this mad dog is made harmless."

Hitler, "this mad dog," no longer knew any moderation.
Scarcely were Denmark and Norway overrun when he took up
his plans of conquest again.

"On May 10, 1940, at about five in the morning, began the
German invasion of Belgium, Holland, and Luxemburg," recalled
Sir Hartley Shawcross. After long vacillations whether he should
pursue the war first in the West or in the East, Hitler had decided
upon the West. With rapid strokes he would knock out France
and England so that he could then turn against Russia.

Hitler and his strategists saw no possibility of breaking through
the apparently impregnable fortified line designed by the Frenchman, André Maginot. Therefore they chose the route through the
undefended neutral countries, Holland, Belgium, and Luxemburg. But the war against France was not the only reason for the
violation to the three neutral states. Already on August 25, 1938,
Goering's Luftwaffe had carried out a special study of the area.
"For the execution of operations in Western Europe," said the
report, written long before the beginning of the war, "the Bel-
gian-Dutch territory assumes an increased importance, especially
as a basis for the war in the air. In German hands, Belgium and
the Netherlands represent an extraordinary advantage in aerial
warfare against Britain and France." Yet shortly before the outbreak of the war, on August 26, 1939, "the King of the Belgians,
the Queen of the Netherlands, and the Government of the Grand
Duchy of Luxemburg were solemnly assured by the German am-
bassadors that their neutrality would be respected." On October
6, Hitler repeated this assurance. On October 9, 1939, nevertheless, he issued an instruction for the conduct of the war: "For
the further conduct of the military operations I command: On
the northern wing of the Western front, an attacking operation
through the territories of Luxemburg, Belgium, and Holland is to
be prepared. This attack must be carried out as powerfully and
as early as possible. Object of this action is to acquire as much
Dutch, Belgian, and Luxemburg territory as possible as a basis
for a prospective air and sea attack on England."

Nothing could reveal the reason behind the invasion of these three countries more clearly than this document. Hitler no longer took the trouble to think up a reasonable excuse. He told an old tale, and thought it was good enough.

The British prosecutor, Roberts, read from a report by the Belgian Government:

> At 8:30 the German ambassador came to the Ministry of Foreign Affairs. As he entered the room he began to draw a paper from his pocket. Monsieur Spaak (the Belgian Foreign Minister) interrupted him:
>
> "Excuse me, Mr. Ambassador, I will speak first. Mr. Ambassador, the German Army has just invaded our country. It is the second time in twenty-five years that Germany has made a criminal attack upon neutral and loyal Belgium. What has just happened is perhaps more shameful than the invasion of 1914. No ultimatum, no note, no protest of any kind has been sent to the Belgian Government. Only by the invasion itself has Belgium learned that Germany has violated the guarantees given by her on October 13, 1937, and voluntarily renewed on the outbreak of the war. The German act of aggression, for which there is no justification, will deeply affect the conscience of the world. History will hold Germany responsible. Belgium is determined to defend herself. Her cause, which is that of justice, cannot be lost."
>
> The ambassador was then allowed to read the contents of the note he had brought: "I am instructed by the Government of the Reich," he said, "to make the following statement: 'In order to anticipate the invasion of Belgium, Holland, and Luxemburg, for which Britain and France have been carrying out preparations clearly aimed against Germany, the German Government finds itself obliged to insure the neutrality of the three countries by force of arms. For this purpose, the Government of the Reich will employ extensive forces so that all resistance is useless. In the event of resistance of any kind Belgium will bring about the destruction of her country and her independence.'"
>
> In the middle of this announcement M. Spaak interrupted the ambassador: "Give me the document," he said, "I would like to spare you such an unpleasant task." After reading through the note, M. Spaak confined himself to saying that he had already replied by the protest he had made.

Almost as embarrassing as the conversation in the morning of May 10, 1940, was the cross-examination by the British lawyer, Roberts, of the former Air Marshal Erhard Milch at Nuremberg.

ROBERTS: You were present at a meeting which was held at the Chancellery on May 23, 1939. I might remind you who else was present: the Führer, Goering, Raeder, Brauchitsch, Keitel, Holder, General Bodenschatz, and Warlimont, all of them leaders of the German forces. Would you, on the basis of your knowledge, call them men of honor?

MILCH: Yes.

ROBERTS: It is one of the qualities of a man of honor to keep his word?

MILCH: Yes.

ROBERTS: Then you knew, did you not, that Germany had given her word to respect the neutrality of Belgium, Holland, and Luxemburg?

MILCH: I suppose so, I don't know the actual occasion, but I assume so.

ROBERTS: Don't you know that scarcely a month before this meeting, on April 28, Hitler had given an assurance in the Reichstag that he would respect the neutrality of a great number of European countries, including the three countries I have mentioned?

MILCH: Yes, I suppose so.

ROBERTS: Do you remember that at that conference Hitler used the following words: "The Dutch and Belgian air bases must be militarily occupied. No heed must be paid to declarations of neutrality. Here, justice and injustice and treaties play no part." Do you remember those words being used?

MILCH: I cannot exactly recall which words were spoken.

ROBERTS: Was a protest raised by any of the men of honor against the breaking of Germany's given word?

MILCH: At this conference it was not possible for any of those present to speak at all, for Hitler stood at a desk in front of us and made a speech, and after the speech he went away. A discussion did not take place and was not permitted by him.

ROBERTS: You mean it was impossible for the men of honor to defend their honor?

Be that as it may, the High Command of the Wehrmacht did their work thoroughly. Belgium could only hold out for eighteen days before King Leopold III was forced to sign the capitulation. In the Netherlands resistance lasted only four days.

"In order to end the campaign in the Netherlands as quickly as possible," Hermann Goering stated on the witness stand, "I proposed the use of the parachute division in the rear of the whole Dutch front turned against Germany, and especially to occupy the three important bridges at Moerdijk, Dordrecht, and Rotterdam. While the matter was quickly accomplished in Moerdijk and Dordrecht, the unit at Rotterdam ran into difficulties. It was surrounded by Dutch forces."

This was the cue for one of the vilest incidents of the war, the bombing of Rotterdam. The destruction of the city by Goering's Luftwaffe, the massacre of the civilian population from crashing buildings, bombs, and fire became a terrible symbol. Field Marshal Albert Kesselring was questioned as a witness about these events in the Nuremberg courtroom, first by Goering's defense.

DR. STAHMER: Did you take part in the attack on Rotterdam?

KESSELRING: Yes, as Luftwaffe Chief 1, which I had become in the meantime. The Air Landing Corps was commanded by General Student, who asked for the defense of his parachutists by an air raid. The attack was carried through according to plan.

DR. STAHMER: How did it come about that there were large fires in Rotterdam?

KESSELRING: It is a matter of experience in war that the chief damage is not caused by bombs but by the spreading of fires. Unfortunately, a bomb struck a margarine factory so that the oil scattered and spread the fire.

DR. STAHMER: What military result did this attack produce?

KESSELRING: The immediate result was the capitulation of the Dutch army.

Cross-examined by Sir David Maxwell Fyfe, Kesselring had to reveal another aspect of the attack.

SIR DAVID: Did you know at what time of the day the bombing of Rotterdam began?

KESSELRING: To my knowledge it began in the early afternoon, about two o'clock, I believe.

SIR DAVID: Did you know that since ten in the morning discussions of the capitulation had been in progress?

KESSELRING: No.

SIR DAVID: Did you know that at 12:15 a Dutch officer had crossed the German lines and met General Schmidt and General Student, and that General Schmidt laid down the proposed conconditions of capitulation at 12:35?

KESSELRING: No.

SIR DAVID: You never heard about that?

KESSELRING: I was not informed, at least not to my recollection.

SIR DAVID: You understand, witness, that this was fifty-five minutes before the beginning of the bombing.

KESSELRING: The attack would have had to be canceled by General Student. This cancellation never reached me, nor my unit.

SIR DAVID: If they had wished to pass this information to the aircraft and the bombing had to be held up, they could easily have done so by wireless?

KESSELRING: In my opinion, yes.

SIR DAVID: Now I put it to you that everyone saw these bombers flying over. Student saw the bombers flying over. You know that, don't you?

KESSELRING: Yes.

SIR DAVID: If this attack had any tactical significance for the support of your troops, he could have called it off, couldn't he?

KESSELRING: Yes, if the tactical position had been known.

SIR DAVID: If agreement is reached on honorably intended conditions of surrender, one might expect a soldier to call off the attack, isn't that so?

KESSELRING: If no other decisions had been made, yes.

SIR DAVID: Given the chance to call off the attack, nothing would have been easier than to do so. I wish to state quite clearly that the attack upon Rotterdam was intended to force the Dutch to capitulation through terror.

Goering himself said later on the witness stand: "I ordered the Air Force to use a squadron. The squadron started in three groups, each group had some twenty-five to thirty aircraft. When the first group flew over, the surrender negotiations were in progress, but so far with no definite aim. Nevertheless red Very lights were fired. The first group did not understand the signals but dropped their bombs according to instructions exactly in the predestined places. The second and third groups which were following saw the red Very lights, turned round, and did not drop their bombs. There was no radio connection between Rotterdam and the aircraft. The radio link was from Rotterdam by way of my headquarters, Air Force 2, to the Division, Division Squadron base. From there, radio connection existed with the aircraft. The important thing is, however, that Rotterdam could not radio direct to the aircraft and had therefore fired red Very lights. No great destruction resulted from the bombs but, as has been said, from fire. The spreading of the fire was caused by the burning of these great masses of fats and oils. I should also like to express the opinion that if the Rotterdam Fire Brigade had acted energetically, the spreading of the fire could have been prevented."

With that, Nuremberg left the subject. The further events of 1940 required detailed discussion. In France, the armored wedges of the German Army were driving ahead.

OPERATION SEA LION: THE BEGINNING OF THE END

As Goebbels later put it in his propaganda campaigns, it was the genius of the "greatest general of all times" which led to the amazingly rapid victory in France. Meanwhile, however, it has been established that not Hitler but General Erich von Manstein designed the plan which defeated his French opponent, General Maurice Gamelin.

Five days after the beginning of the German invasion, the French Premier, Paul Renaud, telephoned in despair to London. The call reached Mr. Churchill at his private residence.

"We are beaten," said Renaud. "We have lost."

"That cannot possibly have happened so quickly," Mr. Churchill replied, startled.

"Our front has been pierced at Sedan," Renaud continued. "The Germans are streaming through the gap with tanks and great masses of infantry."

"We must hold out," said Mr. Churchill.

"The enemy forces are too strong and too quick," said Renaud. "They operate in conjunction with dive bombers. It is devastating. The wedge is growing wider and stronger every hour in the direction of Laon-Amiens. We have lost the fight."

It made no difference that General Gamelin was replaced by General Maxime Weygand who, in turn, was soon superseded by Marshal Henri Pétain. France collapsed. The British Expeditionary Force was forced back to the port of Dunkirk. It looked as though the British could not be saved from annihilation by the forces of General Ewald von Kleist, except by a miracle.

But the miracle happened. Karl von Rundstedt, the Commander in Chief of the central Army group, was telephoned from the Führer's headquarters. The conversation has been recorded for posterity. Hitler himself was listening as Rundstedt was being told: "Regarding your further operations in the Dunkirk region—pass on the order to Kleist's tank group not to cross the line of the St. Omer Canal."

"But you can't be serious," cried Rundstedt, taken aback. "Our tank divisions are on their way to the town."

"The canal is not to be crossed," insisted the voice from headquarters. "This is a personal order of the Führer."

The German tanks stopped. Kleist, who had tried to ignore the order and had gone on, had to withdraw his forces to the canal. Thus the British were able to ship almost their whole expeditionary force—about 338,000 men—back to England.

The cause of the "Miracle of Dunkirk," which only Propaganda Minister Goebbels described as a decisive defeat for the British, has been explained since. Goering had persuaded Hitler to leave Dunkirk entirely to the Luftwaffe. He thought that his airmen could carry out the job alone, and Hitler agreed with him. But after the oil tanks in the port of Dunkirk had begun to burn, a thick cloud of smoke hung over the area for days—and Goering's Luftwaffe could no longer see how the forces of Lord Gort were escaping from its grasp under the cover of the smoke pall.

The evacuated troops soon became the nucleus of Britain's home defense, and one of the chief reasons why Hitler could not risk invading England after the fall of France. Mr. Churchill himself confirmed this in a speech to Parliament on June 4, 1940: "The whole question of Home Defence against invasion is, of course, powerfully affected by the fact that we have, for the time being in this Island, incomparably stronger military forces than we have ever had at any moment in this war or the last."

Goering's vanity and the shortsightedness of the "greatest general of all times" had thus decided the future course of the war at Dunkirk.

On June 22, 1940, Hitler experienced his greatest triumph. On that day, the French signed the German armistice conditions in the forest of Compiègne. As we have seen in the newsreel shots and photographs, Hitler on this occasion performed a dance of joy and slapped his thighs. He was convinced that the war was already won, and that now Britain would have to give in.

Winston Churchill soon shattered Hitler's illusion with his famous speech: "Even though large tracts of Europe and many old and famous states have fallen or may fall into the grip of the Gestapo and all the odious apparatus of Nazi rule, we shall not flag or fail. We shall go on to the end. We shall fight in France, we shall fight on the seas and oceans, we shall fight with growing confidence and growing strength in the air; we shall defend our Island, whatever the cost may be. We shall fight on the beaches, we shall fight on the landing grounds, we shall fight in the fields and in the streets, we shall fight in the hills; we shall never surrender; and even if, which I do not for a moment believe, this Island or a large part of it were subjugated and starving, then our Empire beyond the seas, armed and guarded by the British fleet, would carry on the struggle . . ."

Hitler replied with a secret instruction to Keitel and Jodl. It bears the date of July 16, 1940, and was read out in the Nuremberg courtroom:

> Since England, in spite of her militarily hopeless situation, still does not show any inclination to come to terms with us, I have decided to prepare and, if necessary, to carry out landing operations against her. The British Air Force must be so completely destroyed, morally and factually, that it can no longer offer any effective opposition to the German invasion.

The British chief prosecutor, Sir Hartley Shawcross, added to this: "The defendant Goering and his Luftwaffe doubtless made the most strenuous efforts to carry out this instruction. But although the bombing of the towns and villages of England was carried out during the dark winter of 1940–41, the enemy finally reached the conclusion that Britain could not be brought to heel by these means."

Operation Sea Lion—that was the code name of Hitler's plan for the invasion of England—became his first decisive setback. The Blitz—Goering's air attack on the British Isles—was a succession of losses. For the first time in the war, Hitler met with an opponent he was unable to knock out. General Ironside, at the time the British Commander in Chief, had the whole of Britain turned into a hedgehog on Churchill's instruction. Every man, woman, and child accepted some home defense job; every shotgun became a weapon of war, every house an air-raid shelter protected with sandbags, every golf course a mine field, every strip of land a tank trap. The production of aircraft—in January 1940, 802 planes; in June, 1,591—increased by leaps and bounds. "Our island is a hornet's nest," said Winston Churchill.

"Mr. Churchill has apparently not yet realized England's hopeless position," Hitler complained at a conference at his headquarters on July 21, 1940. The meeting was discussing the preparations for the landing, and the Commander in Chief of the Navy, Admiral Raeder, asked: "I should like to know whether the Reichsmarschall believes that he can accomplish the following tasks: one, destroy the bulk of the Royal Air Force, and two, prevent the British Navy from attacking our invasion troops."

GOERING: I consider this question quite superfluous. In the shortest possible time I shall proclaim total air war, and then I shall let twenty-five hundred aircraft attack the British Isles. The invasion will not fail on account of the Luftwaffe.

HITLER: It must be possible to get ten divisions to land in the first four days, sufficient for the formation of a stable bridgehead. A week after the beginning of the invasion, the first attack must be made along a front line from the mouth of the Thames south of London to Portsmouth, with sufficient reserves in the bridgehead.

JODL: According to preliminary plans, the Sixth Army should follow the first invasion force. The Fleet assures us that it would take six weeks to ferry the major part of only twenty-five divisions to England. There is a contradiction here.

HITLER: It is not a question of twenty-five divisions. We must get at least forty divisions to the island.

RAEDER: The Fleet can give no guarantee of being able to carry forty divisions across.

HALDER: Then this is complete suicide! I might as well push the troops that have landed through a meat grinder.

But Hitler would not give way. Preparations went on at full steam; even river steamers and Rhine tugs were given provisional fittings for the landing operations, and everywhere in the West German troops were trained in embarkation and invasion operations.

On August 15, 1940, Goering's blitz began. With 2,600 aircraft of all kinds he attacked southern England. Seventy-six planes, mostly bombers, were shot down during the first massed raid, the first bitter foretaste of the striking power of the Royal Air Force. In the weeks and months that followed, the Luftwaffe never managed to establish air supremacy over the Channel or over Britain. The uninterrupted air attack on London was far from making the island ripe for capitulation. Goering had to endure losses which were never made good; within three months, he lost 2,500 aircraft over England, and with them the elite of his airmen.

In spite of all this, Hitler proclaimed in the Berlin Sport Palace on September 4, 1940: "Whatever may come, England will be smashed, one way or the other. We shall wipe out her cities. And if they are curious in England and ask, 'Well, why doesn't he come now?' then I tell them, 'Just you wait, he'll be coming all right!' "

Joachim von Ribbentrop, Hitler's Foreign Minister, stated on a visit to Rome, "Contrary to the forecasts of the meteorologists, the weather has been exceptionally unfavorable for intensive operations against England during the last few weeks. Nevertheless, Duce, Germany has won supremacy in the air."

Only the German Admiralty Staff had no longer any illusions. On September 10, 1940, they committed their opinion to paper: "There is no sign to indicate the defeat of the enemy's air force over southern England and in the Channel area, and this is of decisive importance for the further assessment of the situation."

In the end, Hitler himself had to realize that he could not conquer Britain at the time. In Nuremberg, Kesselring was questioned by the American chief prosecutor on this matter.

JACKSON: Did you not advocate the invasion of England, and was not the Air Force ready to invade England?

KESSELRING: The Air Force was subject to certain conditions, in view of the existing situation at that time, ready to fulfill that task.

JACKSON: You recommended very strongly to the Reichsmarschall that the invasion take place immediately after Dunkirk, did you not?

KESSELRING: Yes, and I still advocated that view later on, too.

But the Naval Chief Ernst Raeder said on the same witness stand, "In September 1940, we still believed that the landing could be carried out. But it was recognized as a prerequisite that supremacy in the air must be achieved first. When it became clear that air supremacy could not be established in any satisfactory measure it was decided to put off the landing until the spring of 1941."

In addition, a number of other emergencies had suddenly arisen. Italy, which had until then regarded herself as Germany's ally but not a belligerent, had declared war on the Allies on June 10, 1940, eager to insure her share of the spoils from the collapse of France. In October 1940 Mussolini launched an attack on Greece, and soon the German Wehrmacht had to come to his aid, for the Greeks showed themselves more than a match for the Italians. At the same time, Hitler had to come to Italy's aid in Africa.

His basic aim, however, remained unalterable: the destruction of the Soviet Union. Even while the Battle of Britain was still raging, Hitler issued—on December 18, 1940—his famous Directive 21. It was read out in Nuremberg: "The German Army must be prepared, even before the end of the war against England, to overthrow Soviet Russia in a rapid campaign. Preparations are to be put in hand at once and are to be complete by May 15, 1941." The document bears Hitler's signature and was countersigned by Jodl and Keitel. Code name for the attack was Operation Barbarossa.

But before May 15 drew near, Hitler became involved in other developments, and the deadline had to be postponed. Yugoslavia joined the Berlin-Rome-Tokyo Axis; as a result, her government tumbled—and the Wehrmacht was on the march again.

On March 27, 1941, Hitler held a conference with his senior officers. "Among those present," said the British prosecutor, H. J. Phillimore, "were the defendant Goering, the defendant Keitel, the defendant Jodl, and the defendant Ribbentrop. Hitler spoke, and the report of the meeting says, 'The Führer is determined to destroy Yugoslavia militarily and as a state. The attack will begin as soon as the necessary supplies and troops are assembled.'

"On page five of the report, a short passage says, 'The chief task of the Luftwaffe, beginning as soon as possible, is to destroy the ground installations of the Yugoslav air force, and to wipe out the capital Belgrade in a series of attacks.' We know of course today how ruthlessly these raids were carried out when the residential parts of Belgrade were bombed the morning of April 6."

On that day, Hitler crossed the Greek border; in the first place, to help the Italian forces which were in difficulty, but also to prevent the British from coming to the aid of Greece and gaining a foothold on the peninsula.

Hitler maintained, as usual, that lightning action had been necessary, but in Nuremberg Sir Hartley Shawcross showed that once again it was a matter of an attack planned long beforehand: "On November 12, 1940, Hitler, in a top-secret order to the High Command of the Army, gave instructions to prepare for the occupation of Greece. On December 13 Hitler issued a directive on Operation Marita, as the invasion of Greece was to be called. In this directive it was declared that the invasion was planned and would take place as soon as weather conditions were favorable."

The war assumed monstrous proportions. The folly of destruction and sadism spread everywhere. A frightful example was what took place on the Greek island of Crete. In the courtroom at Nuremberg, part of a report of the Greek government was read: "Shortly after the capture of the island by the Germans, the first reprisal measures were carried out. A large number of almost completely innocent men were shot, and the villages of Skiki, Brassi, and Kanades were burned down as a reprisal for the killing of some German parachutists by members of the local police during the invasion of the island."

With the attack on the Soviet Union, every restraint went by the board; Hitler had by now lost all touch with reality. "To overthrow Soviet Russia in a lightning campaign" had become his *idée fixe*. How disastrously he miscalculated emerges from a few of his pronouncements. To Jodl he said, "All we have to do is smash the door open, and the whole rotten edifice will collapse." To his senior officers he said on July 31, 1940: "The sooner Russia is overthrown the better. The attack is only worth while if the Russian state can be shaken right down to its roots with one blow. If we strike in May 1941, we shall have five months' time in which to complete the job."

There was no aim so fantastic that Hitler did not aspire to it in those days. While Barbarossa was imminent and the invasion of England had been shelved, he was busy with new instructions for further conquests: Under the code name Felix an attack on Gibraltar was being considered, under that of Isabella the occupation of Portugal. His imagination roamed all over Europe.

Did the Russians know what was in store for them? In November 1940 the Soviet Foreign Minister, Molotov, visited Berlin. The partner of the German-Soviet nonaggression pact was received by his colleague, Ribbentrop, with the words: "No power on earth can alter the fact that the beginning of the end has now come for the British Empire. England is defeated, and it is only a matter of time until she is given the final blow."

At that moment the sirens sounded an air-raid warning. Ribbentrop had perforce to ask his guest into the shelter, where they continued their conversation. Afterward, Molotov asked with some amusement: "If England is defeated and powerless, why did we have to carry on our conversation in the air-raid shelter?"

Another guest visited Berlin about that time: the Foreign Minister of Germany's ally, Japan, Yosuke Matsuoka. He was as much in the dark about Hitler's true intentions as the Italians, but in the end he suspected what was going on, and raised his head in surprise when Ribbentrop said to him: "If one day the Soviet Union takes up an attitude that Germany would regard as a threat, then the Führer will strike against Russia."

Matsuoka traveled on to Moscow, where he concluded a pact of neutrality between the Soviet Union and Japan. He had seen the absurd illusions that were entertained in Berlin regarding Russia's strength, and he wanted to keep his own country out of Hitler's adventure.

OPERATION
BARBAROSSA

Two typewritten lines, the most decisive for the German people, were read out at the Nuremberg Trial by the American prosecutor, Sidney S. Alderman. They were from Hitler's secret orders and ran: "Timetable for Barbarossa. The Führer has decided: Barbarossa start—June 22."

On that day, at 3:30 A.M., in accordance with the timetable of its Supreme Commander, the Wehrmacht launched its invasion of the Soviet Union. The dreams in which Hitler and his closest followers indulged emerge in frightening clarity from the

Nuremberg documents. Alderman read out a decree by the Führer, written more than two months before the attack: "I nominate Alfred Rosenberg as my delegate, empowered to handle all matters concerning the Eastern European Territories. April 20, 1941. Adolf Hitler."

Little more than a fortnight after this nomination, Rosenberg had already prepared a memorandum which made his plans clear.

> The political aim of a settlement by war can only be to free the German Reich for centuries from the pressure of Greater Russia. For this reason, these territories must be divided up into Commissariats of the Reich according to their historical and racial affinities. The Commissariat of "Eastland" including White Ruthenia, will have the task of preparing an even closer union with Germany in the form of a Germanized Protectorate. The Ukraine will be an independent state in alliance with Germany, Caucasia with the adjacent northern territories a Federal State under a German representative. Russia proper must make her own arrangements for the future.
>
> The object of the Commissariat for Estonia, Lithuania, Latvia, and White Ruthenia must be to form a German Protectorate, and then by Germanizing of racially suitable elements, by colonization of Germanic tribes, and by expulsion of unwanted elements, to transform this region into a part of the Greater German Reich. The Baltic Sea must become a German inland sea under German protection.

Alderman then continued: "Having thus elaborately prepared on every side for the invasion of the Soviet Union, the Nazi conspirators proceeded to carry out their plans and on June 22, 1941, hurled their armies across the borders of the U.S.S.R. In announcing this act of perfidy to the world, Hitler issued a proclamation on the day of the attack. . . . I should like to refer to it in passing here by quoting therefrom this one sentence: 'I have therefore today decided to give the fate of Europe again into the hands of our soldiers.'

"This announcement told the world that the die had been cast —plans darkly conceived almost a full year before . . . had been brought to fruition. That brings us to the consideration of the motives for the attack. It will, I think, be sufficient to read to the

Tribunal a few entries which include the reports of the German ambassador in Moscow as late as June 1941."

This is what the German ambassador, Count Friedrich Werner von der Schulenburg, wrote on June 7: "Russia will only fight if attacked by Germany. Situation in Moscow is considered much more serious than up to now. All military preparations have been made quietly—as far as can be recognized, only defensive. Russian policy still strives as before to produce the best possible relationship to Germany." On June 7, 1941, Schulenburg reported to Berlin: "All observations show that Stalin and Molotov, who alone are responsible for Russian foreign policy, are doing everything to avoid a conflict with Germany. The entire behavior of the government as well as the attitude of the press, which reports all events concerning Germany in a factual, indisputable manner, support this view. The loyal fulfillment of the economic treaty with Germany proves the same thing."

Naturally the German people were not told what their own ambassador had reported. The German people were told that the Soviet Union was carrying out preparations for an attack upon the Reich. The German invasion was once again to "anticipate" these plans with "lightning speed."

Millions of Germans were thrown ruthlessly into their doom. From the moment of the first plans until the turning point at Stalingrad one man had the opportunity to see behind the scenes: Field Marshal Friedrich Paulus.

Quite unexpectedly he was called as a witness by the Soviet prosecution on February 11, 1946. The former army leader, whose name is irrevocably associated with the collapse of the Sixth Army at Stalingrad, walked calmly and with an inscrutable expression into the floodlights of the courtroom.

Roman Rudenko, the Soviet chief prosecutor, conducted the first interrogation of the witness. After him, the German defense counsels had the opportunity of questioning him.

RUDENKO: What do you know about the preparations of the Hitler government and the German High Command for the armed attack on the Soviet Union?

PAULUS: From personal experience I can report this: On September 3, 1940, I began my service with the Army High Command as Quartermaster General of the General Staff. On taking over my duties I found among other things the incomplete operational plans which concerned an attack on the Soviet Union. These operational plans had been worked out by the then Major General Marx, Chief of General Staff of the Eighteenth Army. The Chief of General Staff for the whole Wehrmacht, General Halder, assigned to me the completion of this task on the following lines: there should be a consideration of the possibilities of attacking Soviet Russia, with regard to the terrain, the forces involved, the requirements, and so on. It was assumed that some 130 to 140 German divisions would be available for these operations. Furthermore, the operation was to be based right from the start on the use of Romanian territory for the advance of the German southern wing. It was also stated that in the view of the OKW the aims of the operation were these:

1. Destruction of the Soviet forces stationed in White Russia; prevention of the escape of fighting units into the depths of the Russian territory.

2. To reach a line from which the Russian air force could not effectively attack Germany, and, as a final objective, to reach the line Volga-Archangel.

The development of the project was completed by two military exercises, the conduct of which General Halder entrusted to me. At that time, on December 18, 1940, the Commander in Chief of the Army issued Directive 21. This was the basis for all military and economic preparations. The first instructions for the invasion were approved by Hitler at Obersalzberg on February 3, 1941. For the beginning of the action the Commander in Chief of the Army had determined a time of the year that would allow the easiest large-scale movement of troops on Russian territory, about the middle of May. This date was changed, however, when Hitler decided, at the end of March, to attack Yugoslavia. As a result of this decision the beginning of Operation Barbarossa had to be put off for some five weeks.

RUDENKO: Under what conditions was the armed attack upon the U.S.S.R. undertaken?

PAULUS: The attack on the Soviet Union took place, as I have indicated, according to a long prepared and carefully camouflaged plan. A great diversion, which was organized from Norway and from the French coast, was to give the appearance of a planned landing in England in June 1941, and distract the attention from the East.

RUDENKO: How would you define the aims which Germany was pursuing in her attack on the Soviet Union?

PAULUS: The target Volga-Archangel, which was far beyond the German potential, was typical of the delusions of the policy of conquest in which Hitler and the National Socialist regime indulged. Strategically the achievement of this target would have implied the destruction of the entire fighting forces of the Soviet Union.

How much Hitler depended upon the acquisition of economic objectives I can illustrate from an example from my personal experience. On June 1, 1942, on the occasion of a meeting of senior officers of the Army Group South in Poltava, Hitler said, "If I do not get oil from Maikop and Grozny, I shall have to stop this war."

Summing up, I might say that the whole aim was conquest for the purpose of colonizing Russian territory; and by exploiting and looting them the war in the West was to be carried to an end, with the object of finally establishing supremacy over Europe.

RUDENKO: Which of the defendants were, in your opinion, guilty of starting the crminal war of aggression against the Soviet Union?

PAULUS: So far as I was able to judge, Hitler's leading military advisers: the Chief of the High Command of the Army, Keitel; the Chief of the Wehrmacht General Staff, Jodl; and Goering in his capacity of Reichsmarschall, as Commander in Chief of the Luftwaffe, and as plenipotentiary of the armament industry.

With the disaster of Stalingrad the fate of Operation Barbarossa was sealed. Hitler's last venture into the world of megalomaniacal lunacy finally brought his downfall and carried the German people with him into the abyss. Everything had been based on fatal fallacies. In a final speech before the attack Hitler, on June 14, 1941, spoke of the "myth of Russian armaments"; but

Kleist, who commanded the 1st Tank Corps, had to admit later: "My tank army comprised 600 vehicles. In comparison, the Army Group Budenny, which opposed us in the south, had some 2,400 tanks."

Hitler's characteristic of closing his eyes to all unpleasant factors came into prominence here. Scarcely a fortnight after the beginning of the attack he was saying in an aside to those near him: "The Russians have practically lost this war already." Even before the beginning of the winter of 1941, he claimed to have destroyed the Soviet Union. He was so confident of this that he was already busy with further plans. Alfred Rosenberg, Minister for the Occupied Eastern Territories, had already coined the term of the "Greater German World Empire"; in fact Hitler, after his victory over Russia, planned to extend his power still further. The American prosecutor, Sidney S. Alderman, produced some surprising documents on this point. He said: "That their [the Nazis] overall plan involved ultimate aggressive war against the United States was intimated by the defendant Goering in a speech, July 8, 1938, when these conspirators had already forcibly annexed Austria and were perfecting their plans against Czechoslovakia. This speech was delivered to representatives of the aircraft industry, and the copy that we have was transmitted as the enclosure to a secret memorandum from Goering's adjutant to General Udet."

In that speech a year before the beginning of the war, Goering stated: "I completely lack the bombers capable of round trip flights to New York with a five-ton bomb load. I would be supremely happy to possess such a bomber which would at last stuff the mouth of arrogance across the sea."

"Even in the fall of 1940," Alderman continued, "the prosecution of war against the United States of America at a later date was upon the military agenda. This is clearly shown in a document which we have found in the German Air Force files. This document . . . is dated October 29, 1940. I shall quote to you numbered paragraph 5: 'The Führer is at present occupied with the question of the occupation of the Atlantic islands with a view to the prosecution of a war against America at a later date. Deliberations on this subject are being embarked upon here. A brief assessment of the possibility of seizing and holding air bases and of the question of supply is needed from the GAF, the German Air Force.'

"In July 1941, in his first flash of confidence resulting from early gains against the U.S.S.R., the Führer signed an order for further preliminary preparations for the attack on the United States. This top-secret order, found in the files of the German Navy, is our Document C-74. 'By virtue of the intentions announced in Directive 32, for the further conduct of the war, I lay down the following principles: the military domination of Europe after the defeat of Russia will enable the strength of the army to be considerably reduced. . . . As far as the reduced strength of the army will allow, the armored units will be greatly increased. Naval armament must be restricted to those measures which have a direct connection with the conduct of the war against England, and should the case arise against America.' "

Five months later, on December 11, 1941, Hitler made his words come true—Germany declared war on the United States.

But how different were the circumstances now! Neither the Soviet Union nor England had been defeated—on the contrary: Britain's supremacy in the air now made itself felt even on the Continent, and in the East the German attack on Moscow was hopelessly bogged down. In addition, Japan's blow against the American fleet at Pearl Harbor on December 7, 1941—which gave Hitler the courage to declare war on the United States—proved to be in no way fatal. In the African theater of war, the Italian and German troops had to give way before the advancing British. The turning point of the war was approaching fast.

The Nuremberg Court did not concern itself with the further phases of the Second World War: they were known to history and formed no part of the evidence. On the other hand, much that happened and was ordered behind the front lines was discussed before the Tribunal under the headings of "War Crimes" and "Crimes Against Humanity." Beyond any doubt, the documents and the statements of witnesses combined to form one of the most horrible pictures in the history of mankind.

5
Behind the Front

SATAN'S
PROGRAM

Among the evidence placed before the Court by the Soviet chief prosecutor, Roman Rudenko, were the memoirs of the former National Socialist President of the Danzig Senate, Hermann Rauschning. In his book [*The Voice of Destruction*], Rauschning recalled what Adolf Hitler once said to him: "We must develop a technique of depopulation. If you ask me what I understand by depopulation I would say that I have in mind the destruction of whole racial entities. This I will certainly do; broadly speaking, I regard it as my task. Nature is cruel, therefore we, too, may be cruel. If I don't mind sending the pick of the German people into the hell of war without regret for the shedding of valuable German blood, then I have naturally the right to destroy millions of men of inferior races who increase like vermin."

The program of Hitler and his Party was Satan's program. Yet it would never have become cruel reality had there not been men who smartened it up philosophically and idealistically. Among the accused at Nuremberg were the propagandists of National Socialism: Rosenberg, Streicher, Schirach, and Fritzsche. It was they who, by their propaganda, prepared the way for the National Socialist dictatorship, and who then brought up German youth in the ideas of the new regime and duped a whole nation.

In this quartet of boosters, Alfred Rosenberg occupied the first place. His importance is described in a few sentences in the judgment of the Court: "He was the acknowledged theoretician of the Party, who developed and propounded the Nazi philosophy in the *Völkischer Beobachter* and *NS-Monatshefte*, which he published, as well as in the numerous books he wrote. More than a million copies of his principal book, *The Myth of the Twentieth Century*, were distributed."

237

As an ideologist, Rosenberg had great influence on National Socialism. He outlined the Party program and the new *Weltanschauung*. At the request of his defending counsel, Dr. Alfred Thoma, he told something of his life on the witness stand.

"Apart from my artistic interest in architecture and painting I pursued, since my early days, some philosophical studies, and as I felt myself very close to Goethe, Herder, and Fichte, I formed myself about them. At the same time I was influenced by the social thought of Charles Dickens, Carlyle, and by the American writer Emerson. At Riga I pusrued these studies further and of course took up Kant and Schopenhauer; above all, I devoted myself to Indian philosophy and related subjects, later naturally to European writers on history and culture, and eventually, in Munich, to a closer study of modern biological research."

Rosenberg the theoretician saw with satisfaction that his ideas became reality. He himself was given the chance to put them into practice—as chief of the Foreign Policy Office of the Nazi Party, as chief of the Special Commando Rosenberg which plundered cultural treasures in the conquered areas, and as Minister for the Occupied Eastern Territories. It was this last position that brought Rosenberg to the gallows.

With particular zeal he took upon himself the so-called Jewish question. He issued the directions for the "Institute for Research into the Jewish Question," which was opened on March 28, 1941. The American prosecutor, Walter W. Brudno, read out to the Court what Rosenberg wrote in the *Völkischer Beobachter:* "For Germany the Jewish question is only solved when the last Jew has left the territory of Greater Germany . . . and for Europe when he has left the Continent."

Julius Streicher, leader of the Franconians and Jew-baiter Number One, expressed himself much less elegantly and academically. In his anti-Semitic weekly, *Der Stürmer*, which for a time had a circulation of 600,000 copies, Streicher's hatred of the Jews assumed a particularly disgusting form. In May 1939, long before the beginning of the war, *Der Stürmer* demanded: "There must be a punitive expedition against the Jews in Russia, an expedition that will bring them to the same end as all murderers and criminals. Sentence of death, execution! The Jews in Russia must be killed. They must be exterminated root and branch!"

How did the former elementary school teacher, Gauleiter, and honorary SA General, Julius Streicher, form his fanatical hatred of the Jews? He, too, pleaded guidance by the Führer when he was asked about it by his defender, Dr. Hanns Marx.

STREICHER: I was already engaged in writing against the Jews before Adolf Hitler was publicly known. But I first understood the historical connections of the Jewish question from his book, *Mein Kampf.* In that book, Adolf Hitler explained to the world why he was an anti-Semite, and said that he knew the Jewish question through and through.

Streicher always maintained that he knew nothing of the mass murders of the Jews. The British prosecutor, J. M. G. Griffith-Jones, took up the issue in cross-examination. "This morning, when you were speaking of a German Jewish weekly, you said, 'In these papers there were sometimes hints that something was going on. Later, in 1943, there appeared an article saying that masses of Jews had disappeared, but no figures were given, and there was no mention of murder.' Do you really mean that in these issues of the Jewish weekly, which you and your editors read, there was nothing but hints about the disappearance of Jews, without mention of numbers or murder? Do you expect the Court to believe that?"

STREICHER: Yes, I stand by that, certainly.

GRIFFITH-JONES: Now I ask you to have a look at this portfolio. It is a portfolio with extracts from that weekly from July 1941 up to the end of the war. Please look at the first page; there is an article of July 11, 1941: "Last year, some 40,000 Jews died in Poland; the hospitals are overcrowded." You needn't turn over the page, we will pass on quickly. On December 12, 1941: "According to reports that have come in from many sides, many thousands of Jews have been executed in Odessa. Similar reports come from Kiev and other Russian cities." Did you read that?

STREICHER: I don't know, and if I had read it, it would not alter the matter. This is not evidence.

Streicher also denied the prosecutor's submission that *Der Stür-mer* had reported on ghetto conditions. On May 6, 1941, an eye-witness account appeared in that journal, and Mr. Griffith-Jones read some sadistic sentences from it: "*The Stürmer* sent its pho-tographer-reporter into various ghettos in the East. A *Stürmer* man knows his Jews through and through; nothing can easily sur-prise him. But what our colleague saw in those ghettos was a unique experience even for him. He writes: 'What offered itself to my eyes and my Leica has convinced me that the Jews are not human, but children of the devil and criminal scum. This satanic race really has no justification for its existence.' You still don't know, even if you don't believe all the figures, that millions of Jews were murdered after the beginning of the war? Do you know that? You have heard the evidence, haven't you?"

STREICHER: I believe so . . .

GRIFFITH-JONES: I only wish to know if you have heard the evi-dence. You can answer Yes or No, but I presume it will be Yes.

STREICHER: The only evidence for me is the testament of the Führer. It states in it that the mass murders took place at his command. That I believe. Now I believe it.

The systematic teaching of anti-Semitism had a special influ-ence upon German youth. The prosecution produced striking examples of the way in which hatred of the Jewish people was implanted in the hearts of the young. In this work, the major part was played by the Leader of the Hitler Youth, Baldur von Schi-rach. The Court condemned him, above all, on account of the crimes which were committed under his rule as Gauleiter and Reich Commissar for Vienna. The indictment states that Schirach was responsible for the deportation of 60,000 Jews from the Aus-trian capital. He was obsequiously faithful to Hitler according to the prosecution, a misled idealist according to the defense. Basi-cally, he was in fact both, idealist and fawning paladin. He was responsible for the fact' that in 1933 all organizations competing with the Hitler Youth were disbanded. He organized the Hitler Youth movement and brought up German youth in the ideas of the regime by means of bloodthirsty mercenaries' songs and pre-military training.

Schirach admitted the premilitary training of the Hitler Youth. Prosecutor Dodd produced some figures during the cross-examination of Schirach; they were confirmed by Schirach. In 1938, the Hitler Marine Youth comprised 45,000 members, the Hitler Motor Youth 60,000 members, 55,000 were given glider training, and 74,000 were organized in flying units. These figures came from an article in the *Völkischer Beobachter* on February 21, 1938, which concluded with the sentence: "In the field of small-bore rifle shooting, 1,200,000 Hitler Youths receive regular training today, guided by 7,000 marksmen."

Baldur von Schirach was one of the few at Nuremberg who confessed to their guilt. His confession said more about the duping of Germany's youth than all the documents of the prosecution. On May 24, 1946, Schirach stated on the witness stand:

"I have trained this generation to believe in Hitler and to be faithful to him. The youth movement which I built up bore his name. I intended to serve my Führer, who was to make our people and our youth great, free, and happy. Like myself, many millions of young people believed in this, and saw their ideal in National Socialism. Many have fallen for their creed. It is my guilt, which I bear before God, before the German people, and before our nation, that I have trained the youth of this people to believe in a man whom I regarded as above reproach as our leader and as head of the state for many a year; that I organized for him a youth that would look up to him as I did. It is my guilt that I have trained youth for a man who became a murderer a million times over."

Hitler Youth drums brought German youth marching to the parade ground. The propaganda drummer who, on the radio and in the press, daily brought the people up to the mark was Hans Fritzsche. He joined the Party only after it had seized power. Through his daily radio commentary, *Hans Fritzsche Speaking*, he became popular and had a meteoric career. In addition Fritzsche, as leader of the German press was the supervisor of 2,300 daily papers. He was the right hand of Propaganda Minister Joseph Goebbels. And as the latter had committed suicide, Fritzsche found himself in his place in the dock at Nuremberg.

Fritzsche was acquitted; the verdict said that he had in fact disseminated false reports, but it had not been proved that he knew they were false. The most famous case was the sinking of the *Athenia* by a German U-boat. Fritzsche had put the blame on Churchill. The Court believed his version that he had only learned the truth in prison from Admiral Raeder.

On the witness stand Fritzsche himself exposed the propaganda machine of the Third Reich when his defending counsel, Dr. Hans Fritz, asked him about his activities.

FRITZSCHE: Press politics were conducted by the National Press Chief, Dr. Dietrich. He gave his instructions in great detail, mostly with the actual wording to be used, the so-called "Daily Statement of the National Press Chief." As a rule he even gave the commentary word for word; this was also issued to the press conference. Dr. Dietrich generally stayed at the Führer's headquarters and received his instructions directly from Hitler. Dr. Dietrich's delegates were Sündermann and Lorenz. Second in importance after Dietrich in German press politics was National Director Amann, who was at the head of the publishers' organization.

A minor sensation was created in Nuremberg when during his cross-examination by the Soviet prosecutor, Roman Rudenko, Fritzsche repudiated the statements he had signed in Moscow, where he had lived after being taken prisoner.

FRITZSCHE: I gave my signature after many months of very strict solitary confinement. I signed because I had heard from another prisoner that once a month judgment was passed by a court only on the basis of such statements without a hearing, and because I hoped in this way at least to get a sentence and thus in time to see some end to my imprisonment. In order not to be misunderstood, I want to state expressly that no kind of pressure was exerted and that I was very humanely treated even though the imprisonment was very strict.

RUDENKO: Good. You never really supposed that after all you have done you would be taken to a convalescent home. Obviously you had to go to prison, and prison is prison after all.

The Court acquitted Fritzsche, perhaps because some of Rudenko's documents were questionable, perhaps on account of the consideration that war propaganda on both sides cannot be measured by the normal standards of journalism. At any rate, Fritzsche, Schirach, Streicher, Rosenberg had all labored at the task of deluding the German people. They were the propagandists of Satan, preparing the way for the criminal plans of National Socialism. Their philosophy had its most dreadful effect in the persecution of the Jews. Less openly, but just as ruthlessly, that philosophy gave battle to that of the churches.

"The essence of the present world revolution lies in the awakening of racial types," Alfred Rosenberg wrote in his philosophical bible, *The Myth of the Twentieth Century*. The American prosecutor, Walter W. Brudno, read some further extracts from the book: "Today a new faith awakens: the myth of the blood, the faith to defend, with the blood, the divine essence of man, the faith that incorporates the clearest knowledge that the Nordic blood represents this mystery, which has replaced and conquered the ancient sacraments."

Rosenberg was shown the bloody fruit of this seed, which he helped to spread in his *Myth*, at Nuremberg: As Minister for the Occupied Eastern Territories he received the written reports of his subordinates—reports like the one from which Jackson read to the Court: "In the presence of an SS man, a Jewish dentist was forced to extract or, if necessary, break out all gold teeth, bridges, or fillings from the mouths of German and Russian Jews before they were executed. Men, women, and children were locked up in barns and buried alive. Peasants, their wives and children, were shot on the pretense that they were suspected of conspiracy." ·

In the National Socialist *Weltanschauung* there was no place for humanity. On June 7, 1941, Martin Bormann wrote in a secret memorandum to all Gauleiters: "The National Socialist and the Christian outlooks are incompatible. Our National Socialist philosophy stands far higher than the conceptions of Christianity . . . If in the future our youth hears nothing about Christianity, whose teaching is much lower than ours, Christianity will disappear of itself."

The Germanic Yule Feast was to replace Christmas, and a

novel ceremony called "name giving" superseded baptism. But these were only external symptoms. Much more important was the active fight against the churches, a fight in which, in the end, all the resources of state and Party were employed in the cause of suppression. Admittedly, the Holy See signed a Concordat with Hitler, because the Vatican hoped to set up a defensive barrier by means of treaties. Admittedly, the clergy of several denominations paid homage to the dictator because they were irresolute or believed they might influence him for the better. Admittedly, the churches made compromises, made tactical concessions, sought ways of coming to an understanding. But against this background the bravery of others, of some higher dignitaries and thousands of anonymous secular and ordained preachers, stands out all the more splendidly. The concentration camps were full of them, any frank word from the pulpit meant arrest, and Catholic and Protestant alike were victims of the Gestapo, as were representatives of other denominations, such as the Christian Scientists.

A favorite propaganda method—the "spontaneous rising of the people"—often enough organized by the Nazis, was also applied in this fight. An example of it was cited in Nuremberg by prosecutor Storey:

"I now offer in evidence Document 848-PS, which is a Gestapo telegram dated July 24, 1938, dispatched from Nuremberg dealing with demonstrations and acts of violence against Bishop Sproll in Rottenburg. I quote: 'The Party, on July 23, 1938, from 2100 hours on, carried out the third demonstration against Bishop Sproll. Participants, about 2,500 to 3,000 were brought from outside by buses, etc. The Rottenburg populace again did not participate in the demonstration. This town took a rather hostile attitude toward the demonstrations. The demonstrators stormed the Palace, beat in the gates and doors. About 150 to 200 people forced their way into the Palace, searched through the rooms, threw files out of the window, and rummaged through beds in the rooms of the Palace. One bed was ignited.' "

Almost every bishop's seat in Germany suffered similar outrages sooner or later. In Nuremberg, prosecutor Storey said:

"I now offer in evidence Document 3268-PS which contains excerpts from the Allocution of His Holiness Pope Pius XII to the Sacred College, June 2, 1945. In this address, His Holiness, after declaring that he had acquired an appreciation of the great qualities of the German people in the course of twelve years residence in their midst, expressed the hope that Germany 'could rise to new dignity and a new life once it has laid the satanic specter raised by National Socialism, and the guilty have expiated the crimes they have committed.' His Holiness declared, and I quote from Document 3268-PS:

" 'The struggle against the Church did, in fact, become even more bitter; there was the dissolution of Catholic organizations; the gradual suppression of the flourishing Catholic schools, both public and private; the enforced weaning of youth from family and Church; the pressure brought to bear by the conscience of citizens, and especially of civil servants; the systematic defamation by means of a clever, closely organized propaganda, of the Church, the clergy, the faithful, the Church's institutions, teachings, and history; the closing, dissolution, confiscation of religious houses and other ecclesiastical institutions, the complete suppression of the Catholic press and publishing houses.'

"But when, after he had tried all means of persuasion in vain, he saw himself clearly faced with deliberate violations of a solemn pact, with a religious persecution masked or open but always rigorously organized, he proclaimed to the world on Passion Sunday, 1937, in his encyclical *With Burning Sorrow* what National Socialism really was: the arrogant apostasy from Jesus Christ, the denial of His doctrine and of His work of redemption, the cult of violence, the idolatry of race and blood, the overthrow of human liberty and dignity. . . .

" 'From the prisons, concentration camps, and fortresses, are now pouring out, together with the political prisoners, also the crowds of those, whether clergy or laymen, whose only crime was their fidelity to Christ and to the faith of their fathers or the fulfillment of their duties as priests. In the forefront, for the number and harshness of the treatment meted out to them, are the Polish priests. From 1940 to 1945, 2,800 Polish ecclesiastics and religious were imprisoned in that camp (Dachau); among them was the auxiliary Bishop of Wloclawek (Vladislava) who died there of typhus. In April last, there were left only 816; all the rest being dead, except for two or three transferred to another camp. In the summer of 1942, 480 German-speaking ministers of religion were known to be gathered there; of these, 45 were Protestants, all the others Catholic priests. In spite of the continuous inflow of new internees, especially from dioceses of Bavaria, Rhenonia (the Rhineland) and Westphalia, their number, as a result of the high rate of mortality at the beginning of this year, did not surpass 350. Nor should we pass over in silence those belonging to occupied territories; Holland, Belgium, France (among whom was the Bishop of Clermont) Luxemburg, Slovenia, Italy. Many of these priests and laymen endured indescribable sufferings for their faith and their vocation. In one case the hatred of the impious against Christ reached the point of parodying on the person of an interned priest, with barbed wire, the scourging and crowning with thorns of our Redeemer.' "

But what Pius XII said shortly after the end of the war does not cover the whole extent of the fight against the Church. The SD and the Gestapo had instructions to suppress and stamp out the Church, and so "prevent its treasonable activity during the German fight for life."

The Gestapo and the SD played an important part in almost all of these criminal acts. The variety of those crimes, quite apart from the many thousands of individual cases of torture and cruelty under the surveillance of Germany, reads like a page from the Devil's logbook. They were the most important organs in the suppression of the Churches. Gestapo and SD—the terms meant concentration camps, and in many thousands of cases death was the only escape. Reverend Bruno Theek, who left the hell of Dachau alive, reported:

> In two barracks, each originally intended for two hundred men, three thousand priests of all denominations and from most Continental countries were forced to live under the most unworthy and undignified conditions; many died as a result of their tortures. I was standing near by when an old Polish priest, who knew no word of German, was asked something by the senior guard of the block—a bestial former SA man, now himself a prisoner. The priest, unable to reply, was struck over the head

with a board by the enraged guard many times until he collapsed, covered with blood; he died the same night.

In Nuremberg, one of the darkest chapters of National Socialist history was opened for all to read. Its heading might have been the distorted commandment: "Thou shalt kill."

Thou shalt kill—the weak, the sick, the old, the infirm, the incapable, the unwanted. Thou shalt kill the useless eater. In Bormann's new catechism there was no place for charity, in Rosenberg's *Weltanschauung* sympathy and love were nothing but a "moral quagmire." The terrifying SS man looming over the teeth extraction, the doctor who injected the fatal poison into the bodies of the helpless—these are consequences and symbol of Rosenberg's "mystery of the Nordic blood, which has replaced and conquered the ancient sacraments."

Here there was a contrast with which the Nuremberg Court had to deal. Closely connected with the complex of religious persecution was the so-called "euthanasia program" of the Nazi leadership, for on this point the churches fought their biggest battle with the system of inhumanity.

The Roman Catholic prior of St. Hedwig's Cathedral in Berlin, Bernhard Lichtenberg, used to say after every Mass: "Let us now pray for the Jews." He ignored the Gestapo spies in his church as he preached: "In a number of Berlin homes an anonymous inflammatory rag against the Jews is being distributed. It says that any German who, from allegedly false sentimentality, helps the Jews, commits treason against his own people. Do not let yourself be led astray by such un-Christian thoughts, but act according to the clear command of Christ: Thou shalt love thy neighbor as thyself." On the way to the concentration camp at Dachau, Lichtenberg's voice was silenced forever. But others spoke up against the cold-blooded mass murders which the leaders of state and Party termed "Mercy Death."

Hans Heinrich Lammers, the chief of Hitler's Chancellery, was questioned in the Nuremberg witness stand by Keitel's defense counsel, Dr. Otto Nelte, about the background of the so-called euthanasia program.

DR. NELTE: Do you know anything about Hitler's efforts to put down painlessly those suffering from incurable insanity?

LAMMERS: Yes. The idea was expressed for the first time by Hitler in the autumn of 1939. The Secretary of State in the Ministry for the Interior, Dr. Conti (the National Medical chief), was given the order to study the problem. I spoke against the execution of this plan. But since the Führer insisted, I proposed that the whole business should be put on a legal footing and be governed by a law. I also had an appropriate draft of a law prepared; as a result, the matter was taken out of the hands of Secretary of State Conti and transferred to National Leader Bouhler in 1940. Bouhler reported to the Führer, who did not approve the draft of the law. He did not, however, expressly reject it, but later, without bringing me into the scheme, he issued authority for the killing of incurable invalids to National Leader Bouhler and the doctor who was then working with him, Professor Dr. Brandt.

The American prosecutor, Robert J. Storey, read the decisive document of September 1, 1939, written on Hitler's personal note paper: "National Leader Bouhler and Dr. Brandt are charged with the responsibility of granting to certain physicians the right to administer the Mercy Death to those who are incurably ill, according to human judgment and a critical evaluation of the state of their illness. Signed: Adolf Hitler."

Martin Bormann, Hitler's deputy, instructed the Gauleiter offices on October 1, 1940. The British prosecutor, Griffith-Jones, read out: "The Führer gave the order. Laws are being drawn up. At present, only clear-cut cases or one hundred per cent incapables are to be dealt with. Later there will be extensions."

For the information of the judicial officials, Bormann wrote on the same day: "The action begins in the immediate future. Failures have scarcely occurred so far. 30,000 cases completed. Further 100,000 to 120,000 are waiting. Keep the circle of those in the know as small as possible."

The murders had begun, and although the murderers made every effort "to keep the circle of those in the know as small as possible," the sudden rise of the death rate in nursing homes and mental hospitals caused some speculation. An increasing number of relatives received notices mentioning quite improbable causes of death.

The Nazi district office at Erlangen, in whose area lay one of the largest sanatoria in Germany, saw cause to send a report on the situation to Berlin on the November 26, 1940. At Nuremberg, Mr. Griffith-Jones read from it: "On orders from the Ministry of the Interior, signed Schulz or Schultze, a commission consisting, among others, of a North German doctor and a number of students appeared some time ago in the local sanatorium and nursing home. The doctor examined the records of the patients who were to be transferred to another institution . . . a Berlin transport company was to carry out the transfer and the head of the institution was to follow the directives of this company, which was in possession of the list of names."

The company was called Public Service Transportation Co., Inc.

"In this way," the report continues, "three transports with a total number of 370 patients were in the meantime transferred to Sonnenstein near Pirna (in Saxony) and to the Linz district (in Austria). A further transport will leave in January of next year. . . .

"Strangely enough, various relatives received notification after the transportation that the patients had died. In some cases pneumonia, and in others an infectious disease, were given as the cause of death. The relatives were further informed that it had been necessary to cremate the body, and that . . . the clothing of the deceased could be sent to them. The registry office in Erlangen was also informed by the institution of the various cases of death, and again, either pneumonia or an infectious disease was given as the cause—illnesses which had no relation with the patients' previous medical history. It must therefore be assumed that false statements have been made. The inhabitants are greatly disturbed about the patients being transferred, as the transfers are quickly followed by reports of their deaths. This unrest among the local inhabitants is especially harmful in time of war. Besides, the events described give the church and religious circles cause to assert anew their opposition to National Socialism."

In August 1941, Bishop Hilfrich of Limburg wrote to the Ministry of the Interior, the Ministry of Justice, and the Ministry for Church Affairs: "Some five miles from Limburg, near the small town of Hadamar, there is an institution which previously served various purposes, and eventually that of a hospital and nursing home; but it has now, according to general opinion, been used for some months—since about February 1941—for systematic euthanasia. Several times a week, buses arrive at Hadamar with a large number of victims. Schoolchildren in the district know these buses and say: 'Here comes another murder box!' After the arrival of these buses, the people of Hadamar can observe smoke rising from the chimney and are moved by constant thoughts of the poor victims.

"Gestapo officials, it is said, are trying to suppress talk about the events at Hadamar by threatening people with reprisals. The knowledge, conviction, and indignation of the inhabitants will not be altered in this way. The conviction will be increased by the bitter knowledge that although talk is prohibited by intimidation, the actions themselves are not being punished."

First the hospitals and mental homes were cleared, then came the turn of the homes for cripples and for the aged; eventually others who were incapable of working, among them even prisoners of war, were no longer safe. "Even the war-wounded were condemned to death," said Bishop Johann Neuhäusler.

Archbishop Konrad of Freiburg proposed to the Reich Chancellery on August 1, 1940: "We declare ourselves ready to meet all expenses with regard to the further care of all mental patients who are to be put to death."

All the Roman Catholic bishops in Germany applied to the Chancellery on August 11, 1940—without success. Bishop Clemens August von Galen even denounced these murders in public, in the pulpit of the Lamberti Church at Münster on August 3, 1941:

"German men and women! Article 211 of the Reich Penal Code is still in force. It says: 'A person who kills a man intentionally, will be punished by death if he has carried out the murder with malice aforethought.' But I have been assured that in the Ministry of the Interior and in the office of the national medical chief,

Dr. Conti, no secret is made of the fact that a large number of mental patients have been intentionally killed, and will be killed, in Germany. I have not yet heard that the Public Prosecutor or the Police have acted in this matter."

Bishop Bornewasser of Trier preached on September 14, 1941: "No state, no government has the right to order the killing of those called 'unworthy to live' or 'unproductive,' of innocent, weak-minded, or insane patients, and no doctor has the right to take part in such a killing. Woe to thee, poor Germany! As the Holy Scripture says: 'Be not deceived; God is not mocked: for whatsoever a man soweth, that shall he also reap.' "

Cardinal Faulhaber spoke openly on March 22, 1942, from the pulpit in Munich: "With deep horror the Christian people in Germany have learned that, by an order of the state, numerous mentally weak people, who have been entrusted to hospitals and nursing homes, have been deprived of their lives as 'unproductive members of the community.' Your archbishop will not cease to protest against the killing of the innocent."

Yet all these protests rebounded from the walls of silence with which those responsible had fenced themselves in. In the institutions of death, fanatical doctors, nurses, and assistants carried on with the lethal syringe. As ever more victims were collected by the "Public Service Transportation Company," the slow method of the syringe was replaced by the gas chamber.

The verdict against an "institution" doctor, Professor Dr. Hermann Paul Nitsche, on November 3, 1947, stated: "At the institution of Sonnenstein, the gassing was carried out as follows: The patients, who were brought in in buses with their windows painted green, were taken into a reception room where their identity was checked. Then they were taken into the next room for an examination by the physicians Dr. Schumann and Dr. Schmalenbach. If the doctor decided on gassing, the patients were taken by attendants into a neighboring room where they had to undress; infirm patients were undressed by the attendants. The patients were told that they would be bathed. From the dressing room steps led down into the cellar—into a room that was next to the gas chamber. There the patients were taken over by the 'disinfectors'—specially reliable SS men. After the attendants had withdrawn, the patients were taken into the gas chamber. The actual gassing was carried out by the institution's physician by the moving of a lever. It took only a few minutes. In the whole action the defendant Dr. Nitsche was chiefly involved. The defendants Felfe, Gräbler, and Räpke—so-called male nurses—were in fact accessories. Gräbler brought some 25 to 30 transports with mentally defective people for gassing to Sonnenstein, altogether 15,-000 to 16,000 souls."

Georg Konrad Morgen, retired SS judge, was asked on the witness stand at Nuremberg how this system of mass murder had been developed, and who could be regarded as its originator. The point at issue in the hearing was the gassing of the Jews in the concentration camps.

MORGEN: Wirth described the methods to me.

HORST PELCKMANN (counsel for the SS): Was Wirth a member of the SS?

MORGEN: No. Wirth was a police inspector in Stuttgart.

PELCKMANN: Did you ask Wirth how he came to arrive at this devilish system?

MORGEN: When Wirth took over the liquidation of the Jews he was already a specialist in the mass murder of humans, and he had already carried out the order to kill those who were incurably insane. To this end, at the beginning of the war, he gathered round him a special unit from among his own officials at the order of the Führer himself. Wirth described to me most vividly how he had gone about the task, as he had no detailed instructions and no assistance, but he had to find out everything for himself. He had only been given an old empty asylum in Brandenburg. There he carried out his first experiments, and there he perfected his system after many studies and trials. The system was then applied on a large scale to the insane.

SS battalion leader and police inspector Christian Wirth was thus, according to the statement of Morgen, the satanic deviser of those methods of extermination which he perfected "after many studies and trials," and by which later millions of people from all over Europe were murdered.

Foreign workers and prisoners of war met their death in Wirth's gas chambers: "This is absolutely established by this document," said the American prosecutor, Robert Kempner, in Nuremberg, "by the verdict of the military commission for Hadamar in Wiesbaden: 'Alfons Klein, Adolf Wahlmann, Heinrich Ruoeff, Karl Willig, Adolf Merkle, Irmgard Huber, and Philipp Blum have been found guilty, of having acted, assisted, and taken part in the intentional and unlawful killing of at least four hundred persons of Russian and Polish nationality, whose exact names and number are unknown, in Hadamar during a period from about April 1, 1944, to April 1, 1945.' "

It was established at the Hadamar Trial, that there were several children among the victims. Klein, Ruoeff, and Willig were condemned to death by hanging. The verdict of the Nuremberg Court also stated: "Furthermore, measures were introduced in Germany as early as the summer of 1940 on the basis of which all old and mentally unbalanced persons, and all with incurable diseases, were imprisoned and put to death, while their relatives were informed that they had died from natural causes. The victims were not only German nationals but also foreign laborers who were no longer able to carry on with their work and consequently had become useless to the German war machine. One estimate suggests that in this way at least 275,000 persons from nursing homes, hospitals, and asylums, which were controlled by the defendant Frick in his capacity as Minister for the Interior, have been killed. It was quite impossible to determine how many foreign workers are included in this total."

These sentences from the Nuremberg verdict outline the whole tragedy and significance of the euthanasia program. Murder had become a coldly calculated system of expediency.

HITLER'S
MANAGERS

Among the prisoners at Nuremberg Hitler's former deputy, Rudolf Hess, was undoubtedly the most mysterious. He presented many problems to the Court, and the question of his sanity gave the Court, prosecution, and defense much to think about. Before the beginning of the Trial the first defense counsel for Hess, Dr. Günther von Rohrscheidt, presented a petition in which he requested the Court to appoint a medical specialist to examine Hess and to report on his condition and his ability to plead.

In fact, the Court entrusted a commission of ten physicians with the examination of the defendant. The three Soviet doctors and the French specialist reported: "No substantial physical deterioration from normal condition has been observed. He is an unbalanced personality. Partly as a result of the failure of his mission, anomalous symptoms have increased, leading to suicide attempts." The British specialists came to the conclusion: "He is at present not insane in the strict sense of the word. His loss of memory does not prevent him completely from understanding the proceedings, but it limits his ability to conduct his defense and to understand details of the past which may be important in the submission of evidence. This symptom of loss of memory may possibly disappear if conditions alter."

Those who had the opportunity of observing Rudolf Hess in the Nuremberg prison could hardly believe that he was the same man who had been Hitler's confidant and one of the most important protagonists and leaders of the Third Reich.

During the whole duration of the Trial, Hess bombarded the German prison physician, Dr. Ludwig Pflücker, with requests for a special diet: "Today's bread is obviously baked from bad flour. Indigestible for my stomach. Can I have other bread?"—"This cheese is too strong for me. Have you anything else?" This went on day after day. Pflücker reported: "He was continually occupied with ordinances for the Third Reich which was soon to be revived, designs for a monument in honor of those who would be condemned to death in the Trial, and in default of a larger audience he addressed manifestos to his fellow prisoners."

These reports from the prison made the question of Hess's state of mind even more urgent. On the ninth day of the Nuremberg Trial, he created a sensation in the courtroom. The afternoon session of November 30, 1945, was devoted exclusively to his case. All the other defendants were left in their cells. In the large dock

Rudolf Hess sat alone, reserved, inscrutable, in the pale light of the fluorescent lights. The places of the legal authorities were empty; only his counsel, Dr. Rohrscheidt, was present. The pros and cons of his mental state and his ability to plead were expounded at length, until Rudolf Hess himself suddenly rose from his seat and made a surprising statement. Looking with a slight smile toward the press gallery, balancing himself on his toes, Hess moistened his lips with his tongue—and waited until the American soldiers had set up a microphone beside him. Only then did he begin to speak:

"Mr. President, I would like to say this: At the start of the proceedings this afternoon I gave my defense a note in which I expressed my opinion that the proceedings could be curtailed if I were allowed to speak. In order to avoid the possibility that I may be declared unfit to plead I submit to the Court the following statement, although I originally meant to submit it at a later stage of the Trial: From now on my memory is at the disposal of the Court. The reasons for the pretense of loss of memory are of a tactical nature. In point of fact only my ability to concentrate is somewhat weak. But that does not affect my ability to follow the proceedings, to defend myself, to put questions to witnesses, or to answer questions myself. I declare that I bear the full responsibility for all that I have done, signed, or co-signed. My basic point of view, that the Court is not competent, is not affected by this statement.

"Up to now I have maintained my loss of memory even to my official defense counsel. He has therefore acted in good faith."

There was a breathless hush in the courtroom as Hess sat down. At the back of the room, doors were opened; some journalists were dashing out to telephones in a hurry. Judge Lawrence said only four words: "The proceedings are adjourned."

Next morning, the President began by announcing the Court's decision: "The Court has carefully considered the petition of the defending counsel of the defendant Hess and has also had the opportunity to discuss it in detail both with the defense and with the prosecution. The Court has also taken into account the detailed medical report which has been made on the condition of the defendant Hess, and has come to the conclusion that no reasons exist to order a further examination of the defendant. Since the defendant Hess has made a statement to the Court, and in view of the existing evidence, the Court is of the opinion that he is at present capable of pleading. The petition of defending counsel is therefore rejected, and the Trial will proceed."

Was the puzzle of Rudolf Hess thereby solved? Not in the least. For a time Hess seemed to be clear in his mind and to follow the proceedings attentively. Then he sank again into a listless, indifferent attitude and expressed himself only in confused sentences.

Along with the former Minister of the Interior, Wilhelm Frick, he was the only defendant who elected not to go on the witness stand. Winston Churchill, who saw all the reports on Hess, wrote in 1950: "He was a medical and not a criminal case, and as such he should be treated."

After Hess had made his statement, the proceedings against him took their course. Mr. J. M. G. Griffith-Jones, the British prosecuting counsel, concerned himself with the mysterious flight to England: What did Hess hope to achieve by this adventurous undertaking? If he really intended to negotiate a peace between Germany and Britain, he went about it rather clumsily—or rather his action showed that Hitler's deputy had no idea of the factual situation, that he was nothing but a muddle-headed dreamer.

Hess had had several opportunities of putting his propositions before officials and representatives of the British Government. Immediately after his landing in Scotland he was able, according to his wish, to speak to the Duke of Hamilton. Two days later, on May 13, 1941, he was visited by a representative of the London Foreign Office, Mr. (now Sir) Ivone Kirkpatrick, later High Commissioner in Bonn. In the presence of a stenographer Hess explained in a rather rambling way what had prompted him to undertake his flight. In the Nuremberg courtroom, Mr. Griffith-Jones later summarized the stenographer's report:

> Hess began with a description of the chain of events that had led to his present position and which really consisted of a history of Europe from the end of the last war to the present moment. He spoke about Austria, Czechslovakia, Poland, and Norway, and said that in each case Germany had been right,

and that it was the fault of England and France that Germany
had had to invade these countries. He made England completely
responsible for the beginning of the present war. He then said
that Germany must win the war; that the bombing of England
had only just begun, and with the greatest reserve. He said that
German U-boat production was enormously large, that vast
sources of raw materials were available in the occupied territories,
and that Hitler's confidence in final victory was complete. He
then gave the reasons for his flight, explaining that the thought
of a long war was repulsive to him, that England could not win,
and should prefer to make peace now.

Mr. Kirkpatrick listened to his clumsy utterances with calm
interest, but—continued the report—"Hess tried to make my blood
boil when he stated that the greedy Americans were aspiring after
the British Empire. Canada would certainly be incorporated in
the United States."

After Hess had shown his diplomatic capabilities by this introduction, he came to speak about the real crux of his mission. The
British prosecutor continued with Mr. Kirkpatrick's report:

> The solution that Hess proposed was that England should
> give Germany a free hand in Europe while Germany would give
> England a free hand outside Europe, with the single condition
> that we should give back to Germany her previous colonies,
> whose sources of raw materials she needed urgently. In order to
> find out something about Hitler's attitude toward Russia, I
> asked him if Russia belonged to Europe or to Asia; he answered,
> to Asia. I replied to him that within the terms of the proposed
> conditions Germany would not be in a position to attack Russia,
> as she would only have a free hand in Europe. Herr Hess re-
> acted at once and declared that Germany had certain demands
> to make of Russia that must be satisfied either by means of
> concessions or by a war. But he added that the rumors of an
> impending attack by Hitler on Russia, which were current at the
> time, were without foundation.

Hess gave these assurances to Mr. Kirkpatrick less than two
months before Hitler's actual attack on the Soviet Union. Was
Hess a hopeless dreamer, or was he consciously bluffing? "When
we were on the point of leaving the room," says Mr. Kirkpatrick's

document, "Herr Hess fired the last shot. He said he had forgotten to say that the proposal was subject to the condition that a government other than the present one would have to negotiate with Hitler. Mr. Churchill and his colleagues were not the kind of personalities with whom Hitler could deal."

On two more occasions, Hess repeated these incredible proposals to Mr. Kirkpatrick. The British Cabinet decided to make quite sure by sending a member of the government to Rudolf Hess. The choice fell on the Lord Chancellor, Lord Simon. On June 10, 1941, Lord Simon and two other officials from the Foreign Office—one of them Mr. Kirkpatrick—visited Hess with an interpreter and a stenographer. The Lord Chancellor introduced himself, but for reasons of security his name was given as "Dr. Guthrie" in the report. The document, from the archives of the British Foreign Office, was classified as "Top Secret." Among other things it reports this conversation:

HESS: I have been told by the Führer the conditions on which Germany is prepared to come to an understanding with England.

LORD SIMON: We have now reached the point where we must hear the conditions.

Mr. Kirkpatrick read out what Hess had put down in writing: "Foundation for an understanding. First, in order to avoid future wars between England and Germany, spheres of interest must be defined. Germany's sphere of interest is Europe, England's sphere of interest is her Empire."

LORD SIMON: Surely that means Continental Europe?

HESS: Continental Europe, yes.

LORD SIMON: Does that include any part of Russia?

HESS: Russia in Europe naturally interests us. If, for example, we were to conclude a treaty with Russia, England would not be involved in any way.

LORD SIMON: Does this include Italy as well?

HESS: Italy? Yes, of course. Italy is part of Europe, and if we conclude a treaty with Italy, England will again not be involved in any way.

LORD SIMON: Let us continue.

KIRKPATRICK: Secondly: Return of the German colonies.

Point Three concerned problems of compensation. Point Four forecast a simultaneous peace treaty with Germany and Italy. Once again Hess spoke about "spheres of interest."

LORD SIMON: If Germany's sphere of interest is to be Europe, does that include Greece?

HESS: These "spheres of interest" concern England in the first instance; in future England shall not be in a position to form coalitions on the Continent against Germany, as little as we shall have occasion to interfere in any way in the British Empire.

LORD SIMON: But there is a slight difference—the internal affairs of the British Empire are British affairs. Are all affairs on the European continent German affairs?

HESS: No, we do not claim that, and we do not intend to bother with the details of these countries as England does with the Empire.

At this point of the discussion Hess struck the table with his fist and said: "If England will not agree to these bases for an understanding, then sooner or later the day will come when she will be forced to agree to them."

The Lord Chancellor remained unmoved. "Yes, but I don't think that that is a very good argument for the British Government. We are a rather courageous people, and do not in any way think much of threats."

HESS: May I say that that was not intended as a threat but as my personal opinion.

LORD SIMON: Yes, I see.

The Minister rose. At the door he turned again and asked: "Return of the colonies—am I to understand that German Southwest Africa is to be included?"

Hess did not notice the biting irony of these words, and answered naively, "Yes."

KIRKPATRICK: And the Japanese islands as well?

HESS: Not the Japanese islands.

With this mention of the formerly German Marshall Islands, which after the First World War became Japanese mandated territory, the meeting was at an end. After this, Hess was no longer of any interest. His ignorance, the awkward arrogance of his manner, and the naïveté of his political ideas made any further discussion with him pointless.

But the prosecution at Nuremberg did not regard Hess as a political dreamer. Detailed charges were submitted against him. They showed how extensive and manifold Hess's functions had been in Hitler's machinery of state. "The defendant Hess," says the indictment, "employed his position, his personal influence, and his very close relationship with the Führer to help the seizure of power by the Nazi conspirators, the establishment of their control over Germany, and their military, economic, and psychological preparations for war; he took part in the political planning and preparation for a war of aggression: he approved, led, and took part in war crimes and crimes against humanity, including many crimes against persons and property."

The British prosecutor, Mr. Griffith-Jones, spent almost a whole day in laying before the Court the details of the charges against Hess. The tactics of confusion had not helped him. From the wealth of material and the statements of witnesses his true personality and his guilt emerged. The Court acquitted him of the charge of war crimes and crimes against humanity. But the sentence passed on him—life imprisonment—showed that Hess, as Hitler's deputy, was regarded as the most important man in the Party hierarchy and as an active participant in the preparations for war.

The Party official who replaced Hess as Deputy Leader was a man named Martin Bormann. At Nuremberg he was the only defendant who was proceeded against in his absence. Bormann joined the Nazi Party in 1925, and rose in the Party hierarchy to become Staff Leader to Hess. Bormann's great chance came when Hess flew to England. He was promoted to Chief of the Party Headquarters and Chief of Staff to the Führer's deputy. In 1943, Bormann became Hitler's secretary and in the last years of the war enjoyed his confidence more fully than anyone else. Things went so far in the end that only people acceptable to him were admitted to Hitler.

Prosecutor Griffith-Jones stated: "Up to the time when Hess flew to England, Bormann was his deputy, and therefore I am of the opinion that for the ordinances that Bormann issued as deputy of the Deputy of the Führer, the defendant Hess is responsible as well."

In point of fact all Bormann's decrees and ordinances were issued at first "in the name of the Deputy of the Führer." The American prosecutor, Thomas F. Lambert, who presented the case against Bormann, produced a document which concerned Bormann and Hess jointly: "I submit as evidence Document 062-PS. According to its cover it is an order by the defendant Hess of March 13, 1940, which is addressed to national leaders, Gauleiters, and other Party functionaries and organizations. Those Party officials are instructed by the defendant Hess to inform the whole of the civil population that Allied airmen who make emergency landings are to be arrested or rendered harmless. I draw the Court's attention to the third paragraph in which Hess lays down that these instructions are to be passed on only by word of mouth. In fact, they were instructions for the lynching of Allied airmen. They were headed, 'Instruction for action in the case of landings of enemy aircraft or parachutists.' The fourth paragraph says— I quote: 'Similarly, enemy parachutists are to be arrested at once or rendered harmless.' This speaks for itself and calls for no further commentary on the part of the prosecution."

"This instruction contains nothing," replied the defense counsel Dr. Alfred Seidl, "that is contrary to the laws and usages of war. Both according to the words and the meaning of this paragraph four there cannot be the slightest doubt that all it says is that an enemy parachutist must be fought and overpowered if he does not surrender voluntarily but attempts to avoid capture by the use of force, and especially by the use of weapons. This meaning is expressed by the word 'or'; in the first instance, their capture is to be attempted."

The objection was successful in the case of Hess: but Bormann was held responsible by the Court for the lynching of Allied airmen. His guilt was proved by a direction of May 30,

1944, to the Party officials; in this he forbade the police and the judicial authorities to take action against people who had participated in lynchings. Already on November 5 he had forbidden that Soviet prisoners of war should be properly buried. Two years later he ordered the Gauleiters to report cases of lenient treatment of prisoners of war. The climax of this policy toward defenseless prisoners was reached on September 30, 1944, with an order which was a virtual sentence of death for thousands of them: Bormann withdrew from the Wehrmacht the jurisdiction over all prisoners of war, and transferred it to Himmler and the SS, who were also put in charge of all internees.

Not all the men around Hitler were such fanatical and unscrupulous bureaucratic types as Bormann. In the dock at Nuremberg there were two men who shared the company of the Party leaders for years, but would gladly have withdrawn from that company. They were Franz von Papen and Hjalmar Schacht— both to be acquitted by the Court. Papen, "Hitler's stirrup-holder," had had a dubious career since 1933. The former Reich Chancellor and Vice-Chancellor was appointed Ambassador to Vienna in 1934 and Ambassador to Ankara in 1939. He was called in by Hitler, who did not have to beg him to accept. Papen kept silent about the crimes that were happening all around him. He was silent about things that must have gone against his innermost convictions, such as the Nazi fight against the churches. The British prosecutor, Sir David Maxwell Fyfe, cross-examined him about an incident which proved Papen's fellow-traveling in Hitler's Party machine.

SIR DAVID: You will remember that you introduced Cardinal Innitzer to Hitler when you came to Austria?

PAPEN: Yes.

SIR DAVID: I want you now to remember what happened to Cardinal Innitzer. Here is a sworn statement by a cleric, Dr. Weinbacher, Secretary to the Archbishop: "On October 8, 1938, there was a severe attack by young demonstrators on the Archbishop's Palace in Vienna. I was present." Then he describes how windows were smashed and the gate was forced open. The priests took the Cardinal to a room at the back and hid him there.

"Shortly after we reached the chapel, the intruders stormed into the Cardinal's rooms. Pieces of wood were thrown about in the chapel; I received a blow which felled me. The demonstrators were youths from 14 to 25 years old, about a hundred in number; meanwhile in the other rooms there was a frenzy of destruction which cannot be described. The youths destroyed tables and chairs, chandeliers and valuable pictures, especially all crosses, with the brass rods with which the carpet was fastened to the stairs."

Then he described how the mirror doors of the chapel were smashed. There was a great tumult when the Cardinal was discovered. Dr. Weinbacher was hauled out by some six people and dragged to the window with shouts: "We're going to fling the dog out of the window."

At long last the police came, "first a lieutenant who apologized, then a representative of the Gestapo who expressed his regret that the policemen felt no inclination to interfere. Meanwhile, other demonstrators had made an attack on the cathedral parsonage on the Stefansplatz where they had thrown the cathedral curate, the Reverend Krawarik, out of the window into the courtyard. This priest was for many months in the hospital with both his thighs broken. That these demonstrations were not just an expression of youthful high spirits or due to momentary indignation, but a well-thought-out plan known to the Nazi officials emerges clearly from the public speech of Gauleiter Bürckel on October 13, when he had the infamy of accusing the Cardinal himself of being the guilty party."

Now, Herr von Papen, you had a great responsibility toward Cardinal Innitzer, had you not? You had introduced him to Hitler. You must have heard of this?

PAPEN: I heard of it later, yes.

SIR DAVID: What protests did you make when you heard of this shameful attack?

PAPEN: I might remind you, Sir David, that I had left the service six months earlier, and that I had no longer anything to do with this matter. Naturally, the details of this attack are in the highest degree regrettable and were criminal acts. But the details were not reported in the German press . . . I made no protest. I was then no longer in any official capacity, I was a private individual, and I only knew about these things what the German papers were allowed to print.

SIR DAVID: But you have told us that you were one of the leading Catholics in Germany. Are you going to tell the Court that the Catholic bishops in Germany and probably the priests did not all know that this shameful offense had been committed upon a Prince of the Church in his own house in Vienna?

PAPEN: That is quite possible. But do you expect me, as a private individual, to take some sort of action?

SIR DAVID: I thought that you might have taken the trouble to protest to Hitler. You could have written to Hitler. What you in fact did was that within six months, in April 1939, you accepted another position under Hitler.

In its judgment, the Court underlined the active part of Papen in the *Anschluss* with Austria, and stated: "In order to carry through this plan he both carried on intrigues and made threats."

Just as Papen had helped Hitler to power, so Hjalmar Schacht had helped Hitler to secure the economic means to achieve his political aims. Schacht placed his financial and political talent and his economic knowledge at Hitler's disposal, although he recognized the criminal character of the Third Reich. The American prosecutor, Jackson, reproached him with this at the beginning of his cross-examination.

JACKSON: Dr. Schacht, according to the transcript of the testimony, you said that in 1938 you told a certain lady while you were dining: "My dear lady, we have fallen into the hands of criminals. How could I have suspected that!" I am sure you want to help the Tribunal by telling us who these criminals were.

SCHACHT: Hitler and his confederates.

JACKSON: Well, you were there; you know who the conspirators were. I am asking you to name all that you put in the category of criminals with Hitler. Hitler, as you know, is dead.

SCHACHT: Mr. Jackson, it is very difficult for me to answer that question fully because I do not know who was in that close conspiracy with Hitler. The defendant Goering has told us here that he considered himself one of that group. There were Himmler and

Bormann, but I do not know who else was in the small circle of men who were trusted by Hitler.

Schacht himself held important economic positions. He was President of the Reichsbank, Minister for Economy, and General Director of the Armaments Industry. He was relieved of the post of President of the Reichsbank in 1939 and remained Minister without portfolio until 1943.

JACKSON: Now, there came in the Four-Year Plan in 1936?
SCHACHT: Yes.
JACKSON: You did not like the appointment of Goering to that position [Minister of Armaments]?
SCHACHT: I thought he was unsuited, and, of course, it made an opening for a policy which was opposed to mine. I knew perfectly well that this was the start of exaggerated armament, whereas I was in favor of restricted rearmament.
JACKSON: That is exactly the point I want to make. Your difference with Goering over rearmament was entirely a question of what the economy of Germany would stand, was it not?

Schacht disputed this strongly, and in this case the Court believed him more than it did the prosecution. In its judgment the Court described Schacht as the central figure in the field of rearmament, but took the position that rearmament as such was not criminal. During the war years Schacht was increasingly in opposition to the State. He may even, as he claimed, have resisted pressure, but he never let it come to an open quarrel. He made numerous propaganda speeches, which mostly ended with a triple "Sieg-Heil to our Führer." For this, Schacht excused himself by claiming that he had chimed in with the usual phrases for purposes of "camouflage." His life had been threatened. "I wish to add," he said, "that if Hitler had ever given me an unethical order, I would have refused to carry it out."

Schacht would not, or perhaps could not, see that the immorality did not begin with any order, but at the instant when he decided to throw in his lot with criminals. His successor as President of the Reichsbank and Minister for Economy, Walther Funk, said in a speech on November 17, 1938—and with this the

Court turned its attention to another of the accused—"State and Industry are a unity. They must be directed on the same principles. The best proof of this is given by the latest development of the Jewish problem in Germany. We cannot expel them from the life of the State but must let them go on working in our economy."

Funk acted on this principle. How far it carried him into the whirlpool of events and crimes was made clear to the defendant in a hearing at a preliminary examination on October 22, 1945.

QUESTION: Were not all decrees by which Jews were excluded from the economy sanctioned by you?

ANSWER: So far as my participation in these Jewish matters is concerned, they were my responsibility. I later regretted that I took part in them; but the Party always exerted great pressure on me to give my approval for the dispossession of Jewish property, which I repeatedly refused. But later, when the anti-Jewish measures and the acts of violence against the Jews were carried out with all severity, something legal had to be done to prevent the looting and the seizure of the entire Jewish property.

QUESTION: You knew that the looting and the other measures which were carried out were done with the approval of the Party, did you not?

Funk began to weep and answered: "I should have withdrawn then, in 1938, therefore I am guilty, I am guilty, I admit that I stand here as a guilty party."

The criminal connection between state and economy became quite clear in the so-called Gold Affair of the Reichsbank. Prosecutor Thomas J. Dodd surprised Funk by confronting him with a statement which seriously incriminated him. It came from the former Vice-President of the Reichsbank, Emil Puhl, and was the more painful to Funk because it came from a man he himself had asked for as a defense witness. "In the summer of 1943," said Pohl, "the Reichsbank President and Minister for Industry Walther Funk had a talk with me and later with Friedrich Wilhelm, a member of the Board of Directors. Funk told me he had reached an agreement with Himmler to take gold and jewelry into the safekeeping for the SS. Funk instructed me to make the necessary arrangements with SS Chief Group Leader Oswald Pohl, Chief of the Economic Department of the SS, who was entrusted with the economic organization of the concentration camps. I asked Funk about the source of the gold, jewelry, money, and other objects which were to be deposited by the SS. Funk replied that it was confiscated property from the occupied Eastern regions, and that I should ask no further questions.

"Among the articles deposited by the SS were jewelry, watches, spectacle frames, gold fillings, and other objects in great number, which had been taken from Jews, concentration camp victims, and other people. It came to our knowledge that the SS were trying to change this material into ready money, and they called on the help of the Bank personnel for this purpose, with the approval and knowledge of Funk. In carrying out my duties I visited the strongrooms of the Reichsbank from time to time and saw what was stored there, and Funk did the same. Under his direction, the Gold Discount Bank also set up a current account, which finally amounted to ten to twelve million Reichsmarks, and was kept at the disposal of the Economic Department of the SS for the financing of the manufacture of products in SS-conducted factories by forced labor from the concentration camps."

Later, SS Chief Group Leader Oswald Pohl confirmed this statement as a witness. In its judgment the Court summed up: "The Court is of the opinion that Funk either knew the articles that were deposited or that he turned a blind eye to this. In spite of the fact, however, that Funk occupied high positions, he was never a leading figure in the various programs in which he co-operated." This saved Funk's life. He seemed to have been only a small, unimportant manager and assistant of Hitler's, in comparison with the SS leaders who conspired in a monstrous murder and plunder organization. Funk accepted the sentence of life imprisonment gratefully—apparently he had expected the death sentence.

One of the defendants had filled more diverse offices in the state machine than anyone else except Himmler—Wilhelm Frick. In pronouncing the death sentence upon him, the Court listed his posts and functions. Frick, the leading Nazi bureaucrat, was appointed Minister of the Interior in Hitler's first cabinet. He held this important post until August 1943, when he was appointed Reich Protector of Bohemia and Moravia. In conjunction with his duties at the hub of the home government he was made Prussian Minister of the Interior, National Director of Elections, Plenipotentiary for the Adminstration of the Reich; and Member of the National Defense Council, of the Ministerial Council for the Defense of the Reich, and of the "Three-Power Council." As the various countries overrun were annexed to the Reich, he was placed at the head of the central offices for their annexation. Frick was the man who, after Hitler's seizure of power in Berlin, energetically subjected the German states to the Nazi regime.

Prosecutor Kempner told the Court about the innumerable laws by which Frick brought the German people under the control of the Party and its machinery. He quoted from a book by Frick's Secretary of State, Hans Pfundtner: "While Marxism in Prussia was being smashed by the hard fist of the Prussian President, Hermann Goering, and a gigantic wave of propaganda was introducing the Reichstag elections of March 5, 1933, Dr. Frick was preparing the seizure of power in all the states of the Reich. All political opposition disappeared overnight, and even the main 'frontier' within Germany vanished. From that moment on, only one will and one leadership prevailed in the German Reich."

Kempner reminded the Court of that fatal law of June 17, 1936, signed by Hitler and Frick, which gave Himmler and his companions a pseudo-legality and a free hand: "In order to insure the uniform control of police activities in the Reich, a Chief of German Police has been appointed to the Ministry of the Interior. He will be responsible for the direction and co-ordination of all police activities." This Chief of Police was expressly "personally and immediately subordinate to the Reich and Prussian Minister of the Interior." Frick was therefore made the superior of Himmler, and—theoretically at least—of the whole police system. In fact his control was slight, even though his name remains inseparably connected with the atrocities of the police committed in the service of the SS.

Particularly the Jews suffered under Frick's measures. "His activities created the basis for the Nuremberg Laws," said the verdict of the Court, "and he was instrumental in carrying them through. He was responsible for banning the Jews from numerous professions, and for the seizure of their property. In 1943, after the massacres of the Jews in the East, he signed a final decree, which made them outlaws and fair game for the Gestapo."

Frick, who, like Hess, elected not to go on the witness stand at Nuremberg, was deeply concerned in the crimes that were concealed behind the harmless name of euthanasia. The British prosecutor, Sir Hartley Shawcross, dealt with this aspect: "In the summer of 1940, Hitler issued a secret decree for the murder of sick and old people in Germany who were of no use for the German war machine. Frick, more than anyone else in Germany, was responsible for what happened as a consequence of that decree. There is a wealth of evidence that he and a great number of other people knew about it."

In July 1940, Bishop Wurm wrote to Frick: "During the last few months, insane, mentally defective, and epileptic patients of national and private hospitals have been taken to other institutions by order of the Reich Defense Council. The relatives are told only later of these transfers. Generally, they receive, a few weeks later, the information that the patient concerned has died of an illness and that for safety reasons he had to be cremated. According to conservative estimates, several hundred patients from Württemberg alone have met their deaths in this way. From numerous inquiries in town and country and among various circles I regard it as my duty to make the Government of the Reich aware that in our small land this matter has attracted a great deal of attention. The transports of the invalids, who disembark at the small station of Marbach on the Lahn, the buses with opaque windows which bring the patients from more distant stations or straight from the hospitals, the smoke rising from the crematorium, which can be noticed from afar—all this disturbs the minds of the people. But, above all, it is the air of secrecy which gives rise to the thought that something is going on that is contrary to all conceptions of right and ethics—something which the government cannot justify like other necessary and severe wartime measures."

Wilhelm Frick was partly responsible for these crimes. In 1943, he was made Reich Protector of Bohemia and Moravia. The Court stated that in this position he was responsible for the terrorization of the inhabitants, for slave labor, and for the deportation of Jews. Thus the state machinery of Adolf Hitler operated from the beginning to the bitter end without a hitch and without much noise. Men were always found who placed their abilities and their devilish cunning at the service of that machinery, irrespective of whether it corresponded to their inner convictions and their consciences or not. That is the guilt of the "managers" who administered Germany as Hitler ordered up until its collapse.

SOLDIERS' HONOR

The group of former high-ranking military officers among the defendants were easily recognizable by their bearing at Nuremberg. The one-time generals and admirals spoke in the curt, clipped manner of professional officers. A few of them were still wearing their old uniforms, but without badges of rank. When the prosecution asked them about their past, they spoke of the duty of obedience and about soldiers' honor. Field Marshal Wilhelm Keitel was found guilty on all four counts of the indictment by the Nuremberg Court. The verdict listed them:

1. Keitel knew Hitler's plans for the attacks on Czechoslovakia, Poland, the Scandinavian countries, and the neutral states of Holland, Belgium, Luxemburg, Greece, and Yugoslavia. He took a prominent part in the preparatory work.

2. On August 4, 1942, Keitel issued the order that allied parachutists should be surrendered to the Security Forces (SD).

3. "When the OKW issued its ruthless directions for the treatment of Soviet prisoners of war on September 8, 1941," the verdict said, "Canaris wrote to Keitel that on the grounds of

international law the SD should not have to deal with them. There exists in Keitel's handwriting the following comment, dated September 23 and signed by him: "These objections arise from a soldier's conception of chivalrous warfare. Here we are concerned with the destruction of a *Weltanschauung*. Therefore I approve the measures and authorize them.' "

4. Keitel ordered the military authorities to work with Rosenberg's operational staff for the purpose of looting culturally valuable objects in the occupied areas.

5. On September 16, 1941, Keitel, in order to counter assaults on German soldiers in the East, ordered that fifty to a hundred Communists should be killed for each German soldier. On October 1 he ordered his Commanders always to have hostages in readiness so that they could be executed for assaults on German soldiers.

6. When the Reich Commissar for Norway, Josef Terboven, wrote to Hitler that making the relatives of workers responsible for acts of sabotage would only be successful if execution squads were allowed, Keitel wrote on that letter, "Yes, that is best."

7. The notorious "Night and Stealth" Decree bears Keitel's signature. When, on January 4, 1944, Hitler ordered Sauckel to squeeze another four million slave workers out of the occupied areas, Keitel was present.

All these things were in contradiction to Keitel's oft-repeated statement that he had only been a soldier in the spirit of military tradition. An attempt was made at Nuremberg to explain this contradiction as a characteristic of the defendant by the statements of witnesses. The former Minister for War and Commander in Chief of the Wehrmacht, Field Marshal Blomberg, said about Keitel: "Keitel was lacking in opposition to any measure of Hitler's. He was a pliable tool in Hitler's hands for any of his decrees. He grew into a position for which he was not big enough."

Hermann Goering said on the witness stand, in reply to a question put to him by Keitel's defense counsel, Dr. Otto Nelte: "Often weeks passed before one could get the required signature from Hitler. There is scarcely a decree or order issued by the Führer which was not signed by Keitel, who was extremely industrious. It was natural that when there was a clash of opinions, the Commander in Chief of the Wehrmacht was pressed from both sides. He was caught between the millstones. One side attacked him for not being critical enough of the Führer; and when he did object, the Führer rebuffed him and said that he would take the matter in his own hands. The task was certainly very thankless and difficult, and I remember how Keitel once came to me and asked me to get him a command at the front; even as a Field Marshal he would take only one division—as long as he could only get away, for he was at the end of his tether."

Keitel himself said on the witness stand about his relations with Hitler: "I was naturally justified and under an obligation to submit my views. How difficult that was only those can judge who know how Hitler, after a few words, cut short any further discussion. Thus it was very hard to return to the subject in question. The conditions that I met there were quite novel to me and frequently made me quite unsure of myself."

Behind the scenes of the case against Keitel, a tug of war took place of which the public heard nothing. Dr. Robert Kempner, one of the American prosecutors, told the authors about it twelve years after the Trial. According to Kempner, Keitel was prepared to make a full confession of guilt on the witness stand and a general statement about the crimes of the Third Reich. Two days before the date fixed for this statement he said he could not go through with it. He had spoken about it to Goering, whom he still regarded as a sort of superior. Goering had forbidden him to admit his guilt with the argument: if one person tries to leave the lifeboat, the boat will capsize.

Thus in this last role of his life, Keitel again fell "between two millstones." As he had so often, he acted according to an order and against his private convictions, with the result that he presented a lamentable picture.

First it was the turn of the Soviet prosecutor, Roman Rudenko, to question Keitel.

RUDENKO: I turn now to the question of the treatment of Soviet prisoners of war. I want to question you about the report by Canaris. In this report Canaris speaks of the mass murders of

Soviet prisoners of war and about the necessity to restrain this lawlessness. Listen to me and pay attention. This is the document by Canaris. Your comment runs: "These objections arise from a soldier's conception of chivalrous warfare. Here we are concerned with the destruction of a *Weltanschauung*. Therefore I approve the measures and authorize them." Was that your decision?

KEITEL: Yes, I wrote that, as a decision after talking to the Führer. I wrote that.

RUDENKO: I ask you, Defendant Keitel, who call yourself Field Marshal and have repeatedly described yourself as a soldier. With your bloodthirsty decision of September 1941, you have approved and sanctioned the murdering of unarmed soldiers who were in your power as prisoners. Is that right?

KEITEL: I signed this decree and therefore bear the responsibility for it in the course of my duty.

In the cross-examination by the British prosecutor, Sir David Maxwell Fyfe, further points came under discussion.

SIR DAVID: Will you please look at Document 769. It is a telegram from General of the Air Force Christiansen in the Netherlands. It comes from his chief of staff: "As a result of a railway strike all traffic in Holland is at a standstill. Railway personnel do not respond to demands that they should return to work. The Army must again be given permission to shoot, with or without court-martial, even people who are not terrorists or saboteurs in the sense of the Führer's order, but hinder the fighting troops by passive resistance. It is requested that the order of the Führer be altered accordingly." Now, defendant, you will admit that the shooting of railwaymen who would not work is a measure that can be described the height of brutality and cruelty. Do you admit that?

KEITEL: That was a cruel measure, yes.

SIR DAVID: What was your answer to this cruelty? Look at Document 770, I believe that was your answer. "If the SD is not capable of the task, other effective measures are to be ruthlessly applied. Under such conditions there must, of course, be no scruples about the passing and execution of death sentences by a summary court-martial."

Especially important is the role that Keitel played in the planned murders of the French Generals Giraud and Weygand. Only by a ruse of Admiral Canaris did the two French soldiers get away with their lives.

The French Chief of Staff, Maxime Weygand, went to North Africa after the collapse of France. General Henri Giraud fell into German hands and was held prisoner in the fortress of Königstein in Saxony. On April 17, 1942, he succeeded in escaping. His escape was an adventure story in itself. With a fifty-yard rope, which he had made in a year from parcel string, he lowered himself down the impregnable fortress walls. "The General," Keitel admitted on the Nuremberg witness stand, "must have been a courageous soldier. When a man of sixty lowers himself fifty yards down a rock wall on a mere length of string—"

While they were searching for the General throughout the whole of Germany, Giraud traveled to Munich, Stuttgart, Metz, Strassburg, and Mühlhausen, and one day he ran, gasping for breath, across the closely guarded border—a hundred yards over open fields toward three fir trees, which a peasant had described to him. The trees stood on Swiss soil. Giraud had made it.

Erwin Lahousen, from the office of the German Chief of Intelligence, Canaris, was cross-examined by the American prosecutor, John Harlan Amen, about what had happened behind the scenes.

AMEN: Do you recall attending a meeting in 1940 at which the name of Weygand was under discussion?

LAHOUSEN: Yes. In this discussion Canaris revealed to us that already for some considerable time Keitel had put pressure on him to arrange for the elimination of the French Marshal Weygand; and that naturally I—that is my division—would be charged with the execution of this task.

AMEN: When you say "elimination' what do you mean?

LAHOUSEN: Killing.

AMEN: What was the reason given for attempting to kill Weygand?

LAHOUSEN: The fear that Weygand together with the unconquered part of the French Army might form a center of resistance in North Africa.

AMEN: What else was said at this meeting?

LAHOUSEN: This request, which was first put to the Military Abwehr so openly and in such an undisguised form by a representative of the Armed Forces, was decidedly and indignantly rejected by all those present. When the other gentlemen had left the room, I spoke with Canaris alone, and he told me at once, "It is quite obvious that this order will not only not be carried out, but it will not even be communicated to anybody else," and that, in fact, happened. On one occasion when Canaris was reporting to Keitel and I was present, Keitel mentioned the subject to me and asked me what had happened or what had been done in this matter up to now.

AMEN: What reply did you make to Keitel?

LAHOUSEN: One thing is certain: I did not answer that I had no intention of carrying out this order. Otherwise I would not be sitting here today. Probably, as in many similar cases, I replied that it was difficult but everything possible would be done, or something of that sort.

Lahousen went on to say that in July, 1942, Keitel, gave the order to Canaris that General Giraud should also be killed. This action was to go under the name of Gustav. The Intelligence Service, however, refused to carry it out. Lahousen continued: "It must have been in September. Keitel, then Chief of the OKW, rang me up in my private apartment. He asked me, 'What about Gustav? You know what I mean by Gustav? How is the matter progressing? I must know, it is very urgent.' I answered, 'I have no information on the subject. Canaris has reserved this matter for himself, and Canaris is not here, he is in Paris.' "

Lahousen flew at once to Paris to report to Canaris, who was at first worried, but then he had an idea. He informed Keitel that he had passed on Action Gustav to Heydrich while the latter was still alive. Thus the matter was sidetracked. Lahousen concluded his statement: "Nothing more happened. Giraud fled to North Africa and much later only I heard that Hitler was very indignant about this escape and said that the SD had failed miserably."

"I don't know what I shall say," Keitel stammered that evening in his cell, when he received the usual visit from the Court psychologist, Dr. Gilbert. "This Giraud affair—of course I knew that it would be brought up—but what shall I say? I know what an officer and a gentleman like you must think—they are things that affect my honor as a soldier. I wouldn't complain if I were accused of having started the war—I only did my duty and obeyed orders. But these murder plots—I don't know how I ever came to be caught up in them."

Keitel spoke for a long time about his honor as an officer. Late that evening, Dr. Gilbert had an opportunity to talk to Lahousen. "Now they speak about honor," said Lahousen when Gilbert had told him, "now, after they have murdered millions. No question about it, it is very unpleasant for them when anyone can stand up and tell them the unpleasant truth to their faces. I have spoken for those whom they have murdered."

A few days later, Dr. Gilbert noticed that the former Chief of the General Staff of the Wehrmacht, Alfred Jodl, no longer sat at Keitel's table at mealtimes as he used to do. The psychologist cautiously brought the conversation in Jodl's cell round to Lahousen.

"There are things that cannot be associated with the honor of an officer," said Jodl.

"Such as murder," suggested Dr. Gilbert. Jodl was silent for a time, then he answered quietly: "Naturally, that cannot be reconciled with an officer's honor. Keitel told me that Giraud was under observation, and that the case was to be handed over to the Chief Office of the Security Service—but never a word about murder. No—that is not honor. Such things have occurred many times in military history, you know. But I never thought that one of our own generals—"

"I notice," said Dr. Gilbert," that you no longer eat at the generals' table, Goering's and Keitel's table?'

"Oh, so you have noticed that?" asked Jodl in surprise. "Yes, but I won't kick a man when he is lying down—especially as we are all in the same boat."

With that the conversation ended. To the end of the Trial Keitel was shunned by the other military men. Even though the plans to murder Weygand and Giraud came to nothing, the moral effect could not be wiped out.

To show that these murder plots were not imaginary, a case in which such a plan was carried out was brought before the Court. The material for evidence came from the archives of the Foreign Office and seriously incriminated the former Foreign Minister, Joachim von Ribbentrop.

"In the Köningstein Camp," ran the first document, of November 1944, "there are 75 French generals. The transfer will take the form that a first batch of five or six French generals, each in a special car, will be taken to another place. In the car will be the driver and a guard. The car has Wehrmacht marks. Both Germans wear Wehrmacht uniforms. It is a matter for specially selected people. On the way, the car of General Deboisse will have a puncture to separate it from the others. Then the General will be shot in the back 'while trying to escape.' For the timing, dusk is suggested. It must be made sure that no local inhabitants are present. For reasons of possible inquiries, the body shall be burned and the urn taken to the cemetery of the fortress of Köningstein. It is to be ascertained that a medical report, identification certificate, and certificate of cremation are supplied in good order."

However, General Deboisse escaped with his life. In his place, General Mesny was simply substituted in the murder plot. Mesny's eldest son was at that time a political hostage in a concentration camp.

The final document, again from the archives of Ribbentrop's Foreign Office, was dated January 12, 1945: "Strictly confidential. A French General who is a prisoner of war will meet an unnatural death by shooting while trying to escape, or by poisoning. The details, such as reporting, post-mortem, verification interment, have been seen to according to plan. The instruction of the Foreign Minister is to discuss the matter with Ambassador Albrecht to ascertain exactly what rights the protecting Power possesses in this matter." On January 18, 1945, shots rang out on a country road near the fortress of Köningstein. General Mesny had been murdered.

The second soldier in the dock at Nuremberg, Alfred Jodl, was not implicated in this action. The case against the former Chief of the General Staff of the Wehrmacht offered quite a different picture. Jodl, like Keitel, was condemned to death on all four counts of the indictment. In his case, too, the counts of the indictment offer a comprehensive survey of his crimes:

1. Jodl was "very active" in the planning of the operation against Czechoslovakia. After the Munich Agreement had been signed, Jodl wrote in his diary: "Czechoslovakia has ceased to play any part in power politics. The genius of the Führer and his determination not to shrink from the risk of a world war have brought victory."

2. Jodl discussed the invasion of Norway with Hitler. He was also active in the planning against Greece and Yugoslavia.

3. As early as July 29, 1940, Jodl ordered the plans to be prepared for the attack on Russia. Hitler's instructions for the preparation of the invasion and the document Barbarossa bear Jodl's initials.

4. The covering letter of Hitler's notorious "Commando Order" was signed by Jodl. On June 25, 1944, after the landing of the Allies in Normandy, he confirmed the validity of this order.

5. When Hitler, in 1945, planned to withdraw from the Geneva Convention, Jodl objected "and by way of example mentioned the sinking of a British hospital ship as a reprisal measure, which would then officially be described as a mistake. He said that he had behaved in this way because it was the only attitude that Hitler would take into consideration, and that moral and legal reasons had become ineffective."

6. On October 28, 1944, Jodl ordered by teletype the evacuation of all civilians from northern Norway and the burning down of their houses so that they could give the Russians no assistance.

7. On October 7, 1941, Jodl signed an order in which it was stated that Hitler would not accept any offer of surrender by Leningrad and Moscow, but on the contrary commanded that these cities should be completely destroyed.

Jodl marched blindly after Hitler, and on November 7, 1943,

in a speech to the national Gauleiters in Munich, he emphasized this when he said, "I am speaking in this hour not only with my lips, but from the depths of my heart in confessing that our trust and our faith in the Führer are unbounded."

How did Jodl behave on the witness stand when he had to answer the prosecutors' questions? Right at the beginning of the cross-examination he gave a typical illustration.

G. D. ROBERTS (British prosecutor): Defendant Jodl, you have told the Court that soldiering is in your blood. Is that so?

JODL: Yes, that is so.

ROBERTS: Very good. And you said that you were here to represent the honor of the German soldiers. Is that so?

JODL: That I am doing to the best of my ability.

ROBERTS: Very well. You have described yourself as an honorable soldier?

JODL: That I have done.

ROBERTS: You have represented yourself as a truth-loving man?

JODL: I have described myself as such a man, and that I am.

ROBERTS: Very well. And do you believe that your honor has been sullied by what you have had to do during the last six or seven years?

JODL: My honor has certainly not been sullied, for I have personally taken care of it.

ROBERTS: Very good. You say that your honor is not sullied. Has your love of truth remained on the same high level during the last six or seven years?

Jodl made no answer.

ROBERTS: Can't you answer the question?

JODL: I think I am too stupid for this question.

ROBERTS: Good. I come now to Document C52. Do you remember this order?

JODL: Yes. I remember this order.

ROBERTS: I believe that you helped in drafting it, didn't you?

JODL: Certainly, because it is an operational order.

ROBERTS: Yes, indeed. Will you look at Point 6: "The troops available for safeguarding the occupied Eastern territories are sufficient for the area only if all resistance is discouraged not by the juridical punishment of the guilty but if the occupying force can spread sufficient terror to drain the population of any desire for resistance." That is a frightful order, is it not?

JODL: No, it is not a frightful order, for it is laid down by international law that the inhabitants of an occupied area have to carry out the commands and orders of the occupying power.

ROBERTS: Good. I come now to the Commando Order. It concerns an announcement broadcast by radio on October 7, 1942, which ran as follows: "In future, all terror and sabotage troops of the British and their henchmen, who act not like soldiers but like bandits, will be treated by German troops as such and, wherever they appear, will be ruthlessly cut down in battle." Do you make any distinction between a British airman who bombs a power station and a British parachutist in uniform who has landed and blows up the power station?

JODL: No, I regard the destruction of an objective by a commando unit as completely permissible in warfare according to international law. But I do not regard it as permissible that a man wears civilian clothes under his uniform and has a shoulder pistol which starts firing as soon as the arms are raised in surrender.

ROBERTS: Good, but if you consider the case you will find many instances in which men were killed without any evidence that they wore anything but a uniform. I have such a report here, it bears Keitel's initials: "On September 16, 1942, ten Englishmen and two Norwegians landed on the Norwegian coast in the uniform of British mountain troops, heavily armed and provided with explosives of all kinds. On September 21 they blew up important installations in the power station at Glomfjord. A German guard was killed in the action. The Norwegian workers were threatened that they would be chloroformed if they resisted. The Englishmen had morphine syringes for that purpose. Seven of the men have been taken prisoner while the others have escaped to Sweden." Then follow seven names. These men were shot on October 30, 1942, on the grounds of the order which you had issued, although it did not even exist when they were taken prisoner. All these men were in uniform. Can you justify this in any way?

JODL: No, I cannot justify that, and I would not justify it. I consider it completely contrary to law. But I did not know of it at the time.

One of the last points that Roberts touched upon was the case of the fifty British airmen who escaped from the prison camp of Sagan, were recaptured, and were then shot.

JODL: At that moment I had the impression that Hitler turned his back on all human conceptions of the law.

ROBERTS: Do you agree with me that it was pure murder that was committed in the case of these fifty airmen?

JODL: I agree completely with you about that. I consider this as a clear case of murder.

ROBERTS: How was it possible that all you honorable generals could continue to serve a murderer with such unquestioning loyalty?

JODL: From that time onward I did not serve with undiminished loyalty, but I tried with all the means in my power to avoid further evil.

ROBERTS: Did you make a speech to your staff shortly after the attempt on Hitler, on July 24, 1944?

JODL: Yes, with my head bandaged.

ROBERTS: Did you begin in the following manner: "July 20 was the darkest day that German history has ever known, and will perhaps remain so for all times."? Was that a more cowardly deed than to shoot these fifty soldiers down like dogs?

JODL: That was murder, there is no doubt about it. But it is not the task of a soldier to act as judge over his supreme commander. Let history do that, or God in heaven.

Two of the defendants were primarily concerned with the German conduct of the war at sea: the former Admiral and Commander in Chief of the German Navy, Erich Raeder, and his successor, U-Boat Commander Karl Doenitz. What charge was brought against them?

On January 3, 1942, a conference with Hitler took place in the presence of the Foreign Minister, Ribbentrop. The ambassador of their ally Japan, Hiroshi Oshima, attended as a guest. As was usual with Hitler's conferences, the contents of the speeches were transcribed; and like so many other documents the minutes of this meeting were discovered by the Allies at the end of the war.

"After he had made further explanations," the British prosecutor, H. J. Phillimore, read from the document, "the Führer declared that however many ships the United States built, one of their biggest problems was the scarcity of crews. For this reason even cargo ships should be sunk without warning, with the intention that as many as possible of the crew should be killed. Once it would be widely known that most seafaring men were lost by torpedoing, the Americans would soon have difficulty in enlisting new crews. The training of seamen takes a long time. We are fighting for our existence, and can therefore not take a humanitarian attitude. For this reason the Führer had also to give the order that where the foreign seamen could not be taken prisoners, which was mostly not possible on the open sea, the U-boats should rise after torpedoing and gun the lifeboats. Ambassador Oshima approved these suggestions of the Führer and said that the Japanese, too, were forced to adopt such methods."

A few months after this meeting, Hitler's deliberations had taken the form of a written order. On September 17, 1942, it was radioed from the staff headquarters of the defendant Doenitz to all U-boat commanders. The important part of the message ran: "All attempts to save crews of torpedoed ships, including the picking up of those swimming and helping them into lifeboats, the righting of overturned lifeboats, and the supply of food and water are to cease. Lifesaving at sea contradicts the primitive requirements of naval war by the destruction of enemy ships and crews. Captains and chief engineers of sunken vessels should be captured and brought back, if possible, on account of their importance. Harden yourselves! Remember that the enemy shows no consideration for women and children in his air raids on German towns."

"It was, of course, a cautiously phrased order," said prosecutor Phillimore. "But now I pass on to the next evidence. It is an extract from Operational Order Atlantic No. 56 of October 7, 1943: 'In every convoy there is, as a rule, a so-called rescue ship, a special ship of up to 3,000 tons, which has the task of picking up shipwrecked men after U-boat attacks. Its destruction is of great value in the desired annihilation of ships' crews.' "

The prosecution produced a series of documents relating to the unrestricted U-boat war ordered by Hitler. One of these was the logbook of the German U-boat U-37. In it, Lieutenant Oehrn described the sinking of the British ship, *Sheaf Mead*: "The stern of the boat is under water. The bow rises higher. The lifeboats are now in the water. They are lying at some distance. The bow rises very steeply. Two men appear from somewhere in the forward part of the ship. They run and jump in great leaps over the deck to the stern. The stern disappears. A boat capsizes. Then a boiler bursts. Two men are blown through the air. The ship breaks up. Then everything is over. A large number of shipwrecked men are swimming about. The crew clings to spars and overturned boats. A young lad in the water shouts: 'Help, help, please!' The others are all very composed. They look gloomy and rather tired. An expression of cold hatred lies upon their faces. Back to our former course."

" 'Back to our former course,' " said Phillimore, "means quite simply that the U-boat sailed away."

Lieutenant Schacht, after sinking another steamer, the *Laconia*, had taken British and Polish sailors on board, as well as shipwrecked Italian prisoners of war. He reported this by radio, and received this reprimand from Doenitz on September 20, 1942. "Your action was wrong. Boat should have been provided to save Italian allies but not Englishmen and Poles."

"There are hundreds of similar tales," said prosecutor Phillimore, "tales of open boats being tossed about for days by the storms of the Atlantic, of men who held on to a raft for hours until one after the other had to let go, of those who were machine-gunned while trying to lower the lifeboats, or while they were drifting away in one."

In a general description of the defendant Doenitz, some passages from his speeches were read out in the courtroom: "I am a strong supporter of indoctrinating people in our philosophy of life." . . . "The whole corps of officers must from the first be so trained that they feel responsible for the National Socialist State in its entirety." . . . "I demand therefore from commandants and commanders of the Fleet that they clearly and single-mindedly follow the path of duty, whatever may happen. I demand of them that they stamp out ruthlessly all symptoms and incipient attitudes that may endanger this course."

Dr. Otto Kranzbühler, defense counsel for Doenitz, questioned him about his order of September 17, 1942: "You said: 'All commanders are again instructed that all attempts to save the crews of sunken ships contradict the primitive requirements of carrying on war by the destruction of enemy ships and crews.'"

DOENITZ: If I am not to conceal anything here I must say that the compiling of a war diary was a difficult problem for me because I did not have competent officers whom I could assign to the job. This entry was made by a former chief mate who attempted to give the gist of my order in this entry.

DR. KRANZBÜHLER: Herr Admiral, the decisive point seems to me to be whether this entry really represents your actual statement, or whether it is only an extract from the radio order, drawn up by a subordinate according to the best of his knowledge and ability.

DOENITZ: The latter is correct.

So much for the hearing. Later, the Nuremberg Court said in giving judgment: "The Court is of the opinion that the evidence has not established with the required certainty that Doenitz intentionally ordered the killing of shipwrecked survivors." But: "The orders were undoubtedly ambiguous and deserve severe criticism."

Doenitz got away with ten years' imprisonment. What saved him from the gallows was another matter: his defending counsel was successful in producing similar orders by the British Admiralty on unrestricted submarine warfare, and he further managed to secure a written statement from the Commander in Chief of the American Pacific Fleet, Admiral Chester W. Nimitz. Nimitz answered a questionnaire which Dr. Kranzbühler read out in the courtroom.

QUESTION: Was it forbidden by order or by general usage to carry out rescue operations for passengers and crews of ships sunk without warning if the safety of one's own ship was thereby jeopardized?

NIMITZ: In general U. S. submarines did not save enemy survivors if this involved an unusual, additional risk for the submarine, or if the submarine was thereby prevented from carrying out its further duties.

"Having regard to an order of the British Admiralty," the Court decided, "and in consideration of the answer of Admiral Nimitz, the verdict on Doenitz is not based on his offenses against the international regulations for submarine warfare." His sentence was based much more on "Crimes Against the Peace," and "War Crimes." The first point arises from the fact that Karl Doenitz was concerned in preparations for the attack on Norway. The second point concerns the handing over of the prisoners from an Allied torpedo boat to the SD: "They were by his order handed over to the SD and eventually shot. Doenitz permitted the 'Commando Order' to remain in full force when he became Commander in Chief, and to that extent he is responsible."

Matters were much the same with Doenitz's predecessor and fellow defendant, Raeder. The sentence on Raeder, imprisonment for life, was based on the facts of "conspiracy," "Crimes Against the Peace," and "War Crimes."

"He was one of the leaders," said the Nuremberg verdict, "who were present at the Hossbach Conference of November 5, 1937," and therefore knew of Hitler's plans of conquest. "The idea for the invasion of Norway was born in Raeder's mind and not in Hitler's. At a conference with Hitler on March 18, 1941, he urged the occupation of the whole of Greece. The evidence shows clearly that Raeder took a full share in the planning and conduct of wars of aggression."

Raeder was also implicated with Hitler's notorious Commando Order. The verdict said: "On December 10, 1942, two commando soldiers were shot in Bordeaux by sailors, not by the SD. The explanation of the naval authorities was that this was in agreement with the special order of the Führer, but that nevertheless it represented something new in international law as the soldiers were in uniform." Raeder admitted that he had passed on the order in the course of his duties, and had not remonstrated against it with Hitler.

The British prosecutor, Elwyn Jones, introduced the famous case of the sinking of the *Athenia:* "On October 23, 1939, the journal of the Nazi Party, the *Völkischer Beobachter,* announced in bold headlines: 'Churchill sinks the *Athenia.'* I will bring before the Court evidence proving that the *Athenia* was in fact sunk by the German U-boat U-30. So unjustifiable was the torpedoing of the *Athenia* that the German Fleet carried out the falsification of a whole number of its records and other dishonorable measures in the hope of concealing their guilt."

RAEDER: The fact was that a young U-boat commander, the commander of U-boat U-30, on the evening of September 3, torpedoed an English passenger ship which was blacked out, because he wrongly assumed that it was an auxiliary cruiser.

JONES: It seems proper to me to refer to Doenitz' order of September 22, 1939, that "a sinking of a passenger ship without warning must be explained by the possibility that it was confused with a warship, or with an auxiliary cruiser."

SIR DAVID MAXWELL FYFE: About a month later the Ministry of Propaganda announced—I believe you said at Hitler's command —that the *Athenia* had been sunk by Churchill. Did you not consider it your duty as an admiral and Commander in Chief of the German Fleet to protest against this shameful lie, that the First Lord of the British Admiralty had intentionally sent a large number of English citizens to their death?

RAEDER: I spoke to Hitler about it—but it had already happened before we knew anything about it. It was extremely painful to me that the First Lord of the British Admiralty should be attacked in this crude manner, but I couldn't alter things afterward.

J. W. POKROVSKI (Soviet prosecutor): It was still possible to make your departure?

RAEDER: Yes.

POKROVSKI: Apparently you retired only in January 1943. Is that right?

RAEDER: There were some favorable conditions then. One was that Hitler himself no longer favored me so that I did not commit an act of disobedience by leaving. Secondly, it was possible to arrange the parting in a friendly manner so that the Fleet would not be drawn into the affair.

POKROVSKI: I didn't ask you about favorable conditions, I put to you the principal question: was retirement possible or not?

RAEDER: What was not possible was to throw up the whole thing in order to create the impression that one wanted to show disobedience. That had to be avoided at all costs, that I had never done, I was too much of a soldier for that.

Hermann Goering belonged only in the wider sense to the group of senior officers, although he held a number of military ranks and orders specially created for him. The former Reichsmarschall and wearer of the Grand Cross was primarily a politician and Hitler's companion; his military offices and functions were the share of the spoils that Hitler owed to his vain friend. Many rumors were current in the Third Reich, and even during the Trial, about Goering's bacchanalian character. One of them said that the Soviet prosecutor, Rudenko, had shot at Goering. This rumor survived for a long time in postwar Germany. There was no truth in it, and yet, like so many rumors, it had a tangible origin. Of course Rudenko never shot at Goering, but once the exasperated American chief prosecutor, Robert H. Jackson, in cross-examining Goering, threw his earphones on the table. Goering was answering questions on a document entitled, "Preparation for the Liberation of the Rhine," which was connected with the occupation of the demilitarized zone of the Rhineland in 1935.

JACKSON: Well, those preparations were preparations for an armed occupation of the Rhineland, were they not?

GOERING: No, that is altogether wrong.

JACKSON: You mean the preparations were not military preparations?

GOERING: They were general preparations for mobilization, such as every country makes, and not for the purpose of the occupation of the Rhineland.

JACKSON: But were of a character which had to be kept entirely secret from foreign Powers?

GOERING: I do not think I can recall reading beforehand the publication of the mobilization preparations of the United States.

At this point Jackson snatched his earphones off and threw them on his desk. For a moment he stood with his hands on his hips, tightlipped. Then he turned to the judges: "Well, I respectfully submit to the Tribunal that this witness is not being responsive, and has not been in his examination and that it is . . . perfectly futile to spend our time if we cannot have responsive answers to our questions. This witness, it seem to me, is adopting, and has adopted in the witness box and in the dock, an arrogant and contemptuous attitude toward the Tribunal which is giving him the trial which he never gave a living soul, or a dead one either."

The President of the Tribunal, Lord Justice Sir Geoffrey Lawrence, looked at the clock and decided: "Perhaps we had better adjourn now at this stage."

As Goering was returning to his seat, the other defendants patted him on the shoulder and shook hands with him. But in the evening he admitted to a lawyer, Werner Bross: "The matter is not over. I feel as though I am walking through a forest with people aiming at me from behind every tree, but I cannot see them."

"Goering Hits Back," said the headlines in the Western press next day. But the defendant Speer said in his cell to the psychologist Dr. Gilbert: "You should have seen Goering earlier: a foul, egotistical, corrupt, irresponsible drug addict. Only your prison discipline has perhaps sobered him up. But why did he not stay in Berlin with his beloved Führer? Because it got too hot there when the Russians were closing in."

Was Speer's verdict just? Admiral Erich Raeder, too, had something to say about Goering; he even wrote it down. Although Raeder's defense counsel, Dr. Walter Siemers, at the last moment decided against reading out the passage, it remained among the documents of the Trial:

Goering's personality had a disastrous effect upon the fate of Germany. His outstanding traits were unimaginable conceit, endless striving after popularity, untruthfulness, inaccessibility, and an egotism which did not stop short of selling his country and people. He was remarkable for his greed, his extravagance and his weak, unsoldierly behavior. I am convinced that Hitler soon recognized Goering's character, but he used him since he served his purpose, and kept him busy with ever new tasks to prevent him becoming dangerous to the Führer. Goering put the greatest emphasis on appearing outwardly to be most loyal to the Führer, but in spite of that he was often unbelievably tactless and rude toward Hitler, which the Führer, however, ignored intentionally.

Goering, who loved to compare himself with the Nibelungs and whom his one-time secretary Paul Körner described at the Trial as "the last Renaissance man," was found guilty on all four counts of the indictment: Conspiracy, Crimes Against Peace, War Crimes, and Crimes Against Humanity. If one considers the most important points on which the Court based its verdict, there really remains little of the Nibelungs and of the Renaissance. Here are a few of them:

1. He built up the Gestapo, created the first concentration camps, and handed them over to Himmler in 1934; in the same year he carried out the Roehm purge, and started the shady intrigues leading to the removal of Blomberg and Fritsch.

2. Goering was one of the five important leaders who took part in the Hossbach Conference on November 5, 1937 (at which Hitler announced his plans for war).

3. On the eve of the invasion of Czechoslovakia and the dismemberment of Bohemia and Moravia, he threatened at a conference between Hitler and President Hácha to bomb Prague if Hácha did not surrender. He admitted on the witness stand to this threat.

4. Goering was present at the meeting in the Chancellery on May 23, 1939, when Hitler said to his military leaders: "The question whether Poland should be spared is unsubstantial." He commanded the Luftwaffe during the attack on Poland and during all the attacks that followed.

5. In the course of the Trial, Goering made many admissions of his responsibility for the use of slave labor. As Commander in Chief of the Luftwaffe he demanded from Himmler more and more slave laborers for the subterranean aircraft factories: "That

I demanded concentration camp prisoners for arming the Luftwaffe is true, and should be regarded as quite normal."

6. As director of the Four-Year Plan, Goering signed an order to the SD on the treatment of Polish workers in Germany— including their "special treatment" (murder). In that capacity Goering was also active in the pillaging of conquered countries.

7. Goering persecuted the Jews, and this he did not only in Germany but also in the conquered countries, to which he extended the anti-Jewish laws valid in the Reich.

8. Although the extermination of the Jews was really Himmler's task, Goering was far from being unconcerned or inactive in the matter. With his decree of July 31, 1941, he instructed Himmler and Heydrich to bring about "a final solution of the Jewish question within the German sphere of influence in Europe."

In conclusion, the verdict on Goering stated: "No mitigating circumstances can be adduced, for Goering was often, indeed nearly always, the driving force, and he was second only to his Führer. He was the leading personality in the wars of aggression, both as a political and a military leader; he was the leader of the slave labor program and the originator of the policy of oppressing the Jews and all other races at home and in other countries. All these crimes were openly admitted by him. In a few definite cases there are perhaps contradictions in the statements; but by and large his own admissions are more than sufficient to establish his guilt. That guilt is unique in its enormity. For this man one can find no excuse in the whole evidence of the Trial."

This is a terrible catalogue of crimes. Its gravamen, no doubt, lies in its final items. These concern the destruction of millions of human beings under the disguise of "a final solution." On July 31, 1941, Goering extended the power that he had given Heydrich in January 1939, concerning the "Jewish emigration." The document found its way into the hands of the prosecution, and Goering knew that it would be under discussion. The nervousness which seized him before the cross-examination can easily be understood. His inner turmoil was so great that he took a piece of cardboard with him to the witness stand, on the back and front of which he had written reassuring words in red pencil.

"Slow, make a pause!" he had written on one side. "Quiet, keep steady!" on the other.

JACKSON: Did you, on July 31, 1941, sign a decree in which Himmler and the Chief of the Security Police, SS Group Leader Heydrich, were commanded to prepare plans for the complete solution of the Jewish problem?

GOERING: No, that is not correct. I know this decree well enough.

JACKSON: I shall put the document before you. This document bears your signature, does it not?

GOERING: That is true.

JACKSON: And it is addressed to the Chief of the Security Police and of the Security Service, SS Group Leader Heydrich?

GOERING: That is true.

JACKSON: So that we may have no difficulty with the translation, correct me please if my version is not accurate. "In conclusion of the task committed to you on February 24, 1939—"

GOERING: There is a mistake here. It says, "in completion," not "in conclusion."

JACKSON: Good. I accept that: "In completion of the task committed to you on January 24, 1939, which was concerned with the wholesale emigration and evacuation of the Jews in as favorable a manner as possible, as a solution of the Jewish problem, I hereby charge you to carry out all necessary organizational and financial preparations with the purpose of achieving a final solution of the Jewish problem in the German sphere of influence in Europe."

GOERING: I find that in no way correct.

JACKSON: Please give me your own translation.

GOERING: Let me read it exactly as it stands here: "In completion of the task committed to you on January 24, 1939, to introduce one of the most favorable solutions for the Jewish problem under the present circumstances in the form of emigration or evacuation, I command you herewith to make all requisite preparations of an organizational, factual, and material nature . . ." And here comes the decisive word that was wrongly translated, it says here in fact: "for a complete solution," not for a "final solution," of the Jewish problem in the German sphere of influence in Europe. "I command you further to submit to me shortly·a complete proposal of the organizational, factual, and material measures suggested for achieving the final solution of the Jewish problem."

Jackson did not pursue the matter further. He had obviously been taken in by Goering, and had not noticed that at the end of the document the significant word "final solution" had in fact been used. Goering was well aware of this, and in his cell even boasted to Bross: "I fooled Jackson properly this time! No lawyer could have handled the document better."

The extermination, the "final solution," took its course. On January 20, 1942, Heydrich informed all departments concerned of his "appointment as plenipotentiary for the preparation of the final solution of the Jewish problem in Europe by the Reichsmarshal." Yet Goering had the impudence, in cross-examination by the British prosecutor Sir David Maxwell Fyfe, to maintain that he knew nothing about the action.

SIR DAVID: Will you look now at a report of a conference which you held on August 6, 1942? Will you look where it says: "Field Marshal Goering: How much butter have you delivered, 30,000 tons?" Lohse, who was taking part in the conference, replied, "Yes." You asked, "Do you also deliver to Wehrmacht units?" Lohse answered, "There are only a few Jews left now; we have already gotten rid of tens of thousands, but I can tell you that the [non-German] civilian population received 15 per cent less than the Germans, as you ordered."

Will you still maintain, in the face of this document, that neither you nor Hitler knew that the Jews were being exterminated, Defendant Goering?

GOERING: I want my remark to be read out properly. It has been rendered quite wrongly. May I quote from the original text:

"Lohse: 'Only a few Jews still live there, tens of thousands have gone.'" It does not say here that they were destroyed. From this remark it is not to be concluded that they had been killed but that the Jews had gone away. They might have been evacuated.

SIR DAVID: I suggest that you explain quite clearly what was meant by the remark: "there were still a few Jews left."

GOERING: Still left—that is how it is to be understood.

SIR DAVID: Do you still maintain that neither Hitler nor you knew anything about the policy of exterminating the Jews?

GOERING: So far as Hitler is concerned I have said that I don't believe it; so far as I am concerned I have said that I had no idea of the extent of the action.

SIR DAVID: You had no idea of the extent—yet you knew that a policy existed that was aimed at the extermination of the Jews?

GOERING: No, about the emigration of the Jews and not about their extermination. I only knew that in individual cases offenses had occurred in that direction.

SIR DAVID: Thank you.

After this cross-examination, Goering's prestige among the other defendants was at a low ebb. After the heroic Nibelung pose which he had adopted at the beginning of the Trial, more had been expected from him than a few naive arguments about words and childish, shabby evasions. Reichsmarschall Hermann Wilhelm Goering had failed: as a man, as a politician, and as a soldier. No one could have demonstrated this more clearly than he did, with his own words on the witness stand at Nuremberg.

THE MASS MURDER
AT KATYN

Never yet in the history of mankind were individual men accused of so many and such terrible crimes as the chief defendants at Nuremberg. The documentary material of the prosecution towered up like mountains. Yet in the extensive documents of the Court some material remained unconsidered because the evidence produced in the opinion of the Court was not sufficient to prove the defendants guilty. And in this sense the Katyn Case ended as a clear victory for the defense.

The chief Soviet prosecuting representative in Nuremberg, Colonel J. W. Pokrovski, spoke about this case: "I wish now to discuss the atrocities which Hitlerists carried out against members of the Polish Army. We see from the bill of indictment that one of the most important of the criminal acts of the war was the mass execution of Polish prisoners of war which was carried out in the woods of Katyn near Smolensk by the German Fascist invaders."

With these introductory words the Soviet prosecutor turned to one of the most puzzling and disputed crimes of the Second World War. Only today, twelve years after the Nuremberg Trial, is it possible to throw a little more light even on the background of this fearful mystery. What happened?

After the German and Soviet invasion of Poland in 1939 the Polish Army ceased to exist, its members were in captivity. Between Moscow and the Polish government in exile in London diplomatic relations were resumed, and soon the London Poles were active in trying to secure the liberation of the prisoners of war who had fallen into Soviet hands. In fact the Soviet Union did let thousands of Polish prisoners of war go free. In London comprehensive lists were compiled. It soon transpired that the numbers did not tally. Several thousand officers had disappeared. The Polish ambassador in Moscow, Jan Kot, on October 6, 1941, visited the Soviet Foreign Minister Andrei Vishinsky. The conversation was reported by Kot:

KOT: I wish to draw attention to the following numbers: Altogether 9,500 officers were taken prisoner in Poland and were taken to various parts of Russia. At present we have only 2,000 in our army. What has happened to the remaining 7,500 men? More than 4,000 officers were taken from the camps of Starobelsk and Kozelsk. There is an impenetrable wall between us and these men, which keeps us apart. We ask you to make it possible for us to surmount this wall.

VISHINSKY: Perhaps you will realize, Mr. Ambassador, that since 1939 great changes have taken place. Men have moved from place to place. Many have been released, many are settled, many have gone home.

KOT: If any of the men of whom I speak had really settled they would at once have reported to us. These men are not children. They cannot stay hidden. If any of them are dead, we ask you to inform us. I cannot believe that they are not here.

The conversation ended with an evasive answer by Vishinsky. The Polish ambassador did not give up, however. On November 14, 1941, he was successful in penetrating to Stalin and in questioning the dictator himself.

KOT: Mr. Chairman, I have already taken up much of your valuable time, but there is a further point that I should like to raise if I may.

STALIN: But of course, Mr. Ambassador.

KOT: I can assume, Mr. Chairman, that you were the originator of the amnesty granted to Polish citizens on Soviet territory. Would you agree to insist that this noble gesture should be fully carried out?

STALIN: Are you telling me that there are still Poles who have not been liberated?

KOT: From the camp of Starobelsk, which was set free early in 1940, we have so far not found a single man.

STALIN: I will certainly look into the matter. But with these liberations funny things often happen.

KOT: Nevertheless I would request you, Mr. Chairman, to issue orders that the officers, whom we require to build up our Army, are to be set free. We have abundant evidence that they were taken away from the camps.

STALIN: Have you detailed lists?

KOT: All the names have been procured from the Russian camp commandant, who held a daily roll call of all his prisoners. Besides the NKVD has carried out separate searches for each single case. Not a single officer of the Army staff which General Anders led in Poland has been found.

Stalin picked up the telephone and was connected with the head office of the NKVD, the Soviet secret police.

"This is Stalin," he said. "Have all Poles been set free from captivity?"

He hung up, turned to Kot again, but spoke of other things. Some eight minutes later the telephone rang. Kot assumed that it was the answer from the NKVD. Stalin listened in silence to what was said, placed the telephone back on its stand, and did not mention the matter again. The problem of the vanished officers remained unsolved.

The Polish Generals Wladislaw Sikorski and Wladislaw Anders also tried to find out the fate of their compatriots. On December 3, 1941, they again tackled Stalin.

SIKORSKI: I have with me a list of some four thousand officers who were abducted by force and who are at present in prison or in labor camps, and this list is not complete because it contains only such names as can be assembled from memory. I have had a search made in Poland, with which we are in continual contact, and have ascertained that they are not there. It appears as though not one of them is there, nor are they among our prisoners of war in Germany. These men are here, not one of them has returned.

STALIN: That is out of the question. They have fled.

ANDERS: But where can they have fled?

STALIN: Oh, for example, to Manchuria.

SIKORSKI: It is impossible that they could all vanish and all correspondence between them and their families cease from the time when they were taken from the prisoner of war camps to labor camps or prisons.

STALIN: They have definitely been set free and just not reached you yet.

Nothing further came of this conversation. The Polish exile government in London sent to the Kremlin in the course of time forty-nine notes, in which the question of the whereabouts of the vanished officers was raised, and all these notes show that in London it was believed that the officers were still alive.

A frightful disillusionment destroyed this belief on April 13, 1943. On that date the German radio announced: "It is reported from Smolensk that the local inhabitants have shown German officials where the Bolshevists have secretly carried out a mass execution and where NKVD executed ten. thousand Polish officers."

Shortly after the German Information Bureau announced further details: "A gruesome find recently made by German military authorities in the forest of Katyn on the Kosegory hill, 20 kilometers west of Smolensk on the road from Smolensk to Vitebsk, leads to a conclusion that is as shattering as it is inevitable, about the mass murder of over ten thousand officers of all ranks, among them numerous generals of the former Polish Army."

The whole world listened in amazement. The announcement struck the Polish exile government in London like a bomb. Were the missing officers lying in the forest of Katyn? General Sikorski at once demanded an inspection of the mass grave by the International Red Cross. The suspicion of having committed the atrocity was clearly directed against the Kremlin.

A few days later, on April 26, 1943, Moscow issued a reply. It consisted in breaking off diplomatic relations with the Polish exile government "because they have been carrying on base fascist slander and conspiracy with Hitler's government." To the British and American governments this split in the Allied camp was highly unwelcome. They exerted unmistakable pressure on Sikorski, and the General in fact withdrew the demand for an international inquiry. That allowed the resumption of diplomatic relations.

Admiral William Standley, the former American Ambassador in Moscow, has admitted that on April 26, 1943, President Roosevelt wrote a letter to Stalin in which he said, "I hope Churchill can persuade Sikorski to show more common sense in future."

Sikorski and his daughter shortly after lost their lives in an airplane accident. En route from Cairo to London their plane crashed near Gibraltar on July 5, 1943. "It was definitely sabotage," declared the former American Undersecretary of State Sumner Welles.

But those are uncertain conjectures. The happenings at Katyn itself speak a more definite language. The course of events is now widely known: In the summer of 1942 some labor units of the Todt organization were working in the neighborhood of Smolensk. Among the men were ten Poles. Through another Pole, by the name of Partemon Kisielev, who lived near Katyn, they learned of a secret grave. One day they went secretly to the site described.

They opened one of the graves without any idea of their full extent, closed it again, and raised a simple wooden cross. No one troubled about it further.

In the following winter a wolf drew attention once again to the gloomy spot. In February 1943 several hills in the northwest of the region were discovered. The rising ground was in a plantation of young firs between the stations of Katyn and Gnesdovo. After the frost had gone the German authorities had the graves opened by Russian workers. In twelve layers, one above the other, they found 4,183 corpses.

Thus came about the German announcement, in which a number of "over ten thousand" was cited. The Soviet news agency Tass announced three days later: "The Polish prisoners in question were taken to special camps in the neighborhood of Smolensk and set to building roads. As it was impossible to evacuate them at the time of the German approach, they fell into their hands. And so if they are now found murdered it means that they were murdered by the Germans, who now claim, for reasons of provocation, that the atrocity was carried out by Soviet forces."

Who actually carried out the crime?

Three inquiries have been carried out. The first was set up by the National Medical Chief Leonardo Conti. Conti invited twelve physicians from Belgium, Bulgaria, Denmark, Finland, Italy, Croatia, Holland, from the Protectorates of Bohemia and Moravia, from Romania, Switzerland, Slovakia, and Hungary, to inspect the graves. In their final report the Commission, on April 30, 1943, affirmed that "the shooting took place in March and April 1940, and so at the time when the Soviets dissolved the officers' camp."

The second inquiry was held by the Poles after the war. The Cracow state official, Dr. Roman Martini, in his report even mentioned the names of the Soviet NKVD officers concerned. According to him the leader of the execution squad was a man named Burjanov. Further Martini could not go: On March 12, 1946, he was murdered in his house in Cracow during the night by two members of the Society for Polish-Soviet Friendship.

The third inquiry took place under the aegis of the Soviet Government itself, shortly after the Smolensk district was recovered. The Soviet prosecutor had this inquiry in mind when he said at the Nuremberg Trial:

"It would take up too much time if I were to read through the detailed document which sets out the conclusions of this inquiry. I shall therefore only read short extracts.

The forensic medical experts gave the number of corpses as some eleven thousand. From the total material at the disposal of the special commission; that is to say, from the statements of more than a hundred witnesses, from the conclusions of the experts, from the documents, and from the evidence of the graves, the following conclusions emerge with irresistible clarity:

1. Polish prisoners of war who were in three camps west of Smolensk and were allocated to road building before the outbreak of war, remained there even after the arrival of the German invaders up to and including September 1941.

2. In the forest of Katyn in the autumn of 1941 mass shootings of the Polish prisoners of war by the German occupying forces were carried out at the place mentioned.

3. The mass shootings were carried out by a German military unit which was disguised under the name of 'Staff of Construction Battalion 537,' and at their head were Lieutenant Colonel Arnes and his colleagues, Lieutenant Rex and Lieutenant Hott.

4. The German occupying authorities in spring 1943 brought the corpses of Polish prisoners of war they had shot elsewhere and placed them in the graves in the forest of Katyn in order to hide the traces of their own bestiality and to increase the number of 'victims of Bolshevist brutality.'

5. From the conclusions of the forensic medical experts of the commission it is established beyond all doubt that the date of the shooting was autumn 1941.

"The German butchers in shooting the Polish prisoners of war used the same method (pistol shot at the nape of the neck) as in the mass murder of Soviet citizens in other cities, especially in Orel, Voronezh, Krasnodar, and Smolensk. The signatures of all the members of the Commission follow."

"As witness for the defense I call Colonel Ahrens to the witness stand," said Goering's defense counsel, Dr. Otto Stahmer. Ahrens was sworn in.

DR. STAHMER: Your regiment was the Intelligence Regiment 537. Was there also a Construction Battalion 537?

AHRENS: No unit of the same number was known to me.

DR. STAHMER: After your arrival at Katyn did you notice that there was a burial hill in Katyn forest?

AHRENS: Shortly after I came—the territory was covered with snow—I was told by my soldiers that a wooden cross could be seen on a kind of hill. I saw this wooden cross. Then in the course of 1942 I heard repeatedly from my soldiers that here in our wood shootings had taken place. In the winter of 1943, in about January or February, I happened to see a wolf in the forest, but didn't believe at first that it could be a wolf. But then I followed the tracks with an expert and saw places where it had dug in the hill where the wooden cross was. I found out what kind of bones they were. The doctors told me: human bones. I then made a report of the matter to the War Graves Officer.

DR. STAHMER: When did the excavations take place?

AHRENS: I am not acquainted with the details of that. One day Professor Dr. Butz came to me and informed me that he must carry out excavations in my wood.

DR. STAHMER: Did Professor Butz later tell you details about the outcome of his excavations?

AHRENS: I remember a kind of diary which he gave me, in which date followed date, with some written remarks which I could not read because they were written in Polish. He explained to me that these entries had been made by a Polish officer over past months and that at the end—the diary ended in spring 1940—the fear was expressed that something dreadful was about to happen.

DR. STAHMER: It has been said that in March 1943 bodies were brought to Katyn on trucks from elsewhere and were buried in this wood. Do you know anything of that?

AHRENS: I know nothing of that.

DR. OTTO KRANZBÜHLER (defense counsel for Doenitz): Have you yourself discussed with any local inhabitants the remarks about 1940?

AHRENS: Yes, early in 1943 I had a Russian man and wife very near us. These people told me that in the spring of 1940 over two hundred uniformed Poles arrived in railway carriages at the station of Gnesdovo and were then taken in the trucks into the wood. They had heard much shooting and shouting.

L. N. SMIRNOV (Soviet prosecutor): Were you there in person in September or October 1941?

AHRENS: No.

SMIRNOV: That means you do not know what actually took place in September or October 1941 in the woods of Katyn?

AHRENS: I wasn't there at that time.

SMIRNOV: I want to give the names of some members of the Wehrmacht. Please tell me whether these persons belonged to your unit: Lieutenant Rex.

AHRENS: Lieutenant Rex was my regimental adjutant.

SMIRNOV: Please tell me, was he already attached to this unit in Katyn before your arrival there?

AHRENS: Yes, he was there before me.

SMIRNOV: And Lieutenant Hodt or Hoth.

AHRENS: Hodt is right. Lieutenant Hodt belonged to the regiment.

SMIRNOV: I will mention other names. Corporal Rose, Private Giesecke, Sergeant Major Krimmenski, Sergeant Lummert, a cook by the name of Gustav. They were all people who belonged to your units?

AHRENS: Yes.

SMIRNOV: You maintain that you were not aware what these people did in September and October 1941?

AHRENS: Since I wasn't there, I cannot tell with any certainty.

SMIRNOV: Have you been informed that the Extraordinary National Commission counts you among those responsible for the crimes committed in Katyn?

AHRENS: It says there: "Lieutenant Colonel Arnes."

IOLA NIKITCHENKO (Soviet judge): You were not present in person when the diary and other documents were found which Professor Butz showed you?

AHRENS: No.

NIKITCHENKO: And so you don't know where he got this diary and these documents?

AHRENS: No.

Another witness for the defense was General Eugen Oberhauser, Intelligence Chief of the Central Army Group.

DR. STAHMER: Did Regiment 537 possess the requisite technical means, pistols, ammunition, and so on, to allow them to carry out shootings on such a scale?

OBERHAUSER: The regiment was less well equipped than the proper fighting troops. They would not be in a position technically to carry out a mass execution.

SMIRNOV: The officers of the regiment were obviously armed with pistols, that is to say either a Walther or a Mauser.

OBERHAUSER: Yes.

SMIRNOV: Perhaps you could tell us roughly how many pistols the Intelligence Regiment possessed.

OBERHAUSER: If we assume that every corporal had a pistol that would be about 150.

SMIRNOV: Why are you of the opinion that 150 pistols would not be enough for a mass shooting?

OBERHAUSER: Because an Intelligence Regiment is an Army group which is scattered over such a wide area and are never together. The regiment was distributed from Kolodov to Vitebsk, and so there were never 150 pistols in the same place at the same time.

DR. STAHMER: The regiment was very scattered. About how many kilometers?

OBERHAUSER: Over five hundred kilometers.

Such were the important questions and answers from this hearing. Finally the Soviet prosecutors produced their witnesses, first the astronomer Boris Bazilevsky, who before the German occupation was the deputy burgomaster of Smolensk. He was interrogated by Counselor Smirnov.

SMIRNOV: How long had you lived in Smolensk before this occupation?

BAZILEVSKY: From the year 1919 onward.

SMIRNOV: Is the so-called Wood of Katyn known to you?

BAZILEVSKY: Yes, it is a favorite spot with the inhabitants of Smolensk.

SMIRNOV: Who was the burgomaster of Smolensk?

BAZILEVSKY: Lawyer Menschagin.

SMIRNOV: What were Menschagin's relations with the German authorities?

BAZILEVSKY: Very good.

SMIRNOV: Could one say that Menschagin held a position of trust with the German authorities and that the Germans gave him secret information?

BAZILEVSKY: Undoubtedly.

SMIRNOV: What did the Polish prisoners of war in Smolensk do, what do you know about their later fate?

BAZILEVSKY: About the Polish prisoners of war, Menschagin told me that it was proposed to execute them.

SMIRNOV: Did you return to the question in your later conversations with Menschagin?

BAZILEVSKY: About two weeks later. I put the question to him, what had happened to the Poles. At first he hesitated, then he said: "It is already the end for them."

SMIRNOV: Did Menschagin tell you why these shootings took place?

BAZILEVSKY: Yes. He said that it was a part of the general system in the treatment of Polish prisoners of war.

After this a man entered the courtroom who had played a changing role in the history of Katyn. He was the Bulgarian physician Dr. Marko Antonov Markov of the Forensic Medicine Institute of Sofia. When Conti in 1943 invited the twelve foreign experts to Katyn, Markov was in the group. His signature occurs on the final communiqué of the Commission. This was the basis for the German claim that the mass murder of Katyn was the work of Soviet troops. Later, when Bulgaria was occupied by Soviet troops, Markov was accused on February 19, 1945, before the People's Court in Sofia. He declared that the members of the Commission had been continually guarded by members of the

Gestapo, and had finally been forced to sign the communiqué. Now Markov appeared on the Nuremberg witness stand.

SMIRNOV: When did the Commission reach Katyn?

MARKOV: The Commission reached Smolensk on the evening of April 28, 1943.

SMIRNOV: How often did the members of the Commission personally visit the mass graves of the Katyn Wood?

MARKOV: We were twice in the Katyn Wood, in the forenoons of the 29th and 30th of April.

SMIRNOV: How many hours each time did you spend at the mass graves?

MARKOV: I believe not more than three or four hours at a time.

SMIRNOV: Did the forensic medical investigations establish the fact that the corpses had already been in the graves three years.

MARKOV: In my opinion these corpses were in the graves a much shorter period than three years. I was of the opinion that the corpse on which I performed a post-mortem had not been buried more than a year to a year and a half.

SMIRNOV: Is it the custom in Bulgarian forensic medicine to divide their inquiries into two parts: description and conclusions?

MARKOV: Yes, it is.

SMIRNOV: Did the report that you made contain conclusions?

MARKOV: My report contained only a descriptive part without conclusions, because I could see from the papers there that they wished to suggest to us that these corpses had already been in the ground for three years. This emerged from papers that were shown to us in the small country house.

SMIRNOV: Were these papers shown to you before the post-mortem or after?

MARKOV: These papers were shown to us a day before the post-mortem.

SMIRNOV: When you signed the general report, was it clear to you then that the murder in Katyn did not take place before the last quarter of the year 1941 and that the year 1940 was in any case out of the question?

MARKOV: Yes, that was clear to me, and for that reason I did not put any conclusions in my report.

smirnov: Why did you sign the general report?

markov: On the morning of May 1 we flew from Smolensk. About midday we landed at the airport of Bela. It seemed to be a military airport. There we ate at noon, and immediately after the meal copies of the report were put before us to sign. They were put before me at this isolated military airport. That is the reason why I signed the report.

dr. stahmer: The report is not signed by you alone, but bears the signatures of eleven scientists, some of world fame. Among them is a neutral, Professor Naville of Switzerland.

markov: On what grounds the other delegates signed the reports I cannot say. They added their signatures under the same conditions as I did.

This very point in Markov's statement was supplemented on January 17, 1947, three months after the end of the Nuremberg Trial. On that day the Swiss physician Dr. Francis Naville, who belonged to the same Commission as Markov, was called before the Great Council of the Canton of Geneva. Naville, so the Council affirmed, "had acted throughout properly and in keeping with his professional standing." And the President of the Geneva Council said: "If it were true that Markov was forced by pressure to behave as he did, it remains problematical whether the pressure would be maintained for three years by German bayonets or whether it is a matter of pressure that is now being brought to bear by Soviet bayonets."

But now back to the questioning of the witnesses in the Nuremberg courtroom.

dr. stahmer: According to your report the bodies of the Polish officers upon which you carried out a post-mortem were clothed. Was it in summer or winter clothing?

markov: It was in winter clothing, winter coat and a scarf round the neck.

dr. stahmer: In the report the following statement occurs: "The documents, diaries, letters, papers found with the bodies date from the autumn of 1939 to March and April of 1940. The last date found is that of a Russian newspaper of April 22, 1940."

I now ask you, is this statement right? Does it reflect what you found?

MARKOV: Such letters and newspapers were shown to us. Some such papers were found by members of the Commission who were conducting post-mortems.

Dr. Stahmer achieved a complete victory in this cross- examination. But there was still a further twist when the last witness for the Soviet prosecution took the stand, the Moscow legal-medical expert Professor Ilich Prosorovsky.

SMIRNOV: In your examination of the corpses did you find cartridges or cartridge cases?

PROSOROVSKY: The cause of death of the Polish officers was a shot in the neck. We found bullets and in the excavations cartridge cases of German origin, for on the base of these cases the name of the firm Geco was engraved.

Later, however, it was established that cartridges with this designation from the Genschow factory in Durlach had been exported to the Baltic countries under the terms of the German-Soviet Rapallo Treaty. In Nuremberg, however, the subject of Katyn was not raised again after this hearing. And so the case remains obscure, or at least no decisive evidence was produced.

In the year 1952 an American Congressional committee attempted to resuscitate Katyn as a symbol of the cold war.

"Is the fact that the Soviet dropped the prosecution in the case of Katyn not a clear acknowledgment of guilt?" Daniel J. Flood, a member of the Committee, asked Robert Kempner, former American prosecutor in Nuremberg.

Kempner's answer: "At least it seemed very strange." Then he added, "We admired Stahmer for the fact that he forced the Soviet to drop the Katyn accusation. It was a victory for the defense."

Till the end of November 1952 the Committee questioned many witnesses, of whom some wished to remain anonymous and made their statements with a sack over their heads. Robert H. Jackson, Chief American Prosecutor in Nuremberg, stated before the Inquiry Commission: "I had already considered the possibility in Nuremberg that the Soviet Union was responsible for Katyn. For that reason we refused to say the Germans were guilty of it."

Another important statement was made by the American Lieutenant Colonel John H. van Fliet, Jr. He was in 1943 in German captivity as a prisoner of war and attached to a group of Western prisoners, who were taken by the German official to see Katyn. About his view of the scene of the crime van Fliet said: "I hated the Germans, but I had to admit that they were telling the truth."

The report that van Fliet made immediately after his return from captivity in 1945 was designated secret material by the American Army—"for fear," as the Congressional committee in 1952 verified, "the Soviet Union would not take part in the fight against Japan nor join the United Nations."

On February 12, 1953, the committee issued an extensive report of 2,362 pages on its inquiries. In it the Soviet Union is held responsible for the extermination of fourteen thousand Poles. Every member of the United Nations was given a copy. But since that February 12, 1953, public opinion has heard nothing further about the matter.

THE TECHNIQUE OF DEPOPULATION

Right from the start, Hitler's policy in the occupied areas was determined solely by his National Socialist outlook. Its principles were: Decimation of whole races and peoples, systematic liquidation of undesired elements, plundering, starvation, forced labor. The chief aim, especially in the East, was depopulation. Territory won by force of arms had to be "politically secured." This neutral official term concealed unbelievable crimes.

Adolf Heusinger, now Inspector General of the new German *Bundeswehr*, submitted in 1945 a sworn statement to the Nuremberg Court from which the American prosecutor, Telford Taylor, quoted: "It was always my personal view that the treatment of the civil population and the methods of combating resistance in operational areas gave the supreme political and military leadership a welcome opportunity to achieve their objectives, namely the systematic reduction of the Slav and Jewish populations. Quite apart from that I have always regarded these cruel methods as military folly, which only went to make the fight against the enemy needlessly more difficult for the army."

What Heusinger meant was explained on the witness stand by the chief of the German antipartisan units, as Group Leader and General of the Armed SS, Erich von dem Bach-Zelewski. He was asked by Mr. Telford Taylor: "Did the highest military authorities issue any detailed instructions on the methods to be used in combating partisans?"

BACH-ZELEWSKI: No.

TAYLOR: What was the result?

BACH-ZELEWSKI: There was, as a result of this lack of instructions, a wild anarchy in the fight against the partisans.

TAYLOR: Did these measures lead to the unnecessary killing of a large number of the civil population?

BACH-ZELEWSKI: Yes.

J. W. POKROVSKI (Soviet prosecutor): Do you know anything about the setting up of a special brigade consisting of smugglers, poachers, and freed convicts?

BACH-ZELEWSKI: At the end of 1941 and the beginning of 1942, a battalion was formed under the command of Dirlewanger for the fight against the partisans. This Dirlewanger brigade consisted largely of convicted criminals, officially called poachers, but there were also pure criminals among them who had been sentenced for burglary, murder, and so on.

POKROVSKI: How do you explain that the German commander was so willing to have the number of his soldiers increased by the addition of criminals?

BACH-ZELEWSKI: I am of the opinion that there is a distinct connection between the speech of Heinrich Himmler at the beginning of 1941, before the start of the Russian campaign, when he said that the object of the Russian campaign was the decimation of the Slav population by about thirty million, and this task should be carried out by less valuable troops.

POKROVSKI: Do you know of any order which concerned the burning of villages as punishment for the help which the partisans have been given?

BACH-ZELEWSKI: No.

POKROVSKI: Am I to understand that when certain commanders burned down villages as a punitive measure against the population, these commanders were acting on their own initiative?

BACH-ZELEWSKI: Yes.

POKROVSKI: Did you say that the fight against the partisan movement was an excuse for the extermination of the Slav and Jewish populations?

BACH-ZELEWSKI: Yes.

POKROVSKI: Did the High Command of the Army know the methods of fighting used in combating the partisan movement and in exterminating the Jewish population?

BACH-ZELEWSKI: The methods were generally known, by the Army High Command.

POKROVSKI: Can you actually and truthfully confirm that the measures applied by the Wehrmacht Command in the district areas then occupied by the Germans were directed to the sole purpose of reducing the number of Slavs and Jews to thirty million?

BACH-ZELEWSKI: I believe that these methods would definitely have resulted in the extermination of thirty million if they had been continued.

Without inhibition or conscience, Hitler planned to create an "empty space" in Eastern Europe, a place for the master race, to be picked and organized by Himmler. "The execution of the crime," said the Soviet chief prosecutor, Rudenko, "was carried out by 'Special Commandos' created for the purpose, which were called into being by agreements between the Chiefs of Police of the SD and of the OKW."

This was also stated to the Court by Otto Ohlendorf, a high official of the Reich Security Office. Ohlendorf, who himself led an action group in the East and was tried in Landsberg, as a mass-murderer in 1951, was questioned by the American prosecutor, John Harlan Amen.

AMEN: How many Einsatz (action) groups were there?

OHLENDORF: There were four Einsatzgruppen. Group A, B, C, and D. Group D was not attached to an army group but was attached directly to the Eleventh Army.

AMEN: Who was the commanding officer of the Eleventh Army?

OHLENDORF: At first, Ritter von Schober; later von Manstein.

AMEN: Did you, personally, have any conversation with Himmler?

OHLENDORF: Yes, in the late summer of 1941 Himmler was in Nikolaiev. He assembled the leaders and men of the Einsatzkommandos, repeated to them the liquidation order, and pointed out that the leaders and men who were taking part in the liquidation bore no personal responsibility for the execution of this order. The responsibility was his alone, and the Führer's.

AMEN: Do you know how many people were liquidated by Einsatz Group D under your direction?

OHLENDORF: In the year between June 1941 to June 1942, the Einsatzkommandos reported 90,000 people liquidated.

AMEN: Did that include men, women, and children?

OHLENDORF: Yes.

AMEN: On what do you base these figures?

OHLENDORF: On reports sent by the Einsatzkommandos to the Einsatzgruppen.

AMEN: Were these reports submitted to you? You saw and read these reports personally?

OHLENDORF: Yes.

AMEN: Did you personally supervise mass executions of these individuals?

OHLENDORF: I was present at two mass executions for purposes of inspection.

AMEN: Will you explain to the Tribunal in detail how an individual mass execution was carried out?

OHLENDORF: The place of execution . . . was as a rule an anti-tank ditch or a natural excavation.

AMEN: In what positions were the victims shot?

OHLENDORF: Standing or kneeling.

AMEN: And after they were shot, what was done with the bodies?

OHLENDORF: The bodies were buried in the anti-tank ditch or excavation.

AMEN: What determination, if any, was made as to whether the persons were actually dead?

OHLENDORF: The unit leaders or the firing squad commanders had orders to see to this, and, if need be, finish them off themselves.

AMEN: Were all victims, including men, women, and children, executed in the same manner?

OHLENDORF: Until the spring of 1942, yes. Then an order came from Himmler that in the future women and children were to be killed only in the gas vans.

The reason why Himmler gave this order came to light only in a later trial. The witness Erich von Bach-Zelewski related the following event: In August 1941 Himmler ordered the action group leader Arthur Nebe in Minsk to execute a hundred people, many of them women, in his presence. Bach-Zelewski was standing quite near Himmler and watched him. When the first shots rang out and victims collapsed, Himmler was upset. He turned giddy, and almost fell to the ground, but pulled himself together. Then he screamed at the executioners because they had shot so badly and some of the women were still alive. Shortly afterward, he issued the decree mentioned by Ohlendorf at Nuremberg, not to shoot women and children any more but to kill them in gas chambers.

AMEN: Will you explain to the Tribunal the construction of these gas vans and their appearance?

OHLENDORF: They looked like closed trucks, and were so constructed that, at the start of the motor, gas was conducted into the van, causing death in ten to fifteen minutes.

AMEN: What organizations furnished most of the officer personnel of the Einsatzgruppen and Einsatzkommandos?

OHLENDORF: The officer personnel was furnished by the State

police, the Kripo (criminal police), and, to a lesser extent, the SD.

LUDWIG BABEL (defense counsel for the SS and SD): Could any individual expect to succeed in evading the execution of these orders?

OHLENDORF: No. The result would have been a court-martial with a corresponding sentence.

Thus the terrible machinery of Hitler, Himmler, and their helpers worked ruthlessly to the end. In the Nuremberg courtroom, the horrible actions were described in detail for days and weeks. The "technique of depopulation" devoured millions of human beings: Jews, Slavs, women, children, old people, whole villages. Eyewitnesses and survivors came to Nuremberg; captured German documents, official reports, and confiscated photographs were put before the judges. It is impossible to comprehend the full extent of this disaster created by the hand of man. Several thousand pages of the Nuremberg Trial report are devoted to them, but even they show only a small portion. A few examples here must stand for all the others. A report sent by Major Rösler of the 528 Infantry Regiment to the Commander of the Ninth Army, General Schierwind, on January 3, 1942, was found after the end of the war, and read at the Nuremberg Trial:

> At the end of July 1941, Infantry Regiment 528, which was then under my command, was on the way from the West to Zhitomir for a rest period. On the day of our arrival, as I left my staff quarters with my staff, we heard not very far off salvos of shots at regular intervals, followed a little later by single pistol shots. I decided to look into the matter, and set out in the direction of the shooting with my adjutant and ordnance officer— Lieutenant von Bassewitz and Lieutenant Müller-Brodmann.
>
> We soon came to the conclusion that something horrible was going on, for after some time we saw numerous soldiers and civilians streaming toward a railway embankment behind which, as we were told, continuous executions were going on. During all that time we could not see over the embankment at first, but we heard after a certain interval the note of a whistle, and then a salvo of about ten shots, followed after a time by single pistol shots.
>
> When we had finally climbed on the railway embankment, we

saw a scene whose horror and brutality had a shocking, terrifying effect on anyone who was faced with it unprepared. A grave had been dug in the ground about seven or eight yards long, perhaps four yards wide, with the excavated earth thrown up at one side. This layer of earth and the wall of the grave below were completely stained with streams of blood. The grave itself was filled with numerous scarcely distinguishable human bodies of all kinds and both sexes, so that the depth of them could not be judged.

Behind the earth wall stood a detachment of police, commanded by a police officer. The uniforms of this detachment showed traces of blood. Numerous soldiers from troops already billeted there stood around in a wide circle, some in bathing trunks, watching the scene, and also numerous civilians with women and children. I approached the grave quite closely and got an impression of it that I cannot forget to this day. Among the others lying in the grave there was an old man with a white beard who still had a little walking-stick hanging over his left arm. As this man still gave signs of life by his convulsive breathing I asked one of the policemen to kill him off, to which he replied laughingly, "I've already chased seven bullets into his belly, he'll pop off all right by himself!"

The people lying in the grave were not specially laid out but remained where they had dropped from the earth wall when they had been shot. All these people were finished off by shots in the back of the neck and by pistol shots from above.

After my war experiences both in the French and the Russian campaigns I do not suffer from exaggerated squeamishness, but I cannot remember ever having watched such a scene.

This description by a German major can be confirmed by a hundred other eyewitness accounts; similar scenes took place everywhere in the vast Eastern areas, around all the big cities.

That this was not a matter of irresponsible actions was proved by another Nuremberg document: the diary of the defendant, Governor General of Poland Hans Frank. On February 6, 1940, Frank gave the correspondent of the *Völkischer Beobachter* Kleiss an interview. Soviet prosecutor Smirnov read from it:

KLEISS: Perhaps it would be interesting to define the difference between Protectorate and General Government.

FRANK: A flexible difference, I can tell you. In Prague, for example, large red posters were displayed saying that today seven Czechs had been shot. So I said to myself: "If I hang up a notice for every seven Poles shot, all the forests of Poland would not suffice to furnish the paper for these posters."

Samuel Harris, the American prosecutor, revealed the basis for the "depopulation theory" with an important document: "It concerns a report of May 23, 1941, a date prior to the invasion of the Soviet Union. It was found in the captured archives of the OKW and carries the heading 'Economic-political directives for economic organization East, agricultural group,' that is to say, the agricultural group that formed an important part of the economic government set up by the defendant Goering for the administration of Russia."

This document states among other things that the products of the surplus-producing areas of the Soviet Union should no longer be distributed in areas where they were needed but should be brought to Germany: "The consequence is nondelivery to the whole forest zone including the important industrial centers of Moscow and Petersburg. The inhabitants of these areas, especially the population of the towns, will have to face starvation. Many tens of millions of people in these areas are superfluous and will die or have to emigrate to Siberia."

Thus the population which escaped the action groups operating under the pretense of combating partisans was condemned to death from hunger by the callous directives from Berlin. Prisoners of war in particular were ruthlessly sacrificed to the policy of depopulation. This was shown by the orders concerning the Commissars, and it reached its dreadful climax in mass murder by starvation. Bogislav von Bonin, who later—from 1952 to 1955— was actively concerned in building up the Federal German Army, made a statement at the Nuremberg Court in 1945. Prosecutor Taylor read out the relevant passage:

"At the beginning of the Russian campaign I was First General Staff Officer of the 17th Panzer Division, which was to attack north of the Brest-Litovsk across the Bug. Shortly before the beginning of the attack, my division received a written Führer order from the OKW. It laid down that Russian Commissars, when being taken prisoner, were to be immediately shot without legal formalities. This order applied to all units of the Eastern Army. Although the order was to have been promulgated down to the companies, the General commanding the VIIth Panzer Corps, General Lemelsen, forbade the announcement to the troops because in his opinion this order was insufferable from a military and moral point of view."

Lemelsen's behavior shows how Hitler's order about Commissars affected the troops, but few commanders had the personal courage of the Panzer General. The murder command assumed dreadful forms. The witness Erwin Lahousen, from the office of Admiral Canaris, was questioned about this matter in Nuremberg by John Harlan Amen.

LAHOUSEN: These orders dealt with two groups of measures which were to be taken. Firstly, the killing of the Russian Commissars, and secondly, the killing of all those elements among the Russian prisoners of war, who under a special selection program of the SD, could be identified as thoroughly bolshevized or as active representatives of the Bolshevist ideology.

AMEN: Yes—according to my recollection—by the Einsatzkommandos of the SD. These SD squads were in charge both of singling out of persons in camps and in assembly centers for prisoners of war, and of carrying out the executions.

AMEN: Will you explain to the Tribunal the exact manner in which the sorting of these prisoners was made and in what way it was determined which of the prisoners were to be killed?

LAHOUSEN: The prisoners were sorted out by Commandos of the SD and according to peculiar and arbitrary ways of procedure. Some of the leaders of these Einsatzkommandos were guided by racial considerations; particularly, of course, if someone were a Jew or of Jewish type or could otherwise be classified as racially inferior, he was picked for execution. Other leaders selected people according to their intelligence. Some had views all of their own.

After the declaration of Lahousen another document was read out:

"The fate of the Soviet prisoners of war in Germany is a tragedy on the greatest scale. Of the 3,600,000 prisoners captured, only a few hundred thousand are still capable of working today. A great number of them have succumbed to hunger or the rigors of the weather. Thousands have gone down with spotted fever. In many cases in which prisoners of war on the march have not been able to carry on because of hunger and exhaustion, they have been shot before the eyes of the shocked civilian population, and their bodies left lying around. In many camps no shelter was provided for the prisoners of war. In rain and snow they were lying in the open air. They were not even given tools to dig a trench or a hole. Finally the shooting of prisoners of war must be mentioned. Thus for example the 'Asiatic' types were shot in various camps . . ."

The amazing thing about this document is its source. It comes from a letter which Alfred Rosenberg wrote to Wilhelm Keitel on February 28, 1942. Mention must also be made of the so-called Bullet Decree, by which escaped officers and N.C.O. prisoners of war were taken to the concentration camp of Mauthausen and there shot. This diabolical action applied to all prisoners, with the exception of the British and American ones.

This decree makes a distinction between East and West, but the Night and Stealth Decree was directed against the inhabitants of all occupied territories. It was the product of a diseased satanic mind.

"Next," said the American prosecutor, Robert G. Storey, "I would like to turn to the charge that the Gestapo and SD took civilian persons from the occupied territories to Germany for secret trial and punishment. It concerns the so-called Night and Stealth Decree, which was issued by Hitler on December 7, 1941." The document bore the signature of the defendant Wilhelm Keitel, Commander in Chief of the Wehrmacht: "It is the long considered wish of the Führer that in cases of attacks against the Reich or the occupying forces in occupied territories, the perpetrators shall be punished by different methods from those used until now. The Führer is of the opinion that in such cases the mere loss of freedom, even life imprisonment, may be regarded as signs of weakness. An effective and enduring intimidation is only to be achieved by the death sentence or by measures which leave the defendants and the inhabitants in uncertainty about the fate of the culprits. Transfer to Germany fulfills this purpose. The attached directives for punitive measures are in line with this decision of the Führer. They have been considered and approved by him. Keitel."

The directives contained the sentence: "The intimidating effects of these measures lie (a) in the disappearance without trace of the guilty person, (b) in that no kind of information must be given about their whereabouts and their fate."

A terrible symbol of the unleashing of every evil instinct—ordered by Hitler and directed by Himmler—was the fate of the Czech village of Lidice.

"Many times," said the Soviet prosecutor, Smirnov, "and in even more gruesome form, the fate of Lidice was repeated in the territories of the Soviet Union, Yugoslavia, and Poland. But the world knows about Lidice and will never forget it. The annihilation of Lidice was carried out by the Nazis as a reprisal for the justified killing of the Protector of Bohemia and Moravia, Heydrich.

"On June 9, 1942, the village of Lidice was surrounded on the orders of the Gestapo by soldiers who came from Slany in ten large trucks. People were allowed to enter the village but no one was permitted to leave. The Gestapo then forced women and children into the school. The men were imprisoned in the cellar, the barn, and the stables of the Horak family. They knew what their fate would be, and awaited it with composure. The seventy-three-year-old priest Sternbeck fortified them with the words of God. Ten men at a time were led from the Horak courtyard into the garden and shot. This mass murder went on from early morning till four in the afternoon of June 10. Later the murderers were photographed with the bodies at the place of execution. One hundred and seventy-two men and youths of sixteen and upward were shot. Seven women of Lidice were also shot in Prague, the remaining 195 women were transported to the concentration camp of Ravensbrück; 42 died of ill-treatment, seven were gassed, three are missing. The children of Lidice were separated from their mothers a few days after the destruction of the village. Ninety children were sent to Lódź in Poland and from there taken to the concentration camp Gneisenau. From that day no trace of the children has been found."

But not only in the East, everywhere in Europe the terror of Hitler's "technique of depopulation" was raging. From Norway to Greece, from Estonia to the Spanish border, villages were burned and innocent men murdered. Another small European community—now a symbol like Lidice—was the French village of Oradour-sur-Glane. The German General Brodowski noted laconically in his war diary on June 14, 1944: "600 men said to have been killed. The whole male population of Oradour was shot. Women and children fled to the church. The church caught fire; explosives had been stored there. The women and children, too, were killed."

Rather different was the official report which the French prosecutor, Charles Dubost, read out:

On Saturday, June 10, 1944, an SS unit, apparently belonging to the Division Das Reich which was in the district, entered the village and ordered the inhabitants to gather in the market place. The men were told to line up in four or five groups. They were then all locked in a barn. The women and children were taken to a church and there locked in. Soon after this, machine-gun salvos rang out and the whole village as well as the surrounding farmhouse were set on fire. The houses were set alight one after the other. During this time the women and children, who heard the noise of fire and the salvos, were frightened out of their senses. About 5:00 P.M. German soldiers entered the church and fixed to the communion bench an appliance to suffocate them, consisting of a kind of chest with smoldering fuses. In a short time the air was no longer breathable; someone managed to wrench open the door of the sacristy to revive some of the women and children who had collapsed. The German soldiers began to shoot through the church windows; then they pushed their way into the church in order to finish off the last survivors with submachine-gun fire, and scattered a highly inflammable material on the floor. One woman managed to escape. She had clambered up to one of the church windows when the cry of a mother who wanted to entrust her child to this woman drew the attention of a soldier to her. He fired and wounded her severely. She was able to save her life only by pretending to be dead. About 6:00 P.M. the German soldiers held up the local train passing near Oradour and made the passengers traveling to Oradour leave the train. They shot them down with submachine-guns and threw the corpses into the fire.

When the burned-out place was visited again after the massacre, a gruesome picture presented itself:

> In the partly caved-in church there were the charred remains of children's bodies. Bones were mixed up with the ashes of the wooden paneling. A witness saw at the entrance to the church the corpse of a mother holding her child in her arms, before the altar the body of a kneeling child, and by the confessional bench two children still embracing each other.

This report was written by the French General Bridoux on the instruction of the Vichy Government which was dependent on Berlin; it was transmitted to the German Commander in Chief West.

Lidice and Oradour were only two items among many hundred similar ones mentioned in the Nuremberg Trial. For days and days the names of towns and villages which had had a similar or even a worse fate were read out, hour after hour of the proceedings were filled with witness accounts of the tragedies, a hundred thousand nameless victims.

"Citizens of western countries were executed without trial by the tens of thousands as reprisal measures for deeds in which they had not taken part," the deputy French chief prosecutor, Charles Dubost, said when speaking about another kind of crime which occurred under the German policy of occupation. It was the murder of hostages, which was considered to be an intimidating measure but in fact sowed new hatred against the occupying power and only helped to make the resistance movement stronger. In France alone, 29,660 hostages were shot by the Germans. Prosecutor Dubost could tell of shocking scenes which took place before the shootings. One must remember that these people were paying with their lives for things which others had done. Two reports may stand here for all the others.

On October 21, 1941, this announcement appeared in the French paper *Le Phare:* "Cowardly criminals who are in the pay of England and Moscow shot the Commandant of Nantes in the back on the morning of October 20, 1941. The assailants have not yet been arrested. As a reprisal for this crime I have ordered the immediate shooting of fifty hostages. If the assailants are not caught by October 23, 1941, a further fifty hostages will be shot in view of the severity of the deed. Signed, Stülpnagel." The shootings were carried out.

A report by the Royal Norwegian Government described another two such instances of murder: "On October 6, 1942, ten well-known Norwegian citizens were executed as hostages as a reprisal for attempts at sabotage. On July 20, 1944, an unknown number of Norwegians were shot without trial. They all came from a single concentration camp. The reason for their arrest and execution was not known, and has never been published. After the German capitulation 44 corpses were found in graves. They had all been shot. It is not believed that they appeared before a court. The execution was carried out by shots in the neck or a revolver shot in the ear. The hands of these victims were tied behind their backs."

These orders to shoot hostages, in which not only the police and the SS but also the Army were involved, speak of the same disregard for human life as Hitler's whole occupation policy. The German soldier, who had conquered the territories in battle, saw little of these atrocities. While he was at the front, the old guard of the Party set about behind his back to render the territory "politically secure" so that they could rule and rape the country according to the Nazi system. The men in the dock at Nuremberg, those who had not committed suicide, were completely united on the principle of their policy, however different their characters were otherwise. There was really no difference as to whether the occupied area was west or east of Germany. The defendant Arthur Seyss-Inquart, who was both chief of the civil government of southern Poland and Reich Commissioner for the Netherlands, said in 1940 when taking leave of Governor General Hans Frank: "I am now going to the West, and I will be quite frank: in my heart I remain here; for by my whole nature I am inclined toward the East. In the East we have a National Socialist mission, in the West we have merely a function; there is perhaps a difference."

The difference between mission and function was only a question of nuance: the principle was the same. Seyss-Inquart's policy in Poland as well as in the Netherlands was based on the principle which he laid down for his leading officials at Lublin in November 1939: "We demand everything that is of use to the Reich, and suppress everything that may harm the Reich." A great deal was "of use to the Reich," beginning with the seizure of foreign property and works of art, and extending to the forced displacement of workers and the deportation of Dutch Jews. Here are a few examples:

Rosenberg's action staff (*Einsatzstab*) collaborated most successfully with Seyss-Inquart's officials. A report on the confiscation of cultural goods says: "The material value of the libraries can only be estimated. But it runs to about thirty or forty million Reichsmarks."

On May 18, 1942, Seyss-Inquart issued an order by which he introduced collective fines for Dutch cities in which elements of resistance were said to exist. The economic exploitation under his direction assumed great proportions. In 1943 he seized textiles and consumer goods for the German population. The property of people who were accused of any activity against the Reich was also confiscated. In addition, Seyss-Inquart sent 500,000 Dutchmen as workers to the Reich; only a small fraction of them were genuine volunteers.

The policy of the Reich Commissioner had the most appalling consequences for the Jews. In his book, *Four Years in the Netherlands*, Seyss-Inquart wrote:

> To us, the Jews are not Dutchmen. They are enemies with whom we can conclude neither an armistice nor a peace. Do not expect from me an order which lays this down, apart from police regulations. We will strike the Jews where we meet them, and he who goes with them has to bear the consquences. The Führer has declared that the role of the Jews in Europe has come to an end, and therefore it has come to an end.

Thus, on the order of Seyss-Inquart, 117,000 of the 140,000 Jews in Holland were deported. Among these Jews was a small girl whose diary of the days when she was hiding from the German police in a loft shocked the whole world: Anne Frank, who perished in Bergen-Belsen.

The policy of depopulation was not limited to the Jews. All the races and social groups which were not acceptable to the "Master Race" were subjected to it. This also applied to the Protectorate of Bohemia and Moravia, the first territory in which the main principles of the German policy of occupation and incorporation were applied. A document of this matter incriminated the defendant Konstantin von Neurath, Reich Protector of Bohemia and Moravia until 1941. It is a secret order of October 15, 1940:

> The Reich Protector, after full consideration of the various possibilities, has laid down his opinion in a memorandum which shows three possible solutions:
>
> a) German penetration (i.e. Germanization) of Moravia and confinement of the Czech population to a limited part of Bohemia. This solution must be considered unsatisfactory as the problem of the Czechs—although in a smaller measure—would continue to exist.
>
> b) The most complete solution, namely the forced emigration of all the Czechs, would raise many contrary arguments. The memorandum therefore comes to the conclusion that it is impracticable within a foreseeable time.
>
> c) Assimilation of the Czechs; that is to say, the absorption of about half the Czech population, insofar as it has any racial value, into the German people; this could also be effected by their transfer to Germany as a labor force, i.e., by breaking up the population group. The other half of the Czech people must be devitalized, eliminated, and taken to other countries. This applies particularly to the racially Mongoloid population groups and the majority of the intellectuals.

Since the administrative policy of Konstantin von Neurath seemed too mild to Hitler, he replaced him by SD chief Reinhard Heydrich in 1941. This, and Neurath's appeal for some arrested Czechs, persuaded the Court to sentence the former German Foreign Minister to only fifteen years' imprisonment.

Nearly all of Hitler's governors, commissioners, and other occupation officials tried to shift the blame for their regime of terror to Himmler's SD and Security Police. There was hardly a document or statement by witnesses which did not show the enormity of the crimes committed by Himmler's organization. But Himmler was dead, and in his place Ernst Kaltenbrunner had to answer for the deeds. Yet Kaltenbrunner was no mere substitute: enormous was the guilt of the man who, as chief of the Security Police and the SD as well as of the Reich Security Headquarters at home and abroad, directed Himmler's machinery and signed many death sentences.

The unlimited cruelty of these orders is borne out by a letter from the Security Police and the SD for the district of Radom, dated July 19, 1944. It says:

> The National Leader of the SS has ordered, with the approval of the Governor General, that in all cases in which attacks or attempted attacks on Germans have taken place or saboteurs have destroyed vital installations, not only the convicted perpetrator will be shot, but in addition all the men of his kinsmen are to be executed at the same time and the female relatives over the age of 16 sent to concentration camps.

The Governor General mentioned in this letter is the defendant Hans Frank, head of the civil government of the occupied Polish territory. The prosecution had an easy task in his case. His war diary, which comprised thirty-eight volumes, is a unique and unassailable indictment of its author. The American prosecutor, William H. Baldwin, declared: "It is incomprehensible to a man with a normal conscience how anyone could set down such a soberly written history of murder, starvation, and mass extermination."

Frank ruled his domain according to his motto: "Poland shall be treated like a colony, the Poles will become the slaves of the Greater German World Empire." He was an absolutist potentate, a tyrant, and mass murderer. Frank himself explained his position on March 8, 1940, to his divisional chiefs: "Here in the Government General of Poland there is no authority higher in rank, no influence stronger than the Governor General's. Even the army has no governing or administrative function: it has security tasks and general military duties. It has no kind of political power. The same applies to the SS and the police. There is here no state within a state but we are the representatives of the Führer and the Reich."

His speeches and his diary gave evidence against him. Thus on January 14, 1944, he made the shocking entry: "Once we have won the war, then as far as I am concerned they can make mincemeat out of the Poles and the Ukrainians. We can do what we like."

During the war, Frank did what he liked. Plunder, terror, and forced labor were the fundamentals of his policy. The Polish inhabitants lived under unimaginable conditions. Frank depicted them faithfully in his diary: "Medical counselor Dr. Walbaum explained the health situation of the Polish population. Investigations which were carried out by his department indicate that the greater part of the Poles get only some 600 calories a day." That was in 1941, early in the war. A year later, on August 24, 1942, Frank stated to his subordinates: "Before the German people reach a hunger crisis the occupied areas and their inhabitants are to be reduced to starvation. The Government General has undertaken to deliver 500,000 tons of grain to Germany in addition to what is required to feed the Army, police, and SS stationed here."

August 18, 1942, Frank had a conference with the Plenipotentiary General for the Allocation of Labor, Fritz Sauckel. On this occasion Frank said: "I am happy to be able to inform you, Party Comrade Sauckel, that up to now we have sent over 800,000 workers into Germany. They have just inquired about the supply of a further 140,000. But over and above these 140,000 they can count on a further number of workers next year. We shall use the police to get them."

The story of slave labor played an extensive part at Nuremberg; especially the defendants Sauckel, Frank, Kaltenbrunner, and Speer were involved in it. This action may well be unique in the history of mankind. At its center stood the defendant Fritz Sauckel, who, on March 21, 1942, was commanded to concentrate under unified control "the employment of all available labor forces, including workers conscripted abroad and prisoners of war." The verdict on him states: "The evidence shows that Sauckel bears the principal responsibility for a program which involved the deportation of more than five million people for the purpose of forced labor, which subjected many of them to terrible cruelty and suffering."

The dreadful program was planned before the war. Hitler stated in a talk with Goering and Raeder on May 23, 1939: "If fate forces us to have a conflict with the West, it will be good to have a large territory in the East. During a war we will be able to count on record harvests even less than in peacetime. The inhabitants of non-German territories do no service under arms and are available for labor purposes."

Gauleiter Sauckel set to work with unrivaled fanaticism. A mere four months after his installation as labor chief he was in a position to report in a letter to Hitler and Goering: "As it was necessary to find some 1,600,000 workers for urgent requirements in the armament and food industries, I made the supply of this number of workers in the shortest possible time an important part of my program. On July 24, 1942, that number of required workers was already exceeded."

"I will not praise Gauleiter Sauckel," said Goering a week later. "That is not necessary. But what he has achieved in this short time, to bring workers with such speed from all over Europe and to supply them to our factories, that was unique."

Among the 1,600,000 slave workers that Sauckel had collected were almost a million from the East and more than 200,000 Soviet prisoners of war. These two groups made up the main part of the program. On April 15, 1943, Sauckel informed Hitler that a further 3,600,000 foreign workers had been brought into industry, as well as 1,600,000 prisoners of war. Armament firms then operated with 40 per cent of foreigners who came from fourteen countries. On March 1, 1944, Sauckel declared quite openly: "Of the five million foreign workers who have come to Germany, less than 200,000 have come voluntarily."

These somber figures conceal tragedies of unimaginable extent. The Netherlands Government declared in a report to the Nuremberg Court: "In November 1944, the Germans began a ruthless campaign to enlist labor forces; they by-passed the labor exchanges. Without warning they singled out whole town areas, arrested people in the streets or in their houses, and deported them."

In the East, slave labor began earlier. Every form of compulsion was used right from the start. "A wild, ruthless manhunt was carried on in town and country, in the streets and squares, at the stations, as well as in churches and at night in private houses; it destroyed any feeling of security among the inhabitants," wrote the leader of the Ukrainian Committee, Professor Volodymyr Kubiyovich to Government General Frank in February 1943. The professor told him that the Ukrainians had not expected to be regarded as Germany's enemies. He said that the German police had even ransacked the Ukrainian holy of holies, the St. George Cathedral in Lemberg, which had never happened once during the Bolshevist revolution.

The director of the Krupp locomotive factory in Essen, Hupe, wrote about the ghastly living conditions of the Eastern workers on March 14, 1942: "We have confirmed in the last few days that the lodgings of the Russians billeted here are miserable, that the people grow weaker from day to day. Investigations have established that individual Russians are no longer in a condition, for example, to work a lathe correctly on account of their failing bodily health. The same thing is reported from all other factories in which Russians are employed."

It seems as though this situation would have grown worse and still more men would have died of exhaustion had not Albert Speer laid down the principle that workers "must be adequately fed so that they can work competently." As National Minister for Armament and Munitions, Speer worked in close collaboration with Sauckel. It seems that Speer gave Sauckel an estimate of his labor requirements and the latter procured the workers and sent them where Speer required them. Speer got away with a sentence of twenty years' imprisonment. The Court considered, among other things, his upright attitude toward Hitler as a reason for leniency. Yet his responsibility for the slave-labor program was beyond doubt.

The German senior camp physician in the camp for foreigners

at the Krupp works, Dr. Wilhelm Jäger, submitted this statement to the Nuremberg Court: "The conditions in all the camps were bad in the extreme. The food for the Eastern workers was completely inadequate. The scarcity of shoes forced many workers, even in winter, to go to work barefoot. The sanitary conditions were specially bad. The number of Eastern workers who were ill was twice that of the German workers. They died off like flies. The camp in Nogerratstrasse (where prisoners of war were housed as ammunition workers) was in a shocking condition. The people lived in ash pits, dog kennels, old baking ovens, and huts they had made." Another document says: "It appeared to me as a physician that the place where they were living was unfit for human habitation. Every day, up to ten people were brought to me whose bodies were covered with black bruises as a result of the continual beating with rubber hoses, steel rods, or sticks. The people were often writhing with pain, but I was unable to let them have even a little medical help. Often the dead lay on their sacks of straw for two or three days until other prisoners carried them out and buried them."

All of them, the innocent hostages, the murdered and starved prisoners of war and slave workers, the decimated peoples and liquidated races, were the anonymous and unexpiated victims of that policy of depopulation which Hitler and his henchmen applied so successfully in the occupied territories.

THE EXTERMINATION
OF THE JEWS

Hitler's attempt to exterminate the Jews in Europe took up a considerable period at the Nuremberg Trial. There was among the defendants scarcely a representative of the Third Reich who did not bear at least some guilt for this ghastly program of annihilation. The anti-Semitism of the Party was not academic; it demanded action and found executioners and hangmen enough to carry it out.

The history of the persecution of the Jews in the Third Reich is filled with unbelievable horror and crimes whose complete extent is still unknown to the German people. It began seemingly harmlessly and ended with the destruction of some six million people. The path that Hitler and his colleagues were to follow was already laid down in the program of the National Socialist Party of 1920. There it says: "A citizen can only be one who is a member of the people, a member of the people can only be one who is of German blood, without consideration of religion. No Jew can therefore be a member of the people."

After the seizure of power the Nazis had the "legal" means of turning their program into action. Numerous decrees curtailed the rights of the German Jews. Immigrant Jews were deprived of citizenship. Jews could not marry "Aryans," they could not vote, they could not follow certain professions or use certain means of transport or places of recreation. Only one thing could they do: pay high taxes and fines and later die.

But that was not enough. The uniformed mobs of 1933 and 1938 were organized, they burned the synagogues, boycotted Jewish businesses, beat up the Jews and shot them down. The measures grew in fierceness. Of the 500,000 Jews living in Germany up to the beginning of the war, 200,000 fled abroad. To those remaining it soon became clear that more was now at stake than their homes, jobs, and friends; their very lives were now in peril.

In his Reichstag speech of January 30, 1939, Hitler expressed himself clearly enough: "If the international financial Jewry inside and outside Europe should succeed in throwing the nations again into war, the result will not be the Bolshevization of the world and with it the victory of Jewry, but the extermination of the Jewish race in Europe."

At that time, Hitler had no clear plans as to how he could achieve this aim, although as early as 1923 he complained in his book, *Mein Kampf*: "If only at the beginning of the war (1914) twelve or fifteen thousand of these Hebrew corrupters of the people had been put away with poison gas!" Perhaps he dallied for a time with the curious plan of the defendant Hjalmar Schacht —to deport the German Jews to Madagascar. This plan was finally interred only in 1942 when the departmental chief of the Foreign Office, Franz Rademacher, gave his officials new instructions: "The war against the Soviet Union has now made it possible to use other territories for the final solution. Accordingly the Führer has decided that the Jews will not be sent to Madagascar but to the East."

Hitler himself later repeated this five times. It was the key to the crimes which led to the extermination of millions of people under the euphemism, "Final Solution." On January 24, 1939, SS Group Leader Reinhard Heydrich was ordered by Marshal Goering to organize the "Jewish emigration." On July 31, 1941, this order was expanded by Goering into the "final solution." From then on, organized by a professional murderer, the extermination of the Jewish "race" was systematically pursued. Everything that had previously happened to the Jews was only a modest prelude to the atrocities that were now to follow. While the German troops swarmed across Europe in their triumphal progress, with final victory almost within their grasp, thousands of Himmler's specialists devoted their labors to the final solution, and destroyed—as efficiently as possible—millions of people. In Nuremberg, Goering maintained on several occasions that he had no radical antipathy against the Jews. But the facts present another picture. Goering's name is forever connected with the order for the final solution, and appears everywhere whenever anything was planned or undertaken against the Jews. The meeting called by Goering on November 12, 1938, at which the fine of one thousand million marks was imposed on the Jews, proves Goering's active anti-Semitism. He demanded a "uniform" for the Jews and their concentration in ghettos. In conclusion he predicted: "If the German Reich in the forseeable future comes into conflict with a foreign country, it goes without saying that we in Germany will think first of all in terms of having a great reckoning with the Jews." In Nuremberg, however, Goering denied all knowledge of the atrocities in the concentration camps.

It is true that up to the middle of 1941 there were no systematic mass murders of the Jews. The reason may be that the German government still wished to conciliate world opinion, especially in America and Russia. Only when both nations were at war with

Germany did the program of the final solution come into full force.

By that time, the fate of the Jewish people in those territories where National Socialism was in power was already grim enough. German Jews in their thousands were deported under unimaginable condititons to the newly created Governor Generalship of Poland. The Viennese Jews, for example, were forced into the already overcrowded Jewish settlements near Lublin. Many Jews never reached their destination. They died on the way of hunger or cold. Governor General Frank had the idea of making some cities, such as Cracow, free of Jews. He achieved it by restricting the Jews to ghettos. This notion occurs first in confidential statements from Rosenberg's ministry, and were read out at Nuremberg: "A first leading objective of the German methods must be to separate the Jews strictly from the rest of the population." The ghettos offered the possibility of starving their inhabitants to death. Life was made a hell for millions of human beings (see also the next chapter on the Warsaw ghetto). All the possessions of the Jews were taken from them before they were sent to the ghettos and later into the gas chambers. The Reinhardt Action alone, this monstrous project of robbing and killing the Jews of Poland, carried out under the leadership of SS Group Leader Odilo Globocnik, brought in spoils to the value of 180,000,000 marks.

The system of starving the Jews to death in the ghettos proved to be too slow. In March 1942 the so-called selections began, the choosing of those Jews who were not working for the Germans. Their path of suffering ended in the gas chambers of Auschwitz or in the mass graves of one of the four action groups. All these massacres go back to the notorious Wannsee Conference of January 20, 1942. Heydrich had called this "international conference" to discuss the spheres of competence and to co-ordinate the final solution. Those present, with Heydrich in the chair, included SS and police officers, a representative of Governor General Frank, Gestapo chief Heinrich Müller and his "Jew specialist" Adolf Eichmann, Gauleiter Alfred Meyer from Rosenberg's Ministry for the Occupied Eastern Territories, Secretary of State Dr. Wilhelm Stuckart from Frick's Ministry of the Interior, Ernst Neumann from Goering's Air Ministry, Martin Luther from Ribbentrop's Foreign Office, Secretary of State Roland Freisler from the Ministry of Justice (the "hanging judge" of the July 20 trials), and others.

The frightening report of this meeting, which was later issued and signed by Ribbentrop's Secretary of State, Ernst Freiherr von Weizsäcker, discloses what Heydrich said to his listeners about the final solution. "Instead of emigration, the evacuation of the Jews to the East has now become possible, subject to the approval of the Führer. Valuable experience has already been gained, and will be of considerable importance in view of the imminent final solution of the Jewish problem. It affects about eleven million Jews."

Then follows a detailed account which shows what unhinged minds were at work here—a list of victims including 330,000 Jews from England, 4,000 from Ireland, 18,000 from Switzerland, and 6,000 from Spain. In their murderous fantasies they completely forgot the political and military realities, especially that final victory was a prerequisite for the final solution. Still, German efficiency achieved the annihilation of nearly half of the intended murders of eleven million human beings. Heydrich concluded the meeting with these directions:

"Jews capable of working will be taken in large labor columns, the sexes segregated, to these (Eastern) areas to build roads; undoubtedly, a large proportion will succumb there to exhaustion. The finally remaining part, since they undoubtedly represent the most resilient ones, must be handled accordingly since these— if they were set free—would form the nucleus of a Jewish revival."

In his own words, the Nuremberg defendant Hans Frank made it clear that he knew exactly what Heydrich meant. It was Frank who said, at a Cracow meeting of his subordinates on December 16, 1941: "The Jews are a nuisance for us because they are noxious eaters. We have in the Protectorate approximately 2,500,000, perhaps 3,500,000 Jews. We cannot shoot or poison all these 3,500,000 Jews, but we must be able to carry out operations which will lead to their successful destruction. The Government General of Poland must be as free of Jews as the Reich. Where and how that is brought about is up to the departments which we have to install, and about whose efficiency I shall keep you informed."

Among the "departments" which Frank demanded, there were, in the first place, the Action Groups of the SD. In Nuremberg the prosecution produced a report from SS Brigade leader Franz Stahlecker to Himmler. The leader of Action Group A reported that 135,567 men, mostly Jews, had been killed by his unit "in the course of the final solution."

In satanic manner the SD leaders succeeded in using the smoldering anti-Semitism in the Baltic countries in bringing about the "final solution." Stahlecker was able to report about this: "Surprisingly enough it was at first not easy to get a pogrom against the Jews going on a grand scale. The leader of the Partisan Group, Klimaitis, whom we employed in this matter, was successful in getting a pogrom started without any German instigation or participation becoming conspicuous. In the course of the first pogrom, on the night of June 25, more than 1,500 Jews were done away with by Lithuanian partisans, many synagogues were set on fire or otherwise destroyed, and a Jewish quarter with about 60 houses was burned down. During the nights that followed, 2,300 Jews were rendered harmless in the same manner."

Otto Ohlendorf, one of the chief agents in Hitler's policy of depopulation, spoke of the purpose of the action groups at Nuremberg: "Himmler declared that an important part of our task consisted in the removal of the Jews, men, women, and children, and of Communist functionaries." Ohlendorf spoke frankly and coolly about the way in which his murder unit—Action Group D —operated:

> The unit selected for the job usually went to a village or a town and instructed the leading Jewish inhabitants to call together all Jews for the purpose of resettlement. They were ordered to give all objects of value to the leaders of the unit and to hand over their outer clothing shortly before the execution. The men, women, and children were taken to a place of execution, which was usually beside a deepened antitank trench. Then they were shot, kneeling or standing, and their bodies were thrown into the trench.

Sir Hartley Shawcross, the British chief prosecutor at Nuremberg, read out a document which shall be reproduced here in its entirety. It was a sworn statement of the German engineer, Hermann Friedrich Gräbe, who from September 1941 to January 1944 was manager of a branch of a Solingen firm of building contractors, Josef Jung, at Zdolbunow in the Polish Ukraine. His duties included visits to the building sites of his firm, among them some grain stores on a former airfield near the small town of Dubno. "When I visited the building site in Dubno on October 5, 1942," Sir Hartley read from Gräbe's report, "my foreman, Hubert Mönnikes, told me that Jews from Dubno had been shot in three large trenches, each some 100 feet long and 10 feet deep near the building site. Some 1,500 men had been killed per day. I went with Mönnikes to the building site, and near it I saw a great mound of earth about 100 feet long and six feet high. In front of the earth mound there were several trucks, from which people were being driven by armed Ukrainian militia under the supervision of an SS man. All these people had the yellow patches prescribed for Jews on the front and back of their clothing so that they could be recognized as Jews.

"Mönnikes and I went straight to the trenches. We were not prevented from approaching. I heard rifle shots in rapid succession coming from behind one of the earth mounds. The people who had been taken from the trucks, men, women, and children of all ages, had to undress and, separating their clothing into shoes, outer and underclothing, had to put it on separate piles at the order of an SS man, who had a riding crop or a dog whip in his hand. I saw a mound of shoes of approximately eight hundred to a thousand pairs, and great piles of underclothes and garments.

"Without crying or tears these people undressed, stood in family groups together, kissed and said goodbye, and waited for a sign from another SS man who stood by the trench and also held a whip in his hand. During the quarter of an hour that I stood near the trucks, I heard no moaning or begging for mercy. I watched one family of some eight persons, a man and wife both of about fifty, with their children, about one, eight, and ten years old, as well as two grown-up daughters of twenty to twenty-four.

An old woman with snow-white hair held the one-year-old child in her arm, sang to him, and tickled him. The child chuckled with joy. The father and mother looked on with tears in their eyes. The father held a youngster of some ten years by the hand, and spoke quietly to him. The boy fought back his tears. The father pointed with his finger to heaven, stroked his head, and seemed to be explaining something to him.

"The SS man at the trench called out something to his comrade. The latter detailed twenty persons and told them to go behind the mound of earth. The family of whom I spoke was among them. I remember exactly how a young woman, dark-haired and slim, pointed to herself and said 'twenty-three years old' as she passed near me.

"I went round the mound of earth and stood before the gigantic grave. People lay in it so closely packed one upon the other that only their heads could be seen. The trench was already three-quarters full. By my reckoning there were already about a thousand people lying in it. I looked round to see who was shooting. An SS man sat at the edge of the trench letting his legs dangle in it; he had a submachine gun resting on his knee and was smoking a cigarette.

"The completely naked people went down a few steps which had been dug in the wall of the trench, scrambled over the heads of those who were lying there to the position that the SS man indicated. They lay down among the dead or wounded people; some stroked those who were still alive, and spoke quietly to them. Then I heard a succession of shots. I looked in the trench and saw how the bodies twitched; blood spurted from the necks. I was surprised that no one told me to go away, but I also saw two or three postmen in uniform standing nearby.

"Soon the next group approached, climbed down into the trench, stretched out on the previous victims, and were shot. When I went back round the mound of earth I noticed a transport of human beings that had just arrived. This time there were invalids and cripples among them. An old woman with a wasted body and dreadfully thin legs was undressed by others who were already naked, while two people supported her. The woman was obviously lame. The naked men carried the woman around the earth mound. I left with Mönnikes and drove back to Dubno."

This report must stand for all the rest.

Incessantly, the overcrowded trains rolled toward the East with their freight that was condemned to death. Tens of thousands of Jews from France and the Netherlands, from Germany, Denmark, and Norway, had to embark on the journey without return. They had already been penned together in the crammed ghetto of Lódź. The longer the war lasted, the bigger were the transports of the deported. Often the path of suffering of the Jews did not lead first to the ghettos but straight to the gas chambers of the extermination camps or to the death trucks of the action groups. The conventional method of execution by shooting was gradually replaced by a more modern one. Ohlendorf reported:

"In the spring of 1942, the chief of the Security Police and of the SD in Berlin sent us gas trucks. These trucks were ordered by Office II of the Reich Security Headquarters. The man who was responsible for the trucks of my action group was Becker. We had received orders to use the trucks for the gassing of women and children. Every time a unit had collected a sufficient number of victims a truck for their liquidation was sent. We also had these trucks stationed near transit camps to which victims were brought. The victims were told that they would be transferred and for this purpose had to get into the trucks. Then the doors were shut, the engine was started, and the gas streamed in. The victims died within 10 to 15 minutes. The trucks were then taken to the burial place, where the bodies were taken out and buried."

The SS man Becker mentioned by Ohlendorf must have had a peculiar frame of mind. He introduced colored shutters for the death trucks, "as they are often seen on peasants' houses in the country," and he complained to his superiors that "the drivers of the trucks often press the gas pedal right down so that the action ends too quickly."

After the Wannsee Conference, the first extermination camps were built. Some surpassed all others in size and in horror. They were those which are forever stamped upon the consciousness of the world as symbols of unsurpassed barbarity and atrocities. Their names are Maidanek, Belsen, Treblinka, and Auschwitz. These camps were unmasked and branded by a legion of authentic statements at Nuremberg as centers of horror. About Treblinka the Report of the Polish Government Commission says: "Toward the end of April 1942, the first three chambers were ready, in which the mass murders were to be carried out by steam. Somewhat later the actual slaughterhouse was prepared, which contained 10 death chambers. It was first used for mass murder early in autumn 1942."

The euthanasia program had given the mass murderers opportunities for the practical testing of their methods of execution. Although carbon monoxide was chiefly used in the gas chambers, in a number of execution camps they worked predominantly with Zyklon B, a crystallized form of hydrocyanide. The longer the mass gassings went on, the more smoothly they went. This is the only explanation for the astronomical number of victims SS battalion commander Dr. Wilhelm Höttl reported in Nuremberg on a talk with Jew murderer No. 1, Adolf Eichmann. At the end of August 1944 Eichmann told him that in the various extermination camps some four million Jews had been killed, while two million had met their deaths in other ways. The greater part of these had been killed by the action groups of the Security Police. In the witness box, Eichmann's representative in Slovakia, SS chief battalion commander Dieter Wisliceny, stated in answer to a question from the American prosecutor Smith Brookhart:

"I last saw Eichmann at the end of February 1945 in Berlin. He said then that if the war were lost he would commit suicide."

BROOKHART: Did he say anything about the number of Jews killed?

WISLICENY: Yes, he expressed that in a specially cynical way. He said: he would jump into his grave laughing in the knowledge that he had five million people on his conscience, which was extremely satisfying to him.

Wisliceny also described to the Court the organization of the SS for the annihilation of the Jews: "The division IV-A-4-b had to deal with the Jewish question for the National Security Headquarters. Eichmann had special powers from Group Leader Müller, Chief of Section IV, and from the Chief of the Security Police. He was responsible for the so-called solution of the Jewish problem in Germany and all territories occupied by Germany."

One man more than any other at Nuremberg spread paralyzing horror among judges, defending counsels, and defendants: Rudolf Franz Hoess, Camp Commandant of Auschwitz. Here was a mass murderer reporting at firsthand. The mountains of statements about the gruesomeness in the camps had less weight than what Hoess said so calmly on the witness stand, as though he were talking of everyday matters. First, Kaltenbrunner's defense counsel, Dr. Kurt Kaufmann, questioned him:

KAUFMANN: You were Camp Commandant of Auschwitz from 1940 to 1943?

HOESS: Yes.

KAUFMANN: And in that time hundreds of thousands of human beings were put to death there. Is that true?

HOESS: Yes.

KAUFMANN: Is it true that Eichmann told you that altogether over two million Jewish people were killed in Auschwitz?

HOESS: Yes.

KAUFMANN: Men, women, and children?

HOESS: Yes.

Hoess went on: "In summer 1941 I was personally ordered to Berlin to the National Chief of the SS, Himmler. He gave me to understand—I can no longer recall the exact words—that the Führer had ordered the final solution of the Jewish problem, and that we, the SS, had to carry out this order. If we did not do this now, then later the Jews would destroy the German people. He had therefore chosen Auschwitz because it was most favorably situated with regard to transport, and the extensive grounds offered space for seclusion."

Hoess' examination by prosecutor John Harlan Amen was limited to securing from him confirmation of his written statement. Amen read from it: "I commanded Auschwitz up to December 1, 1943, and estimate that at least 2,500,000 victims were killed and disposed of there by gassing and burning; at least a further half million died of starvation and illness, which makes a total of about 3,000,000 dead. This number represents about 70 or 80 per cent of all the people who were sent to Auschwitz as prisoners; the others were sorted out and used for slave labor in the workshops of the concentration camp. The total number of victims comprises about 100,000 German Jews and a great number of mostly Jewish inhabitants of Holland, France, Belgium, Poland, Hungary, Czechoslovakia, Greece, and other countries. About 400,000 Hungarian Jews alone were executed by us in Auschwitz in the summer of 1944.

"The camp commander of Treblinka told me that he had liquidated 80,000 in the course of six months. His task was chiefly the liquidation of all Jews from the Warsaw ghetto. He had used carbon monoxide, and I regarded his methods as not very effective. So when I put up the execution buildings in Auschwitz, I began to use Zyklon B, a crystallized hydrocyanic acid, which we threw into the death chamber through a small opening. It required, according to climatic conditions, 3 to 15 minutes to kill the people in the death chamber. We knew when the people were dead because their screaming stopped. We usually waited half an hour before we opened the doors and took out the corpses. After the bodies had been dragged out our special detachments took off their rings and drew the gold from the teeth of the corpses. A further improvement as compared with Treblinka was that we built gas chambers which could hold 2,000 people at a time, while the ten gas chambers at Treblinka could only take 200 each.

"The manner in which we chose our victims was as follows: Two SS doctors were employed in Auschwitz to inspect all the incoming convoys of prisoners. The prisoners had to march past them while they made their decision on the spot: those capable of work were sent into the camp, the others at once to the extermination block. Very young children, being incapable of working, were killed as a matter of principle. Often women tried to hide their children under their clothes, but when they were found they were at once sent to their death. We tried to carry out these executions in secret, but the foul and nauseating stench which rose from the incessant burning of corpses penetrated the whole area."

AMEN: Is all this true and accurate?

HOESS: Yes.

General Reitlinger, who studied the matter thoroughly, gives this description in his book, *The Final Solution:*

> Slowly the gas escaped from the perforations in the sheet metal columns. Generally the victims would be too tightly packed in to notice this at first, but at other times they would be few enough to sit in comfort, gazing up at the douches, from which no water came, or the floor, which, strange to say, had no drainage tunnels. Then they would feel the gas and crowd together away from the menacing columns and finally stampede toward the huge metal door with its little window, where they piled up in one blue, clammy, blood-spattered pyramid, clawing and mauling each other even in death.
>
> Twenty-five minutes later the "exhauster" electric pumps removed the gas-laden air, the great metal doors slid open, and the men of the Jewish *Sonderkommando* entered, wearing gas masks and gum boots and carrying hoses, for their first task was to remove the blood and defecations before dragging the clawing dead apart with nooses and hooks, the prelude to the ghastly search for gold and the removal of the teeth and hair which were regarded by the Germans as strategic materials.

Conveyor belts or small electric railways took the bodies to the cremation furnaces. Ashes and bone remnants were pulverized: nothing was to survive as evidence. SS Group leader Oswald Pohl, chief of the SS Economic Direction Headquarters, had the task of changing the belongings of the murdered victims into cash with the help of the Reichsbank—gold from teeth, jewelry, cigarette cases, clothing, watches, spectacle frames, shoes, linen in tremendous quantities. Pohl devoted himself to all details with barbaric thoroughness. On August 6, 1942, he wrote to the Commandants of sixteen extermination camps ". . . that the human hair cut in all concentration camps shall be put to industrial use. Human hair will be processed into felt and spun into yarn. Women's combed-out and cut hair is to be made into inner soles for U-boat crews and felt stockings for railwaymen. It is therefore commanded that the hair of women prisoners is to be collected after disinfection. Hair cut from male prisoners is only of value if over ¾ ins. long . . ."

It would be easy to add many more documents of this kind, but the facts are impressive enough without reiteration. Only one further statement may be cited here, the report of SS battalion chief Kurt Gerstein, who went to Lublin with SS Group Leader Globocnik in the middle of August 1942:

"Globocnik told me: 'This is one of the most secret matters that we have at present, one might say the most secret one. At the moment we have three plants working:

1. Belzek, on the Lublin-Lemberg railway; full capacity, 15,000 persons a day.

2. Treblinka, 75 miles northeast of Warsaw; full capacity 25,000 persons a day.

3. Sobibor, also in Poland, 20,000 persons a day.'

"Globocnik then turned to me and said: 'It is your special duty to carry out the disinfection of the very extensive textile material. After all, the whole collection of woven goods at home is only being carried on to explain the ample supply of clothing for the workers from the East and so on, making the thing look like a sacrifice on the part of the German people. In fact, the output of our plants amounts to ten or twenty times the whole collection of woven goods.'

"I then took up with the largest firms the question of washing and disinfecting such a mass of textiles—it was a matter of an accumulated stock of some forty thousand tons, that is to say sixty complete freight trains. It was, however, quite impossible to place an order for such quantities.

" 'Your other and more important task,' said Globocnik, 'is the adaptation of our gas chambers, which now work with Diesel exhaust gases, into something better and faster. I am thinking chiefly of cyanide. The day before yesterday the Führer and Himmler were here. On their instruction I have to take you there in person; I am not to issue anything in writing.'

"Thereupon SS Chief Pfannenstiel asked: 'What did the Führer say?'

" 'Faster, carry out the whole thing faster.' Hitler's companion, Counselor Dr. Herbert Linden of the Reich Ministry of the Interior, had then asked: 'Herr Globocnik, do you think it right and proper to bury whole corpses instead of burning them? After us there might come a generation that may not understand the whole thing.'

"Globocnik replied: 'Gentlemen, if ever a generation comes after us that is so flabby and weak at the knees that it does not understand our great task, then the whole National Socialist movement has been in vain. On the contrary, I am of the opinion that bronze tablets should be buried which tell posterity that we have had the courage to carry out this great and necessary work.' To which the Führer replied: 'Good, Globocnik, that is also my view.'

"But later another view prevailed. On the approach of the Russians the bodies were dug up and burned on huge grates, improvised from railway rails, with the help of gasoline and Diesel oil.

"Next day we went to Belzek. The stench of the whole area in the heat of August was pestilential, and millions of flies were present everywhere. Next morning the first train arrived from Lemberg. Forty-five cars with 6,700 people, of whom 1,450 were already dead on arrival. Children, terribly pale and frightened, peered out from behind the barred windows, their eyes full of the fear of death, and also men and women. The train came to a halt. Two hundred Ukrainians pulled open the doors and drove the people out of the cars with their leather whips. A powerful loudspeaker gave the following instructions: They were all to undress, remove artificial limbs, spectacles, and so on. Valuables to be surrendered at an office window. Shoes to be carefully tied together. Then the women and girls had to go to the barber, who cut off their hair with two or three sweeps of his scissors, and put it in potato sacks.

"Then the procession started, in front a beautiful young girl; they went along the alley, all naked, men, women, children, without artificial limbs, mothers with children at their breasts, small naked children. Most of them knew what was coming, the smell told them their fate. They hesitated, but they entered the death chambers, pushed by those behind them or by the whips of the SS. Most of them went without saying a word. A Jewess of some

40 years with flaming eyes called down upon the murderers' heads the blood that was being shed here. She was given five or six strokes across the face with a riding crop from Captain Wirth himself; then she too disappeared into the chamber. Many prayed.

"The chambers filled. Well packed—as Captain Wirth had ordered. The people stood on each other's feet—seven to eight hundred in a space of 25 square yards—no more than 45 cubic yards. The SS packed them together as tightly as was physically possible. The doors closed. My stop watch timed it all. 50 minutes, 70 seconds—the Diesel engine would not start. The people were waiting in the gas chambers. In vain. We could hear them weeping, sobbing. Captain Wirth struck the Ukrainian who helped with the engine twelve or thirteen times across the face with his whip. At last the Diesel started up. The people were still alive after all that time in those four chambers, four times 750 people in four times 45 cubic yards. A further 25 minutes passed. Many were now dead. One could see through the small window as the electric light lit up the chambers for an instant. After 28 minutes only a few were still alive. Finally, after 32 minutes, all were dead.

"From the other side, men of the working detachment—Jews themselves—opened the doors. Like pillars of basalt the dead stood there, pressed upright in the chambers. There was no room to fall or even to bend. Even in death one recognized families. They still held hands, embraced tightly in death, so that it was difficult to tear them apart to clear the chambers for the next charge. They threw out the bodies, wet with sweat and urine, smirched with feces, menstrual blood on their legs. Children's bodies flew through the air. There was no time. The riding whips of the Ukrainians flailed the working detachment. Two dozen dentists opened the dead people's mouths with hooks, looking for gold. Other dentists broke the gold teeth and crowns out of the jaws with pincers and hammers. Some workers searched the genitals and anuses for gold, precious stones, and valuables. Wirth called me over: 'Just lift this can with gold teeth, that's only from yesterday and the day before. You won't believe what we find every day in gold and precious stones.'"

Even for those who were able to work, life was an indescribable horror. "There were no beds," a woman witness reported, "but only wooden planks, about two yards square, on which we had to sleep without straw mattresses or covers. We spent several months in blocks of this kind. About 3:30 A.M. the yelling of the women overseers woke us up. We were driven out of our bunks with truncheon blows to roll call. Nothing in the world could exempt us from this roll call. Even the dying had to be carried there. We had to stand in rows of five till day broke, that was till 7 or 8 A.M. in winter."

In the summer of 1944, this witness continued, the newly arrived prisoners were received by the gay tunes of an orchestra before they were directed to the labor camp or to the extermination block. They were sent into the gas chambers to the strains of *The Merry Widow*.

For days, eyewitnesses told of their experiences at Nuremberg. The evidence also included films. They came either from the private ownership of the SS chiefs or were shot by Allied cameramen after liberation. The unspeakable atrocities heavily oppressed the whole courtroom. Even the defendants appeared shaken. During the performance Funk wept, Doenitz hid his face, others hung their heads and said only one word: "Terrible!" The court psychologist, Dr. Gilbert, spoke about it later with some of the defendants.

In his cell Fritzsche squatted on his small bed, his head in his hands, and was weeping when Dr. Gilbert visited him. Slowly the one-time radio commentator raised his head, and looked at the psychologist with a distraught expression. Then he said, shaken time and again by sobs: "No power in heaven or on earth can take this shame away from my country—not in generations—not in centuries." He sobbed again, struck his temples with his fists, drew in his breath, and rapped out: "Excuse me, I lost my self-control."

"Do you want a sleeping pill for the night?" Dr. Gilbert asked.

"What good would that do?" Fritzsche answered. "Could I shut all that out of my mind with a pill?"

With the psychiatrist Dr. Kelley, Dr. Gilbert went into the other cells. Baldur von Schirach said, "I never knew that Germans could behave in such a way." Walther Funk was incapable of speaking to his visitors. Tears ran down his face and he kept murmuring only one word: "Terrible, terrible . . ."

At Dr. Gilbert's entry Hans Frank began to weep. "We lived like kings, and believed in that monster," he said finally when he had regained his composure. "Don't let anyone tell you that they knew nothing about it. Everyone felt that there was something frightful about this system, even if we did not know the details. We didn't want to know. It was too comfortable to be in the swim at top, and believe that everything was in order." He pointed to the supper which was still untouched on his table. "You treat us too well," he said. "Your prisoners of war and our own people starved to death in our concentration camps. May God have mercy on our souls. Yes, doctor, this trial is God's will. At first I tried to come to an understanding with my fellow prisoners—but that is past."

"Do you want a sleeping pill?"

"No, thank you. If I don't sleep I can pray."

For many a prisoner in the concentration camps, death in the gas chamber might perhaps have come as a release. The tortures that many had to endure until death freed them put all else in the shade. They served as guinea pigs for the unfeeling and fanatical SS doctors. They were misused for experiments whose scientific value was nil. It is impossible to indicate the whole extensive program of human experiments to which thousands were subjected in the most gruesome way. In Auschwitz there were operations on Jewish women suffering from cancer, experiments with identical Jewish twins, injections and X-ray radiation to make women sterile. In Buchenwald, tests were made with phosphorus burns, sex hormones, and hunger edemas. Spotted-fever tests cost the lives of nearly 600 prisoners. The French chemist Alfred Balachowsky stated as a witness at Nuremberg that these prisoners were injected with blood from a typhoid patient who was at the height of his crisis. These injections were always followed by death. Other tests were concerned with yellow fever, smallpox, cholera, and diphtheria.

A special kind of experiment in the camps were the biological ones. In this field, SS physician Dr. Sigmund Rascher especially distinguished himself by his work on high and low temperatures.

Himmler followed these experiments of Rascher's with sadistic interest and gave long prognoses how, in his opinion, the individual tests would turn out. Rascher put his victims in water of a temperature between 36.5 to 53.75 degrees F. In 1943, he asked Himmler to be moved from Dachau to Auschwitz, as his experiments would arouse less commotion there: "The persons under test yell when they begin to freeze," he explained. In other camps the prisoners were shot through the thighs with poisoned bullets. They died in horrible pain within two hours. Death was just as frightful for those who had air injected into their veins, and petroleum under the skin of both legs.

The proportion of women among the human guinea pigs was high. It was within the framework of the "negative population policy" of the SS to sterilize the Jewish people. In this program, the foremost worker was SS Brigade Commander Professor Hans Clauberg, who boasted that he could render sterile a thousand women a day. In the concentration camp of Ravensbrück even children were used in these tests.

But the experiments with women were not limited to sterilization. "When we left Auschwitz, they sent us to Ravensbrück," Mme. Couturier told the Court. "There we were taken to the N.N. block where there were Polish women with the registration number 7,000, and some others who were called the hares, because they were used as guinea pigs. They had been picked out from the prisoners' columns because of their straight legs and their good state of health. They were subjected to various operations. Some had parts of the bones of their legs removed. Others had injections. I don't know what kind of injections. The death rate among those who had been operated on was high. When they wanted to take others away for operations they refused to enter the hospital. These were then taken by force to special cells, and there operated on by a professor in uniform who came from Berlin, and who never took the slightest antiseptic precautions. He wore no gown and did not even wash his hands."

The scale of the atrocities spread ever wider. In Buchenwald, prisoners were killed who had tattoo marks. Their skin was removed, cured, and made into lampshades and "souvenirs." The witness Maurice Lampe spoke of the atrocities in Mauthausen:

"Yes, they were the order of the day at Mauthausen as in all other camps. I believe we have two pieces of evidence which were found: two skulls which the SS chief surgeon used as paperweights. The skulls came from two young Dutch Jews who were selected from a transport of 800 people because they had specially good teeth. The SS surgeon who made the choice had let it be known that the two young Dutch Jews would have to suffer the fate of their comrades in the transport. He said to them: 'No Jews are alive here. I need two young strong men for surgical experiments. You have the choice of offering yourselves for these tests or you can die with the others.' Both were taken into the sick quarters, from one a kidney was removed, from the other the stomach. Then they were given injections of benzine in the heart. Finally they were beheaded."

Whence came the terrible masses of humanity who in the sick quarters of the camps were tortured and gassed to death, shot by the action groups, and starved in the ghettos? The victims of the Nazi race policy came from the whole of Europe. In talking of the deportations, of this terrible trail of suffering of the Jewish people, we must limit ourselves to a few sober figures: 160,000 German Jews fell victims to the "final solution," that is to say, almost all who had not emigrated. From Austria came 60,000; some 230,000 of the 350,000 Jews from Czechoslovakia perished after deportation; from France, some 60,000. Holland alone mourns some 104,000 Jews. Many of the deported Jews came from Yugoslavia, Hungary, Greece, and Romania.

Germany's Axis partner, Italy, and even Bulgaria did not share in Hitler's drastic racial policy. Only in 1944, when Mussolini was completely powerless, Jews from Rome were sent to Auschwitz. On the other hand, Hitler found much sympathy in Romania, where some 220,000 Jews were killed. Of the 3,500,000 Polish Jews, some 2,600,000 perished. In the Soviet Union, about 750,000 Jews fell victim to the action groups. Reitlinger came to the conclusion that altogether some 4,200,000 to 4,600,000 Jews were murdered, which is about 1,500,000 less than the prosecution in Nuremberg assumed, but Reitlinger also quoted the German writer Walter Dirks: "It is a disgraceful thing that there are Germans who see an exoneration in a reduction of the number of victims from six million to four million."

After the liquidation of the Warsaw ghetto by Himmler's order in 1943 and 1944, the remaining Polish and Russian ghettos were also destroyed. Some 300,000 Jews who had been lingering on in the ghettos of Lódź, Bialystok, Sosnowiec-Bedzin, Lemberg, Vilna, Kovno, and Riga fell victims to the massacre. This took place under circumstances which mock any description. After the turning point of the war, Stalingrad, Himmler set about having the traces of the SS crimes removed. He gave SS Unit commander Paul Blobel the order to liquidate the mass graves before the Soviet Army could recover the territory. Blobel began his ghoulish activity in August 1943 with Special Detachment 1005, which carried out the first exhumations in Kiev. Wherever it was possible the Special Detachments opened the mass graves and burned the remaining bodies. This gruesome work had to be carried out by prisoners whom the SS then shot. Where exhumation was not possible the graves were blown up with dynamite, leveled, and covered with grass.

As the Allied troops drew the circle ever closer around Germany, the finale of this tragedy began. In Auschwitz, the gas chambers ceased to work in autumn 1944, but the arrival of prisoners continued. At Himmler's command, Auschwitz and many other camps were evacuated. On foot or in open trucks, clad only in their thin rags, the prisoners started on their last march. Epidemics raged in the camps; 300 prisoners died daily in Belsen. When the Allies reached this camp they found 12,000 unburied corpses; 13,000 prisoners died in the days following liberation. When the Soviet Army occupied Auschwitz on January 26, 1945, they found only a few hundred invalid prisoners. Himmler had made a clean sweep at the last moment.

"A thousand years will pass and this guilt will not be taken from Germany," said the defendant Hans Frank at Nuremberg. Only a few years of that millennium have passed since. Have these things been consigned to oblivion already?

THE END OF THE
WARSAW GHETTO

In the annihilation of the Jewish people, ordered by Hitler and conducted by Himmler, there was an intermediate stage which originated in the mind of Hermann Goering. According to the verbatim report of the notorious Conference of November 12, 1938, he said: "My dear Heydrich, you can't get away from it, we must have ghettos on a large scale in the towns. They must be built."

Reinhard Heydrich, who later took the "final solution" so actively in hand, was then, a year before the outbreak of war, still against ghettos "on political grounds." But with the conquest of the Eastern European territories, new possibilities were opened. In Poland, the domain of the late Nuremberg defendant Hans Frank, the idea of a distinguishing badge for all Jews emerged. Shortly after the German invasion, on October 24, 1939, all Jews in the Polish city of Wloclawek were ordered by the occupying authorities to wear white arm bands showing the Star of David. Hans Frank liked this so much that on November 23 of the same year he signed a decree which extended the arrangement at Wloclawek to all the Jews in Poland, altogether several million people. A few months later a beginning was made to realize Goering's ghetto idea. The Jews, who were plainly distinguished by their arm bands and had long been officially registered, had to move to special quarters. They had to leave their homes, businesses, and places of work, their villages and hamlets, and start on their pitiful trek to the ghettos of Cracow, Warsaw, Lublin, Radom, and other towns.

Heydrich, the one-time opponent of the ghetto idea, was suddenly interested in concentrating all Jews, for now the ultimate objective of the "final solution" had been decided upon, and for the murderers it represented a technical convenience to have their victims ready for seizure in great collecting centers. With the expansion of Hitler's conquests, ghettos arose everywhere in the East, in the Baltic states up to Riga, in Galicia with its main centers at Lemberg, and behind the central sector of the Eastern front in Minsk and Smolensk. Only when the German troops had advanced as far as Simferopol in the Crimea, the temporary solution of the ghettos had served its purpose, and the action groups could at once begin with the mass shootings.

In building the ghettos, walls, palisades, and barbed-wire fences were erected round the newly created Jewish areas as soon as the transports arrived. Millions of people thus found themselves suddenly in a prison of unimaginable extent. What happened from now on behind the walls has been described by survivors, and also by eyewitnesses from the outside who were able to have a view of that living hell.

The executioners found and tried several solutions in succession for the problem of how the Jews could best be destroyed in the ghettos. Himmler's first plan was simply to let the walled-in people starve to death. Right from the start, the victims' food rations were below the minimum for existence, and this was in accordance with a decree which Herbert Backe of the National Ministry for Food and Agriculture had issued on September 18, 1942. Prosecutor Walsh quoted from it: "From the 42nd rationing period, Jews will no longer receive the following forms of food: meat, meat products, eggs, cereals, unskimmed milk, skimmed fresh milk, and all foodstuffs issued against the blank coupons in the ration book."

Governor General Frank did even better than Berlin, and reduced the daily bread ration for the ghetto inhabitants to 5 ounces—later even down to three-quarters of an ounce, with 3½ ounces of jam and 1¾ ounces of fat per month. He knew he was signing a collective death sentence, and remarked coolly in his diary: "During the winter months no doubt the mortality will rise, but this war brings with it the complete annihilation of the Jews." On August 24, 1942, he had already written: "Just a marginal remark—we have condemned a million and a half Jews to death by starvation."

The artificially created scarcity of food did in fact account for the deaths of thousands of the interned Jews. In the streets of the ghettos lay skeletons of emaciated children. Men and women who simply succumbed to exhaustion were put in the gutters until the death carts came and gathered their gruesome harvest the following morning.

Nevertheless Himmler and his henchmen had to realize in the end that the method of starvation was too slow and brought with it the danger of uncontrollable epidemics for the whole territory behind the fighting line. Moreover, the growing scarcity of labor created for the Jews a temporary respite; the inhabitants of the ghettos could be pressed into war-important production processes. Himmler did not sign the order to liquidate the ghettos completely, and to send all Jews who were still alive to the gas chambers of Auschwitz and Treblinka, until June 11, 1943.

The "annihilation by work" which followed the "destruction by starvation" was discussed at Nuremberg by prosecutor Walsh. Of the Party philosopher, Rosenberg, Walsh said: "The defendant Rosenberg, as National Minister for the occupied Eastern territories, established within his organization a department which, among other things, sought a solution of the Jewish problem by forced labor. His plans are contained in a document which I put forward as evidence. Jewish workers were sought out from the ghettos and taken to collecting points. Here the usable Jews were separated from those regarded as useless. From a contingent of, say, 45,000 Jews 10,000 to 15,000 were expected to be picked out as capable of working. The source of my information is a telegram from the National Security Headquarters to Himmler, which is marked *Urgent* and *Secret*, and bears the date December 16, 1942. I read the last lines: 'Among the number of 45,000, those incapable of working (old Jews and children) are included. By applying a reasonable standard the total number of Jews mustered up as workers in Auschwitz would come to at least 10,000 to 15,000.' "

These words conceal the transition to the next and last phase. At the "mustering" the stream of helpless Jews was divided into two branches: some were sorted out for "destruction through work" and were allowed to stay alive for a while, the others trod the path to the gas chambers. In his incredible diary, Hans Frank wrote: "With the Jews—this I say quite openly—an end must be made one way or the other . . . We must essentially have sympathy only with the German people, and with nobody else on earth. As an old National Socialist I must say: if the Jewish clan should survive the war, then this war would be only a partial success. We must be on our guard against any considerations of sympathy. We must destroy the Jews, wherever we meet them, and wherever it is possible."

This was the Nazi program. Only in a few places did a spark light up in that terrible darkness, and one of them was the courageous, desperate action of the Jews of the Warsaw ghetto who, on April 18, 1943, rose in arms against their persecutors. At Nuremberg, prosecutor Walsh read from a report of SS brigade leader Jürgen Stroop:

"The Jewish quarter in the city of Warsaw"—an area two and a half miles long and one and a half miles wide—"was inhabited by some 400,000 Jews. There were 27,000 homes with an average of two and a half rooms each. It was separated from the rest of the city by fireproof walls and by the bricked-up streets, windows, doors, and gaps in buildings." Walsh added: "An impression of the conditions inside this ghetto can only be formed from the fact that on an average six persons lived in each room."

In 1941 there were 44,630 deaths in the Warsaw ghetto, mostly as a result of lack of food. The death rate was increasing, but a commission of Jewish doctors who looked into the problem came to the conclusion that it would be five years before all the inhabitants were starved to death. Two facts were clear. First, that in addition to the official rations there were other sources of sustenance; second, that the inhabitants of the ghetto had organized to study their problems in an attempt to deal with them.

The wall round the ghetto was in fact not an unsurmountable obstacle. There were still some gaps, there were Polish police who turned a blind eye, there were sewers which led out of the ghetto. Above all, there were children who by these secret paths carried on a smuggling service by day and by night, and if several hundred thousand people did not die of hunger as Frank had planned, they could thank these indomitable children. Indomitable—for the German police guards fired at them, and it was an everyday spectacle in Warsaw to see the police at the boundary of the ghetto shooting the smuggling children down like rabbits.

There were other "gaps" in the wall. Jewish workers were conducted out of the ghetto every day because their places of work lay in other parts of Warsaw. It was impossible to search them all thoroughly on their return. The guards made random searches, and contented themselves with beating up their victims on the spot.

Inside the ghetto there was a streetcar line—only for Jews, marked with the Star of David instead of a number. The ghetto was also crossed by another line at its narrowest part. The drivers had instructions to travel through here at top speed; there were no stops, and yet this short track was an important spot for secret dealings: from the platforms of the cars, Polish children used to drop little sacks onto the street, and Jewish children would shoot out of a house door, pick up the sacks, and disappear with them behind the nearest cover.

It was a desperate organization, but it even succeeded somehow in smuggling a few cows into the ghetto, keeping them hidden on the third floor of a house, and thereby supplying milk at least for the newly born.

On the other hand it was a great help that the SD, the Gestapo, and the SS were corrupt; even their highest representatives in Warsaw could be bribed. Globocnik, for example, had a share in the firm of a man named Walter Többens, who became a millionaire from the slave labor of fifteen thousand Jews. Globocnik had no interest in seeing his partner's slave workers die of hunger or dragged off to the gas chambers, although such was his official duty. It is also known that by the end of 1942 Globocnik and some other hangmen were so deeply involved in the ghetto business that they wished the ghettos would never cease to exist. Thus the Jewish resistance organization succeeded in buying, at fantastic prices, rifles, pistols, ammunition, hand grenades, machine guns, and even heavier weapons, in smuggling them into the ghetto, and keeping them hidden. The sources of these dark deals were German soldiers, quartermasters, and in part the Italian divisions stationed in the neighborhood of Lemberg.

July 20, 1941, was a turning point in the fate of the Warsaw ghetto. On that day the Jewish Council—a powerless body set up by the German authorities—was ordered to pick out 60,000 Jews who were to be taken away during the coming weeks and months. The object of this measure was to rid the ghetto of all "unproductive elements." Children, invalids, beggars, paupers, women, old men, all who were unable to work in the armament factories, had to come to a certain assembly point. From here they were to go direct into the trucks and off to the extermination camps. Officially, however, they were told that they were going to be "resettled" somewhere in the East, in the region of Minsk. The president of the Jewish Council, who knew the truth, put an end to his life with poison.

Bernard Goldstein, a member of the Jewish resistance, wrote in his memoirs:

> We had not the slightest doubt that these wagonloads of unfortunates were going to their certain death. We assigned the difficult task of finding out more about this to Zalman Friedrych, one of our most courageous and untiring comrades in the underground movement. A Polish railwayman, who knew the direction taken by the deportation trains, told Friedrych their route.
>
> Friedrych at last reached Sokolow under great difficulties. There he learned that the Germans had built a short branch line to the village of Treblinka. Trains laden with Jews were sent daily along this new track. In Treblinka there was a large camp. A citizen of Sokolow had heard that dreadful things happened in Treblinka, but he did not know the details.
>
> In Sokolow, Friedrych happened to meet one of our comrades, Azriel Wallach, a nephew of Maxim Litvinov (the former Soviet Foreign Minister). He had just escaped from Treblinka and was in a fearful state, badly burned, bleeding, his clothing in rags. Friedrych learned from Wallach that all Jews taken to Treblinka were immediately killed. They were unloaded from the trains, and they were told that they must bathe and wash before they could be admitted to the working quarters. Then they were taken to large, hermetically sealed chambers and gassed. Wallach was saved from this fate because he was ordered to clean out the freight trains. There he had succeeded in escaping.
>
> With this information, Friedrych returned to Warsaw. So we

were in a position to give the ghetto an eyewitness account of what really happened to the wagonloads of deportees who were sent off daily.

But the report found few believers. Desperately, the majority clung to the illusion that it was really only a removal for settlement at some other place of labor. The transports rolled on, and there were even some volunteers who came to the assembly point because they thought things might be better at some other place in the East. Only gradually did this self-deception vanish. The ghetto was emptying, and eventually even a job in the factory of Walter Többens no longer protected people from being sent away.

But on January 18, 1943, a column of selected victims on the way to the assembly point suddenly drew pistols from their pockets and opened fire on the accompanying SS. Before the Germans could shoot back, the column had scattered and vanished.

It was a fantastic event. Ferdinand von Sammern-Frankenegg, Superior SS and Police Chief, started a great police raid in the ghetto, and had several Jewish houses demolished by gunfire; but he never succeeded in discovering the leaders or those who had taken part.

A month later, on February 16, 1943, Himmler ordered the Warsaw ghetto to be destroyed. Sammern-Frankenegg and Odilo Globocnik, however, seem to have hesitated, and so there suddenly appeared on the scene SS Brigade leader and General of Police Jürgen Stroop to take over. On April 19, he drove into the ghetto with three guns and three armored cars. On that day began the tragic fight to the death of the Warsaw Jews. It lasted almost a month, until May 16, 1943. The German forces stamped out all resistance, but the victory, which will remain a shining example for many centuries, went to the Jewish people.

In the Nuremberg courtroom the American prosecutor, John Harlan Amen, tried to elicit details from Ernst Kaltenbrunner.

AMEN: What did you have to do with the final razing of the Warsaw ghetto, nothing, as usual?

KALTENBRUNNER: I had nothing to do with it.

AMEN: We will find out whether Stroop confirmed what you are trying to tell the Tribunal.

With these words Amen produced a sworn statement by Stroop: "I received a teletype from Himmler which ordered me to evacuate the Warsaw ghetto and raze it to the ground. Dr. Hahn was Commander of the Security Police of Warsaw at that time. Hahn gave the Security Police their orders concerning their tasks in this action. These orders were not given to Hahn by me, but came from Kaltenbrunner in Berlin. All executions were ordered by Reich Main Security Office, Kaltenbrunner."

AMEN: Do you say that that statement of Stroop's is true or false?

KALTENBRUNNER: It is untrue.

But Kaltenbrunner's statement could not diminish the value of another Nuremberg document, the day-by-day account by Stroop of the destruction of the ghetto. Here, under the title *There is no longer a Jewish quarter in Warsaw!* the SS Brigade leader had produced a unique historical testimony.

"This distinguished specimen of German handicraft," said prosecutor Walsh, "bound in leather, richly illustrated, printed on heavy, handmade paper, contains an almost incredible report by Stroop, who has signed this report with a bold hand. General Stroop boasts in this report of the bravery and heroism of the German forces who took part in the ruthless and merciless action against a group of Jews who, to be exact, amounted to 56,065 persons, including, of course, women and children."

The report was read in Nuremberg:

> Before the beginning of this extensive action, the boundaries of the Jewish quarter were sealed off by barricades in order to prevent a sally by the Jews. At our first entry to the ghetto the Jews succeeded, by means of a prepared surprise attack, in driving back our forces including the armored vehicles. In spite of a repetition of the counterattack, the second attempt succeeded in penetrating the built-up area according to plan. Our opponents were forced to withdraw from the roofs and other high vantage points into cellars, bunkers, and sewers.
>
> The principal fighting group of the Jews, who were reinforced

by Polish bandits, withdrew to the so-called Muranowskiplatz. They planned to establish themselves in the ghetto with all their resources in order to prevent us from penetrating. The jewish and the Polish flags were raised on a concrete building as an appeal to others to join the fight against us.

Soon after the first days I recognized that the original plan could not be carried out. The Jews had everything at their disposal, from chemical means to prepare explosives to pieces of clothing and equipment of the Wehrmacht, arms of all kinds, especially hand grenades and Molotov cocktails. The Jews had also succeeded in turning some workshops into centers of resistance. One such center had to be attacked by means of a pioneer squad using flame-throwers and artillery fire on the second day.

At first it was assumed that only a few shelters had been prepared, but in the course of the action it became obvious that the whole ghetto had been systematically provided with cellars, bunkers, and passages. All these passages and shelters had access to the sewer system. In this way, the Jews had created a safe system of communication below ground. How carefully the Jews had worked was shown in many places by the provision of the shelters with living accommodation for whole familes, washing and bathing equipment, toilets, rooms for weapons and ammunition, and large stores of food, sufficient for several months.

While it was at first possible to catch the Jews, who are by nature cowards, in great numbers, this became increasingly difficult as the action went on. Fighting groups of twenty to thirty and more Jewish youths, aged 18–25, kept turning up, sometimes with a corresponding number of women who kindled fresh resistance. These fighting groups had been ordered to defend themselves to the last and, if need be, to escape capture by suicide. The women belonging to the fighting groups were armed in the same way as the men. Sometimes these women fired pistols from each hand at once. It happened time and again that they kept their pistols and hand grenades hidden in their bloomers till the last minute, and then used them against the armed SS, police, and Wehrmacht.

On April 23, 1943, the Reich Leader of the SS ordered the complete destruction of the ghetto in Warsaw with the greatest severity and ruthless thoroughness. I decided, therefore, to carry out the total destruction of the Jewish quarter by burning down complete blocks of houses. This made the Jews, as a rule, come out of their hiding places and shelters. But it was not uncommon for the Jews to remain in their burning houses until the heat or the fear of being burned to death forced them out; then they jumped from the upper stories after having thrown down mattresses and other bedding into the street. With broken bones they then tried to creep across the street into other houses which were not yet or only partly on fire.

The longer the resistance lasted, the more implacable became the men of the SS, the police, and the Wehrmacht, who continued untiringly in the fulfillment of their duties in true comradeship in arms. The action went on often from early morning till the late hours of night. Nightly patrols, with rags tied round their feet, kept on the heels of the Jews, and maintained unrelenting pressure on them. Often, Jews who used the night to build up their food stores from deserted shelters, or to get into contact with neighboring groups, were discovered and finished off. . . . Only by the continued and untiring efforts of all our forces did we succeed in achieving a total of 56,065 Jews captured and proved killed. To this number must be added those Jews who lost their lives by explosions, fires, and so on, but could not be accurately counted.

The action was completed on May 16, 1943, with the blowing up of the Warsaw Synagogue at 8:15 P.M. All the ghetto buildings have been destroyed. Since even after the action one had to consider that under the ruins of the former Jewish quarter individual Jews might still survive, the territory had to be firmly barricaded off from the Aryan sector and well guarded. By the destruction of all buildings and hiding places and by the cutting off of the water supply, the possibility of survival of any Jews or bandits was removed.

This comprehensive description by Stroop was supplemented by numerous telegrams on the course of the battle which he sent to Cracow. Thus he wrote on April 23: "The whole of the former ghetto was divided into twenty-four zones today for the purpose of searching it. The result of this action—600 Jews and bandits ferreted out and caught, some 200 shot dead, 48 shelters blown up. A number of bandits sniping from balconies were brought down by our shots. Altogether to date those captured, including those already transported, number 19,450 Jews. The next train goes on April 24, 1943."

May 6: "Today we searched those blocks of buildings which were destroyed by fire on May 4. Although it was scarcely to be expected that here people would be found still alive, we discovered a large number of shelters, in which a terrible heat had developed. From these and other shelters a total of 1,553 Jews were taken away. A gun fight developed, during which 356 Jews were killed. In this action the Jews used pistols and threw Polish hand grenades."

May 8: "Today again a number of Jewesses, carrying pistols hidden in their bloomers, were captured. The undersigned is determined not to end this action until the last Jew is destroyed."

In fact only a few Jews who managed to escape and hide in other parts of Warsaw survived the horror of those days; only a few survived the extermination camp of Treblinka where they had been sent and were able to tell the story of the fight of the defeated.

What are words? At Nuremberg, prosecutor Walsh concluded: "The prosecuting authorities could lay before the Court masses of evidence concerning the total number of Jews who died at the hands of the Nazis, but I believe that no additional evidence could affect the guilt of these defendants."

6

The Final Chapter

CLOSING WORDS
AND VERDICTS

The Trial of the International Military Court was approaching its end.

"These two score years in the twentieth century," said the American chief prosecutor, Robert H. Jackson, "will be recorded in the books of years as one of the most bloody in all annals. Two World Wars have left a legacy of dead which number more than all the armies engaged in any war that made ancient or medieval history. No half-century ever witnessed slaughter on such a scale, such cruelties and inhumanities, such wholesale deportations of people into slavery, such annihilations of minorities. The terror of Torquemada pales before the Nazi Inquisition.

"Of one thing we may be sure. The future will never have to ask with misgiving what could the Nazis have said in their favor. History will know that whatever could be said, they were allowed to say. They have been given the kind of a trial which they in the days of their pomp and power never gave to any man. The fact is that the testimony of the defendants has removed any doubt of guilt which, because of the extraordinary nature and magnitude of these crimes, may have existed before they spoke. They have helped write their own judgment of condemnation."

Jackson raised another point: "We are not trying them for the possession of obnoxious ideas. The intellectual bankruptcy and moral perversion of the Nazi regime might have been no concern of international law had it not been used to goose-step the *Herrenvolk* across international frontiers. It is not their thoughts, it is their public acts which we charge to be crimes."

The defendants had the last word. So the Statute of the Tribunal had decided, and thus on August 31, 1946, the twenty-one

361

men in the Nuremberg courtroom had a further opportunity to take the microphone and speak.

Almost fifty pages of the report of the Trial are filled with these final speeches, and it seems appropriate to quote their most significant parts. All the defendants had carefully prepared these concluding statements, and read them from typescripts or from notes.

Goering, who spoke first, said among other things, "I wish to state expressly that I condemn these terrible mass murders to the utmost, and cannot understand them in the least. But I should like to state clearly once more before the High Tribunal that I have never decreed the murder of a single individual at any time, and neither did I decree any other atrocities or tolerate them, while I had the power and the knowledge to prevent them.

"The German people trusted the Führer, and as a result of his autocratic direction of the state they had no influence on events. Without knowledge of the serious crimes which have now been made known, the people, faithful, self-sacrificing, and brave, fought and suffered in their fight for life or death. The German people are free of guilt.

"I have not wished or caused any war, I did everything I could to avoid it by negotiations. When it had broken out I did all I could to achieve victory. Since the three greatest world powers and many other nations fought against us, we were overcome in the end. I stand by what I have done. But I deny most emphatically that my actions were dictated by the desire to subjugate foreign nations by war, to murder, to rob, or to enslave, to carry out atrocities or crimes. The only motive that inspired me was passionate love for my people, its happiness, its freedom, and its life. I call the Almighty and my German people as witness to this."

Next, Rudolf Hess was allowed to speak. His speech was confused and obscure, it did not come to an end until he was eventually interrupted by the President.

Ribbentrop: "I have been made responsible for the conduct of foreign policy which someone else determined. But I know this much about it, that it was never concerned with plans for world domination, only with removing the consequences of the Ver-

363 THE FINAL CHAPTER

sailles Treaty and with the problem of feeding the German people.

"Before the Statute of this Court was drawn up, the signatory Powers of the London Conference must have had opinions on international law and policy different from those they hold today. When I went to Marshal Stalin in Moscow in 1939 he gave me to understand that if he could have half of Poland and the Baltic countries, I could fly back at once. Apparently in 1939 warfare was not yet an international crime against the peace, otherwise I could not explain Stalin's telegram at the conclusion of the Polish campaign. It ran: 'The friendship of Germany and the Soviet Union, founded on the blood which we have shed together, has every appearance of being enduring and firm.' At that time I strongly wished for that friendship. Today the key problem for Europe and the world still remains: Will Asia dominate Europe, or will the Western Powers restrict the influence of the Soviets to the Elbe, the Adriatic coast, and the Dardanelles? In other words, Great Britain and the U.S.A. today face practically the same dilemma as Germany did at the time I carried out my negotiations with Russia. I hope with all my heart for my country that in the event you may be more successful."

Keitel: "I have believed, I have erred, and I was not able to prevent what should have been prevented. That is my guilt. It is tragic to have to admit that the best that I had to offer as a soldier, obedience and fidelity, were exploited for obscure purposes, and that I did not see that a limit is set even for a soldier's fulfillment of duty. From a clear recognition of the causes, the disastrous methods, and the terrible consequences of the events of this war, may the hope grow for the German people of a new future in the community of nations."

Kaltenbrunner: "The prosecution has made me responsible for the concentration camps, for the destruction of Jewish life, for the action groups, and many other things. All this does not correspond to either the evidence or the truth. Himmler, who in masterly manner was able to split up the SS into small groups, and Müller, the chief of the Secret State Police, carried out the crimes of which we have heard. I was deceived about the Jewish problem just like the other higher officials. I have never approved or allowed the biological destruction of Jewry. Hitler's anti-Semitism, as we now know it, was barbaric. I only know that, in my faith in Adolf Hitler, I put all my ability at the disposal of the German people."

Rosenberg: "I know my conscience is completely free of any participation in the murder of nations. Instead of destroying the culture and the national feeling of the people of Eastern Europe, I was called in for the furtherance of their physical and psychological conditions of existence; instead of destroying their personal security and human dignity I used all my faculties to resist any policy of forcible measures, and I demanded with all severity a correct attitude on the part of German officials and humane treatment of the Eastern workers. In Germany, in accordance with my convictions, I desired freedom of conscience for any opponent, and never caused any religious persecution. The thought of a physical destruction of Slavs and Jews—that is, of an actual murder of a people—never entered my head, much less did I ever propagate such an idea. I was of the opinion that the Jewish problem would have to be solved by creating a minority law, emigration, or the resettlement of Jews in their own national territory during the course of decades. The methods, here proved in court, of the German government in wartime were entirely contrary to my opinion. Adolf Hitler drew to an increasing degree upon men who were not my comrades but my opponents. Of their monstrous deeds I must say: This was not the practice of the National Socialism for which millions of trusting men and women have fought, but an outrageous abuse, an abuse which I condemn most strongly."

Frank: "Adolf Hitler, the chief defendant, owes an account to the German people and the world. In the direst need of his nation he found no word of solace. He hardened and did not carry out his function of a leader, but escaped by committing suicide. Was it obstinacy, doubt, or spite against God and men which made him take the attitude, 'If I go down, let the German people too sink to the depths.' Who is to know? We—and by that I mean myself and those National Socialists who are united with me in this admission, not those accused here with me, for whom I cannot speak—we do not wish to leave the German people to its fate in a similar manner without a final word. We will not simply say: 'Now see how you get on with the mess we have left you.' Even now, perhaps more than ever, we accept our great intellectual responsibility. At the beginning of our journey we never dreamed that our turning away from God would have such destructive, fatal consequences and that we would inevitably sink ever deeper into guilt. We could not have known then that so much faith and self-sacrifice by the German people would be so abused by us. By turning away from God we have broken down, and deserved to founder. It was not technical shortcomings and unfortunate circumstances alone that lost us the war; neither was it bad luck or treason. It was more than anything else that God pronounced sentence on Hitler, and carried it out on him and on the system which we served in a godless state of mind.

"May therefore our people turn back from the road along which Hitler and we with him have led it. I beg our people that it should not continue on that road, not for another step. For Hitler's road was the presumptuous way without God, the road of the denial of Christ, and in the end the road of political folly, of destruction and death. His progress became more and more that of a terrible adventurer without conscience or honor, as I now know, at the end of this Trial."

Frick: "As far as the charge against me is concerned I have a clear conscience. My whole life was service to my people and fatherland. By the fulfillment of my legal and moral duty I think I have earned punishment just as little as the tens of thousands of dutiful German officials who have now been imprisoned only because they carried out their duties."

Streicher: "At the beginning of the Trial I was asked by the President whether I was guilty within the sense of the charge. I answered that I was not. The proceedings and the evidence have confirmed the truth of my statement. Neither in my capacity as Gauleiter nor as a political writer have I taken part in any crimes, and so I await your verdict with a clear conscience."

Funk: "Hideous crimes have been disclosed here, in which also officials in my departments have been implicated. This I have learned for the first time here in this court. I did not know of these crimes and had no means of knowing. These criminal acts fill me, like every German, with deep shame. Before this Trial I knew nothing of the millions of Jews in concentration camps or killed by action groups in the East. The existence of such extermination camps was quite unknown to me; I have never entered a concentration camp. I, too, assumed that some of the gold and valuables delivered to the Reichsbank came from the concentration camps, but according to German law everyone had to give up such valuables. Besides, the nature and amount of these deposits by the SS were not known to me. How could I ever imagine that the SS had obtained these valuables by the mutilation of corpses! Had I known of these ghastly transactions, my bank would never have accepted these valuables for deposit and evaluation. I would have refused even at the risk of losing my life. Then the world would have been a better place for me than this painful life fraught with suspicion, calumny, and evil accusations. No man has lost his life through an order of mine."

Schacht: "The only charge against me is that I wanted war. The overwhelming weight of the evidence in my case has proved that I was a fanatical opponent of war, and actively and passively tried to prevent it by resistance, sabotage, ruse, and force. My opposition to Hitler's policy was known at home and abroad. Admittedly I erred politically. My political error was that I did not recognize early enough the extent of Hitler's criminal nature. But I have not soiled my hands with a single illegal or immoral act. The terror of the Secret State Police did not frighten me, for any terror must fail before an appeal to conscience. Herein lies the great source of strength that religion affords to us. At the end of this Trial, I stand deeply moved in my innermost heart by the indescribable misery which I tried to prevent with all my personal strength and with all available means, but which I was unable to prevent through no fault of mine. Therefore, I hold my head erect and I am unshaken in the faith that the world will recover not by the power of violence but only through the strength of the spirit and the morality of its actions."

Doenitz: "I wish to say three things. First: You can adjudicate the legitimacy of the German U-boat war as you like. I consider that the conduct of the war was justified, and have acted according to my conscience. I would do just the same again. Second:

authoritarianism has proved itself best in the military leadership of all armies in the world. On the basis of this experience I considered it was also right in political leadership, especially for a people in the hopeless condition of the German people in 1932. But this has been proved wrong, for human nature apparently is not capable of applying the power of this principle for good ends. Third: My profession was my life, dedicated to service to the German people. As the last Commander in Chief of the German Fleet and as the last Head of State I feel responsible toward the German people for all I did or did not do."

Raeder: "As a sailor I have done my duty because I was of the conviction that I thereby best served the German people and the fatherland, for which I have lived and for which I was ready to die at any time. If I have to any extent become guilty it was in the fact that in spite of my purely military position I had also to some extent to be a politician. That was, however, a moral guilt toward the German people and I can never in any way regard myself as a war criminal; it was not guilt before a human criminal court, but a crime before God."

Schirach: "At this hour, as I speak to the military court of the four victorious Powers for the last time, I wish to state, with a clear conscience, to our German youth that they are completely innocent of the excesses and atrocities of the Hitler regime as proved by this Trial. They know nothing of the innumerable acts of horror that have been committed by Germans. My lords, please help by your verdict to create for the young generation an atmosphere of mutual respect, an atmosphere that is free of hatred and vengeance. That is my last request, a request from the heart for our German youth."

Sauckel: "I am shocked to the utmost by the atrocities as disclosed in the Trial. I bow in deep respect and humility before the victims and the fallen of all nations and before the unhappiness and sorrow of my own people. I had no part in any conspiracy against the peace or against humanity, nor have I tolerated murders or ill-treatment. My intentions and my conscience are clear; the inadequacies and miseries of war, the frightfulness of its repercussions affect my heart deeply. I myself am prepared to submit to any fate to which Providence may subject me. God protect my beloved people, may the Lord God bless once more the labor of the German worker, to whom I have dedicated all my life and efforts, and may He send peace to the world."

Jodl: "It is my unshakable belief that a later historical judgment will achieve an objective and proper opinion of our supreme military leaders and their assistants. They did not act in the service of hell, nor of a criminal, but of their people and their fatherland. So far as I am concerned, I believe that no man can act better than if he strives toward the highest of all attainable aims. That and nothing else has always been my guiding principle, and therefore, whatever verdict you, the judges, may pass on me, I shall leave this court with my head as high as I entered it many months ago. In such a war as this, in which hundreds of thousands of children and women were killed in air raids in which partisans used any form of violence that seemed serviceable to them—in such a war severe measures, even though they may not perhaps seem in keeping with international law, are not crimes against morals or conscience. For I believe and know: the duty toward people and fatherland stands above all others. To fulfill that duty was my honor and my supreme law. May this duty in a more fortunate future be superseded by a still higher one—by the duty toward mankind."

Papen: "My lords, the power of evil was stronger than that of virtue; it has driven Germany inevitably into disaster. But should on this account those be condemned who in the fight of faith against ungodliness carried the banner of the former? And is Mr. Justice Jackson justified in his assertion that I was only the hypocritical agent of a pagan regime? Or what gives Sir Hartley Shawcross the right to say, with scorn and mockery and contempt, that I preferred to rule in hell, instead of serving in heaven? This verdict is not for you to pronounce, it is for another Judge. I believe that I can face my responsibility with a clear conscience. Love of my country and of my people alone were the mainspring of all my acts. I did not serve the Nazi regime but my fatherland. Does the prosecution really want to condemn all those who offered their collaboration with honorable intentions? Only if the High Court knows and acknowledges the truth will the historic mission of this Trial be fulfilled. Only then will the German people, although its Reich is destroyed, recognize its errors, but also find the strength for its future tasks."

Seyss-Inquart: "I owe the Court an explanation of my attitude to Adolf Hitler. For me he remains the man who made Greater Germany a reality in German history. This man I served. What came of it? I cannot shout today, 'Crucify him!' as I cried yesterday, 'Hosanna!' My last word is the principle by which I have always acted and to which I will adhere to my last breath: I believe in Germany."

Speer: "After this Trial the German people will despise and condemn Hitler as the proved cause of its misfortune. The world will learn from these events to hate and fear dictatorship as a form of government. The dictatorship of Hitler differs in a fundamental point from all historical precedents. It was the first dictatorship in this period of modern engineering, a dictatorship which in subjecting its own people made the fullest use of technical means. By these means, such as radio and loud-speakers, eighty million people were deprived of independent thought: thus they were subjugated to the will of a single individual. Earlier dictators required for subordinate positions men with great qualities, who could think and act independently. The authoritarian system in our technical age can dispense with them. The means of communication alone allow the work of subordinates to be mechanized. As a result there arose a new type of uncritical receivers of orders. We are only at the beginning of this development. Every country in the world now stands in danger of being terrorized by technical means. The more technical the world becomes, the more necessary is the demand for individual freedom and independent thought of the individual as a counterweight. This war has ended with remotely controlled rockets, with aircraft traveling with the speed of sound, with new kinds of submarines and with torpedoes that can find their own targets, with atom bombs, and with the prospect of a dreadful chemical war. The next war will of necessity be fought by means of these new destructive discoveries of the human intelligence. In five or ten years' time the technique of war will have made it possible to fire rockets from continent to continent with uncanny precision. An atomic rocket, operated perhaps by only ten men, may be able to destroy a million people in the center of New York within seconds, without prior warning, invisible and faster than sound, by day or by night. Science will be able to spread disease among men and beasts and to destroy harvests by an insect war. Chemistry has found terrible means of inflicting unspeakable suffering upon helpless mankind.

"Will there be another nation which will use the technical experiences of this war in preparation for a new one? As a former minister of a highly developed armament industry it is my last duty to say: another world war would end with the destruction of human culture and civilization. Nothing prevents unfettered science and engineering from completing its work of destruction upon mankind. For this reason this Trial must be a contribution toward preventing wars in the future and in laying down the fundamental laws of human co-existence. What does my fate matter, after all that has happened?"

Neurath: "Sustained by the conviction that in this High Court, too, truth and justice will prevail, in spite of all the hatred, slander, and distortion, I believe that there is only one thing left to say, that my life was dedicated to truth, honor, the maintenance of peace, and the reconciliation of nations, to humanity and justice, and that I stand here with a clear conscience not only before myself, but before history and the German people."

Fritzsche: "I must not waste the great opportunity of my final words in this important Trial by a recital of details. I wish I had in my radio talks carried out the propaganda of which the prosecution accuses me now! Had I only expounded the theory of the Master Race! Had I only preached the hatred of other nations! Had I only urged wars of aggression, acts of terror, of murder, and inhumanity! Then, gentlemen, if I had done all these things, the German people would have turned away from me, and would have rejected the system for which I spoke. But the misfortune lies in the fact that I did not propagate these attitudes which were the secret motives of Hitler and a small circle of his henchmen. I believed in Hitler's assurances of his honorable desire for peace. I believed the official German denials of all foreign reports of German atrocities. That is my guilt—no more, no less. The prosecutors have expressed the indignation of their peoples about the atrocities that have been committed. They did not expect any good of Hitler, and are shocked at the immensity of what actually happened. But I beg you to try to grasp the indignation of those who expected nothing but good of Hitler, and who now see how their good faith, their good will, and their idealism were abused. I find myself in this situation of the disillusioned men together with many, many other Germans, of whom the prosecution says that they ought to have known what was happening from the smoking chimneys in the concentration camps or from the mere sight of the prisoners. But it is time to break the eternal circle of hate which has till now ruled the world. It is high time to stop the vicious circle of seed, harvest, new seed, and new harvest of hatred. After all, the murder of five million people is a grim warning, and mankind today possesses the technical means for its own destruction. It may be difficult to separate German crimes from German idealism, but it is not impossible. If one achieves this separation, then much suffering will be prevented for Germany . . . and for the world."

With these concluding words, here abridged, of the twenty-one defendants, the taking of evidence at the Nuremberg Trial had come to an end. All that there was to say had been said: much of it was merely declamatory, much of it in bold contradiction of the established facts, but much of it also came from truly honorable motives, and some of it had prophetic validity.

For the last time the President of the Tribunal, Lord Justice Lawrence, announced an adjournment: "The Court adjourns now until September 23, in order to consider the verdict. On that date the verdict will be announced. If a postponement should be necessary, this will be promptly announced."

In fact a postponement did become necessary, for the consideration of the Court took more time than was originally foreseen. In complete seclusion the judges of the four nations worked on the final document that was to be read out at the Trial: the verdict and its detailed explanation. Even the telephone lines to the council rooms were disconnected during these weeks. Security officers guarded the entrances, searched the wastepaper baskets, removed every trace from which an outsider could draw premature conclusions about the outcome of the deliberations.

While the British, French, and Russians worked independently, the American judges, following the usage of the Court of Appeal in the United States, had qualified jurists as advisers, among them Professor Quincy Wright of the University of Chicago, Attorney General Herbert Wechsler, formerly professor of law at Columbia University, and Adrian S. Fisher, later the State Department legal advisor. The judges knew that every word of the verdict would go down in history. Complete agreement was not achieved. The Soviet judge, Nikitchenko, was of a different opinion from his Western colleagues on many points, and so in the end a vote had to be taken and the majority decided, as the Statute had provided. Nikitchenko made use of the Anglo-Saxon legal practice and gave a "minority opinion." It was not read out, had no practical importance, and was more or less intended for judicial literature and historical research.

September 30, 1946, was the day of the verdict. At seven in the morning everything was the same as usual in the Nuremberg Court building: doors and windows were open, it was drafty in the corridors, the Palace of Justice was still the domain of the charwomen. But shortly before eight, the first of the officials, stenotypists, and technicians, who wished to avoid the crowd that would gather later at the entrance, began to arrive.

The patrol of police vehicles around the Court buildings was considerably strengthened. All controls were tightened up, the guards looked carefully through the contents of the brief cases, examined passes on both sides, compared pass photographs with their holders. The old passes for the courtroom were no longer valid, everyone had been cleared again before receiving a special pass for the hearing of the verdict. Everyone was subjected to the same procedure: newsmen, officials, soldiers, even generals.

From the throng outside the entrance to the courtroom faces emerged that had been seen only in the early days of the Trial. They had gathered from all corners of the earth, and now, as they approached the last barrier, all excitement disappeared. The proximity of imminent events produced calmness. There was yet another highly embarrassing formality: a physical search. Only then—after showing the pass for the last time to the guard at the entrance door—one was allowed to enter the hall with its babel-like confusion of tongues, mixed with the humming of the ventilating fans. Shortly before half past nine, the defense counsels, accompanied by military police, were brought into the hall in a body. The stenographers and interpreters had already taken their places. Every seat in the press gallery was occupied. Announcers and technicians were crowded behind the glass panes of the radio booth. Photographers and their staffs were on their platforms.

The defendants appeared in groups of twos or threes, brought up by elevator from the prison, at intervals of exactly half a minute. Most of them made a good-humored impression, talked to each other, and greeted their fellow defendants with nods or handshakes. Only a few took their places in silence, among them Funk and Schacht. Last of all Goering appeared, alone. As always, he was wearing his altered light-gray uniform. Before he took his place in the first row he shook hands with Keitel and Schirach.

The ceremony of announcing the verdicts was laid down: First the indictment was read out; next, each of the defendants would be informed on which count of the indictment he had been found guilty or not guilty. Only then—in the ensuing afternoon —the defendants would be conducted once more, and this time singly, into the courtroom, in order to hear their sentences.

"The Court," called the marshal of the Court.

Everybody rose. Silence fell. The eight judges entered the room with inscrutable expressions. The time was three minutes past ten.

Then hour after hour passed. The members of the Tribunal took turns reading the document. The voices of the interpreters came from the earphones in a droning monotone. Everyone in the hall listened with great tension, most of all the defendants.

But only next morning, on October 1, 1946, was the reading of the verdict so far advanced that the names of the twenty-one were listed. Goering, his head bowed, holding the earphone against his right ear, heard "guilty on all four counts of the indictment," and knew for certain that this could only mean sentence of death; but not a muscle in his face betrayed agitation. His eyes were hidden by dark glasses, his lips pressed together in an imperceptible smile.

Rudolf Hess, who was next, did not appear to grasp that it concerned him. He seemed completely indifferent, had a few sheets of paper on his knees, and wrote continuously. Goering leaned over, trying to make him understand that it was now his turn. But Hess brushed him away with an angry wave of the hand and continued to make his secret notes without troubling to hear what was said about him. Not once did he put on the headphones, and when Goering finally whispered the verdict in his ear, he acknowledged it only with an absent-minded nod.

Most of the defendants heard the verdicts with outward passivity. Keitel sat rigidly upright. Kaltenbrunner was working his jaw. Rosenberg sat stooping, showing no interest. Frick, hitherto motionless, sat up with a jerk at the mention of his name. Frank shook his head almost imperceptibly. Julius Streicher, his arms crossed, made a show of leaning back comfortably on the backrest of the bench when his turn came, but interrupted for the first time his eternal gum-chewing during the reading of the verdict. Walther Funk fidgeted restlessly, tears in his eyes, his mouth twitching nervously, his shoulders hunched up to his ears. Schacht sat with arms folded in his corner and acknowledged his acquittal as a formality with an ironical smile.

After the announcement of Fritzsche's acquittal—he was the last of the twenty-one—his counsel jumped up and waved to him excitedly. Fritzsche and von Papen left the benches of the defendants, and shook hands with Goering and Doenitz. Only Schacht kept aloof.

By 1:45 P.M. the first part of the reading of the verdicts was at an end. The Court withdrew for the midday break. The sentences would be pronounced after lunch. Meanwhile, journalists from all over the world discussed in the pressroom of the Palace of Justice the morning's sensation, the acquittal and liberation of Fritzsche, Papen, and Schacht. These three were in the best of moods, smiling and smoking with enjoyment; Schacht wore a gray fur coat. Questions were fired at them from all sides.

"Where will you live now?"

Schacht: "I too would like to know."

"Will you spend the night in jail?"

Fritzsche: "No, rather in a Nuremberg ruin: no more gray walls and window bars."

"What are your plans?"

Papen: "I will go to my daughter in the British zone or to my wife and children in the French zone."

Schacht: "I will go to my wife and my two children who live in the British zone, and I hope I shall never again see anyone from the press!"

Fritzsche: "The problem of freedom is quite new for me, I can't say yet what I shall do."

The flash bulbs of the photographers popped continuously. While questions and answers were exchanged, the acquitted men were approached on all sides with requests for autographs. Suddenly Schacht held up his hand and asked for silence. Then he said: "My two children, aged three and four, have never had any chocolate. I will only give further autographs in return for chocolate." General laughter, but clearly audible above the noise the voice of a Frenchman: "*C'est dégoûtant.*"

It was time to return to the courtroom.

At 2:50 P.M. the Court began its 407th and last session.

The atmosphere was now different from the previous months, different from the morning session. No spotlight lit up the room, only the cool gray-blue light of the fluorescents fell shadowless upon the walls, the empty dock, on the faces of the judges, prosecutors, defending lawyers, stenographers, assistants, and newspapermen.

A decision of the Court had banned all photographers and newsreel cameramen from the room. At the moment when the prisoners were to hear whether they were going to live or die, their faces were not to be photographed or filmed. A brittle tension lay upon the scene. Every cough, every rustling of papers sounded like an unexpected detonation. People sat almost motionless. Were they expecting drama, sensation, a historical scene?

All eyes in the hall were directed to one point: the built-in door behind the dock that was almost invisible in the paneling. From the shadowy door, Hermann Goering emerged into the gray light of the room, behind him two military police stood to the right and left of him. His face was flabby and sunken. He took the headphones that were offered to him.

"Defendant Hermann Wilhelm Goering! In accordance with the counts of the indictment"—the expressionless voice of the interpreter began to translate the words of the President. Suddenly, Goering made signs with both hands. He could hear nothing. The relay system had broken down. A technician hurried over and put things right.

"Defendant Hermann Wilhelm Goering! In accordance with the counts of the indictment, on which you were found guilty, the International Military Court sentences you to death by hanging."

Motionless, his head bowed, Goering heard the sentence. He took the headphones from his ears, made a smart, military-style about-face, and left the room.

Smoothly, as though moved by a ghostly hand, the door closed behind his broad back. Seconds passed. Then it opened again to admit Rudolf Hess.

With an effeminate movement of the hand he rejected the headphones. He stood rocking on his toes, turned the dark sockets of his eyes this way and that, looked at the ceiling—one almost expected him to start whistling.

"Defendant Rudolf Hess! In accordance with the counts of the indictment, on which you were found guilty, the International Military Court sentences you to life imprisonment."

Hess did not hear the verdict, and only when a military policeman tapped him on the shoulder did he amble around and disappear through the exit.

Ribbentrop's face was ashen. His eyes were half closed. Under his arm he carried a bundle of documents. He held onto his file in the face of death.

"...death by hanging."

Keitel faced his sentence erect and with a reserved expression.

"...death by hanging."

For the first time, Kaltenbrunner's stony visage changed to a slight smile as he heard the words:

"...death by hanging."

Rosenberg seemed to have some difficulty in remaining calm.

"... death by hanging."

Frank held his hands, after putting on his headphones, still half raised in a beseeching attitude. His lower lip was drooping and he nodded when he heard the decisive words:

"... death by hanging."

He turned quickly to hide his face.

Julius Streicher stood with legs apart, his head bent forward, as though expecting a hammer blow.

"... death by hanging."

Sauckel raised his glance gloomily to the judges' bench, then turned around jerkily.

"... death by hanging."

Jodl listened, slightly bent forward, took the phones formally from his head, and breathed a scornful hiss before he drew himself up bravely and withdrew stiffly.

"... death by hanging."

Funk, who had undoubtedly counted on a death sentence, broke into sobs at the words "life imprisonment" and made a helpless bow toward the judges.

Eighteen times the sliding doors opened and closed. Each sentence took an average of three minutes. At 3:40 P.M., the Court withdrew in silence. Its part in world history was over.

A solid stream of humanity rushed out of the courtroom, split up in the corridor into individuals racing to the telephones and teletypes. Papers were waved in the air. Someone fell, picked himself up, hurried on. The newspapers all over the world, the radio stations had to get their copy within minutes:

"The International Military Tribunal in Nuremberg has given its verdict. Twelve of the accused have been condemned to death by hanging: Goering, Ribbentrop, Keitel, Kaltenbrunner, Rosenberg, Frick, Frank, Streicher, Sauckel, Jodl, Seyss-Inquart, and Martin Bormann in his absence. Hess, Funk, and Raeder have been condemned to imprisonment for life, Schirach and Speer to twenty years, Neurath to fifteen years, and Doenitz to ten years."

The curtain had come down on the courtroom.

What happened then behind the scenes, in prison, has been

described by another observer, the court psychologist, Dr. Gustave M. Gilbert. He wrote in his diary:

"Goering came down first and strode into his cell, his face pale and frozen, his eyes popping. 'Death!' he said, as he dropped on the cot and reached for a book.

"His hands were trembling," the psychologist noted, "in spite of his attempt to be nonchalant. His eyes were moist and he was panting, fighting back an emotional breakdown."

Some time later, Goering said to the prison barber, Hermann Wittkamp: "Now we know. They will hang me—they can't shoot. I have bet on twelve death sentences without Bormann— and eleven it is. Only the sentence against Jodl I can't understand; I had someone else in mind in his place. I was thinking of Raeder."

About the other condemned men Gilbert wrote: "Hess strutted in, laughing nervously, and said that he had not even been listening, so he did not know what the sentence was. Ribbentrop wandered in, aghast, and started to walk around the cell in a daze, whispering, 'Death! Death! Now I won't be able to write my beautiful memoirs. Tsk! Tsk! So much hatred! Tsk! Tsk!'"

Keitel stood with his back to the door of his cell. When Dr. Gilbert entered he wheeled around and snapped to attention at the far end of his cell, his fists clenched and arms rigid, horror in his eyes: "Death by hanging! That, at least, I thought I would be spared."

"Frank smiled politely," Gilbert went on, "but could not look at me. 'Death by hanging,' he said softly, nodding his head in acquiescence. 'I deserve it, and I expected it, as I've always told you. I am glad that I have had the chance to defend myself and to think things over in the last months.'

"Rosenberg sneered: 'The rope! The rope! That's what you wanted, wasn't it?' Kaltenbrunner's clasped hands expressed the fear that did not show in his insensitive face. 'Death!' he whispered, and could say no more. Funk watched the guard unlock his handcuffs in simpering bewilderment. Then he walked around his cell with bowed head, mumbling, as if he couldn't quite grasp it, 'Life imprisonment! What does that mean? They won't keep me in prison all my life, will they? They don't mean that, do they?'

"Von Schirach's face was grave and tense as he walked to the cell, head high. 'Twenty,' he said, as the guard unlocked his handcuffs. I told him his wife would be relieved that he had not gotten the death penalty, which she had feared. 'Better a quick death than a slow one,' he answered.

"Jodl marched to his cell, rigid and upright, avoiding my glance. After he had been unhandcuffed and faced me in his cell, he hesitated a few seconds as if he could not get the words out. His face was spotted red by vascular tension Then he said: 'Death—by hanging. That, at least, I did not deserve. The death part—all right. Somebody has to stand the responsibility. But that—' his mouth quirked and his voice choked for the first time, 'that I did not deserve.'"

Sauckel found it more difficult than the other prisoners to accept the death sentence. He pestered the barber, the doctor, and the psychologist with the idea that the verdict of the Court must have been due to an error in translation. He was firmly convinced that the mistake would still be discovered and the verdict revised. The story of his doubts quickly went around the prison, and eventually it was Seyss-Inquart, himself sentenced to death, who wrote a letter of condolence to Sauckel. Dr. Ludwig Pflücker, the German prison doctor, brought it to the one-time leader of slave labor:

"Dear Party Member Sauckel, You are bitterly critical of the verdict. You think that the verdict has been given against you because a word of yours has been wrongly translated. I do not share this impression. The fact that we obeyed the Führer cannot take the responsibility from those of us who had the courage and strength to stand in the front line in this fight for the existence of our people. In the days of triumph we stood in the front rank, and thus we have the privilege of standing in the front rank in misfortune. By our example we help to build a new future for our people. Yours, Seyss-Inquart."

DEATH
BY HANGING

Two long weeks passed.

On the night of October 15–16, 1946, the executions were to be carried out. The day and the hour were strictly secret, but the condemned men somehow believed that it would be October 14. Meanwhile, there were several official appeals for mercy, addressed to the Allied Control Commission in Berlin, as well as a number of private efforts such as letters to Field Marshal Montgomery, to President Truman, and to Prime Minister Attlee; even the Curia was approached by roundabout ways and asked for intercession. But all this was in vain; the sentence stood. In the Nuremberg prison, increased security measures had been introduced: at night the cells remained brightly lit, the guards were not allowed to take their eyes off the prisoners. Dr. Pflücker described in his memoirs how they passed their last days:

"Jodl read Wilhelm Raabe. Frank showed a cheerful countenance and spoke to the doctor enthusiastically about Franz Werfel's book *The Song of Bernadette*. Ribbentrop always had only one question on his lips—where the execution would take place. Keitel begged Dr. Pflücker 'that the organist, who often played a few tunes of an evening, should not play the folk song, *Schlafe, mein Kindchen, schlaf ein*, as it stirred up particularly nostalgic memories in him.'"

On October 15, their last day, the prisoners seemed to sense that the end was near. From all the cells there came sudden requests for the Bible; only Rosenberg would have nothing to do with it.

Goering declined the usual morning and evening walk. He lay almost the whole day on his bunk, reading Fontane's *Effie Briest*. Betweentimes he wrote a letter and received one. Ribbentrop complained about sleeplessness and headaches, turned absent-

mindedly the pages of a novel by Gustav Freytag, read five
letters, and wrote one himself. Rosenberg read *The Violin*, a
novel by Binding, received three letters in the course of the day,
but wrote none himself.

Streicher also read on that last day: a novel by Jelusich entitled *The Soldier*. He also wrote six letters and received one.
Jodl read Hamsun's *The Wanderer*, wrote a letter, and received
seven. Keitel had expressed the wish "to be informed beforehand
so that he could put his cell in good order." He read stories by
Paul Alverdes, received three letters, and wrote one.

Hans Frank told the German prison personnel about the
beauties of St. Peter's in Rome, read Thomas' poem *Holy Night*,
and repeatedly leafed through the nine letters he had received;
he wrote two himself. Seyss-Inquart read Eckermann's *Conversations with Goethe*, Frick Jelusich's novel, *Hannibal*. Sauckel
read a volume on the youth of great Germans.

Frank, Kaltenbrunner, and Seyss-Inquart, the three practicing
Catholics among the condemned, made their confessions and
took Communion in their cells.

"Something is going on," said Goering. "There are strangers
in the corridors, and there are more lights on than usual." Already that morning Goering had said to Hermann Willkamp,
the prison barber: "Tomorrow you will leave, a barber will no
longer be required. You can keep my razor, which you have used
all this time, and also the badger's-hair brush—at least I know
who has got them. I won't need them any more. I would like
to give you also my pipe, but I can't. When I leave this cell for
the last time, I will break it to bits and throw it out of the
window."

Wittkamp mused: "I did not understand his strange smile at
the time, but there must have been something special about that
pipe. When I heard of his suicide everything became quite clear:
he could have hidden his ampule of cyanide of potassium only
in that pipe."

Goering was lying on his bunk with his eyes open, gazing into
space, his hands resting on the blanket as the rules required. It
was 10:45 P.M. For over half an hour he lay like that. The sentries looked through the peephole. There was nothing out of

the ordinary about the man on the bunk. Only his hands seemed restless. They plucked the cover, quivered, moved to and fro, grasped the cloth, pulled at it. The guard looked more closely. The prisoner's face was now distorted in a convulsed grimace. His legs jerked under the covers, his body heaved and tossed.

The guard shouted for the officer on duty. The door was opened. The guard and the officer burst into Goering's cell. Right on their heels was the Protestant minister, Reverend Gerecke. Goering's convulsions ceased. His heavy body was bent, slightly raised, resting on his elbows. His breath was rattling in his throat. Beads of sweat covered the face of the dying man.

They were unable to save him. Everything they did was meaningless, and was done only for the sake of doing something. They held up his head, slapped his cheeks as though he were only in a faint, moved his arms a little to restore respiration. Some water was brought. Dr. Pflücker arrived.

"Have you had a heart attack?" he shouted at Goering. No answer. Suddenly, as Dr. Pflücker says in his memoirs, "Goering's face turned blue as though from the light of an ultraviolet lamp. He sank back. Another short rattle in the throat, and all was over."

When Colonel Andrus entered, Goering gave no further sign of life. The American put the paper he was holding in his hand in the pocket of his uniform. It was no longer required. A few minutes before he had received it in his office by courier, and was on the way to inform Goering of its contents. It was the rejection by the Allied Control Commission in Berlin of his appeal for mercy.

Dr. Pflücker took Goering's wrist and detected a slight pulse. He listened for heartbeats, but could no longer hear them. The pupils also remained motionless; the corneal reflex had ceased. "This man is dead," said the doctor.

"Thanks, doctor," replied Colonel Andrus. "He has taken poison, hasn't he?"

"Yes, presumably cyanide of potassium."

"Here," said the sergeant, and handed Andrus a small brass capsule which he had picked up from the floor of the cell. It was the container of the poison vial. Dr. Pflücker had already found the vial under Goering's left hand. Later the glass splinters of the ampule were found in the dead man's mouth by the American prison doctor, Dr. Martin.

How did Goering come into possession of the poison? Where had he hidden it? How was he able to take it without anyone noticing? American police and CIC spent days upon the task. The guard on duty at the peephole had seen nothing; there were no other witnesses or evidence.

Where had Goering hidden the poison? This secret, too, the dead man took with him. During the regular or sporadic searches nothing suspicious had been noticed. The clothing and other belongings of the former Field Marshal gave no clues, and neither did the prisoner's body at a post-mortem examination.

Under the security system that Andrus had built up it was simply unthinkable that a prisoner in a Nuremberg cell could ever possess so much as a pinhead which would not be instantly discovered; or so Andrus thought.

After the executions, the prison cells were cleaned up thoroughly. Colonel Andrus was amazed when he saw the things that were found. Although he thereby admitted the failure of his own security methods, he gave the foreign press an exact account:

1. A steel screwdriver was found in Konstantin von Neurath's cell. With its point the prisoner could have opened an artery. It was large enough to be fatal if swallowed.

2. In the cell of Joachim von Ribbentrop the cleaners discovered a glass bottle. Its splinters would have been suitable for suicide.

3. In Wilhelm Keitel's cell they found a large safety pin, carefully concealed in a shirt. The prisoner also had four metal nuts, two sharp-edged metal bolts, and a knifelike piece of steel under the fold of his uniform collar.

4. In the cell of the acquitted Hjalmar Schacht there was a length of cord a yard long, strong enough for hanging oneself. The one-time president of the Reichsbank also collected ten paper clips, and kept them carefully hidden.

5. In the cell of Alfred Jodl the cleaners discovered a twelve-

inch length of wire, several sharp pencils, and a mechanical
pencil that had been taken to pieces.

6. In Karl Doenitz's cell they found five shoelaces, tied together.

7. In Fritz Sauckel's cell was a broken-off, sharp-edged spoon.

Altogether, it was a whole arsenal of suitable implements for
suicide. After these discoveries the American investigation group
gave the answer to the question where Goering had kept the
poison hidden. It was now clear that there were apparently dozens
of possibilities, especially his pipe. Only the question how he
had come into possession of the poison remained unanswered.
Unfortunately, Colonel Andrus never disclosed the contents of
a private letter which Goering addressed to him in his last hour.
This letter was one of three that Goering wrote in the death
cell: one "to the German people," one to his wife, and one to
Burton C. Andrus.

Two men have since claimed to have smuggled the poison
secretly to Goering: the Austrian journalist Petermartin Bleibtreu, and the one-time SS General Erich von dem Bach-Zelewski.
Bleibtreu's adventurous account of how he went furtively into the
empty courtroom and stuck the ampule of potassium cyanide with
a piece of chewing gum to the railing at Goering's seat disin-
tegrated into a tale of fantasy upon closer examination.

Bach-Zelewski's statement was to be taken more seriously.
During the preliminary hearing before the opening of the Trial,
the former chief of the antiguerrilla forces claimed to have given
Goering the poison in a piece of soap when he met him in the
corridor of the prison. Bach-Zelewski said that weeks before he
had begun, at every meeting with Goering, either in passing or
during sessions, to greet him ceremoniously and to show him all
kinds of preposterous marks of respect, in order to offer the
guards an amusing show and lull their attention. By this trickery,
claimed Bach-Zelewski, it was eventually possible for him once
to shake Goering by the hand, although this was strictly forbidden. On this occasion the poison changed hands. As a proof
for his story, he handed a second ampule of poison to the
American authorities in 1951. The glass was tested and compared

with the carefully preserved splinters that Dr. Martin in 1946 had retrieved from Goering's mouth. The glass was in fact identical with that which was found in Goering's mouth.

In Nuremberg, however, on October 15, 1946, nearly everyone fell under suspicion of having saved Defendant No. 1 from the gallows. The sensational event struck the whole world like a thunderbolt, eclipsing even the news of the actual executions.

Goering's suicide, however much it may have thrown the security and prison authorities into confusion at the last moment, did not alter the carefully worked-out plan for the executions. Shortly before one in the morning, on October 16, 1946, the bolts rattled open in Ribbentrop's cell.

"I trust in the blood of the Lamb that bears the sins of the world," said Ribbontrop, his eyes closed.

Two American military policemen with white web belts took him across the courtyard to the gymnasium.

In the brightly lit room, there stood three scaffolds painted in black. Thirteen wooden steps led to the platforms on which the gallows had been erected. "The prisoner stood upon a trap door, which was opened after the fixing of the noose," wrote Dr. Pflücker. "The prisoner fell the height of a story. The lower story of the gallows was draped with a curtain so that nothing could be seen. Here two American doctors examined the hanged and certified their death.

"It must be mentioned," continued Dr. Pflücker, "that death does not occur at once in hanging, but loss of consciousness, a consoling assurance that I was able to give all the prisoners beforehand."

Everything had to happen quickly. The faces of the few witnesses remained in the dark: four Allied generals, Colonel Andrus, eight selected representatives of the press, and the Bavarian Premier, Dr. Wilhelm Hoegner, who had been hastily summoned to Nuremberg as "witness for the German people." The smell of whisky, Nescafé, and Virginia cigarettes lay over the scene.

Master Sergeant John C. Woods from San Antonio, Texas, the United States hangman, had two assistants. Every condemned man was brought in, had his hands tied behind his back with shoelaces, and had to mount the steps of the scaffold, with a military policeman on his right and left. A few seconds remained for spiritual consolation, for last words. Then the black cap covered the prisoner's world in darkness. Woods pulled the noose over the head, and immediately the trap door opened under the condemned man's feet.

At one minute past one, Ribbentrop was led into the gymnasium. The hangman's assistants bound his hands. He was told to state his name clearly. Then he said:

"God protect Germany. My last wish is that Germany's unity shall be preserved and that an understanding may be achieved between East and West."

The black hood, the trap door . . .

The journalists who had not been granted admission, and who were now secretly crouching behind the attic windows of the Palace of Justice to catch at least a glimpse of the gymnasium door, heard the dull rumble of the trap door at 1:14 A.M.

Next it was Keitel's turn.

"I beg the Almighty to be merciful to the German people" were his last words. "For Germany—everything! Thank you."

Alfred Rosenberg only gave his name. To the cleric who asked him whether he should pray for him, he said morosely, "No, thank you."

Frick said nothing. Hans Frank said, "I am grateful for the mild sentence I have received. I pray God to receive me mercifully."

From the attic windows the journalists saw two soldiers who dragged rather than led a man in long white underclothes across the courtyard. Streicher had refused to get dressed, he refused to make his last journey on his own feet. Without a pause, his voice rang out over the courtyard: "Heil Hitler! Heil Hitler! Heil Hitler!"

"Heil Hitler!" was his last cry, audible even from the attic windows of the Palace of Justice, already half drowned by the rumbling noise of the trap door.

Fritz Sauckel, who was next, clung to the alleged error of translation even under the scaffold, shouting: "I pay my respect to the American officers and soldiers but not to American justice!"

Twice more after Sauckel's execution the trap door rumbled—for Jodl and Seyss-Inquart. At 2:45 A.M. the last act of the drama ended. "Most of them tried to show courage," reported Kingsbury Smith of the International News Service, who attended the executions as a representative of the American press. "None of them broke down."

Twelve minutes after the announcement of Seyss-Inquart's death, at 3:09, the dead Goering was brought on a stretcher into the gymnasium. His body was set down at the head of the row of the executed at the foot of the gallows. It was a symbolical act.

The last official act was left to a photographer of the American Army. He had to photograph each of the dead men twice, once dressed, as he was taken from the gallows, and once naked. These pictures have been classified Top Secret, and they will remain in the secret archives for a few more decades, until they will be of interest only to historians. Nevertheless, an American newspaper managed to publish pictures of the dead men, taken shortly after their execution. In these photographs, several of the dead show injuries which give them a repulsive appearance. An explanation was given by the German physician. Dr. Pflücker, in his memoirs: "None of them suffered unnecessarily, and none of them bore external wounds except Frick, who had always a tendency to sudden movements, and at the opening of the trap door moved backward, so that he struck the edge of the trap door and suffered a wound in the neck."

Pflücker's statement agrees with the accounts of witnesses of the execution, but he erred in one point: Frick was not the only one injured in his fall; several other prisoners suffered abrasions of the nose and forehead, because the opening of the trap door was too small. This explains the patches of blood.

At four o'clock in the morning, two American Army trucks pulled up outside the gymnasium. The vehicles were accompanied by a jeep and a limousine, both armed with machine guns. An American and a French general were in charge. Eleven coffins were loaded. The trucks turned in the courtyard, rolled out on to the street, and set off in the direction of Furth. A procession of private cars joined them, packed with newspapermen. At Erlangen the column stopped.

The jeep with the machine gun was maneuvered behind the two trucks, and an American officer declared that whoever tried to follow them would do so at the risk of his life. Then the trucks disappeared in the morning mist, apparently to the airfield near Erlangen for further transport to Berlin, as the journalists conjectured.

The truth was disclosed only many years later. The corpses were taken to Munich by roundabout ways. There they were reduced to ashes in the crematorium of the East Cemetery on the same day. The American military government had taken over the crematorium, and two German employees who could not be dispensed with were sworn to secrecy for the rest of their lives. The official announcement said merely that the ashes of the executed men "were scattered in a river somewhere in Germany at an undisclosed place so as to prevent that at any time a shrine should be made of it."

Today the river is known—the Isar; the place, too, is known. But no one has made a shrine of it. Somehow the men and events of 1946 have become incredibly remote.

INDEX

389

ABOUT THE AUTHORS

Joe J. Heydecker was born on February 13, 1916, in Nuremberg. At sixteen he had already written his first novel, which the authorities of the Third Reich were to suppress. From 1933 to 1938, Heydecker was a correspondent in Austria and the Balkans for the German-language newspapers. On his return to Germany, he was temporarily taken into custody by the Gestapo. Then he served as a soldier for six years. Heydecker was present throughout the Nuremberg Trial as a newspaper correspondent. He then worked as a reporter for the *Münchner Illustrierte*. Since 1960, Heydecker has lived with his wife and daughter in São Paulo, Brazil.

Johannes Leeb was born on March 25, 1932, in Berlin. He was too young to have had firsthand experience of the Third Reich, but the end of that regime and the subsequent occupation years made a deep impression on him. When the Nazis wanted to put bazookas into the hands of the twelve-year-old boys for the defense of the German capital, his mother fled with him to her native Bavarian countryside. He graduated from the school of journalism in Munich and worked on various daily newspapers. His travels as a reporter for the *Münchner Illustrierte* have taken him over the whole world. He lives in Munich with his wife and two sons.